ALLOCATING AUTHORITY

The question of which European or international institution should exercise public authority is a highly contested one. This new collection offers an innovative approach to answering this vexed question. It argues that by viewing public authority as relative, it allows for greater understanding of both its allocation and its legitimacy. Furthermore, it argues that relations between actors should reflect the comparative analysis of the legitimacy assets that each actor can bring into governance processes. Put succinctly, the volume illustrates that public authority is relative between actors and relative to specific legitimacy assets. Drawing on the expertise of leading scholars in the field, it offers a thought-provoking and rigorous analysis of the long debated question of who should do what in European and international law.

Allocating Authority

Who Should Do What in European and International Law?

Edited by
Joana Mendes and Ingo Venzke

•HART•
PUBLISHING
OXFORD AND PORTLAND, OREGON
2018

Hart Publishing
An imprint of Bloomsbury Publishing Plc

Hart Publishing Ltd
Kemp House
Chawley Park
Cumnor Hill
Oxford OX2 9PH
UK

Bloomsbury Publishing Plc
50 Bedford Square
London
WC1B 3DP
UK

www.hartpub.co.uk
www.bloomsbury.com

Published in North America (US and Canada) by
Hart Publishing
c/o International Specialized Book Services
920 NE 58th Avenue, Suite 300
Portland, OR 97213-3786
USA

www.isbs.com

First published 2018

British Library Cataloguing-in-Publication Data
A catalogue record for this book is available from the British Library.

ISBN: HB: 978-1-50991-193-6
ePDF: 978-1-50991-191-2
ePub: 978-1-50991-192-9

Library of Congress Cataloging-in-Publication Data

Names: Mendes, Joana. | Venzke, Ingo.

Title: Allocating authority : who should do what in European and international law? / edited by Joana Mendes and Ingo Venzke.

Description: Oxford ; Portland, Oregon : Hart Publishing, an imprint of Bloomsbury Publishing, 2018. | Includes bibliographical references and index.

Identifiers: LCCN 2017039020 (print) | LCCN 2017040733 (ebook) | ISBN 9781509911929 (Epub) | ISBN 9781509911936 (hardback : alk. paper)

Subjects: LCSH: International and municipal law. | International and municipal law—European Union countries. | International agencies—Law and legislation.

Classification: LCC KZ1263 (ebook) | LCC KZ1263 .A425 2018 (print) | DDC 340.9—dc23

LC record available at https://lccn.loc.gov/2017039020

Typeset by Compuscript Ltd, Shannon

CONTENTS

LIST OF CONTRIBUTORS

Maurizia De Bellis is tenured Assistant Professor in Administrative Law in the Department of Public Law of the University of Rome II 'Tor Vergata'.

Jochen von Bernstorff holds the Chair for Constitutional Law, International Law and Human Rights at the Eberhard Karls Universität Tübingen.

Eoin Carolan is Associate Professor at University College Dublin.

Joseph Corkin is Senior Lecturer in Law at Middlesex University London.

Deirdre Curtin is Professor of European Union Law at the European University Institute in Florence and a Joint Chair of the Law Department and of the Robert Schuman Centre for Advanced Studies.

Diane Desierto is Associate Professor of Law and Michael J. Marks Distinguished Professor in Business Law at the University of Hawaii and Co-Director of the ASEAN Law & Integration Center.

Chantal Mak is Professor of Private law, in particular fundamental rights and private law, at the Centre for the Study of European Contract Law and director of the Amsterdam Research Institute for Legal Studies.

Joana Mendes is Professor of Comparative Administrative Law, University of Luxembourg.

Mikael Rask Madsen is Professor of Law at the University of Copenhagen and Director of iCourts—Centre of Excellence for International Courts.

Dominique Ritleng is Professor of European Law at the University of Strasbourg and a Visiting Professor at Uppsala University.

Susan Rose-Ackerman is Henry R. Luce Professor of Law and Political Science, Yale University.

Andreas von Staden is Professor of Political Science at the University of Hamburg.

Ingo Venzke is Associate Professor at the Department of International and European Law, University of Amsterdam, and Director of the Amsterdam Center for International Law.

Bruno De Witte is Professor of European Union law at Maastricht University, and part-time professor at the European University Institute in Florence.

1

Introducing the Idea of Relative Authority

JOANA MENDES AND INGO VENZKE*

I. Authority in Global Governance

The exercise of public authority in global governance is contested, both in public opinion and in the academia.[1] We see challenges to international public authority flare up, for instance, in the backlash against investment arbitration, which is a topic that has made it even onto market squares where citizens campaigned against the Trans-Atlantic Trade and Investment Partnership (TTIP). With different nuances, this topic has also drawn significant attention in scholarship. Questions include not only how balances between investment protection and other public policy objectives are struck, but also who should strike them.[2] The exercise of public authority in the field of trade regulation has faced similar challenges for a while now. Should international adjudication in that field decide about the legality of import prohibitions of hormone treated beef or of seal products? Should it defer to the normative output of specialised standard-setting bodies when it comes to these issues or others? The division and allocation of authority between different institutions is decisive with regard to such questions, and for the contestation of

* A different, longer version of this introduction is forthcoming in the *International Journal of Constitutional Law*.

[1] By exercise of public authority, we mean acts based on law that have the capacity to impact the freedom of others. For this conception of public authority see A von Bogdandy, M Goldmann and I Venzke, 'From Public International to International Public Law: Translating World Public Opinion into International Public Law' (2017) 28 *European Journal of International Law* 115. On the contestation of international public authorities see M Zürn, 'The Politicization of World Politics and its Effects: Eight Propositions' (2014) 6 *European Political Science Review* 47; JK Cogan, 'Representation and Power in International Organization: The Operational Constitution and its Critics' (2009) 103 *American Journal of International Law* 209.

[2] SW Schill and M Jacob, 'Trends in International Investment Agreements, 2010–2011: The Increasing Complexity of International Investment Law' (2012) *Yearbook on International Investment Law & Policy* 141.

public authority more generally. This is evident at the European level just as well, despite its very different institutional structure and constitutional framework. Should highly political decisions, such as the programme of the European Central Bank on outright monetary transactions, be allocated to non-majoritarian institutions?[3] Should the European Commission have the authority to reject national budget drafts and request changes? What is the legitimate reach of the European Court of Justice when interpreting EU laws that constrain Member States' social policies?[4]

These exemplary questions have stirred heated debates. By and large, however, the underlying legitimacy concerns that fuel the contestation of public authority remain quite diffuse. They are trapped between the oftentimes unappealing and practically unrealistic option of retreating back to the state, on the one hand, and the limited legitimacy resources of international or supranational administrations and courts, on the other. Tying the authority of inter- and supranational actors closer to the input of actors on the domestic level may often be a good option, but it comes with practical limitations. Experience, together with a wealth of research, has shown that supra- and international actors outgrow the terms of delegation, develop their own agenda, and, using a variety of mechanisms to increase their leverage, they exercise authority in relation to their one-time creators.[5] That is especially the case where treaty frameworks create administrative and judicial bodies, which then contribute to the dynamic development of the law, including their own statute and their own competences.

These starting points leave us with multiple, scattered sites for the exercise of public authority.[6] Those sites are spread horizontally, across different institutions, and vertically across different levels of governance. In particular, the stark quantitative increase of international adjudication over the past two decades has pushed courts and tribunals onto the agenda of global governance as actors who exercise public authority, next to bureaucracies and standard-setting bodies.[7] If one accepts that the exercise of public authority cannot be tied back to any single level

[3] See BVerfG, 2 BvR 2728/13 of 14.1.2014, and Judgment in Case C-62/14 *Gauweiler v Deutscher Bundestag* [2015] EU:C:2015:400.

[4] eg Judgment in Case C-438/05 *International Transport Workers' Federation and Finnish Seamen's Union v Viking Line ABP and OÜ Viking Line Eesti* [2007] EU:C:2007:772.

[5] Mikael Rask Madsen supports this view in greater detail and, at the same time, argues that savvy actors on the supra- and international level are compelled to take the consequences and likely repercussions of their actions among domestic institutions into account in their decision-making. See Madsen, in this volume.

[6] S Casese, *The Global Polity* (Sevilla, Global Law Press, 2012).

[7] See A von Bogdandy and I Venzke (eds), *International Judicial Lawmaking: On Public Authority and Democratic Legitimacy in Global Governance* (Berlin, Springer, 2012); KJ Alter, 'Agents or Trustees? International Courts in their Political Context' (2008) 14 *European Journal of International Relations* 33; A von Bogdandy, R Wolfrum, J von Bernstorff, P Dann and M Goldmann, *The Exercise of Public Authority by International Institutions: Advancing International Institutional Law* (Berlin, Springer, 2010).

of governance or any single actor, the question strongly suggests itself how such authority should be divided and allocated.

We have thus focused on precisely this allocation at two workshops at the University of Amsterdam, and we continued our debates beyond that with the authors of this volume. As we continued to learn, the terms of the debates have shifted. We started out by framing our concerns above all in the language of the separation of powers or checks and balances, but became increasingly convinced of the difficulties of this framework.[8] In the present chapter we introduce the arguments at which we arrived, especially the idea of relative authority, and explain the limits of separation of powers thinking.[9] We speak of the allocation of authority. Allocation presupposes a division of authority and, at the same time, points to its more specific distribution. Allocated authority does not, however, presuppose a deliberate design, or even a constitutional settlement. Instead it can emerge through iterations and institutional interactions.

We conceive of public authority as a law-based capacity to influence the freedom of others. In our conception, authority does not imply normative legitimacy.[10] Public authority is the phenomenon whose normative legitimacy we wish to critique and aspire to improve. Furthermore, we do not purport or intend to define threshold conditions of ultimate (il)legitimacy—conditions under which authority may justifiably demand obedience.[11] Our approach is reconstructive. And normative legitimacy, in our understanding, comes in degrees.

We see public authority as relative in two specific and closely connected ways. First, any actors' exercise of public authority in global governance can best be understood and assessed *if put into relation to other actors*. This shift towards seeing actors in context—especially international courts and supranational agencies—contributes to understanding and assessing the legitimacy of their authority.[12] For example, should an international investment tribunal defer to the authority of an international governmental commission when it comes to the interpretation

[8] On the appeal and difficulties of this idea in the European Union, see Carolan and Curtin in this volume; and for the context of international law see, in particular, von Bernstorff, in this volume.

[9] The term 'relative authority', we note, is also used in N Roughan, *Authorities* (Oxford, Oxford University Press, 2013) to convey that authority's interdependence impacts the assessment of its legitimacy (see in particular 138). Roughan characterises international law's claim to authority as interdependent with that of other authorities and stresses that appropriate relationships need to be established between them. Our approach complements Roughan's work and, at the same time, distinguishes itself first of all by its aim of providing a framework for normative critique that draws on the institutional characteristics of each actor and on the specific legitimacy assets that they are able to mobilise.

[10] For an overview with an argument in support of this position, see B Peters and JK Schaffer, 'The Turn to Authority Beyond States' (2013) 4 *Transnational Legal Theory* 315; see also von Bogdandy, Goldmann and Venzke, above n 1.

[11] For such a focus see, in particular S Besson, 'The Authority of International Law—Lifting the State Veil' (2008) 31 *Sydney Law Review* 343. This is another way in which our approach is different from that of N Roughan, 'Mind the Gaps: Authority and Legality in International Law (2016) 27 *European Journal of International Law* 329–51.

[12] On the diversity of relations see in further detail von Staden, in this volume.

of a vague treaty provision? Under which conditions should it do so? Should the EU legislator and the European Medicines Agency incorporate guidelines on the technical requirements of medicines that ensure their safety, efficacy and quality as adopted by an 'International Conference on Harmonisation', and, if so, in which terms? Second, we see the public authority of any actor as relative in the sense that it *relates to different legitimacy assets*. With legitimacy assets we refer to the argumentative resources that an institutional actor can invoke in support of its authority. As we will argue, those resources specifically connect to the actor's inclusiveness, functional specialisation, and its capacity to protect rights.[13]

We highlight how exercises of public authority need to be justified in relation to other actors and in view of different legitimacy assets. An actor can seek to justify its authority with reference to its composition and organisation, to its procedures or its function in support. It can point to the way in which it is embedded within a context of other institutional actors. For example, the UN General Assembly supports its authority above all with reference to its inclusiveness whereas an arbitral tribunal would point to its independence, impartiality and to the fairness of the judicial procedure. In the European Union, the European Parliament grounds its authority on inclusiveness and, specifically, on the direct representation of citizens at the EU level, whereas the Council and the European Council draw from the representation of Member States at different levels. The authority of the European Commission is anchored on its independence and collegiality.[14]

This way of setting up the idea of relative authority suggests that it is not per se satisfactory that authority be divided so that no single institution rules, so to speak, or encroaches upon the authority of others. Especially at the international level, the point is typically not that authority is too concentrated. Often it is too dispersed and fragmented.[15] In fact, such dispersion and fragmentation may even exacerbate legitimacy concerns as it may undercut accountability mechanisms and opportunities for critique. The point is that authority ought to be justified not by its sheer division, but by virtue of its specific allocation. In other words, we aim at articulated rather than diffused governance.[16]

The two ways in which we think of authority as relative are closely connected: the way in which each actor's public authority should relate to that of others presupposes a comparative analysis of their respective legitimacy assets.[17] The mere

[13] See below S III.

[14] This is of course a stylised view that, given the complex ways in which the European Union operates, may lack explanatory value in specific instances. See Carolan and Curtin in this volume.

[15] See E Benvenisti and GW Downs, 'The Empire's New Clothes: Political Economy and the Fragmentation of International Law' (2007) 60 *Stanford Law Review* 595 (showing how fragmentation serves the powerful).

[16] C Möllers, *The Three Branches: A Comparative Model of Separation of Powers* (Oxford, Oxford University Press, 2013) 41–44; J Waldron, 'Separation of Powers in Thought and Practice' (2013) 54 *Boston College Law Review* 433; M Goldmann, *Internationale öffentiche Gewalt. Handlungsformen internationaler Institutionen im Zeitalter der Globalisierung* (Berlin, Springer, 2015) 317–19.

[17] This is also basic premise in Mattias Kumm's work, with the difference that he grants the higher level of governance a default benefit of the doubt, see M Kumm, 'The Legitimacy of International Law: A Constitutionalist Framework of Analysis' (2004) 15 *European Journal of International Law* 907.

coordination and cooperation between actors is not a sufficient condition of public authority's normative legitimacy.[18] At the same time, looking for a specific allocation of authority does not necessarily call for a deliberate institutional design or constitutional settlement.[19] Even where overarching institutional frameworks existed, their capacity to guide concrete allocations of authority is often limited. The allocation will thus be a product of institutional practice.

What, then, ought to guide a specific allocation of authority? This is of course a grand question that has neither an easy solution, nor is there a settled way for approaching it. One might cling to first principles of great abstraction or to concrete practices without critical distance. We adopt a meso-level of theorising and analysis that is akin to reconstructive approaches.[20] We see the allocation of authority as a fundamental aspect of democratic legitimation, which provides us with some normative guidance. Concrete allocations of authority may result from institutional practices, but they should be assessed and re-enacted in view of their democratic justification. We see actual practices in European and international law in which the allocation of public authority is both sanctioned and contested. In the reconstruction of such practices, we draw further inspiration from the domestic level of governance and, specifically, from separation of powers thinking, despite the problems that we will discuss in further detail. The institutional set-up on both the European and international level does not readily emulate the domestic context, nor is it clear that it should. And yet, the normative programme that underlies the theory and practice of the separation of powers thinking is instructive, and it can travel across levels of governance.[21] It is by way of induction from practices on different levels of governance and by way of deduction from concerns for democratic legitimation that we identify the three main legitimacy assets that we already mentioned: inclusion, functional specialisation and rights protection.[22]

At the same time, the state may plausibly claim to be left alone in some domains, see M Kumm, 'Sovereignty and the Right to be Left Alone: Subsidiarity, Justice-Sensitive Externalities, and the Proper Domain of the Consent Requirement in International Law' (2016) 79 *Law and Contemporary Problems* 239.

[18] Unlike Roughan's work, our analysis focuses on allocation of authority and on comparative legitimacy analyses that may ground critique and contribute to the democratic justification of authority (cf N Roughan, above n 11, 349), rather than on interdependencies and relationships as grounds for legitimate claims to obedience.

[19] See, similarly, the contributions in T Broude and Y Shany (eds), *The Shifting Allocation of Authority in International Law: Considering Sovereignty, Supremacy and Subsidiarity* (Oxford, Hart, 2008).

[20] Largely in that line, A Honneth, *Das Recht der Freiheit: Grundriß einer demokratischen Sittlichkeit* (Frankfurt, Suhrkamp, 2011). Methods under the name of normative inductivism or even immanent critique come very close, see K Nicolaïdis, 'European Demoicracy and Its Crisis' (2012) 51 *Journal of Common Market Studies* 351, with reference to A Azmanova, *The Scandal of Reason: A Critical Theory of Political Judgement* (New York, Columbia University Press, 2012). For an early systematic treatment see already N Lacey, 'Normative Reconstruction in Socio-Legal Theory' (1996) 5 *Social & Legal Studies* 131. For an application of such a method that comes close to ours, see R Howse and K Nicolaïdis, 'Democracy without Sovereignty: The Global Vocation of Political Ethics' in Broude and Shany, ibid, 163.

[21] See also Bruno Simma, *Foreword*, in von Bogdandy and Venzke, above n 7, v–xii.

[22] These standards are widely shared and supported by comparative public law analyses, see Möllers, above n 16; E Carolan, *The New Separation of Powers: A Theory for the Modern State* (Oxford, Oxford University Press, 2009).

Those assets, we add, are particularly significant in present theory and practice. They are not exhaustive, nor cast in stone. Other considerations may certainly be relevant for assessing an authority's normative legitimacy, especially concerns for redistribution in worlds of inequalities. But these legitimacy assets, we submit, provide a backbone for arguments on how authority ought to be allocated. That, once more, is our ambition: to provide a framework for arguments on who should do what to which extent.

Discussing relative authority both in the context of the European Union and on the level of international law, we add, is insightful for two reasons. First, the conceptual and practical developments at the European level are potentially instructive for international law. Drawing lessons or inspiration does not mean to emulate.[23] Differences may even become more apparent with a deeper understanding of contexts and underlying normative programmes. Second, the exercise of authority within the European Union and in international settings poses similar normative problems. In particular, it moves the exercise of authority in the form of rule- or law-making away from inter-governmental fora (a feature that is perhaps more salient in international law, but also present in EU law) and away from the oversight of national parliaments, notwithstanding their involvement in EU affairs.[24] Our approach brings to the fore the important structural differences between the European Union and international settings. By highlighting them, it also critiques the existing iterations of separations of powers in the EU.

We develop our argument as follows. First, we briefly outline the main scholarly responses to the contested public authority of supra- and international institutions in order to highlight the specific contribution that the idea of relative authority makes in this regard (section II). We move on to develop the idea that authority is relative also because it connects to different legitimacy assets. While this idea originates in separation of powers thinking, there are good reasons to take distance from that specific framework of analysis. A functional division of powers, as it has developed in domestic settings, does not map well onto existing institutional arrangements. But its normative programme bears promise. It teaches precisely that any authority should be divided in a way that is attuned to the specific legitimacy assets that each actor can bring into the governance process (section III). Finally, we trace iterations of our normative programme in practice—we focus on how this programme may be reflected in practice and how it may inform that same practice (section IV). We conclude by summarising how the different chapters of the book discuss the strengths, but also the limitations, of the idea of relative authority in European and international law, and the contributions that they make to shaping this idea (section V).

[23] For such a charge against other strands of scholarship, see JE Alvarez, 'The New Dispute Settlers: (Half) Truths and Consequences' (2003) 38 *Texas International Law Journal* 405, 42.

[24] See, eg, D Jančić, 'National Parliaments and EU Fiscal Integration' (2016) 22 *European Law Journal* 225 (arguing that despite the enhanced role of national parliaments in EU fiscal governance following the Euro crisis, democratic disconnect still favours executive federalism and marginalises parliaments).

II. Towards Relative Authority: Comparative Institutional Assessments

In order to respond to concerns about the legitimacy of supra- and international institutions' exercise of authority, many scholars have turned their attention to issues of accountability and transparency.[25] The normative programme of Global Administrative Law (GAL) further adds obligations of reason giving and opportunities of judicial review to the response.[26] Sure enough, transparency is a virtue, at least within certain limits, and accountability is a core element of democratic rule. In our view, however, these considerations are not sufficient. They do not respond to the more profound questions of legitimacy that the idea of relative authority may, at least in part, be able to capture.[27]

Accountability is concerned with who gives account to whom, with the question of how an actor gives account, and with which possible consequences.[28] It questions the legitimacy of authority only insofar as such authority is exercised without control. One could maybe claim that accountability networks counter potential black holes in settings of scattered authority.[29] But, regardless of which functions those networks may or may not fulfil, they are ill-suited to inform the ways in which decision-making competences are in fact divided and allocated. The focus on holding authority to account only gives secondary consideration to a division and justification of authority that is informed by legitimacy assets. Discourses on transparency, in turn, emphasise the visibility of decision-making, potentially to enable control. At the same time, they have nothing to say regarding the relative role of decision-makers in exercising public authority. As much as accountability and transparency are important elements of legitimation, they are silent when it comes to the question that leads us: who should do what to which extent?

Speaking to the international level specifically, the GAL approach paints with a rather broad brush, prescribing the same cure against legitimacy concerns arising with regard to quite different actors and quite different kinds of acts.[30] It treats

[25] See J Black, 'Constructing and Contesting Legitimacy and Accountability in Polycentric Regulatory Regimes' (2008) 2 *Regulation and Governance* 137; A Bianchi and A Peters (eds), *Transparency in International Law* (Oxford, Oxford University Press, 2013).

[26] B Kingsbury, N Krisch and RB Stewart, 'The Emergence of Global Administrative Law' (2005) 68 *Law and Contemporary Problems* 15; L Casini and B Kingsbury, 'Global Administrative Law Dimensions of International Organizations Law' (2009) 6 *International Organizations Law Review* 319.

[27] See also Rose-Ackerman in this volume, who places these legitimacy claims in specific constitutional contexts and highlights how they may conflict with others.

[28] M Bovens, D Curtin, and P' t Hart, 'The EU's Accountability Deficit: Reality or Myth?' in M Bovens, D Curtin and P' t Hart (eds), *The Real World of EU Accountability What Deficit?* (Oxford, Oxford University Press, 2010) 1.

[29] See Corkin, in this volume; C Scott, 'Accountability in the Regulatory State' (2000) 27 *Journal of Law and Society* 38.

[30] For a discussion of its achievements and limitations, see the symposium in (2015) 13 *International Journal of Constitutional Law* 465.

under the overarching concept of *administration* such different acts as the practice of international adjudication of the World Trade Organization (WTO), decisions of the Basel Committee about capital requirements, and refugee status determinations of the United Nations High Commissioner for Refugees (UNHCR).[31] By and large, GAL is concerned with institutions and regulatory structures, the legitimacy and accountability of which may fail to match their exercise of authority. This approach has guided impressive empirical research, analysing whether and how such institutions and structures correspond with administrative law principles, namely participation, transparency, reason-giving and review.[32] A merit of the GAL approach, relevant to our concept of relative authority, has been the unveiling of the interactions between different actors.[33] Yet, overall problems of legitimacy are confronted with the same toolkit applied to quite diverse realities.[34] We contend that normative assessments of exercises of authority and possible responses need to be more fine-tuned. Is the WTO Appellate Body the most apt institution, in terms of its organisation, composition and procedures, to develop trade law and to take decisions that have far reaching socio-economic and political implications? Which reasons can it offer to support its authority, which legitimacy assets can it tap into? The same questions could be asked with regard to the Basel Committee or the UNHCR, leading to very different answers. Assessments of exercises of authority would need to differ between different kinds of institutions, the legitimacy assets that they do enjoy, and the main effects that their acts produce.[35] GAL approaches are not attuned to this type of analysis.[36]

Similarly, but with a different impetus, global constitutionalism has reacted to the shift of authority beyond the state by articulating an alternative to the

[31] See N Krisch and B Kingsbury, 'Introduction: Global Governance and Global Administrative Law in the International Legal Order' (2006) 17 *European Journal of International Law* 1; RB Stewart and MR Sanchez Badin, 'The World Trade Organization: Multiple Dimensions of Global Administrative Law' (2011) 9 *International Journal of Constitutional Law* 556; L Casini, 'Beyond Drip-painting? Ten Years of GAL and the Emergence of a Global Administration' (2015) 13 *International Journal of Constitutional Law* 473.

[32] eg S Cassese et al, *The Global Administrative Law Casebook* 3rd edn (Cheltenham, Edward Elgar Publishing, 2012).

[33] B Kingsbury, 'Three Models of "Distributed Administration": Canopy, Baob, and Symbiote' (2015) 13(2) *International Journal of Constitutional Law* 478.

[34] On the normative contributions of this approach, see RB Stewart, 'The Normative Dimensions and Performance of Global Administrative Law' (2015) 13 *International Journal of Constitutional Law* 499. Acknowledging the diversity of the phenomena, M Savino, 'What if Global Administrative Law is a Normative Project?' (2015) 15 *International Journal of Constitutional Law* 492, who argues that 'GAL focuses on three functional dimensions—global regulation, global execution, and global adjudication' (at 493).

[35] Also see, placing emphasis on the effect of the acts, M Goldmann, 'Inside Relative Normativity: From Sources to Standard Instruments for the Exercise of International Public Authority' (2008) 9 *German Law Journal* 1865.

[36] While Savino argues that different functions (regulation, execution and adjudication) postulate different legitimacy problems and that GAL recipes differ accordingly, the solutions he identifies still return to the same principles of administrative law. See M Savino, 'What if Global Administrative Law is a Normative Project' (2015) 13 *International Journal of Constitutional Law* 492.

contractual paradigm.[37] With due regard to its variations, global constitutionalism is mainly geared towards the effective pursuit of community values and their protection, be they articulated in the form of *jus cogens*, human rights or other constitutional aspirations. On the whole, the focus of global constitutionalism rests on citizens' rights and protections, democratic self-determination, and on the conditions therefore in regional and global settings. By suggesting the concept of relative authority we too draw on constitutional thinking, relying on the normative programme of separation of powers and proposing a reconstruction that may fit the reality of global governance. Yet, our ambitions are more limited as we do not suggest that there is a constitutional set-up or settlement, at least not at the international level. Our point is that the concern to guide politics in the direction of the pursuit of public goods has so far only led few scholars of global constitutionalism to focus on the allocation of authority between actors.[38] Even those who embrace constitutional pluralism—ie the plurality of authority between different levels of governance—do not readily break down their argument to specific institutional actors.[39]

Against this background of two dominant responses to the exercise of authority in global governance, we recall the gist of comparative institutionalism and place the assessment of any actor in relation to its 'imperfect alternatives'.[40] Institutional choice is what the idea of relative authority places centre-stage.

The lack of comparative institutional assessments haunts most pointed critiques of specific exercises of authority. When it comes to judicial decisions, one may critique, for instance, an arbitral tribunal's extensive definition of investment to include the mere purchase of bonds, the broad interpretation of expropriation to include regulatory takings or the narrow reading of circumstances precluding wrongfulness. One may also call into question the authorisation to market pesticides for overlooking environmental concerns, critique a decision based on the scientific opinion of the European Medicines Agency to approve a drug that research has shown to have dangerous side effects, or a Council regulation imposing anti-dumping duties based on a contested finding of threat of injury to Union

[37] See, eg, P Dobner and M Loughlin (eds), *The Twilight of Constitutionalism?* (Oxford, Oxford University Press, 2010); J Klabbers, A Peters and G Ulfstein, *The Constitutionalization of International Law* (Oxford, Oxford University Press, 2009); M Payandeh, *Internationales Gemeinschaftsrecht* (Berlin, Springer, 2010); T Kleinlein, *Konstitutionalisierung im Völkerrecht: Konstruktion und Elemente einer idealistischen Völkerrechtslehre* (Berlin, Springer, 2012). On the similarities with the GAL approach, see Savino, ibid.

[38] A Peters, 'Compensatory Constitutionalism: The Function and Potential of Fundamental International Norms and Structures' (2006) 19 *Leiden Journal of International Law* 579. Stressing that constitutionalism, in its pluralist variant, facilitates the acceptance of claims of authority, D Halberstam, 'Local, Global and Plural Constitutionalism' in G de Búrca and JHH Weiler (eds), *The Worlds of European Constitutionalism* (Cambridge, Cambridge University Press, 2012) 164.

[39] See, eg, M Kumm, 'Rethinking Constitutional Authority' in M Avbelj and J Komárek (eds), *Constitutional Pluralism in the European Union and Beyond* (Oxford, Hart Publishing, 2012) 39–65.

[40] NK Komesar, *Imperfect Alternatives: Choosing Institutions in Law, Economics, and Public Policy* (Chicago, Chicago University Press, 1997).

industry. That is a worthwhile endeavour. Pointed critique may be well received by decision-makers. The trajectory of the WTO Appellate Body, for instance, shows how it—*sub silencio*, usually—reacts to debates in the Dispute Settlement Body and, arguably, to scholarly criticism. But this kind of critique has its limits, too. More forward-looking and lasting answers oftentimes turn towards institutional questions.

We suggest looking for a better allocation of authority with reference to the legitimacy assets of their authors.[41] It will never happen that a single right balance between competing interests will be found and the job is done. Balances need to be constantly re-enacted and renegotiated. Neil Komesar rightly writes in his manifesto for institutional comparison: '[g]oal choice, no matter how elegantly executed, is no substitute for institutional choice'.[42] Thinking on relative authority leads us to asking not only *how* to strike balances but also *who* should have the authority to strike them. Such a comparative assessment is a principled petitum.

If we situate our inquiry within the landscape of larger theoretical work, we place ourselves in line with research on international public authority.[43] This line of research notably suggests zooming in on specific exercises of authority, to standardise specific acts and their effects, and to ask what kind of legitimacy is required for those acts.[44] We build on this general approach to authority beyond the state and focus more specifically on how authority should be allocated. Building on the more general approach to international public authority, we stay attuned to the way in which authority is exercised in processes of governance where combinations of different actors shape a specific issue area.[45] We claim that it is in their interaction that we can best understand and assess public authority.

Actors use, contest and legitimise the authority of others. Authority is exercised via the combined effect of a series of mutually reinforcing acts. It is instructive to look at the dynamic process in which authority unfolds and thus to better understand and assess it.[46] The guidelines on pharmaceutical testing of the International Conference on Harmonization serve as an illustrative example. They have a significant impact within the Union because of European regulations referencing them. To offer yet another example: formally non-binding food safety standards amount to weighty exercises of authority through their incorporation in WTO law

[41] Such a critique can of course also be articulated in light of specific decisions. See G Shaffer and JP Trachtman, 'Interpretation and Institutional Choice at the WTO' (2011) 52 *Virginia Journal of International Law* 103.

[42] NK Komesar, *Law's Limits* (Cambridge, Cambridge University Press, 2001) 151.

[43] von Bogdandy, Golmann and Venzke, above n 1; A von Bogdandy, P Dann and M Goldmann, 'Developing the Publicness of Public International law: Towards a Legal Framework for Global Governance Activities' (2008) 9 *German Law Journal* 1375.

[44] See M Goldmann, 'Inside Relative Normativity: From Sources to Standard Instruments for the Exercise of International Public Authority' (2009) 9 *German Law Journal* 1865; J Bast, *Grundbegriffe der Handlungsformen der EU. Entwickelt am Beschluss als praxisgenerierter Handlungsform des Unions- und Gemeinschaftsrechts* (Berlin, Springer, 2006).

[45] For an overview of the theoretical terrain also see Peters and Schaffer, above n 10.

[46] J Mendes, 'Rule of Law and Participation: A Normative Analysis of Internationalized Rulemaking as Composite Procedures' (2014) 12(2) *International Journal of Constitutional Law* 22–24.

and jurisprudence.[47] Thorny questions about who should adopt these acts—and critiques of how authority is allocated in existing institutional solutions—can best be answered if placed in this relational setting. It is also in that interaction that we can best see the legitimacy resources that specific actors bring to the table, which legitimacy assets they possibly feed into the process of global governance and which combination of inclusion, rights protection and functional specialisation can support the legitimation of authority.

The idea of relative authority emphasises and links these two thoughts—that an institutional actor's authority be put into relation to other actors and that its authority connects to different legitimacy assets.[48] It links them through the recognition that no exercise of authority can ultimately rely on inclusion, specialisation or rights protection alone. Relative authority is as much about connections as it is about divisions. A parliament cannot do without expertise. Decisions of the executive leaning on the specialised knowledge of its authors may fall short of inclusion. Each may conflict with fundamental or contractual rights. The legitimacy of a court judgment, conversely, ought to be assessed in light of possible politico-legislative responses.[49]

Importantly, each actor should be embedded in a political context in which choices regarding the way in which specific exercises of authority ought to be justified may be challenged and re-enacted. The division between questions deemed to be of a political nature and therefore in need of inclusive decision-making processes, on the one hand, and those that are deemed to be of a technical nature, and thus best in the hands of a functionally specialised institution, on the other, is itself of a highly political nature and best dealt with through inclusive political processes. This division must at least be subject to possible contestation. Too often has a claim to expertise in European and international law shielded the exercise of authority from scrutiny.[50]

III. Normative Traction: Towards a Framework for Assessment

A. Legitimacy Claims

Different actors make different legitimacy claims with which they justify their authority. Authority is relative in this sense even on any single level of governance.

[47] R Howse, 'A New Device for Creating International Legal Normativity: The WTO Technical Barriers to Trade Agreement and "International Standards"' in C Joerges and E-U Petersmann (eds), *Constitutionalism, Multilevel Trade Governance and Social Regulation* (Oxford, Hart Publishing, 2006) 383.

[48] On the former dimension of relative authority also see Roughan, above n 9, 137–45.

[49] See further Corkin and Mak in this volume.

[50] In EU law, this may come in the guise of deferential judicial review of discretion. See Ritleng, in this volume).

In basic terms, the ideal type of judicial adjudication gains its legitimacy from the law that it applies, from party consent, independence and impartiality. Its legitimacy bases are different from those assets that underlie the idea of legislation (representativeness, inclusion) or the idea of administration (competence, expertise).[51] Specific actors feed different legitimacy assets into global governance.

To illustrate the point, the European Commission for instance draws its legitimacy to act 'in the general interest of the Union' mainly from the competence and independence of its members, from its collegial way of acting, and from the way in which it is embedded in the EU institutional system (not only via the powers of oversight of the Parliament).[52] These are the core constitutive elements that define the institutional capacity of the Commission and that explain the authority that the Treaty allocated to this institution.[53] In view of the democratic provisions of the Treaty, and depending on its concrete functions, the procedures of the Commission should be transparent and politically inclusive. Arguably, the extent to which they ought to incorporate such concerns depends on the effects of the acts they adopt. To illustrate the argument further, most EU agencies derive their legitimacy mostly from the expertise that they bring into EU decision-making. Because they incorporate, in different ways, bureaucrats from Member States, the knowledge that they provide also reflects the views of national administrations and, eventually, national social and cultural perceptions. The actual practices of governance complicate this account significantly.[54] Nevertheless, it illustrates that the composition, organisation, procedures of the Commission and of EU agencies provides them with legitimacy assets when exercising authority. Those assets justify their authority to determine whether aid granted by Member States or concerted practices between undertakings are compatible with the rules of the Treaty (in the case of the Commission), and to provide an opinion on the safety of chemicals, food or aircrafts (to name the tasks of some of the EU agencies). They also inform a critique of their authority. Thus, for instance, the Commission's legitimacy to give opinions on draft budgetary plans of Member States is questionable, given inter alia the potential re-distributional effects of those opinions in policy areas that are outside the competences of the EU (even if such a mandate is given by an act of the Parliament and of the Council).[55]

[51] See Möllers, above n 16; B Ackerman, 'The New Separation of Powers' (2000) 113 *Harvard Law Review* 633.

[52] See, respectively, arts 17(3) TEU and 245 TFEU; art 17(6)(b) TEU; arts 226, 230 and 234 TFEU.

[53] See, in more detail, J Mendes, 'La legittimazione dell'amministrazione dell'UE: tra istanze istituzionali e democratiche' in L de Lucia and B Marchetti (eds), *L'Amministrazione europea e il suo diritto* (Bologna, Il Mulino, 2015) 89–116. See also Ritleng in this volume, for a discussion of the different legitimacy assets of EU administrative bodies.

[54] On the importance of including them in an analysis of relative authority, see Carolan and Curtin in this volume.

[55] Reg (EU) No 473/2013 of the European Parliament and of the Council of 21 May 2013 on common provisions for monitoring and assessing draft budgetary plans and ensuring the correction of excessive deficit of the Member States in the euro area [2013] OJ L 140, 11–23.

The same applies to the legitimacy of the outright monetary transactions programme adopted by the European Central Bank at the height of the Euro crisis. It is capable of having redistribution effects and economic consequences unsupported by the Central Bank's mandate and legitimacy assets.

Our argument runs close to separation of powers thinking, which indeed emphasises the distinct legitimacy assets that different actors and institutions bring into the process of governance. In this way the idea of the separation of powers—however odd it may sit at first sight with modern forms of governance—continues to express a normative programme that in our view aids critique. In a prominent formulation of the German Federal Constitutional Court, the

> institutional and functional differentiation and separation of powers serves the distribution of political authority [*politischer Macht*] and responsibility as well as the control of those in power. It pursues the aim that, as much as possible, decisions are right. This means that they be taken by those institutions, which, according to their organization, composition, function, and procedure, are best suited for taking them.[56]

When asking 'who should do what to which extent?' we are indeed opening up towards a rich tradition of political-philosophical and legal-doctrinal work in which normative criteria have ripened to fine-tune institutional balances and allocations of authority. But the idea of separation of powers is also one of functional separation and specialisation. That holds promise but also comes with limits, in particular for supra- and international exercises of authority.[57]

B. The Separation of Powers: Dividing Governmental Functions

We are concerned with how authority is allocated in supra- and international settings. Revisiting thinking on the separation of powers allows us to go back to the underlying ideas for divisions of authority between institutions that are bound to act in specific ways.[58] Notably, it reminds us that the ways in which specific institutions can act is tied to the legitimacy assets that they can bring forward.[59] Discourse theory's reconstruction of the separation of powers is insightful in this regard. It suggests that the legitimacy assets that an institutional actor can claim for itself impact the way it should be allowed to reason and justify its decisions. Jürgen Habermas distinguishes discourses of norm justification (the work of the legislature) from discourses of norm application (the work of the administration and the judiciary, in distinct ways). Only the legislature enjoys unlimited access

[56] 68 Bundesverfassungsgericht (BVerfG) I, 86; 98 BVerfG 218, 251-2.

[57] On those challenges more generally see Carolan, above n 22. See also Carolan and Curtin in this volume.

[58] Möllers, above n 16, 93; Waldron, above n 16, 457, 466.

[59] Möllers, above n 16.

to normative, pragmatic and empirical reasons while the norm application of the judiciary has to stay within the bounds of what is permitted in *legal* discourse.[60] The separation of powers is reflected in the 'distribution of the possibilities for access to different sorts of reasons'.[61]

The idea of the separation of powers has oftentimes been caricatured and easily dismissed. Reasons for dismissive tones are that powers do not necessarily come neatly packaged in the three branches of the legislature, judiciary and executive, nor are those powers neatly separated. Neither reason is compelling for abandoning the normative programme of separation of powers thinking or its more specific and doctrinal manifestations. Critiques tend to set up a straw man. Their take on the separation of powers as hermetically split into three cannot even be attributed to Montesquieu.[62] Already James Madison argued in the Federalist Papers that powers are 'by no means totally separate and distinct from each other'.[63] He clarified that Montesquieu's concern was not with clinical separation. To the contrary, it is clear that '[d]epartments must be connected and blended, as to give so each a constitutional control over the others'.[64] What is more, in its dominant reading, the separation of powers postulates a tripartite distinction of functions. While a *tripartite* division is by no means a necessity, any suggestion of a clear-cut distinction of functions may indeed be a reason to take some distance from separation of powers thinking when analysing supra- and international exercises of authority.

In the dominant reading of separation of powers, an allocation of authority that focuses on the links between the legitimacy claims and ways of acting presupposes a distinction between legislative, executive and judicial functions.[65] Roughly, the legislator, as the most *representative and inclusive* institution, is tasked with laying down general and abstract laws. A court exercises public authority in the context of adjudication, retroactively and not on its own motion, in concrete disputes. It is set up at some distance to the political-legislative process dominated by majority voting. At least when it comes to constitutional adjudication, but also in the enforcement of private contracts or statutory provisions, it aims

[60] J Habermas, *Between Facts and Norms: Contributions to a Discourse Theory of Law and Democracy* (W Rehg trans, Cambridge MA, MIT Press, 1998) 192, 229–37; see further T Lieber, *Diskursive Vernunft und formelle Gleichheit: zu Demokratie, Gewaltenteilung und Rechtsanwendung in der Rechtstheorie von Jürgen Habermas* (Tübingen, Mohr Siebeck, 2007).

[61] Möllers, above n 16, 192.

[62] In this sense questionable, B Ackerman, 'Good-bye Montesquieu' in S Rose-Ackerman and PL Lindseth (eds), *Comparative Administrative Law* (Cheltenham, Edward Elgar Publishing, 2010) 128. See also J Ziller, 'Separation of Powers in the European Union's Intertwined System of Government. A Treaty Based Analysis for the Use of Political Scientists and Constitutional Lawyers' (2008) 73 *Il Politico* 133, 137.

[63] A Hamilton, J Madison and J Jay, *The Federalist Papers* (New York, Bantam Books, 1982) 294.

[64] ibid, 300. On the early American constitutional experiences as revealing of the practical impossibility of hermetic divisions, and generally on the problems of a tripartite division, see Carolan, above n 22, 19–21.

[65] Möllers, above n 16, 79–80, distinguishes between the effect of certain acts according to their scope (who is subject to them?) their temporal orientation (are they directed towards the past or prospective?) and their degree of legalisation (to which degree is the decision already framed by law?).

at the effective *protection of rights*. In this respect, courts are by far the most constrained institutions. Administrations, too, follow highly formalised procedures when acting as adjudicators, or less so when they act as rule-makers.[66] They rely on *competence* or *specialised knowledge* to implement policies, whether enshrined in legislation or not. They carry forward democratic constitutional government.[67] It is this way in which the division and allocation of authority is enmeshed in separation of powers theory with a functional specialisation that can be particularly problematic when analysing supra- and international authority.

C. Limits of the Separation of Powers and its Potential

Revisiting the normative programme of separation of powers thinking is one thing, quite another would be to attempt to project onto the supranational and international realms any ideal-type of a balanced constitution anchored in a tripartite division of functions. The difficulties in delimiting the borders of these functions and the typical absence, at least in international settings, of functioning politico-legislative processes are important reasons to take such distance. A workable theory of separation of powers would also presuppose a division attuned to the specificities of a sufficiently defined system of government in a given constitutional framework.[68] While European constitutionalists could argue that this condition is fulfilled in the European Union, the evolutionary character of the Union also continuously questions the institutional design.[69]

That thinking in terms of a tripartite division of functions could lead us to ask the wrong questions is illustrated by the hitherto vain attempts in European law to delimit delegated acts from implementing acts by reference to their quasi-legislative or executive nature.[70] The division between the two categories of acts was intended to 'guarantee that acts with *the same legal/political force* have the *same foundations* in terms of democratic legitimacy'.[71] This normative ambition comes quite close to our emphasis on relative authority. However, the prism of

[66] The degree to which this is the case varies across legal systems and fields. Variations across legal systems and fields will necessarily temper such a sweeping statement. Further note that the borderline between what is adjudication and what is rule-making can certainly be contested.

[67] On democracy, rights and competence as three core principles of legitimacy, see Rose-Ackerman, in this volume. Also see S Rose-Ackerman, S Egidy and J Fowkes, *Due Process of Lawmaking: The United States, South Africa, and the European Union* (Cambridge, Cambridge University Press, 2015).

[68] Also see Carolan, above n 22.

[69] As shown by P Craig, 'Institutions, Power, and Institutional Balance' in P Craig and G de Búrca (eds), *The Evolution of EU Law* 2nd edn (Oxford, Oxford University Press, 2011) 41–84. See also Carolan and Curtin, in this volume.

[70] For a systematic attempt, see Case C-427/12 *Commission v European Parliament and Council (Biocides)* [2013] EU:C:2013:871, Opinion of AG Villalón. For those difficulties in the context of financial governance, see de Bellis, in this volume.

[71] Secretariat of the European Convention, *Final Report of Working Group IX on Simplification* (Conv 424/02, WG IX 13, 2002) (henceforth 'Final Report') 2 (emphasis added).

the separation of powers turned the question of which acts have the same legal or political force into one of demarcating the substantive realms of legislation and execution.[72] Core to this interpretation was the claim that the 'more technical aspects or details of *legislation*' still belong to the legislator, so to speak. Reasons of efficiency and flexibility arguably justify their delegation to the executive.[73] As 'quasi-legislative matters', they could not be fully taken out of the purview of the legislator at the risk of jeopardising the legitimacy of the delegated acts. This means enhanced controls. By contrast, when the Commission exercises 'purely executive' power, controls by the legislator are not required. They are in fact barred by the Treaty.[74] Where to draw this line has become the core of institutional struggles that found their way to the Court.[75]

In the *Biocides* case—the first after the entry into force of the Lisbon Treaty where the Court of Justice was faced with the question of delimitation between delegated and implementing acts—the Commission argued that the power to specify the fees, which need to be paid to the European Chemicals Agency, was of a quasi-legislative nature and could not be lawfully exercised via implementing acts. The Court sided with the Council and the Parliament, to whom it granted virtually full discretion in deciding what is 'supplementing' a legislative act or 'implementing' a legally binding act of the Union (the Treaty terms). According to the Court, given the detail of the legislative act, the Council and the Parliament could 'reasonably take the view' that the Commission was entitled to 'provide further detail' to the normative content of the legislative act, and thus implement it rather than supplement it.[76] There is no satisfactory substantive criterion to distinguish between supplementing and implementing a legislative act. No substantive criterion may ground a normative assessment on whether the legislative choice complies with the scheme of the Treaty.[77] The alternative, the Court seems to indicate, is to leave the decision on the negotiation table of the Commission, the Council and the Parliament.[78] Ultimately, inter-institutional bargaining

[72] ibid, 8; Commission Communication, 'Implementation of Article 290 of the Treaty on the Functioning of the European Union' [2009] COM 673 final, Brussels, 3; European Parliament Resolution of 5 May 2010 on the power of legislative delegation 2010/2021(INI), recital B; and the respective Explanatory Statement in Committee on Legal Affairs, *Report on the power of legislative delegation* (2010/2021(INI), A7-0110/2010, 2010) 8–9.

[73] ibid; Secretariat, *Final Report* (2002) 8. Commission Communication, *Implementation of Article 290* (2009) 3. Parliament.

[74] Art 291 TFEU.

[75] Judgment in Case C-427/12 *Commission v European Parliament and Council (Biocides)* [2014] EU:C:2014:170; Case, C-65/13, *European Parliament v Commission* [2014] EU:C:2014:2289 (on the scope of implementing powers); Case C-88/14, *Commission v European Parliament and Council* [2015] EU:C:2015:499; Case C-286/14, *European Parliament v Commission* [2016] EU:C:2016:183 (on different types of delegated acts).

[76] ibid, paras 40 and 52; the same approach was confirmed in Judgment in Case C-88/14 *Commission v European Parliament and Council (Visa requirements)* [2015] EU:C:2015:499, paras 28–30.

[77] See, further, Ritleng in this volume, arguing that the degree of discretion left to the institution adopting the act could be a distinguishing criterion.

[78] Case C-88/14, *Commission v Parliament and Council* [2015] EU:C:2015:499, para 32.

(which different agreements between the institutions have tried to stabilise) will determine which checks apply: those of Article 290 (delegated acts) or those of Article 291 of the Treaty on the Functioning of the European Union (implementing acts). In both cases, the Commission will be the author of the act,[79] but, crucially, the role and power of the Parliament and of the Council will be different.

The key question then is: if the distribution of powers of the institutions is currently determined solely by their practice under the imprecise Treaty rules,[80] how can one critique, from a democratic perspective, the legitimation of the adopted acts? The question reaches well beyond the example we mentioned. How far can the authority of the Commission to oversee the national implementation of its budgetary recommendations to Member States be justified solely on the basis of the mandate attributed jointly by the Parliament and by the Council? One could maybe invoke the principle of institutional balance as a possible source of limits to institutional practice. But this principle has neither prevented deep changes in the division of authority in the Union (by the combined effect of Treaty change and case law) 'pulled along the by the strongest current', nor a general judicial endorsement of the institutions' creative use of their powers.[81] Returning to our example, is it enough that the Council and the Parliament (together with the Commission) determine 'on a case-by-case basis whether and to what extent it was necessary to have recourse to "delegated" acts and/or to implementing acts and what their scope would be'?[82] If one tries to argue on the basis of the legislative/executive distinction, the answer is downheartedly positive. Then, however, one is forced to rely on the expectations, political weight and negotiating capacities of each institution under Articles 290 and 291 of the TFEU, on EU non-legislative acts. The logic and rationality of this process may or may not be the satisfaction of legitimacy concerns that grounded and pervade the distinction, ie which acts have 'the same legal/political force' is what the Council, the Parliament and the Commission define, possibly in view of mutual power trade-offs. Their 'foundation in terms of democratic legitimacy'[83] may be a secondary, perhaps uncertain, effect of the schemes of institutional collaboration or conflict that the Treaty rules originated and only partially and imperfectly contain.[84] There are thus good reasons to be critical of attempts to shape the Union's system of governance along the lines of a separation of powers thought as functional differentiation.[85]

[79] The Council may adopt implementing acts in restricted circumstances (art 291(2) TFEU).

[80] For an analysis of institutional practice and its consequences, see M Chamon, 'Institutional Balance and Community Method in the Implementation of EU Legislation Following the Lisbon Treaty' (2016) 53 *Common Market Law Review* 1524.

[81] See, in detail, de Witte in this volume. See also JP Jacqué, 'The Principle of Institutional Balance' (2004) 41 *Common Market Law Review* 383, 387.

[82] Secretariat, *Final Report* (2002) 8. The Court endorsed this position in the *Biocides* and in the *Visa requirements* cases.

[83] Secretariat, *Final Report* (2002) 2.

[84] A similar argument is made in J Mendes, 'The Making of Delegated and Implementing Acts: Legitimacy Beyond Inter-institutional Balances' in CF Bergstrom and D Ritleng (eds), *Comitology and Commission Rule-making after Lisbon: The New Chapter* (Oxford, Oxford University Press, 2016).

[85] Carolan and Curtin, in this volume.

Beyond the context of the European Union, thinking about tripartite division according to governmental function faces a yet steeper uphill battle. Neither the UN, nor the WTO—one of the international institutions with most elaborate set-ups—ultimately implement a separation between legislative, executive and judicial powers. The legislative function is generally lagging behind.[86] Historically, only one power of the state was internationalised: administration.[87] Even the WTO only seemingly relies on the conventional separation of powers. It effectively exercises only one of them: adjudication.[88] Article III section 1 WTO Agreement pertains to the executive, and it states that the WTO shall simply *facilitate* the implementation, administration and operation of the Agreement. The role of many bodies, such as the array of committees, in fact goes beyond that.[89] But that is not reflected in this Article III on the WTO's functions. Section 2 pertains to politico-legislative law-making, but suggests that the WTO merely *provides a forum* for negotiations. Only with regard to adjudication does Section 3 state that the WTO shall *administer* the Dispute Settlement Understanding.[90] This imbalance creates difficulties and escapes any tripartite separation of powers.[91]

It may thus be questionable to look at the allocation of authority in international and European law in light of an idea of the separation of powers that has matured in a domestic context of governance that has taken a different, more defined, constitutional setup. We indeed suggest taking distance from a specific tripartite division of powers that closely ties functions to specific branches of government. But the core normative programme that is vested in separation of powers thinking—above all that authority be divided and connected in specific ways that combines ways of acting with legitimacy assets—that is an idea that does travel well and that is insightful for the exercise of authority beyond the state. It also finds resonance in concrete practices.

IV. Iterations in Supra- and International Practices

The complexity of governance dynamics in the European Union and in international settings confirms our claim that the authority of any actor can only be

[86] See A von Bogdandy and I Venzke, *In Whose Name? A Public Law Theory of International Adjudication* (Oxford, Oxford University Press 2014) 119–28.

[87] Von Bernstorff, in this volume.

[88] ibid. Also see R Howse, 'The World Trade Organization 20 Years On: Global Governance by Judiciary' (2016) 27 *European Journal of International Law* 9–77; P Eeckhout, 'The Scales of Trade—Reflections on the Growth and Functions of the WTO Adjudicative Branch' (2010) 13 *Journal of International Economic Law* 3.

[89] A Lang and J Scott, 'The Hidden World of WTO Governance' (2009) 20 *European Journal of International Law* 575.

[90] See already A von Bogdandy, 'Law and Politics in the WTO—Strategies to Cope with a Deficient Relationship' (2001) 5 *Max Planck Yearbook of United Nations Law* 609; L Bartels, 'The Separation of Powers in the WTO: How to Avoid Judicial Activism?' (2004) 53 *International and Comparative Law Quarterly* 861.

[91] Desierto, in this volume.

assessed in relation to others. This complexity may also hinder the feasibility of our normative proposal of linking authority to legitimacy assets. But there are sufficient indications to think that it is indeed a fruitful endeavour—an endeavour that is met halfway by practice. The case law of the Court of Justice of the European Union has in different ways attempted to align authority exercised in heterarchical schemes with procedures that would render certain actors more suitable to adopt certain kinds of acts or decisions. While this practice does not amount to re-defining the allocation of authority within the EU, such 'process-perfecting' review may adjust the legitimacy assets that EU institutions and bodies may mobilise in support of their authority to legitimately produce acts with given effects.[92] In particular, judicial review of discretion tests the boundaries of legitimate action both by administrators and courts. To a great extent, it has been the role of the Court of Justice to define these boundaries, in ways that some may consider too invasive of discretion and others too deferential. It may seem that there are no normative yardsticks against which to approach these often shifting boundaries, other than the general claims of institutional and material capacity of courts in reviewing acts of the EU institutions and bodies.[93] Nevertheless, on the basis of recent case law reflecting the institutional framework of legislative and non-legislative acts of the Union, the argument can be made that the legitimacy assets of the EU legislator and its 'reserved' authority to make policy choices should entail a different degree of review (and deference) when compared to review of non-legislative acts.[94] At the same time, one may query the limits of judicial action in improving existing institutional and procedural frameworks of authority to make sure that, as far as feasible, decisions are right, ie taken by those that are best suited because of their legitimacy assets.[95] One may question in particular whether courts are themselves the institutions that are well placed to make such adjustments. But first, courts may be well-positioned to further the democratic legitimacy of political processes by shaping and upholding procedural principles.[96] And second, in a somewhat counter-intuitive way, in circumstances of societal change, judicial institutions might in fact be the venue for democratically more legitimate law-making.[97]

When it comes to international practices, it may first of all be reminded that thinking in terms of relative authority faces an uphill battle not only because of repercussions of the long-dominant contractual paradigm, but also because historically, international institutions were constructed only to enhance national

[92] See Corkin, in this volume; also see J Corkin, 'Constitutionalism in 3D: Mapping and Legitimating Our Lawmaking Underworld' (2013) 19 *European Law Journal* 636, 659–60; K Lenaerts, 'The European Court of Justice and Process-oriented Review' (2012) 31 *Yearbook European Law* 3 (defending the argument that process-oriented judicial review may contribute to align political decisions with their legal framework).

[93] P Craig, *EU Administrative Law* 2nd edn (Oxford, Oxford University Press, 2012) 405–09 and 438.

[94] Ritleng, in this volume.

[95] Corkin, in this volume.

[96] Rose-Ackerman, in this volume.

[97] Mak, in this volume.

administration. They did not set up checks and balances, but an administration for limited and specific tasks. This historical origin still resonates in the present day.[98] And yet, the proposed focus on relative authority, and the set of questions that comes with it, does inform a whole host of different inquiries. For example, it helps to respond to questions such as how much weight to attribute to international standards in trade law. Pieter Jan Kuijper opines in this regard that '[i]f one really wants to understand how the WTO functions, it is necessary to take into account the large number of organs and Committees of the organization, their interrelationship, and the division of powers between them.'[99] While the WTO Appellate Body has not found a principle of institutional balance in WTO law, it is surely sensitive to the relative allocation of authority.[100] The notion of 'institutional sensitivity' that it uses stands as a placeholder for a more nuanced normative framework for the division and allocation of authority.[101]

In the field of investment law, too, there are sightings of an explicit discussion of relative authority. One prominent example, which testifies to the analytical purchase of discourse theory and its reconstruction of the separation of powers in terms of available reasons, stems from the controversial *Abaclat* award. The investment tribunal's majority concluded that it had jurisdiction to hear the collective claim of Italian holders of Argentine bonds because 'it would be unfair to deprive the investor of its right to resort to arbitration based on the mere disregard of the 18 months litigation requirement'.[102] The dissenting arbitrator, Georges Abi-Saab, took issue with the invocation of fairness in his elaborate dissent. In his view, the majority 'strike[s] out a clear conventional requirement, on the basis of its purely subjective judgment'.[103] According to Abi-Saab, a balance of interests has been struck 'at the appropriate legislative level, by the parties themselves'.[104] The balance is reflected in the treaty text, which opens up an avenue towards international arbitration but subjects it to an 18 month domestic litigation requirement. Arguments of fairness or expediency were on the table of drafting the treaty text and they have led to a certain outcome. The tribunal must not unravel the legislative agreement. It is at that level, the legislative or conventional level, that the balancing of interests takes place—at the level of establishing the law—not at the level of

[98] von Bernstoff, in this volume.

[99] PJ Kuijper, 'WTO Institutional Aspects' in DL Bethlehem et al (eds), *The Oxford Handbook of International Trade Law* (Oxford, Oxford University Press, 2009) 80.

[100] *India—Quantitative Restrictions on Imports of Agricultural, Textile and Industrial Products*, Appellate Body Report (adopted 23 August 1999) DS90/ABR, para 98, with reference to India's appellant's submission, para 27.

[101] *EC—Measures concerning Meat and Meat Products (Hormones)*, Appellate Body Report (adopted 16 October 2008) DS26&48/ABR, para 118.

[102] *Abaclat and Others v Argentine Republic*, 4 August 2011, Decision on Jurisdiction and Admissibility, ICSID CASE NO ARB/07/5, para 583.

[103] *Abaclat and Others v Argentine Republic*, 28 October 2011, Decision on Jurisdiction and Admissibility, Dissenting Opinion, ICSID CASE NO ARB/07/5, para 30.

[104] ibid, para 31.

adjudication, whose domain is the application of the law.[105] It is not open to the tribunal to arrogate to itself the legislative jurisdiction or power of re-examining the rules in order to revise or refashion them, in the name of a rebalancing of interests of its own, according to its whim.[106]

Thinking about relative authority is instructive not only when it comes to the interpretation of substantive law, but also in procedural questions and institutional design. The so-far only case in the field of investment arbitration in which the interplay between the political-legislative and judicial process was a real issue was *Pope Talbot*, when the NAFTA Free Trade Commission (FTC) adopted an interpretation of the fair and equitable treatment standard with an eye on influencing ongoing proceedings.[107] The arbitral tribunal largely side-stepped questions about the role of the political-legislative branch, noted concerns about undue intervention and retroactivity, and held that its interpretation of the applicable standard in fact coincides with what the FTC had submitted to be the law.[108]

Beyond adjudication, the way global regulatory regimes are designed reveals by and large a concern with allocating authority to those bodies that are best fit for purpose. In some cases, a functional allocation of agenda-setting and standard-setting may be discernible, even if intricate relationships between different bodies may end up lumping them together to a significant extent, and thereby question the attempted coherence of the original design (eg the allocation of agenda-setting to technical bodies).[109] However, the point is not one of neatness of institutional designs, whereby the authority to define the agenda in a given policy field would be allocated to a body composed of representatives at the ministerial level and technical issues (such as the equivalence of technical standards) would be relegated to experts from national or supra-national bureaucracies, subject to duties of transparency and participation and, eventually, duties to report to parliaments. Whether agenda-setting and regulatory bodies anchor their authority on legitimacy assets capable of justifying the effects of their decisions on the life of citizens across the globe (and how their authority relates to that of other actors at various levels of governance) has been arguably one of the core issues in dispute regarding the institutional design of TTIP and of other mega-regional trade agreements.[110]

[105] The argument does *not* deny the law-making dimension of international adjudication but instead highlights the different kinds of reasons that are available at different stages of the law-making process. For the discourse theoretical reconstruction of this argument, see above nn 79–80 and accompanying text.

[106] Above n 103, para 251.

[107] NAFTA Free Trade Commission, Notes of Interpretation of Certain Chapter 11 Provisions, 31 July 2001, www.international.gc.ca/trade-agreements-accords-commerciaux/disp-diff/NAFTA-Interpr.aspx?lang?en.

[108] *Pope&Talbot Inc v Canada*, Damages, 31 May 2002, NAFTA Ch 11 Arb Trib, 41 ILM 1347.

[109] See de Bellis, in this volume.

[110] See R Bull, N Mahboubi, RB Stewart and J Wiener, 'New Approaches to International Regulatory Cooperation: the Challenge of TTIP, TPP, and Mega-Regional Trade Agreements' (2015) 78 *Law and Contemporary Problems* 1.

V. Relative Authority in European and International Law

Who should do what in European and international law? We approach authority as relative, thereby drawing on the normative programme of the separation of powers without emulating at the supra- and international levels the division of governmental functions. We have offered the idea of relative authority in order to critique existing institutional arrangements, and to assess institutional practices that shape current allocations of authority. Because it conveys the demand for a specific allocation of authority that is attuned to the legitimacy assets of those actors exercising authority, the idea of relative authority ultimately aspires to contribute to democratic governance.

The contributions of the volume's first part ('Empirical and Normative Traction') situate and complement our reconstruction in a more general fashion, by clarifying both the phenomenon and the normative questions it triggers. *Susan Rose-Ackerman* analyses the way in which different constitutional systems have addressed the democratic accountability of executive policy-making. Drawing on the cases of the United States, South Africa, Germany and the European Union, she shows the trade-offs between different legitimacy assets (democratic accountability, rights protection and technical competence) that clash or converge in executive rule-making in different constitutional frameworks. In her analysis, positive political theory explains the solutions that each legal system provides. It also explains how legitimacy assets may favour or condition the role of courts in furthering democratic accountability and competence.

Eoin Carolan and *Deirdre Curtin* take as their starting point those approaches that have analysed the EU through the lens of separation of powers thinking. While agreeing with the normative value of such approaches, they argue that any transposition of separation of powers thinking to the EU should be attuned to the actual governance practices that allocate authority in the EU. They call for a realistic assessment of the legitimacy assets that each institution brings into the governance process, one which takes into account the 'de facto power relations'. In their analysis, they highlight both the dialogical institutional processes that are capable of promoting procedural values and the shortcomings of formal analyses oblivious of informal practices, capable of subverting the formal allocation of authority.

Mikael Rask Madsen turns to the exercise of public authority by the European Court of Human Rights (ECtHR), one of the most prolific international courts. Against the background of the ECtHR's remarkable authority, Madsen focuses on the interplay between the ECtHR and other actors in four specific instances, discussing the ECtHR's authority as a legal and political actor in relation to domestic law and politics. Each case gives rise to distinct kinds of challenges to the ECtHR's authority and to different opportunities for the Court to meet them—which it did in each of the cases. While an informal system of checks and balances is indeed at work, Madsen argues that better feedback loops are still needed, especially with the Court's political interlocutors. The further institutionalisation of such feedback loops would involve actors with different legitimacy assets and would thus meet the idea of relative authority. In particular, Madsen suggests a different role of the Committee of Ministers in this regard. He also looks at the possibilities of increased participation before the ECtHR, and at the potential of appeals to the Grand Chamber.

Jochen von Bernstorff then draws attention to the uphill battle that the idea of relative authority faces in international law. Von Bernstorff's historical sketch shows how international organisations have emerged as the long arm of national governments in an attempt to increase the capacity of national administrations in a world increasingly marked by cross-border interaction. This dynamic with its origin in the nineteenth century has essentially remained the same in the twentieth century, and arguably remains entrenched in international organisations today. Von Bernstorff thus speaks of 'authority monism'. Seeing the internationalisation of authority from the perspective of national administrations places emphasis on the dominance of sectorial, fragmented interests that prevail in any specific organisation. An additional, interesting pathway of legitimation thus rests in tying the particular interests of specific administrations at the national level to institutions that aspire to pursue the general interest. Conversely, von Bernstorff sees ambivalence, if not strong limits, in the legitimation of international organisations' authority by way of inclusion and participation.

The contribution by *Andreas von Staden* also focuses on the interplay between horizontal and vertical mechanisms of control, arguing that the strength of the latter explains the relative weakness of the former. Von Staden provides a circumspect overview of how authority in global governance is checked and balanced in different relationships, not only horizontal versus but also vertical, intra-organisational versus inter-organisational and specific versus general. A series of institutional mechanisms controls the allocation of relative authority, especially in vertical relationships. More specifically, domestic actors may be able to veto international action, they may threaten exit, change the law, refuse to comply, or comply in a minimalist fashion. Such a set-up, von Staden notes, privileges national executives. While normatively problematic, this is unlikely to change unless domestic constituencies demand such a change and exert pressure on their representatives in that regard.

The contributions in the volume's second part ('Iterations in Practice') probe the purchase of the idea of relative authority by turning to specific actors or specific fields of European and international law. They trace the influence, vel non, of separation of powers thinking as well as the potential and the limits of the idea of relative authority.

Bruno de Witte's chapter provides much-needed guidance through the ways in which the Court of Justice of the European Union (CJEU) has ruled on the principle of institutional balance—a principle inspired by the requirement of limiting the power of EU institutions. He shows how the principle has enabled the Court to rationalise the complex allocation of authority of the Treaties. In this process, the Court entrenched the Member States' choices, refusing to correct inconsistences across policy sectors in the name of an overarching normative conception of separation of powers. At the same time, in some instances, the Court also gave new meaning to that allocation. Overall, the CJEU has straddled a fine line between a deferential approach to the Treaty and legislative choices, on the one hand, and a re-constitutive effort of rationalising institutional practices and disputes, on the other. De Witte further argues that the case law has been largely guided by the concern for a smooth functioning of the institutions, and even for the Member States' possibility to take EU integration ahead in ways not envisaged in the Treaties.

Joseph Corkin's analysis sheds a different light on the role of the Court of Justice. He focuses on the complexity of interdependences that underpin the exercise of public authority, specifically in EU law-making. Such a complexity may both confirm our claim that authority can only be assessed in relation to others and hinder the feasibility of linking authority to legitimacy assets. Corkin, mindful of the difficulties, argues that the idea of relative authority has purchase all the same. He sheds light on how the Court may contribute to reaching the 'subtle blend of relational legitimacies' that may underpin what he terms a 'new separation of powers', one that can be applied also to the heterarchical relations that are part and parcel of law-making processes in the EU. He concludes that the Court has had a significant role in this respect, even if it has fallen short of accomplishing that role in important instances.

Judicial review of administrative discretion tests the boundaries of legitimate action by administrators and courts. To a great extent, it has been the role of the Court of Justice to define these boundaries, in ways that some may consider too invasive of administrative discretion and others too deferential. There are no normative yardsticks against which to approach these often-shifting boundaries, beyond the general claims of institutional and material capacity of courts in reviewing acts of the EU institutions and bodies. Could our normative proposal help critique the spaces of discretion the Court has granted them?

In his analysis of judicial review of discretion in the EU, *Dominique Ritleng* examines the way in which separation of powers has influenced judicial review of administrative discretion in the EU. He recalls that the differentiation between legislative acts and administrative acts, first in the Court's case law and later in the Lisbon Treaty, is one of the main manifestations of separation of powers thinking in EU law—one where the Court had a pivotal role. Ritleng thus returns to one of the arguments made by Bruno de Witte: the distinction between these different types of acts is the result of an institutional evolution that shaped—or attempted to shape—the allocation of authority in the EU according to domestic-inspired separation of powers. Yet, unlike de Witte, he argues that the rationale of the separation of powers has coincided with that of the principle of institutional balance. This different interpretation of the function of institutional balance in the EU—anchored too on the case law—may be explained by the focus of Ritleng's analysis. Ritleng concludes that, contrary to what could be expected on the basis of the Treaty, the differentiation between legislative and administrative acts did not lead to a distinct degree of review of these acts, even if it has influenced case law in other respects—a sign of the difficulties of transposing separation of powers thinking onto the EU level, or at least, as Ritleng argues, a demonstration of the Court's inconsistency when it comes to separation of powers thinking.

Chantal Mak shakes up received ways of thinking about the allocation of authority in the field of European private law, arguing that, in times of societal change, courts may end up being the democratically more legitimate law-makers. That is certainly at odds with received understandings of how the process of law-making should be divided between legislatures and judiciaries, at least in reconstructive theory. However, if we adopt a more realist perspective, Mak argues, we can start to see how courts open up new ways for citizens to access and influence the law-making process. This insight should lead us to reconsider institutional arrangements in this field and to imagine different ones, ultimately with a view to rethinking the concept of democratic legitimacy in European private law.

Maurizia De Bellis turns to the fragmented and shifting spheres of relative authority in both global and EU financial regulation. She combines the analysis of both levels of governance to develop two main arguments. She argues, first, that inquiries into the legitimacy of EU institutions in this sphere must take into account the ways in which they are constrained by global regulation. Second, and rather counterintuitively, given the abundant critique of EU financial governance, De Bellis also argues that the EU may in fact contain lessons for the global architecture. She draws specific attention to the rather well-developed procedural framework, though not without its faults, in which EU agencies in the financial sector act. De Bellis thus demonstrates both the analytical and normative potential of thinking in terms of relative authority in this domain of financial regulation. The complex interplay between different institutions is on view just as well as the potential of rethinking this interplay by linking the exercise of authority with specific legitimacy assets.

Diane Desierto shows how the idea of relative authority works in the contrasting fields of international trade and investment law. She draws specific attention to the ways in which challenges to the exercises of public authority in both fields reflect an understanding of how different legitimacy assets should be brought to bear. To start with, authority is certainly allocated very differently in the highly institutionalised field of trade law, where the secretariat of the WTO, an underbelly of committees, and a rich practice of adjudication shape the law. Adjudicators are also influential in the making of international investment law, but state governments remain in the driving seat, Desierto argues. In both contexts, she carves out internal checks and external constraints on law-makers. Desierto then pays particular attention to the different practices of judicial deference as a mechanism for allocating authority, and to the potential of public participation in strategies for contributing to the legitimacy of law-making.

The jury on the idea of relative authority now lies with the readers of the volume. We hope that they will be convinced by the idea and that, even if doubts remain, they will find the texts of the volume instructive.

Part I

Empirical and Normative Traction

2

Democratic Legitimacy and Executive Rule-making: Positive Political Theory in Comparative Public Law[1]

SUSAN ROSE-ACKERMAN

All modern democracies promulgate rules or 'secondary norms' inside the executive. Such rules are the result of the complexity and technical requirements of modern policy-making. Legislatures are not competent to write detailed rules in such areas as environmental law, financial policy, and health and safety regulation. Hence, they delegate those tasks to the executive or to independent agencies. The resulting rules make policy; they do not just resolve individual cases or decide technical questions. The administrative procedures are linked to democratic institutions and need to be accountable to the citizenry—not just to organised interests and to those subject to the rules. As a result, modern governments ought to infuse executive policy-making with democratic values. Unfortunately, absent constitutional requirements, there may be little or no incentive to legislate in this area or for the executive to voluntarily engage with the public. Reforms consistent with democratic principles cannot be expected to arise from political expediency alone.

In this chapter I take as given both the inevitability of policy-making delegation and the value of democratically accountable rule-making processes inside the executive. I concentrate here on the incentives for providing such processes that are created by alternative constitutional structures—in particular, presidential and parliamentary systems. The cases I consider are the United States (US), South Africa, Germany and the European Union (EU). The basic empirical differences are clear and striking. Under the United States presidential system the law is fundamentally concerned with the public accountability of rule-making in

[1] This paper builds on material in S Rose-Ackerman, S Egidy and J Fowkes, 'The Law of Lawmaking: Positive Political Theory in Comparative Public Law' in F Bignami and D Zaring (eds), *Comparative Administrative Law and Regulation* (Cheltenham, Edward Elgar Publishing, 2015) and on: S Rose-Ackerman, S Egidy and J Fowkes, *Due Process of Lawmaking: The United States, South Africa, and the European Union* (Cambridge, Cambridge University Press, 2015). My discussion of Germany and South Africa draws heavily on the work of my co-authors.

agencies and cabinet departments.[2] In contrast, the German administrative courts and the Constitutional Court provide almost no review of rule-making procedures inside the executive. The applicable law is fragmented and leaves wide gaps. Judicial review focuses on the violation of rights; courts rarely check rule-making procedures. Their focus is on individual adjudications. The South African Constitution, as interpreted by the courts, includes a rich concept of democracy, but South Africa is closer to Germany than the US when it comes to rule-making. Although its Constitution provides several grounds for reviewing administrative rule-making processes, no legal instrument specifically provides for their review and the Constitutional Court has yet to treat rules as analogous to statutes when it comes to process (although the issue is not yet settled).[3] The EU courts struggle to balance deference to the EU treaty values of human dignity, freedom, democracy, equality, the rule of law and respect for human rights, including the rights of minorities (article 2 Treaty on European Union (TEU)). The Lisbon Treaty has broadened the democratic basis of the EU by emphasising participatory values in addition to the core principle of representative democracy. However, it remains unclear exactly what these broad statements of principle mean in practice. I claim that these differences are tied to the constitutional structures of the four cases. A presidential system creates different incentives for legislators compared with a parliamentary system or with the EU's complex framework. Hence, certain kinds of judicial review would be more intrusive in one system compared to another.

The basic comparative analysis is positive, but my goals are ultimately normative. My focus is on the democratic accountability of executive policy-making, and the ways that it complements or conflicts with the protection of rights and the competent application of expertise to public policy-making.[4] States gain legitimacy by acting competently—incorporating relevant technical, expert knowledge into the development of policy. Unless their actions are an effective response to

[2] The terminology is not standardised. I use the terms 'rules' or 'regulations' to refer to government policy documents issued by any executive body or independent agency that have external legal force. Other umbrella terms are 'secondary legislation' or 'statutory instrument', as used in the (unofficial) English translation of the German Basic Law. I distinguish this category of policy-making both from policy built up through adjudication and from 'guidelines' or 'policy statements' that merely create a framework for implementation without creating legal rights or duties. In Germany the term 'agency' is sometimes used only to refer to independent or quasi-independent bodies that regulate particular sectors or that provide oversight of the government itself. However, I use the term in the looser American sense to also cover core executive branch bodies, such as the Environmental Protection Agency.

[3] In South Africa it remains unclear if the term 'administrative acts' in the Promotion of Administrative Justice Act includes rule-making. If the Court does read rule-making into the Act, then rule-making will be subject to an array of procedural standards and duties.

[4] S Rose-Ackerman, *From Elections to Democracy: Building Accountable Government in Hungary and Poland* (Cambridge, Cambridge University Press, 2005) 5–7; for a slightly different trichotomy see JL Mashaw, 'Judicial Review of Administrative Action: Reflections on Balancing Political, Managerial and Legal Accountability' (2005) 1 *Revista Direito GV* 153, 168. See also the classic texts R Dahl, *Polyarchy, Participation and Opposition* (New Haven, Yale University Press, 1971); R Dahl, *Democracy and Its Critics* (New Haven, Yale University Press, 1989); G O'Donnell, 'Horizontal Accountability in New Polyarchies' (1998) 9 *Journal of Democracy* 112; G O'Donnell 'Delegative Democracy' (1994) 5 *Journal of Democracy* 55.

social and economic problems, their claims to public legitimacy ring hollow.[5] Rights constrain democratic choice, but competence is required to implement policies. Over and above, competence and the protection of rights is democratic legitimacy. Transparency, citizen participation in executive policy-making, and the requirement to give reasons help citizens monitor the state beyond the ballot box. The proper design of bureaucratic institutions is a central task of constitutional government. One route to the political legitimacy and policy-making accountability of the executive is procedural, but the appropriate response is not always obvious. Procedures that further one type of legitimacy—based on, say, individual rights—may limit others—for instance, democratic legitimacy and competence.

I also ask what role the courts should play in furthering this goal given the judges' own lack of technical training and management experience. Drawing on the insights of positive political theory, the argument tries to explicate the role of courts in the review of policy-making procedures and aims for a normative evaluation of that role under different executive structures. A key feature of judicial review is the link between the separation of powers and checks and balances. The separation of powers counsels courts to show restraint especially when dealing with politically sensitive issues. The doctrine of checks and balances holds that, in exercising its own particular powers, each branch should constrain the others' potential abuses. Some scholars stress that the separation of powers permits independent action by each branch; others see institutional separation as a route to oversight without direct hierarchical supervision.[6]

The fundamental normative issues are comparable across the cases. Do policy-making processes for rules further public legitimacy? Can constitutional courts uphold this value without overstepping their bounds? Can checks and balances be compatible with the separation of powers?

I. Positive Political Theory

Positive political theory (PPT) assumes self-interested political and bureaucratic actors who behave strategically to further their goals. The focus is on the re-election motives of politicians and the civil servants' desire for influence and promotion as well as future employment in the private sector. This perspective is prominent in much recent American scholarship dealing with the behaviour of the legislature and of executive agencies.[7] The approach takes certain aspects of the institutional

[5] G Majone, 'Two Logics of Delegation: Agency and Fiduciary Relations in EU Governance' (2001) 2 *European Union Politics* 103; G Majone, 'From the Positive to the Regulatory State' (1997) 17(2) *Journal of Public Policy* 139.

[6] See B Ackerman, 'The New Separation of Powers' (2000) 113 *Harvard Law Review* 633 for a review of the debate and proposals for constitutional reform.

[7] S Rose-Ackerman (ed), *Economics of Administrative Law* (Cheltenham, Edward Elgar Publishing, 2007) reprints many of the most important PPT articles dealing with the executive branch and with its oversight by Congress.

structure as given and explores the behaviour of political and economic actors within that structure. PPT, although more fully developed in the United States, need not be limited to a presidential system with a two-house legislature and a Supreme Court. The claim that political actors behave strategically subject to institutional constraints is a broad and general one. Here, I apply the PPT model to compare executive branch policy-making in the US presidential system with two parliamentary systems, Germany and South Africa, and with the EU. In doing so I take as given the basic institutional framework in each polity and ask how it affects the behaviour of politicians, bureaucrats and judges as they enact rules, make policy and resolve issues in court.[8] The fundamental difference between presidential and parliamentary systems that frames the inquiry is the existence of a powerful, independently elected president. Hence, the executive may be under the control of a different political party or group than the legislature. In a parliamentary system the same party or party coalition controls both the Lower House and the executive. A powerful upper house may complicate the picture, but the key distinction is the unity of interest between executive and the majority in the legislature. Of course, this unity may be fragile, and minority governments can occur, but in a wide range of cases the link between executive and legislative policy-making is much tighter in parliamentary than in presidential systems.

Although drawing on the PPT model, the argument recognises that members of the legislature, political appointees and civil servants are not necessarily motivated only by narrow self-interest. They may have public-regarding motives, endorse a particular theory of constitutional law, aim to be faithful agents of the voters, or seek to further a political agenda.[9] However, it seems reasonable to assume that most politicians seek re-election and wish to preserve their own freedom of action tempered by the collective action problems that dog the legislature—a multi-member decision-making body that persists over time. Politicians and political parties seek to claim credit for benefits to their constituents and to society at large and to avoid blame for imposing costs.[10]

The motivations of judges are left open. The argument follows William N Eskridge, Jr and John Ferejohn in supposing that judges may be driven by constitutional and legal principles that do not easily translate into the rubric of day-to-day politics.[11] Although they are likely to temper their decisions in the

[8] Some research in the PPT tradition considers the incentives facing those who draft constitutions. See RD Cooper, *The Strategic Design of Constitutions* (Princeton, Princeton University Press, 2000) and the articles collected in S Voigt (ed), *Design of Constitutions* (Cheltenham, Edward Elgar Publishing, 2013).

[9] See the similar perspective of D Farber and AJ O'Connell (eds), *Research Handbook on Public Choice and Public Law* (Cheltenham, Edward Elgar Publishing, 2010).

[10] DR Mayhew, *Congress the Electoral Connection* 2nd edn (New Haven, Yale University Press, 2004); MP Fiorina, *Congress Keystone of the Washington Establishment* 2nd edn (New Haven, Yale University Press, 1989). On the connection to judicial review see PP Frickey and SS Smith, 'Judicial Review, the Congressional Process and the Federalism Cases: An Interdisciplinary Critique' (2002) 111 *Yale Law Journal* 1707.

[11] WN Eskridge and J Ferejohn, *A Republic of Statutes: The New American Constitution* (New Haven, Yale University Press, 2010) 22–28.

light of political reality, they do not flout clear legal mandates. They may bend the interpretation of open-ended texts toward preferred policies, but they are committed to 'the rule of law' even if it leads them to rule against their own policy preferences in particular cases. Judges are sensitive to their status as unelected officials who should not interfere too aggressively with political processes.[12] This sense of their role constrains them from imposing doctrines that are deeply at odds with the practical operation of the political system. Such behaviour is both principled and strategic.[13] It derives from a normative commitment to a particular judicial role, but it also acknowledges that the judiciary cannot enforce controversial decisions without political and popular support.

Given that introduction, consider the incentives for legislatures in presidential and parliamentary democracies to delegate policy-making to the executive while constraining executive power through judicial oversight. Legislators have neither the time nor the expertise to solve all policy problems—delegation to the executive is inevitable. Furthermore, their constituents may benefit from a regulatory system that can respond to changes in underlying conditions without requiring statutory amendments. The alternatives of relying on private lawsuits or on very detailed statutes are not realistic responses to many issues. These motives for delegation apply to all democracies, but they are expressed differently in presidential and parliamentary systems.

A. Presidential Systems

In a presidential system the legislature has an additional reason to support delegation beyond expertise, namely time constraints and the need for flexibility. Legislators can increase their re-election chances by shifting hard choices onto the shoulders of cabinet departments and agencies while taking credit for the benefits a statute provides.[14] However, even if the legislature shifts the burden of implementation to the executive, legislators will seldom want to be completely isolated from executive actions. They will want to be informed, even if only to better criticise the president and his top officials. Members will hold hearings, demand reports, control agency budgets and threaten to repeal or amend statutes.[15] Without checks, a new presidential administration might want to change policy-making priorities by

[12] In the US some state judges are elected. It is an open question whether such judges act as if they have a stronger mandate from the public to oppose other political actors. See E Leib and A-A Bruhl, 'Elected Judges and Statutory Interpretation' (2012) 79 *University of Chicago Law Review* 1215.

[13] On judges' motivations, see FB Cross, 'The Judiciary and Public Choice' (1999) 50 *Hastings Law Journal* 355; and FB Cross and EH Tiller, 'Judicial Partisanship and Obedience to Legal Doctrine: Whistleblowing on the Federal Courts of Appeals' (1998) 107 *Yale Law Journal* 2155.

[14] JQ Wilson, *The Politics of Regulation* (New York, Basic Books, 1980); MP Fiorina, 'Legislative Choice of Regulatory Forms: Legal Process or Administrative Process' (1982) 39 *Public Choice* 33.

[15] MD McCubbins, RG Noll and B Weingast, 'Administrative Procedures as Instruments of Political Control' (1987) 3 *Journal of Law, Economics, and Organization* 243.

repealing old rules and enacting new ones with no statutory changes—especially if it is governing with a hostile legislature. Even when there is a unified government, with the same party controlling both the legislature and the presidency, politicians may favour some review of executive actions to improve their own re-election chances and policy-making influence.

Hence, some legislators might support formal statutory pathways to review executive rule-making ex post, but only if these mechanisms do not implicate them in unpopular decisions. For example, a statute might require that rules be submitted to the legislature for an up-or-down vote or to give the legislature time to pass a vote of disapproval. Even more intrusively, the law could permit the legislature or its relevant committees to participate directly in drafting the text. The legislature may not favour such second chances, however. First, the enacting legislature may want to lock in future legislatures and prevent them from interfering with the implementation of a favoured policy. Second, second chances undermine many of the arguments for delegation in the first place. A legislature that delegates because it lacks expertise, time and flexibility will not want to be able to veto rules in subject areas where these elements are salient. Of course, there are cases where other factors trump these concerns. The legislature may acknowledge the executive's superior expertise but want to be able to check its discretion ex post.

But there is an alternative to ex post legislative review of rules. Because legislation is difficult to enact and to repeal in a presidential system with a strong legislature, incumbents may try to prevent their substantive policies from being immediately undermined by a new administration. The legislature can exercise indirect policy control by requiring procedures, such as notice, an open hearing and reason-giving before the executive announces its final rule. Such requirements further the goals of transparency, openness to outside input, and justification in ways that help the general public and affected interests to learn about and to influence the policy-making process.[16] They raise fewer separation-of-powers concerns than a legislative vote on rules, but they still constrain the executive. In addition, they aid legislative review. Interested legislators can find out what rules are in the pipeline and seek to affect their development. Hence, a law covering rule-making procedures may gain the support even of legislators with no strong commitment to the public accountability of the executive per se.

A key feature of administrative procedure laws concerns provisions for judicial oversight of the rule-making process. The incentives and bottlenecks of a presidential system suggest that the legislature may support such review. Legislators opposed to an executive policy-making initiative cannot change the law without

[16] JL Mashaw, 'Reasoned Administration: The European Union, the United States, and the Project of Democratic Governance' (2007–08) 76 *George Washington Law Review* 99 argues that reason-giving enhances the public legitimacy of policies because it 'treats persons as rational moral agents who are entitled to evaluate and participate in a dialogue about official policies on the basis of reasoned discussion'.

surmounting numerous veto gates.[17] Their control of agency budgets and oversight activities may not be effective. Hence, statutes that permit judicial review of executive policy-making processes are a rational response to the separation of powers between the president and the legislature.[18] Judicial review of administrative policy-making processes provides a check that alerts the legislature to particularly serious problems. In the terminology of Matthew McCubbins and Thomas Schwartz judicial review acts as a 'fire alarm' that relieves the legislature from costly, day-to-day monitoring activities, analogous to 'police patrols'.[19]

However, one might wonder why a president would ever support such a law. Are such laws only feasible if passed over the president's veto? In practice, a president is likely to be opposed unless he expects his party to lose the next election and believes that procedural constraints will make it difficult to undo his legacy. In other situations, a president may accept such constraints, not with enthusiasm, but as part of a political compromise that provides other benefits.

B. Parliamentary Systems

Now, consider an archetypal parliamentary system, where the same party coalition controls both the legislature and the cabinet.[20] In that case, the distinction between statutes and executive rules is less clear-cut than in a presidential system. The same political coalition is behind both forms of policy-making. So long as the Constitution's non-delegation principle is not too stringent, the government can decide how much detail to include in the statute and how much rule-making authority to keep inside the cabinet. This decision can be made on technical grounds based on the relative expertise of government officials inside and outside the legislature. Ministerial drafts may be enacted into law with little or no input from the legislature after their submission. Then, there is almost no delegation at all in political terms. Delegation is usually not a way for the legislative majority to avoid blame for hard choices.

The legislature is the prime locus of political legitimacy, and there is no independent executive with its own political power base. The statutes themselves can be rather general because clear and detailed laws are not a feasible way to bind future governments. If a new coalition comes into power, it can modify existing laws comparably easily. It may be in the government's interest to bind

[17] G Tsebelis, *Veto Players: How Political Institutions Work* (Princeton, Princeton University Press, 2002).

[18] McCubbins, Noll and Weingast, above n 15; WM Landes and R Posner, 'The Independent Judiciary in an Interest Group Perspective' (1975) 18 *Journal of Law and Economics* 875–901.

[19] MD McCubbins and T Schwartz, 'Congressional Oversight Overlooked: Police Patrols versus Fire Alarms' (1985) 28 *American Journal of Political Science* 165.

[20] The text ignores some special features of the German and South African cases discussed in Rose-Ackerman, Egidy and Fowkes, 'The Law', above n 1, and it also leaves aside the complications introduced by minority or coalition governments.

its own hands—perhaps in response to popular demands or external pressure from domestic business and international investors. But it cannot be sure that its actions will carry over to a new government, which can always repeal the act. In practice, few statutes may be overruled because a current majority anticipates this risk and drafts statutes accordingly, but the post-war United Kingdom provides a striking example. The steel industry was nationalised and privatised in successive waves as the government changed hands.[21]

Opposition parties in the legislature do have a strong incentive to complain about the government's lack of transparency. Opposition members may chair important committees, giving them a forum to voice complaints or oversee inquiries. The possibility of a contested debate in the Parliament is another reason why the government would propose barebones, framework statutes with little specific policy content that can be filled in through government rule-making after passage.[22]

Votes of no confidence are an important way for the legislature to control the executive in parliamentary systems—an option not available in presidential systems. If members of coalition governments or disgruntled back-benchers join with the opposition, oversight and the veto of individual rules might morph into an effort to bring down the government. Unlike a presidential system with fixed terms, members of the governing coalition must balance the benefits and costs of actions that may cause the government to fall, triggering elections.[23]

In such systems the legislature does not have an incentive to empower the courts to review administrative policy-making. The reason for this is straightforward. So long as the lower house has primary law-making authority, the governing coalition has no interest in a statute that would limit its exercise of policy-making discretion.[24] The legislative majority might seek to provide input into rule-making directly, but it would not want to open these processes to outsiders or to allow the courts to review the degree of openness and the reasons given. The government may promulgate internal rules of procedure, but these are likely to be pruden-

[21] Parliament voted to nationalise British Steel in 1949; that law was repealed by the Conservatives in 1951. In 1967 Labor nationalised the company, and it was then privatised by Margaret Thatcher's Conservative government in 1988. British Steel Corporation PLC, Encyclopedia Online Academic Editions (2014), <www.britannica.com/topic/British-Steel-Corporation-PLC.

[22] In France some advocate for broad framework laws that will be implemented by the professional bureaucracy based on an understanding of the proper division of responsibilities. But to political leaders in the cabinet such laws could also be a way to enact their agenda with a minimum of controversy. See S Rose-Ackerman and T Perroud, 'Policymaking and Public Law in France: Public Participation, Agency Independence, and Impact Assessment' (2013) 19 *Columbia Journal of European Law* 225.

[23] In Germany, the main constitutional constraint on the government is the constructive vote of no confidence. Parliament can bring down a government, but only if it also approves a new government to take its place, art 67, Grundgesetz.

[24] CB Jensen and RJ McGarth, 'Making Rules about Rulemaking: A Comparison of Presidential and Parliamentary Systems' (2011) 64 *Political Research Questions* 656; Rose-Ackerman, Egidy and Fowkes, 'The Law', above n 1.

tial matters, not open to outside checks by the courts. Even if some parts of the governing coalition seek to control other parts, they will be unlikely to obtain majority support for formal judicial oversight. An Administrative Procedure Act, if one exists, will mostly govern official dealings with citizens and businesses seeking to obtain individualised benefits or avoid costs, not secondary legislation.

In short, the legislative majority in parliamentary systems has little incentive to enact procedural statutes that govern administrative rule-making. Oversight of the administration by opposition parties, coalition partners and back-benchers is likely, but passage of a judicially enforceable statute governing rule-making seems unlikely absent acute external pressure. In contrast, presidential systems face a more complex situation. So long as one party does not control both the executive and the legislature, the legislature has an incentive to mandate procedures for executive policy-making and to make them subject to judicial review. The chief executive may go along if he expects that his party will lose power in the next election or is in an otherwise weak bargaining position. These procedures help keep both the legislature and the citizenry engaged in and informed about policy. Court review is a complement to direct legislative oversight, provided that the courts are not dominated by the executive or by the political opposition.

II. Judicial Review and the Democratic Legitimacy of Executive Rule-making: Four Cases

The PPT framework stresses the real-world incentives of the executive and the legislature that arise from differing constitutional frameworks. I argue that judges can draw on the insights of PPT to understand how government works. If courts adopt that posture, they can play a role in upholding democratic institutions, not just protecting rights.

Judges in the cases under review gravitate toward the protection of individual rights and the due process values that protect these rights. Their mandate to protect rights is uncontested; other justifications for review are less secure. Yet preserving democratic legitimacy and checking competence are appropriate judicial roles, but ones that need to be exercised with restraint. Judges are neither politicians nor technocrats, but they can help prevent abuses and encourage positive developments.

As argued above, the political incentives to pass procedural statutes that govern executive rule-making differ in presidential and parliamentary systems, and the statutory law illustrates these incentives. In contrast, legislators in both parliamentary and presidential systems are unlikely to support judicial review of their own legislative procedures. They have no interest in giving the courts authority to review their internal activities. Any procedural constraints that exist will likely be the result of constitutional texts as interpreted by the courts.

A. The United States

The present Administrative Procedure Act (APA) fits well with the incentives of Congress under divided government to create oversight mechanisms. At present, the main challenges to the law are proposals by members of Congress to impose *more* procedural constraints on rule-making inside the administration.[25] Not surprisingly, members of Congress have not proposed a similar statute governing their own procedures.

The US Constitution says little about administrative procedures. The APA is the primary legal route to bureaucratic control.[26] Passage of the Act in 1946 depended on the joint efforts of Republicans seeking to constrain the exercise of delegated power and of New Deal Democrats seeking to entrench the accomplishments of their fragile political coalition. President Roosevelt vetoed an earlier more restrictive bill. President Truman signed the 1946 bill in spite of the limits it placed on the presidency.[27]

The notice and comment provisions in APA §553 set out the barebones of the rule-making process: public notice, an open-ended hearing and reason-giving. The statutory language helps guide the court, which seldom considers regulatory decisions de novo. Checks and balances dominate concerns for judicial overreaching. The courts are constrained by the language of the APA that imposes limits on their review authority. True, the judges' opinions may not track the policy positions of the legislature, but the statute mandates that review should concentrate on the rule-making process and on means/end rationality under the 'arbitrary and capricious' standard. Even the alternative 'substantial evidence' test concentrates on evidence, not the policy itself. The APA forces the courts to monitor democratic values and competence inside the executive and the independent agencies.

However, the courts' role is constrained by a standing doctrine that limits those who can challenge administrative policy-making—a doctrine that is poorly crafted to further democratic values.[28] In addition, the ostensible policy-neutrality of APA review is often violated in practice even if judges do not explicitly take policy positions. In interpreting statutes, the Supreme Court justices claim to be enforcing a set of 'canons', not following their own whims and policy preferences. Debate over

[25] Regulatory Accountability Act of 2017, H.R. 5 (115th Congress, 1st Session), passed by the House, January 11, 2017; Regulatory Accountability Act of 2017, S. 951 (115th Congress, 1st Session), introduced in the Senate, April 26, 2017.

[26] APA, 5 USC §§ 551–59, 701–06 (1946).

[27] President Truman may well have sought to maintain New Deal accomplishments by signing the bill. Studies of the passage of the APA in 1946 contrast its fate with the earlier Walter-Logan bill of 1939–40. The latter, supported by conservative Republican opponents of the President, was vetoed by President Roosevelt. The APA passed by a voice vote. See McNollgast, 'The Political Origins of the Administrative Procedure Act' (1999) 15 *Journal of Law, Economics & Organization* 180.

[28] APA §702 gives the federal courts wide jurisdiction. The Supreme Court has, however, read the Constitution to limit their jurisdiction and to limit standing under the clause that limits the courts to hearing 'cases and controversies'.

these canons has long raged with inconclusive results. Nevertheless, as Abbe Gluck and Lisa Bressman demonstrate, only a few canons appear to be clear and visible enough to affect the legislative drafting process.[29]

Congress has also included legislative vetoes and other ex post oversight mechanisms in statutes, but they face constitutional restrictions. Congressional vetoes of administrative actions were declared unconstitutional in *INS v Chadha*.[30] Congress continues to enact them, even though they are not enforceable. However, they were never a general requirement, and their prevalence did not prevent the passage of the APA. Apparently Congress deemed its own direct oversight either insufficient or undesirable.

Bruce Ackerman designates the APA a 'landmark' statute and gives it quasi-constitutional status.[31] It could be repealed like any other statute, but, in practice, it has become part of the structure of government. However, even if the APA did not have de facto landmark status, its repeal would be unlikely because it satisfies the interests of members of Congress. It remains to be seen if contemporary efforts to add additional restrictive procedures to rule-making will prevail in Congress, and even a president seeking to deregulate the economy might resist additional procedural mandates. In contrast, no general statute governs the internal operation of Congress, and the courts seldom review legislative procedures so long as basic constitutional conditions are fulfilled, such as passage by both houses followed by a presidential signature.

B. South Africa and Germany[32]

Both South Africa and Germany are parliamentary systems, but their constitutional backgrounds differ. South Africa's Post-Apartheid document emphasises democratic inclusiveness and participation. In Germany a long list of individual rights introduces the post-war Constitution, and popular sovereignty has a problematic history.

Consistent with the positive political theory argument, my *Due Process of Lawmaking* co-authors studied the cases of Germany and South Africa. Neither country has a statute mandating notice and comment rule-making subject to judicial enforcement. There are no statutes that explicitly tie judicial review of rules to democratic legitimacy and policy-making competence. The German government

[29] AR Gluck and L Schultz Bressman, 'Statutory Interpretation from the Inside—An Empirical Study of Congressional Drafting, Delegation, and the Canons; Part I' (2013) 65 *Stanford Law Review* 901; 'Statutory Interpretation from the Inside—An Empirical Study of Congressional Drafting, Delegation, and the Canons; Part II' (2014) 66 *Stanford Law Review* 725.

[30] *INS v Chadha*, 462 US 919 (1983).

[31] B Ackerman, 'The Living Constitution' (2007) 120 *Harvard Law Review* 1737.

[32] This section is based on the research of Stephanie Egidy and James Fowkes, and readers who want a more in-depth treatment should consult the chapters on South Africa and Germany in Rose-Ackerman, Egidy and Fowkes, 'The Law', above n 1.

has issued internal guidelines for rule-making, but these have no external legal force. In contrast, legislatures themselves sometimes monitor and participate selectively in rule-makings in both countries. Delegation is not a one-way street, as it is in the US presidential system. Back-benchers and members of the opposition have pushed to include statutory requirements for legislative oversight or approval of rules. If party control of the legislature is strong, as it is in the South African Parliament, members of the majority party may seek greater powers of legislative oversight to constrain the cabinet. In coalition governments in Germany, even cabinet ministers who are members of Parliament may support its involvement in rule-making. They might do so to limit the discretion of ministers who represent parties in the coalition other than their own. As a result of these pressures, the government might have to include such oversight as part of a deal to pass a law. However, it seeks to avoid provisions that build in considerable delay or that give legislative committees too much power. In these parliamentary systems, even given their strong principled commitment to legislative dominance, there is only so much that the legislature can do to intervene in rule-making once it has delegated policy-making to the executive. Of course, in principle, the majority can always entirely withdraw the delegation, but if it does so, the legislature would need to set policy itself—a costly and time-consuming effort for which it may have little aptitude or inclination. The German case is exemplary here. Some statutory delegations to the executive mandate Bundestag involvement in the drafting or the approval of executive rules, but these provisions are all relatively modest in terms of added delay and hassle, given the fact that the same majority controls both the cabinet and the Bundestag. Even when the legislature must pass a statute part way through a major executive policy-making process, it may do so as a routine matter with little independent debate. Such was the result for a statute that determined the general route of new electric power lines as part of the German shift to renewables. Some South African provincial legislatures are experimenting with bolder measures for ex post legislative involvement, but they have yet to yield results.

i. Constitutional Checks on Rule-making Processes

Both the South African and German Constitutional Courts have held certain legislative procedures unconstitutional, but they have not extended those holdings to executive rule-making. In South Africa the legislature failed to carry out a required consultation. In Germany a decision protecting individual social rights had implications for the legislative process—imposing standards of expertise and reason-giving that can enhance both democratic legitimacy and competence.

a. South Africa

In South Africa—a parliamentary system—the Constitutional Court seeks to promote openness and participation as democratic values and not merely as an aid to judicial review, and it engages in limited judicial oversight of law-making processes on that basis. The Constitution enshrines a broad conception of democracy, and the Constitutional Court has read the text to require broad participation in the legislative process. This emphasis on democratic accountability affects the judicial review of procedures in substantive rights cases. It would not be a major leap for the Court to foster public participation in rule-making more generally based on the rich conception of democracy in South African constitutionalism. South African constitutional developments hold that the promotion of transparency is an explicit aim of legislative rule-making and of constitutional checks on legislative behaviour.

The 1996 South African constitution (section 59(1)(a)) provides that the National Assembly must 'facilitate public involvement in the legislative and other processes of the Assembly and its committees'. Equivalent provisions apply to the National Council of Provinces, which is the Second House of Parliament similar to the German Bundesrat, and to the provincial legislatures (section 72(1)(a), s 118(1)(a)). The text offers no further guidance.

However, in a leading case, *Doctors for Life*,[33] the Court treated this language as the basis for a judicially enforceable obligation of legislative bodies to take reasonable steps to facilitate public participation in the drafting of legislation. The case concerned a challenge to several pieces of legislation, including statutes on the sensitive issues of abortion and traditional healers. The National Council of Provinces determined that provinces should hold public hearings or receive submissions from the public on the bills. Most provinces, however, did not do so.

The majority judgment held that citizens have an implied fundamental right to political participation, and that the Court will apply a relatively demanding reasonableness standard in assessing legislative efforts to give effect to that right, although there is no mention of reasonableness in the relevant text. It held that public participation is one of the requirements for the passage of legislation, so a failure to take reasonable steps to facilitate participation in the legislative process makes the legislation constitutionally invalid. With respect to the controversial bills on abortion and traditional healers, where there had been a good deal of public interest, it held that the paltry efforts made by several provincial legislatures were not reasonable. It placed considerable reliance on the fact that several legislatures had stated that hearings would be appropriate but had not held them. However, the Court held that the scope of the duty to facilitate public participation varies with context, but so far the case law has not entirely clarified that duty.[34]

The judicial findings in *Doctors for Life* represent a bold, purposive reading of the text. The Constitution does not explain what it means to 'facilitate public involvement', and it does not grant citizens explicit political rights beyond the right to vote and to participate in the activities of political parties. One might read the text as simply requiring the legislature to have a general policy for facilitating public participation, just as it must have in place measures providing for openness to the public and the media, the topic of the rest of the relevant sections. Read that

[33] *Doctors for Life International v Speaker of the National Assembly* 2006 (6) SA 416 (CC).
[34] ibid, para 43.

way, judicial review would go no further than inquiring whether the legislature had such a policy in place.[35] The majority's approach goes much further. It reads these sections as implying significant judicial scrutiny of public participation processes. It is based on a robust conception of the inclusive, participatory democracy that the 1996 Constitution is said to envisage, and the opinion supports its arguments by reference to international and foreign sources that emphasise citizen participation as an important basis of established democracies. These findings potentially expand judicial oversight of parliamentary procedures considerably, but it is not clear how far the Court will go. So far, it has invalidated four pieces of legislation on this basis—one of them a constitutional amendment. *Doctors for Life* invalidated two, and *Matatiele v President of the Republic of South Africa (2)* handed down the same day, invalidated the other two.[36]

The most revolutionary premise of this line of cases is that a court can get involved in judging how legislatures choose to conduct their business. But this premise has provoked little resistance from the legislatures. Opposing arguments have been confined to contending that whatever the justiciable threshold is, the legislature had met it—not that judicial review is inappropriate in the first place. Indeed, in *Doctors for Life*, the jurisdictional questions and the question of the Court's competence to invalidate Acts of Parliament in these circumstances were not raised by any of the respondents. The Court itself had to ask for argument on these points.[37]

This attitude suggests that government actors have come to accept judicial authority, even with respect to their own procedures. But it also reflects the extent to which the dominant African National Congress (ANC) government agrees with the idea behind the Court's findings. The ANC has long stressed the importance of involving the public in government.[38] In 2005—prior to the decision in *Doctors for Life*—a report to the Second World Conference of Speakers of Parliaments in New York took note of the 'whole range of activities' initiated by the South African Parliament to involve the public.[39] So the Court is being less radical than it may appear; it is codifying what legislatures already do or feel should be done, rather than imposing novel obligations in the face of political resistance. Furthermore, the ANC has responded to citizens' complaints and demands for further engagement even in cases where the Court's ruling upheld its original process.[40]

[35] ibid.

[36] *Matatiele v President of the Republic of South Africa (2)* 2007 (2) SA 477 (CC).

[37] *Doctors for Life*, above n 34, paras 8–10.

[38] H Ebrahim, *The Soul of a Nation: Constitution-making in South Africa* (Cape Town, Oxford University Press, 1998) 13–14; M Putu, *The Role of Ward Committees in Enhancing Public Participation in Rustenberg Municipality: A Critical Evaluation* (Pretoria, IDASA, 2006).

[39] Inter-Parliamentary Union, *Parliamentary Involvement in International Affairs* (Report to the Second World Conference of Speakers of Parliaments, 2005) 21, www.ipu.org/splz-e/sp-conf05/involvement-rpt.pdf.

[40] See eg Staff Reporter, 'ANC meets Forum over Merafong Demarcation' *Mail & Guardian* (Cape Town, 25 June 2008), http://mg.co.za/article/2008-06-25-anc-meets-forum-over-merafong-demarcation; Staff Reporter, 'Merafong to be returned to Gauteng' *Mail & Guardian* (Cape Town, 9 April 2009), http://mg.co.za/article/2009-04-09-merafong-to-be-returned-gauteng.

The *Doctors for Life* line of cases is the most striking application of constitutional values to areas courts have traditionally avoided, but it is not alone. A parallel doctrine concerning local government law-making is emerging in other courts.[41] Courts have also reviewed other internal parliamentary processes on democratic grounds, overturning rulings by the Speaker on two occasions to date.[42] As noted, the logic of these decisions readily applies to executive rule-making, and article 195 of the Constitution stresses the importance of openness and public participation in public administration. Nevertheless, the courts have been cautious, partly because executive rule-making is not specifically included in the administrative procedure statute, and partly because South African administrative law historically has focused on the review of individual adjudications. However, the sources suggest that the courts eventually will come to review executive rule-making on one basis or another. A number of the emerging review doctrines, such as those relating to democracy and public participation, are potentially of general application, and as a result, the lines between legislative and executive law-making are becoming blurred, similar to developments that one can observe in Germany.[43]

b. Germany

In Germany abstract review of a statute can raise structural issues of constitutional law. If an individual challenges a statute in a concrete case, the only route to review is a claimed violation of rights. The long list of fundamental rights guaranteed in the German Basic Law mandates a strict level of proportionality review independent of the form of state activity. The German Constitutional Court is more willing than US courts to consider the adequacy of the legislative process. It sometimes scrutinises the quality of the information underlying a statute, but only in the interest of protecting rights. The Court's efforts to protect rights, however, could have a marked impact on both legislative and executive law-making processes.[44] These effects result from the text of the Constitution, not the activities of the legislature to control its own procedures.

The most important recent developments arose in February 2010 when the Constitutional Court in *Hartz IV*[45] imposed a new level of procedural obligations on the legislature, although the constitutional basis was substantive rights, not democratic legitimacy.[46] The Court reviewed the validity of the legislature's

[41] *Democratic Alliance v eThekwini Municipality* 2012 (2) SA 151 (SCA); *South African Property Owners Association v Johannesburg Metropolitan Municipality* 2013 (1) SA 420 (SCA).

[42] *Speaker of the National Assembly v De Lille* 1999 (4) SA 863 (SCA); *Oriani-Ambrosini v Sisulu, Speaker of the National Assembly* 2012 (6) SA 588 (CC).

[43] These issues are discussed further in Rose-Ackerman, Egidy and Fowkes, 'The Law', above n 1.

[44] ibid.

[45] *Hartz IV*, 125 BVerfGE 175, 1BvL 1/09 of 9 February 2010.

[46] Available in English at www.bverfg.de/entscheidungen/ls20100209_1bvl000109en.html; this section relies heavily on S Egidy, 'Case note—The Fundamental Right to the Guarantee of a Subsistence Minimum in the *Hartz IV* Decision of the German Federal Constitutional Court' (2011) 12 *German Law Journal* 1961.

information-gathering processes when it enacted a law on social benefits that amended the German Code of Social Law. In July 2012, the Court ruled on the adequacy of the basic cash benefits included in the Asylum Seekers Benefits Act and essentially affirmed *Hartz IV*.[47] Both decisions were based on the 'fundamental right to the guarantee of a subsistence minimum' derived from human dignity in Article 1(1) of the German Basic Law in conjunction with the principle of the social welfare state in Article 20(1), which is a human right that is independent of citizenship. It obligates the legislature to create statutes that ensure a subsistence minimum to all individuals. In doing so, the legislature has latitude to specify the levels of standard benefits because they depend on the state of society and the prevailing conditions of life.[48]

In *Hartz IV*, the Court declared that the social law's standard benefits for adults and children were unconstitutional, primarily because the provisions were not entirely based on an underlying statistical investigation by the legislature. The Court found that instead of conducting separate empirical research, the legislature based parts of the calculation of standard benefits on 'random estimate(s)'.[49] Even though the legislature has discretion to choose which statistical models to use to calculate benefits, the Court ruled that it must exercise this discretion consistently and transparently. Instead of declaring the level of social benefits unconstitutional, the Court concentrated on the procedure used to determine the subsistence minimum and found that it violated the Constitution. It intensely examined the statistical analysis underlying the legislature's determination of the standard benefits and concluded that even though the empirical methods employed were suitable, the legislature had failed to apply these tools consistently throughout the calculations. In contrast to prior case law, this decision emphasises the necessity of conducting certain procedures that compensate for the substantive latitude the Court gives to the legislature in this area of law.[50] With this reasoning, the Court imposes procedural duties on the legislature en route to an acceptable substantive result.[51]

The legislature's duty of consistency could ultimately be construed to give individuals the possibility of challenging the legislative process as long as the

[47] *Asylum Seekers Benefit Case*, 121 BVerfGE, 1 BvL 10/10 of 18 July 2012, available in English at www.bundesverfassungsgericht.de/SharedDocs/Entscheidungen/EN/2012/07/ls20120718_1bvl001010en.html.

[48] *Hartz IV*, above n 45, para 138.

[49] ibid, paras 171 and 175.

[50] M Brenner, 'Das innere Gesetzgebungsverfahren im Lichte der Hartz IV-Entscheidung des Bundesverfassungsgerichts' (2011) 26 *Zeitschrift für Gesetzgebung* 394; J Nolte, 'Rationale Rechtsfindung im Sozialrecht: Die vom Bundesverfassungsgericht aufgestellten Anforderungen an die Bestimmung des Existenzminimums im Lichte neuerer sozialgerichtlicher Rechtsprechung' (2013) 52 *Der Staat* 245; P Dann, 'Verfassungsgerichtliche Kontrolle gesetzgeberischer Rationalität' (2010) 49 *Der Staat* 630; N Petersen, 'Gesetzgeberische Inkonsistenz als Beweiszeichen, Eine rechtsvergleichende Analyse der Funktion von Konsistenzargumenten in der Rechtsprechung' (2013) 138 *Archiv des öffentlichen Rechts* 108, 114.

[51] Brenner, ibid 394; Nolte, ibid 247, 250; Dann, ibid 636; Petersen, ibid 114.

statute touches on a fundamental right.[52] The principle of consistency obliges the legislature to adhere to a chosen standard, which is a stricter requirement than the prohibition against arbitrary decisions.[53] The Court used transparency as a second key aspect of *Hartz IV*,[54] stating that: 'In order to facilitate this constitutional review, there is an obligation for the legislature to disclose the methods and calculations used to determine the subsistence minimum in the legislative procedure'.

It is noteworthy that the procedural violations before the Constitutional Court involved harm to an individual rights holder, not the problems facing the general public as it seeks to evaluate the policy impact of the law and hold politicians to account. The procedural requirements are linked to the violation of individual rights, not the promotion of broad democratic values.[55] The Court demands transparency primarily to facilitate judicial review, not to improve the democratic accountability of the legislature. One might think that basing a decision on improper procedures would be less confrontational than subjecting social welfare legislation to full substantive control and ordering an increase in benefits. However, process control is not always less intrusive than substantive review.

The required link to individual rights leaves a gap. There is no concrete ex post review of statutes that indirectly affects the general public in a way that cannot be pulled apart into a set of individualised harms—for instance, where legislative decisions concern the allocation of monetary resources or economic policy. In these cases, no ex post review is possible.

Judicial review of secondary legislation in Germany is not fundamentally different from review of the legislative process and of the substance of statutes. Here too, the violation of rights plays a prominent role. As a result, the system produces some of the same lacunae as for statutes. The ministries and agencies that make rules and the bodies that produce ordinances have less of a claim to democratic legitimacy than does the directly elected legislature. For that reason, judicial review of administrative rule-making could help strengthen the democratic legitimacy and transparency of policy-making by reviewing compliance with the statutory frame. Indeed, that is one of the motivations for judicial review of administrative rule-making in the United States. It plays a less important role in Germany. In addition to rights-based judicial review, the delegation of law-making authority to the executive is constrained and checked by formal and informal inter-branch and internal executive control mechanisms. Broad public participation is not seen as a separate strand providing democratic legitimacy. Therefore, German law often

[52] S Rixen, 'Verfassungsrecht ersetzt Sozialpolitik? "Hartz IV" auf dem Prüfstand des Bundesverfassungsgerichts' (2010) 14 *Sozialrecht Aktuell* 81; R Rothkegel, 'Ein Danaergeschenk für den Gesetzgeber, Zum Urteil des Bundesverfassungsgerichts vom 9 Februar 2010—1 BVL 1, 3, 4/09' (2010) 49 *Zeitschrift für die sozialrechtliche Praxis* 135, 141.

[53] M Lothar, 'Folgerichtigkeit als Wettbewerbsgleichheit, Zur Verwerfung von Rauchverboten in Gaststätten durch das BVerfG' (2008) 63 *Juristenzeitung* 875, 879.

[54] *Hartz IV*, above n 45, para 144.

[55] ibid, para 133 ff.

requires inter-branch or inter-governmental consultation but not broad public participation.

In July 2014 the Constitutional Court upheld *Hartz IV* in reviewing a decision of the Social Court of Berlin, but it read the decision narrowly. It overturned a lower court holding that a revised version of the standard benefits violated the fundamental right to a subsistence minimum.[56] The Constitutional Court upheld the legislature's response to *Hartz IV* and stressed the limitations expressed in the original decision. In this decision, it is beginning to delineate the precise scope of the doctrine of consistency and transparency. The Court is wary of becoming widely involved in second guessing the legislature. This caution seems warranted; going forward, it should apply the doctrine expressed in *Hartz IV* as a procedural, not a substantive requirement. A reason-giving requirement inevitably mixes process and substance, but the Constitutional Court should articulate how it will strike the balance in future cases.

The legislative margin of discretion in shaping fundamental rights protection does not extend to executive rule-making. Hence, unlike legislation, executive rules are often subject to detailed substantive review because the empowering statute limits subsequent rule-making. In cases of wide delegation in complex subject areas, the executive has some discretion to create certain policies. Nevertheless, the empowering statute has to determine the content, purpose and scope of the regulation. As a result, there is less reason to use the review of process as a way of avoiding substantive review. However, as I argued for the US case, procedural review can be valuable in its own right as a way of furthering democratic values over and above substantive concerns. It remains to be seen if German law will develop in that direction.

C. The European Union

Whether one views the European Union as a proto-state or as a confederation of independent countries, its law-making procedures are unique. It draws on the experience of Member States and of the United States, but its sources of political legitimacy are more problematic and diverse. The democratic legitimacy of European institutions remains contentious, and the democratic status of the EU has been the subject of some Member State/EU conflicts, especially involving the German Constitutional Court.

The European Union courts tend to stress scientific and technical competence sometimes to the detriment of public accountability.[57] Nevertheless, both democratic values and rights protection are central to debates over the future of the Union, and challenges based on competence, democracy and rights all come before EU courts. As a result, those courts must resolve claims based on rights that may

[56] BVerfG, 1 BvL 10/12, July 23, 2014.
[57] Rose-Ackerman, Egidy and Fowkes, 'The Law', above n 1.

clash with claims based on expert competence or democratic values. Furthermore, the relationship between the European Code of Human Rights and the EU's own Human Rights Code remains unsettled after a 2014 European Court of Justice (ECJ) opinion disapproving of the Commission's efforts to reconcile the two codes and their enforcement.[58]

In the other cases, legislatures with strong democratic credentials delegate policy-making authority to executive departments and to independent agencies. The key difference between the EU and the other cases is the European Parliament's weak position relative to the Council and the Commission. Its role and status have improved over time, but its struggle for influence is part of the ongoing debate over how to characterise the EU—as a federal state or a treaty-based association of states.[59]

Even though members of Parliament are directly elected, the Council and Commission are key sources of political power. This may have implications for the law of the administrative process. Given its lack of clear dominance in the EU structure, the EU Parliament may prefer to avoid imposing procedural requirements on the Commission or the agencies out of concern that they will end up being applied to the Parliament itself. Furthermore, statutes must be initially drafted by the Commission, and its officials are unlikely to submit legislative proposals that impose judicially reviewable APA-like constraints on themselves. Although both the Commission and the separate EU agencies often express a commitment to broad participation and have created a range of consultation procedures, they do not endorse judicial enforcement of their participatory procedures.[60]

The EU courts themselves have not reached out to review legislative and rule-making procedures. Review of substance is quite aggressive as is review of Member State actions, but the EU courts have little to say about process unless it has a clear basis in the EU treaties. Thus, the main ECJ cases dealing with the administrative process were based on the Aarhus Treaty that applies only to environmental procedures.[61] This deference is reinforced by the contrasting constitutional and

[58] European Court of Justice, Opinion 2/13 [18 December 2014].

[59] For an argument that the latter is more accurate, see P Lindseth, *Power and Legitimacy: Reconciling Europe and the Nation-State* (New York, Oxford University Press, 2010).

[60] Rose-Ackerman, Egidy and Fowkes, 'The Law', above n 1.

[61] The Aarhus Convention (art 2(2)) does not apply to legislative action. ECJ Case C-182/10 *Marie-Noëlle Solvay and others v Région Wallone* [2012] ECR-00000 required the Court to rule on the meaning of 'legislative' under the Convention and the implementing EU Directive. The Belgian Constitutional Court asked for a preliminary ruling on whether a Member State could avoid the requirements of Aarhus and the Directive by passing a statute whose only purpose was to legally approve a major project. The ECJ held that a statute, even if formally fulfilling the Member State's requirements for passage, might still violate the Aarhus requirements. The ECJ held that pro forma legislative approval is not an adequate substitute for the open and participatory processes required by the Convention. The ECJ, however, could only interpret EU law and indicate how the Belgian Court should proceed by expressing strong reservations. The case articulates in clear language the way an open administrative process can serve democratic values and recognises that following the forms of statutory enactment may not further democracy especially if the government in a parliamentary system uses the statutory route to supersede more accountable procedures.

administrative traditions of the judges of the various Member States. Rather than exposing these differences in their opinions, they may be reluctant to impose views that would be a direct challenge to the existing practices of the Commission, Council and Parliament under the Treaty. A move by the EU courts in that direction would be a break with established practices.

But an opening might exist. Although there are no concrete procedural requirements for rule-making, the founding principles of the Lisbon Treaty include elements such as openness, participation and transparency. These could provide a framework for judicial review. The European Union's concept of democratic legitimacy extends beyond representation. If the courts take the abstract norms of participation and transparency seriously, they could transform these principles into concrete and specific norms governing executive and legislative behaviour.

As for secondary rule-making, the Treaty of Lisbon permits delegation to the Commission to 'supplement or amend certain non-essential elements' of legislation (TFEU Article 290) and gives it 'implementing powers' if uniformity across Member States is needed (Treaty on the Functioning of the European Union (TFEU) Article 291(2)). The text does not lay out any required procedures; however, in at least one case the Court has deferred to a legislative choice of which form to use against a challenge by the Commission.[62] Hence, the ECJ may take a hands-off approach. The decision suggests that the Court may be reluctant to issue judgments with procedural implications for Commission behaviour but will rather leave such actions to the legislative process.

The US courts give a broad reading to the APA's demand for public participation. Given the weak democratic credentials of the European Parliament, transparency and broad public participation in rule-making seem especially important. Despite the difficulties, this aspect of public accountability should not be ignored by scholars and judges in the years ahead.

III. Review for Democratic Legitimacy—Old Habits and New Challenges

There are three parts to my positive claims about judicial review of executive branch rule-making—they concern positive political theory, constitutional texts and the role of constitutional courts in furthering both democratic legitimacy and competence.

First, especially in times of divided government, legislative majorities in presidential systems have an incentive to impose procedural constraints on executive branch policy-making and to enforce them through judicial review.

[62] Case C-427/12 *European Commission v European Parliament and European Council (Biocides)* [2014] EC:C: 2014:170.

In parliamentary systems where the executive and the legislature are controlled by the same political coalition, there is little incentive for the government (or its accompanying parliamentary majority) to support statutes that constrain the process of policy-making in either the executive or the legislature. Opposition parties and disgruntled coalition members along with outside pressure and citizen complaints might force the Government's hand—for example, in the aftermath of a scandal—but the Government's actions will be purely defensive. It may face the same coordination and time inconsistency problems as a presidential system, but it has fewer tools to combat them in a credible manner.

Second, modern Constitutions sometimes contain explicit provisions dealing with the democratic legitimacy of policy-making in the executive. These arise out of the particular conditions that framed the debate over the creation of a new polity. In the country cases considered in my book with S Egidy and J Fowkes,[63] only South Africa falls into that category. In Germany, in contrast, popular sovereignty was not seen as an unambiguously good thing. The EU was initially formed by a treaty signed by Member States; it was not the result of a popular movement. The United States' written Constitution has little to say about administrative processes, but Supreme Court opinions as well as legislature and executive actions have essentially given constitutional status to the APA's rule-making procedures.[64]

Third, consider the role of courts in furthering democratic legitimacy and competence. Constitutional courts regulate policy-making procedures indirectly through the protection of individual rights and through the enforcement of other constitutional provisions. Constitutions may give rights-holders access to policy-making processes.[65] In such cases, those with protected rights are not guaranteed substantive results, but they must be part of the debate. Court enforcement of other constitutional provisions can spur certain kinds of procedural responses as policy-makers try to satisfy the courts' burden of proof. However, except in South Africa, the justices have crafted procedural requirements to satisfy the courts, not to improve democratic accountability. In contrast, the South African Court has built on the text to implement the Post-Apartheid emphasis on openness and inclusion and has positioned itself as a conscious promoter of participatory democracy. However, it has not yet applied those principles to executive rule-making.

There is a key issue related to democratic legitimacy and the courts. Holding the constitutional text constant, a statute providing for review of administrative policy-making is more likely in a presidential system than in a parliamentary system. In presidential systems constrained judicial review is a necessary but second-best alternative because direct legislative oversight is difficult. However, executive rule-making in a parliamentary system may also lack democratic accountability and transparency to the citizenry.

[63] Above n 1.

[64] B Ackerman, *We the People; vol 1, Foundations* (Cambridge, Harvard University Press, 1991). B Ackerman, *We the People; vol 3, The Civil Rights Revolution* (Cambridge, Harvard University Press, 2014).

[65] D Levinson, 'Rights versus Votes' (2012) 121 *Yale Law Journal* 1286.

Review of technical competence raises vexing problems in all polities. Few judges will be knowledgeable about science, social science or public administration. Their reluctance to base decisions on non-legal expertise is consistent with the separation of powers as an institutional constraint. If the courts are reluctant to provide substantive review of technical matters, the executive will have greater freedom to act in such areas than in other fields. However, science and data quality frequently interact with claims based on either democratic legitimacy or the protection of rights, and they push the courts into the awkward position of judging mixed questions of fact and law.

I conclude with some normative observations based on the claim that courts should consider the broader impacts of their decisions. Even when a case ostensibly concerns rights, not the structure of government, judges ought to ask how their rulings will be implemented in practice. Constitutional provisions and statutes can permit courts to promote the democratic accountability of executive rule-making procedures. If courts do reach out to further procedural values, however, they should take institutional structures very seriously. Otherwise misalignments between judicial orders and political reality can create other problems. The challenge is to create judicial doctrine that harmonises with the teachings of positive political theory.

Where administrative procedure law tracks the incentives of political actors, the courts need to recognise that efforts to counteract these tendencies will meet with serious opposition. Judicial opinions interpreting the rule-making process of the US Administrative Procedure Act have produced a drumbeat of criticism that claims that the judiciary has gone beyond its monitoring role as envisaged in the original legislation. These criticisms threaten to obscure the key role of the APA in furthering the democratic legitimacy of the modern American regulatory state. Conversely, if the German Constitutional Court, on its own, required notice and comment for major executive rules, such a holding would fit awkwardly with German traditions of internal drafting of rules and could produce a backlash. Constitutional courts ought to act in ways that respect and enhance deliberation over policy.

Political opposition to reforms that could further public accountability means: first, that the institutions will not reform themselves, and, second, if courts try to spearhead reforms, they must be prepared to confront serious resistance. Recognising this, courts tend to shy away from confrontations that impose a contested view of constitutional meaning on the political branches.

Old habits of legal thinking sometimes interfere with the courts' response to new situations. South Africa is still working its way free from an administrative law historically focused only on individual adjudicative decisions. The German courts mainly review executive rules as applied in particular cases if they implicate rights. In both cases the review of executive rules is a contested area of concern. In part, this is because courts recognise that review of rules should not be based on classic notions of due process that rely on court-like procedures. If they did begin to review rules, the focus should be on the strength of democratic links, with a background check assuring the protection of rights.

If legal reformers seek to use the judiciary to respond to the problems of the modern state, they must recognise the courts' limited capacity for substantive review and acknowledge the value of procedure as it relates to all aspects of legitimacy—protection of rights, democratic legitimacy and competence. Modern regulatory tasks make it necessary to delegate to the executive and to defer on substance. Given this reality, the legislature, backed up by the courts, can require the executive and the agencies to consult experts and the public. Procedural reform can respond to the challenges of combining delegation with democratic accountability.

Using the courts to enhance the democratic functioning of elected assemblies is more problematic than administrative law reform. Yet it has been responsibly carried out by the South African court. If democratic values mandate strong links to the citizenry, the courts could be given the authority to be sure that they operate well in practice in the executive as well as in the legislature. These new roles for the courts may clash with standard constitutional interpretations in some systems, but they can be consistent with democratic and republican values.

3

In Search of a New Model of Checks and Balances for the EU: Beyond Separation of Powers

EOIN CAROLAN AND DEIRDRE CURTIN

I. Introduction

The failure of the Constitutional Treaty and the consequent diminished ambition of subsequent agreements has left European institutions and jurists to find alternative means of balancing the Union's 'assumption of independent normative authority' with the necessity to 'adop[t] … constitutional doctrines to constrain and legitimate that authority'.[1] This has been achieved in part through specific amendments to the Treaties. In addition, however, efforts have continued to describe and understand the Union's atypical governance arrangements in ways which resonate more closely with the ideas and values of domestic constitutional law—what Maduro has described as 'low-intensity constitutionalism': 'a gradual judicial and political development that [is] often constructed by reference to national constitutional sources'.[2]

In this context, there has been evidence in recent years of renewed interest in the theory of the separation of powers.[3] Most notably, the Treaty of the European Union draws upon the logic and language of separation of powers theory to, for example, prohibit the European Council from 'exercis[ing] legislative functions',[4] to formally introduce and qualify categories of non-legislative acts[5] and to give

[1] M Poiares, 'The Importance of being Called a Constitution: Constitutional Authority and the Authority of Constitutionalism' (2005) 3 *ICON* 332, 340.

[2] ibid, 337.

[3] The theory of the separation of powers referred to here is the notion, most popularly associated with Montesquieu, of a tripartite division of power between institutions exercising legislative, executive and judicial functions.

[4] Art 15(1) TEU.

[5] Arts 290 and 291 TFEU.

power of review to the European judiciary over EU agencies.[6] Advocates of a stronger EU executive have rested their case in part on a separation-of-powers inspired analysis that this would encourage a more even inter-institutional balance.[7] More generally, Conway—echoing, to some degree, arguments previously advanced by Lenaerts[8] amongst others—has advocated the wholesale move to what he describes as 'a Montesquieu-style separation of powers',[9] suggesting that there is 'potential for reconsidering a tripartite separation of powers as a useful normative framework for the EU'.[10] The implication seems to be that the separation of powers principle could contribute to the *democratic character* of the EU legal and political order.[11]

The central preoccupation of much of this academic literature is the question of whether the EU's sui generis institutional structures *can* plausibly be described in such traditional tripartite separation of powers terms. In this essentially exploratory piece, we argue that a logically prior and arguably more fundamental question must be addressed: whether the EU *should* be so described. This requires us to re-examine whether institutional separation is normatively desirable at all in the contemporary world of European governance (Section II). We argue that it is: but also that a normatively legitimate model of institutional separation for the EU must be based not on the borrowing of an unsuitable constitutional concept[12] but rather on a realist analysis of how the Union *actually* operates. This is an approach which—similar to the idea of relative authority—is based not on abstract or elusive classifications of power or function but instead on a candid assessment of the contributions which specific institutions (and their separation) can make to a normatively legitimate system of checks and balances.

Section III of our chapter focuses on some real-world examples of evolving institutional realities that demonstrate how formal and functional tripartite models of powers are out of kilter with the dynamic realities of who is exercising power where in a political system that is characterised by fragmentation, multi-actorness

[6] Art 263 TFEU.

[7] SG Calabresi and K Bady, 'Is the Separation of Powers Principle Exportable?' (2010) 33 *Harvard Journal of Law and Public Policy* 5; T Chopin, 'Towards a Genuine European Executive Power: from Governance to Government' (2013) Foundation Robert Schuman Policy Paper no 274, www.robert-schuman.eu/en/european-issues/0274-towards-a-genuine-european-executive-power-from-governance-to-government.

[8] K Lenaerts, 'Some Reflections on the Separation of Powers in the European Community' (1991) *28 Common Market Law Review* 11.

[9] G Conway, 'Recovering a Separation of Powers in the European Union' (2011) 17 *European Law Review* 304, 319.

[10] ibid, 322.

[11] Lenaerts, above n 8. See also Möllers' discussion of the democratic legitimacy of the European Union in C Möllers, *The Three Branches: A Comparative Model of the Separation of Powers* (Oxford, Oxford University Press, 2013) 169–95.

[12] On the perils of constitutional borrowing, see Y Hasebe, 'Constitutional Borrowing and Political Theory' (2003) 1 *ICON* 224; CF Rosenkrantz, 'Against Borrowings and Other Nonauthoritative Uses of Foreign Law' (2003) 1 *ICON* 269.

and multi-levelness. The EU political and decision-making system has always involved inter-institutional cooperation rather than strict separation. Indeed, that dimension has arguably increased in recent years, albeit in a fragmented and non-unitary fashion. Even seemingly autonomous actors (the Commission, the European Central Bank (ECB), even the Court of Justice of the European Union (CJEU)) are often forced—in order to realise their policy goals or decision-making objectives—to engage in on-going processes of articulation, explanation and clarification with other institutions and actors (for example, iteratively in the European Semester process or the recent amendment of the CJEU's Statute and proposals to reform the European judicial architecture).[13] Autonomous actors such as the European Council, the ECB and the Commission engage, in the person of their respective Presidents, in political, monetary and economic dialogues with, for example, the autonomous European Parliament (EP)[14] in a manner that has intensified in recent years as the institutions acquire and exercise new and significant powers. The Court of Justice refuses to impose substantive criteria to distinguish between supplementing and implementing a legislative act but rather leaves it as a matter of institutional bargaining.[15] Within the EU political and legal systems we can thus discern the beginnings of a system of semi-organised separation that applies across a wide variety of institutional and policy contexts. It is in these processes, we argue, that scholarship should look for a 'new' model of checks and balances for the EU.

II. Reconsidering the European Union's Institutional Balance

A. Institutional Separation: Where are we Now?

The distribution of authority and influence is, of course, a core concern for any exercise in constitutionalism-as-legitimacy of the sort being discussed here. The complex multi-actor and multi-level character of the Union's political and institutional dynamics means that its allocation of institutional powers has usually

[13] This is obviously not unique to the EU but occurs also in domestic systems.

[14] For details see, MAP Bovens and DM Curtin, 'An Unholy Trinity of EU Presidents? The Political Accountability of Post-crisis EU Executive Power' in D Chalmers, C Joerges, and M Jachtenfuchs (eds), *The End of Eurocrat's Dream* (Cambridge, Cambridge University Press, 2016) 190.

[15] See the CJ's judgment in Case C-427/12 *European Commission v European Parliament and Council of the European Union (Biocides)* [2014] EU:C:2014:170. For a critical assessment of the case, see D Ritleng, 'The Dividing Line between Delegated and Implementing Acts: The Court of Justice Side-steps the Difficulty in *Commission v Parliament and Council (Biocides)*' (2015) 52 *Common Market Law Review* 243.

been conceptualised as a model of 'institutional balance' rather than tripartite separation.[16] Citing the Court of Justice's decision in *Meroni*, Jacqué explained:

> For the Court, the principle [of institutional balance] is a substitute for the principle of the separation of powers ... In the absence of a separation of powers, the principle of institutional balance made it possible to guarantee to undertakings that a modification of the institutional balance would not call into question the decision-making process envisaged by the treaties and the accompanying guarantees provided by the treaties.[17]

However, it is questionable whether this notion of institutional balance has substantially influenced the practical distribution of power within the Union. The balance between the Parliament, Commission and Council has oscillated in accordance with the respective political powers of the institutions at a given moment in time. These changes in what purports to be the organising principle of inter-institutional affairs have 'taken place without prior reflection, simply pulled along by the strongest current'.[18] This reflects the fact that the notion of 'institutional balance' is, in large part, an empty one. This indeterminacy may have a certain pragmatic appeal in an evolving institutional framework as it allows the model to be adjusted to take account ex post facto of political bargains. Craig, for example, has suggested that the studied imprecision of this institutional balance allows it to operate as 'a device which enables the Community to move forward in an incremental manner, without ever really resolving the issues of democracy and legitimacy which lie at the heart of the debate about its future.'[19] However this malleability means that the concept lacks genuine explanatory or analytical power, with the consequence that it contributes little of substance to either descriptive or normative accounts of the Union's arrangements. Too ambiguous to be objectionable, it is also, however, too indeterminate to be effective.

This has been most starkly illustrated perhaps by the ad hoc nature of Europe's response to the economic crisis. If the point of a constitutional system is to establish a system of clear and foreseeable pre-commitments as a safeguard against the future (arbitrary) exercise of discretionary authority by the powerful, there are legitimate questions to be raised about the rule of law within the Union. The response to the economic and banking crisis has been driven by those bodies presently in a position of political or economic power with little evidence of decisions being shaped by institutional, procedural or formal constraints. Dawson has argued that the response can be explained largely from the personal viewpoint of the German Chancellor because of her 'willingness ... to frequently agree

[16] G de Búrca, 'The Quest for Legitimacy in the European Union' (1996) 59 *Modern Law Review* 349.
[17] J-P Jacqué, 'The Principle of Institutional Balance' (2004) 41 *Common Market Law Review* 383, 384.
[18] ibid, 387.
[19] See PP Craig, 'Democracy and Rulemaking Within the EC: An Empirical and Normative Assessment' (1997) 3 *European Law Journal* 105, 113. See further PP Craig, *Public Law and Democracy in the United Kingdom and the United States of America* (Oxford, Clarendon, 1990).

measures during the crisis through inter-governmental fiat, in concert with selected eurozone states'.[20] The references here to fiat and to 'selected states' speak to the ad hoc, agenda-driven and largely rule-free nature of this decision-making.[21] Where formal limitations existed in the Treaties, they have been circumvented by the device of separate international agreements like the Fiscal Compact Treaty. Where forms of governance have been established, they—seemingly deliberately—'carry few mechanisms to ensure political control and legal scrutiny'.[22] In this environment, it is unsurprising that the more ambiguous idea of institutional balance has exerted even less influence.

Given these deficiencies as an organising principle of inter-institutional engagement, the sense in recent scholarship and Treaty reforms that 'institutional balance' might usefully be replaced by a more sharply defined system of institutional separation seems well founded. This does not mean, however, that the tripartite model of the separation of powers is a suitable candidate concept for this replacement role. It is true that the tripartite model's clarity, simplicity and status make it a strong prospect on paper. However, a more detailed interrogation of the model casts doubt on its utility as a guiding principle for the Union.

B. Institutional Separation: Where are we Going?

i. The Broad Case for the Separation of Powers

In considering the benefits of a separation of powers analysis of the European Union, it is logical to examine the claims that have been advanced in favour of its adoption. Broadly speaking, the suggestion is that the establishment of a tripartite separation of powers system would augment either the effectiveness or the legitimacy of the Union's government. Arguments for effectiveness contend, in essence, that 'the governance structure of the EU is a mess',[23] and that a re-organisation of the Union along tripartite lines would give rise to a clearer, less fragmented and more comprehensible form of decision-making. Arguments for legitimacy suggest—sometimes for reasons associated with the enhanced effectiveness that is also claimed—that a tripartite model would enrich the democratic and normative quality of the Union's government. Conway, following Lenaerts' earlier lead, connects the model's descriptive and normative strengths in this way by arguing first, that the model would have certain operational advantages and secondly, that this would also improve legitimacy by reason of the fact that 'normatively, a separation

[20] M Dawson, 'The Legal and Political Accountability Structure of Post-crisis EU Economic Governance' (2015) 53 *Journal of Common Market Studies* 976, 981.

[21] See S Fabbrini, 'Inter-governmentalism and its Limits: Assessing the EU's Answer to the Euro Crisis' (2013) 46 *Comparative Political Studies* 1.

[22] M Dawson, 'The Legal and Political Accountability Structure of "Post-crisis" EU Economic Governance' (2015) 53 *Journal of Common Market Studies* 976, 977.

[23] Calabresi and Bady, above n 7, 9.

of powers framework is appealing because it serves to uphold democracy and the rule of law'.[24] These arguments are examined below.

ii. The Claim to Effectiveness

It was noted above that the primary difficulty with the current concept of 'institutional balance' is its basic imprecision. This limits the concept's normative utility but also leads to ongoing uncertainty about the basic mechanics of the Union's complex institutional structure. This uncertainty about the respective roles of the Union's multiple institutional actors impedes strong and effective decision-making. It is this indeterminacy which Conway specifically cites as a justification for the adoption of a more Montesquian scheme.[25] In his view, '[t]he difficulty with this concept [of institutional balance] appears to be the lack of clear criteria for determining its correct application'.[26] By contrast:

> This problem does not arise in a similar way with a tripartite separation of powers because that depends on a conceptual definition of function (legislative, executive, judicial); it is thus a matter of defining the type of power involved, rather than weighing the exercise of functionally undefined power by one institution with its exercise by another.[27]

The argument here is that the indeterminate idea of institutional balance ought to be replaced by the more concrete criteria supplied by the tripartite model of the separation of powers. This claim is based, however, on a naïvely optimistic understanding of how a theory of separate powers operates. Domestic experience shows that the tripartite model which Conway favours is not only similarly indeterminate but can, in fact, serve to undermine the normative values which it is supposed to secure. This indeterminacy has seen domestic courts struggle to perform the exercise envisaged by Conway in a reliable or consistent manner.[28]

[24] Conway, above n 9, 322.

[25] It is important to note that the phrase Montesquian is used here to refer to the popular conception of the tripartite separation of powers theory: the 'Montesquieu-style separation of powers' Conway refers to (above n 9, 319). While legitimate questions can be raised about the accuracy of this view, the widespread popular understanding of Montesquieu's work is that it favoured a tripartite allocation of powers along functional lines. This gap between separation of powers scholars and those (including more generalist constitutional scholars and courts) who more commonly refer to the popular understanding can lead to a dismissive and unhelpful unwillingness on the part of some separation of powers scholars to engage with this more widespread (and therefore arguably more influential) view. The more popular terminology is used here because the chapter engages with some of this more generalist work (such as Conway), and because the point of the argument is (in part) addressed to non-separation of powers specialists. For further discussion of Montesquieu's methodology and reasoning, see L Zucca, 'Montesquieu, Methodological Pluralism and Comparative Constitutional Law' (2009) 5 *European Constitutional Law Review* 481. For discussions about the historical accuracy of his model, see L Claus, 'Montesquieu's Mistakes and the True Meaning of the Separation of Powers' (2005) 25 *Oxford Journal of Legal Studies* 419.

[26] Conway, above n 9, 319.

[27] ibid.

[28] See, for example, *Myers v US* [1926] 272 US 52 (1926); *Youngstown Sheet & Tube Co v Sawyer* [1952] 343 US 579; *TD v Minister for Education* [2001] 4 IR 259. See further, the cases discussed in E Carolan, *The New Separation of Powers: A Theory for the Modern State* (Oxford, Oxford University Press, 2009) 19–46.

While there are certain core functions that may clearly be associated with and thus reserved to a particular branch—such as the enactment of statutes, for example—there is a general lack of definitional clarity about what makes a particular power legislative, executive or judicial in character. In many situations, functions are associated with a particular institution because that institution has traditionally exercised those functions. Such an allocation of power owes more to historical happenstance and circular reasoning than conceptual coherence. As Stevens J observed:

> [T]he exercise of legislative, executive and judicial powers cannot be categorically distributed among three mutually exclusive branches of government [because] governmental power cannot always be readily characterised with only one of those three labels. On the contrary … a particular function, like a chameleon, will often take on the aspect of the office to which it is assigned.[29]

Furthermore, even activities that are commonly associated with one of the three traditional branches of government may, on closer inspection, involve the exercise of powers or functions that might more properly be thought to belong to one of the other branches. Take the exercise of adjudicative functions by bureaucratic officials, for example. These officials may be subject to the control and scrutiny of the (political) executive while exercising powers of a character, and in a manner, which come close in appearance and effect to a judicial process. An obvious EU example is the adjudicative functions performed by Commission Hearing Officers and other officials in the context of EU competition policy. When confronted with such messy institutional realities, formalists are forced to sacrifice the clean lines of the tripartite ideal and acknowledge the existence of intermediate categories of activity. Yet, this collapses the ideal of an institutional trinity, thereby destroying the definitional integrity upon which this approach to the separation of powers depends. How can an approach premised on the application of a formal tripartite model survive when the model proves inapplicable in practice? As Jackson J conceded:

> The mere retreat to the qualifying 'quasi' is implicit with confessions that all recognized classifications have broken down, and 'quasi' is a smooth cover which we draw over our confusion as we might use a counterpane to cover a disordered bed.[30]

The processes of government are simply too complex and multi-faceted to be neatly divided along functional lines—a complexity which is, of course, particularly pronounced in the EU system.

Conway acknowledges this to some degree when referring to 'the partial exercise of the power of one branch by another' as an aspect of the 'idea of checks and balances in separation of powers theory'.[31] This could indicate some support for

[29] *Bowsher v Synar* [1986] 478 US 714, 749.
[30] *FTC v Ruberoid Co* [1952] 343 US 470, 488.
[31] Conway, above n 9, 319.

a more functionalist account of the theory under which the focus of any analysis should be on whether a particular exercise of power imperils the system's overall balance. This, however, comes close to re-introducing the ambiguous notion of 'institutional balance' which the tripartite theory ought to replace. The model's synchronous attachment to separation and blending means that indeterminacy intrudes once again. At what point does too much separation threaten the system's overall checks and balances? Conversely, at what stage does a system of checks and balances intrude to too great a degree on an institution's autonomous exercise of its distinct functions? And most critically, how should any conflict between these objectives be resolved? The tripartite model is, in its basic form, silent on these issues.

Thus, whether considered in its formal or functionalist incarnations, it is clear that the traditional tripartite conception of separation of powers lacks the determinacy of detail which advocates for its adoption have assumed. As Verkuil explained:

> Certainly broad propositions of republican and democratic government [like the separation of powers], premised on the thoughts of profound political thinkers and our constitutional forebears, are appealing departure points; but they are also unrelentingly open-ended. Left without context, they prove too much. Maxims produce slogans, not workable themes of jurisprudence.[32]

This undermines the central claim of advocates of the effectiveness of the tripartite model: that it would provide greater clarity and guidance than the notion of 'institutional balance'.

iii. The Claim to Legitimacy

The alternative argument for applying the tripartite model to the EU is that it would enhance the legitimacy of the Union government. Here again, however, the ambiguity of the tripartite model requires the claim to be further defined before it can be properly considered. This follows from the fact that the separation of powers has—in normative terms—been justified by reference to a number of distinct, if sometimes overlapping, values. Classically, the model is associated with the protection of political liberty against the potential tyranny of absolute power.[33] However, the model's normative value has been expressed in various other forms, from the familiar establishment of checks and balances,[34] as a method of promoting public goods in government,[35] as an accountability mechanism,[36] as a safeguard

[32] PR Verkuil, 'Separation of Powers, the Rule of Law and the Idea of Independence' (1989) 30 *William and Mary Law Review* 301, 302.

[33] See A Hamilton, J Madison and J Jay, *The Federalist Papers* (London, Penguin, 1987) especially Books 47 and 51. See also MJC Vile, *Constitutionalism and the Separation of Powers* (Oxford, Clarendon, 1967) 14.

[34] *Myers v US* [1926] 272 US 52, 293; E Barendt, 'Separation of Powers and Constitutional Government' [1995] *Public Law* 599.

[35] NW Barber, 'Self-defence for Institutions' (2013) 72 *Cambridge Law Journal* 558.

[36] T Persson, G Roland and G Tabellini, 'Separation of Powers and Political Accountability' (1997) 112 *The Quarterly Journal of Economics* 1163.

against arbitrary decision-making,[37] or more generally, as a prerequisite for the more compendious concept of the rule of law.[38] Thus, in order to examine the normative case for the separation of powers, it is necessary to understand more precisely the case that is being made.

In terms of the literature on the European Union, the most common claim appears to be that the separation of powers would enhance the democratic legitimacy of the system as a whole.[39] This emphasis likely reflects the fact that the perceived democratic deficit of the Union has long been amongst the more prominent concerns of European constitutionalists. However, it also represents a particular strand of separation of powers thought which highlights the broader democratic benefits of a system of institutional checks and balances. On this analysis, the establishment of a system in which independent institutions fulfil a mutual checking function promotes more democratically robust decision-making. The existence and exercise of these independent institutional checks leads not only to more balanced government but also to a way of governing in which the exercise of institutional power is more visible, more subject to account, and more likely to promote the broader public interest.

Here again, however, difficulties arise on closer examination of this claim. In particular, the notion of the tripartite model as an assurance of checked and balanced government seems, at the very least, naive. The model's indeterminacy means its checking function may be less rigorous than its advocates assume. In fact, by focusing attention on artificial and often meaningless definitions of function, the model may even hinder the pursuit of the normative goal of effective checks and balances.

It is a critical weakness of arguments in favour of the traditional tripartite theory that it necessarily obliges its advocates to shut their eyes to the realities of significant areas of institutional activity. A tripartite model of separated powers—with its characterisation of government as comprising three types of function—constitutes an anachronistic and unduly narrow account of how contemporary government operates. The model is based on an understanding of government as a hierarchical and rule-based operation in which power is exercised by central institutions issuing specific commands. This is a legalistic model which focuses on the processes by which laws are created, issued, interpreted and enforced. It focuses on law as the primary means of exercising power and influence and assumes that a decision by one of the three central organs represents a final exercise of power. It also assumes a level of finality or absoluteness in the exercise of institutional authority. The reality, of course, is very different.

One difference is the extent to which powers are exercised today through non-statutory, or even non-legal, means. Rule-based government has given way in

[37] RL Brown, 'Separated Powers and Ordered Liberty' (1991) 139 *University of Pennsylvania Law Review* 1513; Carolan, above n 28.

[38] WB Gwyn, *The Meaning of the Separation of Powers* (Tulane, Tulane University Press, 1965); Verkuil, above n 32; J Waldron, 'Separation of Powers in Thought and Practice' (2014) 54 *Boston College Law Review* 433.

[39] Lenaerts, above n 8; Conway, above n 9.

many areas to 'soft' governance. A second difference is that power is no longer the sole and exclusive preserve of the central organs of the state but is exercised by an array of bodies and officials that exist at various levels of government. The EU has, perhaps even more than most domestic states, witnessed this familiar 'veritable mushrooming of agencies, coupled with an increase in agencies' tasks touching on issues of adjudication, regulation and decision making, functions quite discretionary in nature'.[40] The power and influence vested in these sub-central agencies belies any conception of government as a hierarchical system of command and control. Third, there is the related point that the apparatus of government has itself been the subject of significant evolution. As government has expanded to regulate a wide range of social activities, so it has also seen a proliferation of organisations in the penumbra between classically public and private bodies. Various aspects of this expanded government process have been privatised, contracted out, entrusted to expert bodies or delegated to local or voluntary groups. Yet, the traditional model takes no account of these bodies or functions.

This criticism is even more apposite in an EU context. The EU has always functioned as a multi-level organisation in which power is shared between the central institutions of the EU and the Member States. Even at EU level, power has been broadly dispersed amongst a variety of disaggregated actors. Agencies, committees, officials and other social stakeholders wield significant powers in particular EU contexts. This in turn reflects the fact that the actual exercise of power within the EU is frequently a complex and context-sensitive process of multi-actor inputs. Belying constitutionalist talk of institutional balance, the EU is more accurately characterised by non-linear processes and states of imbalance.[41] The fragmentation of executive power is particularly pronounced in the EU system as there is no one institution, or clearly delineated set of institutions, in which EU executive power is vested.[42] Differentiation in legislative power and even judicial power is also present across different policy areas and has evolved, quasi-systemically, over time. This fragmented and differentiated reality bears little resemblance to the rule-based system of command and control described by the traditional tripartite model.

[40] M Busuioc, 'Accountability, Control and Independence: The Case of European Agencies' (2009) 15 *European Law Journal* 599.

[41] AS Sweet and W Sandholtz, 'European Integration and Supranational Governance' (1997) 4 *Journal of European Public Policy* 297.

[42] See B Crum, 'Executive Accountability in the European Union' (2013) paper presented at the EUSA Thirteenth Biennial Conference, Baltimore, USA, 9–11 May 2013; D Curtin, 'Challenging Executive Dominance in European Democracy', (2014) 77:1 *Modern Law Review,* 1; D.Curtin, *Executive Power of the European Union, Law, Practices and the Living Constitution* (Oxford, Oxford University Press, 2009).

C. Separated Powers: Where should we Go?

That is not to say, however, that there is no point in considering the possibility of developing an improved scheme of separation for the EU. The problem discussed in the previous section is that the tripartite model of 'the separation of powers' has come to dominate the way in which we think about separating power. Yet the persistence of this tripartite model reflects, to some degree at least, the extent to which the notion that power should not be vested in a solitary institution or actor resonates with basic intuitions about good government. Furthermore, the claim that the Union's effectiveness or legitimacy could be improved by the articulation and application of a concrete theory of institutional relations also seems well-founded, especially given the Union's long-standing problems with the complex impenetrability of its processes. The project of recovering a separation of powers for the EU appears a worthy one. The key challenge for the EU—and indeed for any workable theory of institutional separation—seems to be to translate this intuition to action.

The remainder of this chapter provides a preliminary and first-step response to that challenge. The intention is to provide an example of the type of realist enquiry which is, in our view, crucial to developing an improved understanding of how institutional separation within the EU can and could operate. In doing so we further interrogate the notion of institutional separation so as to more precisely identify the values which the system could promote. Once these values are identified, it may—at a later stage and as part of a much more comprehensive enquiry—be possible to design a system which would, in practice, serve such ends. However, the operationalisation of a model of separate powers must correspond to, and be capable of influencing, the patterns of power that are *actually* present in the system in question. This requires as a prerequisite precisely the sort of empirical assessment of power that formal separation of powers theories lack.

D. What Values Could a System of Separation Promote Within the EU?

It has already been observed that the argument for a separation of powers system in the EU has tended to be phrased in terms of the model's normative or democratic potential. This is a form of argument which goes beyond the negative dimension to separating power to focus on the potential for institutional separation to make a positive contribution to the quality of government action. After all, if the purpose of the separation of powers is to protect liberty, simply providing for multiple forms of separation is arguably sufficient. The essence of this strategy is that separating power complicates its exercise such that government itself becomes more difficult. Given that the goal of separation of powers advocates in the EU context has generally been to alleviate some of the difficulties that currently hinder government action at the level of the Union, their focus on the positive potential of institutional separation is unsurprising. Thus, if the purpose of developing a separation of powers model is to enhance the legitimacy of the Union, a system of negative checks is insufficient. Those checks must be designed in a way that ensures that their exercise tends to produce these positive effects.

What effects might the separation of powers advocates have in mind? It was previously pointed out that domestic constitutional theorists have associated a separation of powers structure with an array of positive process values. Given the exploratory nature of this chapter, it is beyond its purpose to contend that any one of these values could or should be identified as the primary concern of an EU system of separation. These values—whether individually or as a composite notion like the rule of law—are all, in principle, consistent with the claim that their instantiation in the guise of a system of institutional separation would enhance the Union's normative or democratic legitimacy. For the purposes of the first step of its analysis, this chapter accordingly treats the separation of powers as concerned in a normative sense with the promotion of a family of related rule-of-law type process values.

The reality is that 'important intellectual traditions comport with the basic view that multiple configurations of our separations of powers are possible as well as normatively acceptable'.[43] Different models of separation may suit different political and institutional realities. This underlines the relevance of this discussion to the institutional structures of the European Union. The fact that the Union's institutional arrangements do not resemble those typically associated with domestic governments need not preclude the development at European level of a legitimising model of separated powers. Equally, however, the simple establishment of some form of institutional separation does not make a system of checks and balances.

Having identified broad rule-of-law values as the normative objective of instituting a model of institutional separation within the EU, the second stage is thus to consider how a system of institutional separation could, in practice, promote these values *in the context of the European Union's particular structures.*

This requires, at the outset, a more interstitial assessment of how a system of separated (or relative) authority operates. A government structure composed of autonomous institutions creates a situation in which a single institution is typically unable to unilaterally accomplish a policy end. In seeking to pursue a particular objective, that institution may require the assistance of another agency or agencies, whether by way of positive support or forbearance from interference. This compels the lead institutional actor to engage in a process of communication with the other branches or agencies of government. Furthermore, the autonomous nature of independent agencies should mean that it is unlikely to be sufficient for

[43] BG Peabody and JD Nugent, 'Toward a Unifying Theory of the Separation of Powers' (2003) 53 *American University Law Review* 1, 34.

the lead actor to issue a policy command. If the position, powers and/or normative legitimacy of institutions are broadly equivalent, the lead institution is more likely to be obliged to persuade the other institutions of the value or permissibility of its policy programme. Indeed, given the extent to which even lower-level agencies may exert discretionary influence over government actions, the pursuit by one institution of a policy end within a system of separated powers will usually involve that institution in an ongoing process of articulation, explanation and clarification, regardless of its position in the ostensible hierarchy of government.

Before looking at specific EU examples, it may be helpful to think in the abstract about the various ways in which requiring institutional separation *may* bring about the kind of dialogic (or collaborative)[44] inter-institutional processes that promote certain procedural values. Separation engenders inter-branch communication, which provides a degree of *transparency* and *publicity*.[45] The *independence* of the branches increases the informational (and thus political) costs of pursuing policy objectives, which tends to encourage *generality* and discourage attainder. If an institution wishes to target a particular group but is dependent on the assistance of other institutions to achieve this, it can only be certain of success if it makes its intentions clear. Separation does not preclude this, but it does limit the potential for surreptitious tyrannies. The burden of persuasion identified above also means that an institution may, in practice, be required to explain its favoured course of action. The provision of this type of institutional *justification*, in turn, means that the actions of that institution are more *susceptible to challenge and/or review* by other agencies of government. This also has the potential to enhance the degree of *expertise* in government by allowing other agencies with particular experience or specialisations to identify and correct errors in the reasoning provided. Taken together, these process values promote institutional *accountability*, which in turn fosters the substantive principle of *non-arbitrariness* which is at the core of legitimate governance.[46] That a separation between institutions can have such significant effects on the legitimacy of government is underlined by the fact that it was, after all, this concern to prevent arbitrary government which animated much of the original scholarship on the separation of powers.[47]

A close analysis of the positive inter-institutional dynamics sketched out in the previous paragraphs makes clear that institutional separation, of itself, is insufficient to support the process values identified therein. In particular, this account suggests that a model of separated powers must take some account of the nature,

[44] E Carolan, 'Dialogue isn't Working: the Case for Collaboration as a Model of Legislative–Judicial Relations' (2016) 36 *Legal Studies* 209.

[45] Whether within government or to the public at large.

[46] For this argument in more detail, see Carolan, above n 28, 82–105.

[47] R Brown, 'Accountability, Liberty and the Constitution' (1998) 98 *Columbia Law Review* 531; LS Bressmann, 'Beyond Accountability: Arbitrariness and Legitimacy in the Administrative State' (2003) 78 *New York University Law Review* 461.

context and content of inter-institutional relationships if it is to operate as an effective model of checks and balances. Separation does not, of itself, inculcate positive institutional attributes.

In particular, it seems to be a prerequisite for the majority of the process values identified in this abstract account that the institutions involved enjoy both de jure and de facto autonomy. The proposition that the interactions between separated institutions supports values such as transparency, publicity, generality and justification depends upon the assumption that these are arms-length transactions between independent institutions. The presence of accountability seems logically prior to the achievement of these other process values. Genuine accountability, however, requires independence of outlook as well as of action. This suggests that there may be two essential components of an effective system of checks and balances: that the institutions involved are psychologically independent; and that they are capable of holding each other to account. These conditions seem necessary for the establishment of the sort of contestatory inter-institutional engagement from which the other process values may flow.

Applying these insights, the next section of this chapter seeks to investigate the European Union's system of institutional separation. This, for the reasons already articulated, requires an empirical understanding of power relations that goes beyond a mere consideration of the Union's formal structures. A workable model of institutional separation within the EU must, at a minimum, be based on and be sensitive to the realities of institutional independence and accountability.

III. Autonomy and Accountability in the EU's System of Separated Powers

The EU system is already fragmented and separated so it meets some of the basic elements of a separation of powers strategy. Furthermore, there is a division of interests between some of its key institutional actors (eg some more EU-focused, some more domestic-government-focused) so again there are the basic elements of a genuine checks and balances. But the analysis shows that the fact that these institutions are formally independent, formally accountable and have different instincts is not enough to enhance the legitimacy of the system as a whole. As this section will show, the rules of engagement matter. Independence and accountability are necessary conditions but not sufficient of themselves. Accountability, in particular, forms a particular challenge in the EU because executive power is straddled across the European and the national level and dispersed over a wide range of actors, including national governments, the Commission, the European Council and EU agencies. These de facto power relations are critical to both the reality and the potential of the Union's checks and balances.

A. The Impact of Informal Practices on Formal Autonomy

The Union's institutional structure has from the very beginning been built on the division of powers between the various institutions established by the Treaties.[48] They are ascribed specific competences and have to act within the scope of those competences. The separate interests of the institutions were protected at least formally by this notion of division of powers. As the years have gone by, new institutions have been added to the list (in particular, the European Central Bank and more recently the European Council) and others, growing in practice, have been largely ignored by the Treaties (agencies, for example). In formal terms, the autonomy of the European Central Bank and the CJEU is ring-fenced in the Treaties. The fact that these two institutions are clearly designed to be institutionally separate and 'autonomous' means that both are instructive examples of the gap between formal separation and the informal influence of other institutions.

The CJEU is an example of an institution with its independence and separateness enshrined in the Treaties, in its own internal rules and in its own psychology. In the system of the Treaties, the Court acts as independent and ultimate arbiter of the law (both Treaty and secondary legislation) and enjoys a formal separation of its overarching judicial power from the other institutions or actors and from the national courts which enforce and apply Union Law. There has been a great deal of discussion as to the precise nature of that judicial power, both as a Supreme Court through its exercise of preliminary rulings jurisdiction[49] and as a Constitutional Court. Psychologically, it can be said to be very independent about its role as, in effect, the leading institution with regard to what the law means.[50] The individual judges must 'be chosen from persons whose independence is beyond doubt'[51] and in extra-judicial writings the judges illustrate strong levels of psychological independence but also of considerable freedom from inter-institutional constraints.

There is little real checking from the outside as to the exercise of this judicial function nor indeed, on the whole, the means to do so. When the Court decides upon inter-institutional conflicts or about the division of powers, for example, it receives input and information in the context of the court procedures. In this context, there may be a dialogue of sorts with a limited number of representatives of other institutions at the oral hearing, but this does not affect its 'independence' in reaching judgment. The Court has always vigorously resisted any perceived political interference with its ability to impartially reach judgment.[52]

[48] Art 13(2) TEU.
[49] Lenaerts, above n 8, 32.
[50] K Lenaerts, 'The Court's Outer and Inner Selves: Exploring the External and Internal Legitimacy of the European Court of Justice' in M Adams et al (eds) *Judging Europe's Judges. The Legitimacy of the Case Law of the European Court of Justice* (Oxford, Hart Publishing, 2013) 13.
[51] Art 19(2) TEU, third subpara.
[52] See, in general, Lenaerts, above n 50.

This does not mean, of course, that the situation remains the same or indeed that the Court remains as in control of its own institutional environment as it would wish. In common with (higher) courts elsewhere, it is dependent on the political actors (government and sometimes legislature) for budgetary and other more procedural/architectural reforms. The Vice-President of the Court now spends a considerable proportion of his time talking on behalf of the CJEU with these institutions in order to put the rules it wants in place.[53] The selection committee put in place by the Lisbon Treaty[54] does provide some supranational checks on Member State appointments and could be considered a nascent part of a wider system of checks and balances on the Court itself.[55] This underlines the point made in the previous section that the formal rules that prescribe and protect the independence and separation of a specific institution—even a strongly independent one such as the CJEU—provide, at best, an incomplete picture of how it engages with and may be influenced by other institutions.

This point is reinforced by the experiences of the other institution whose independence is constitutionally protected, the ECB.[56] Whereas the CJEU demonstrates how formally separate institutions can become informally subject to external constraints, the unprecedented actions, new responsibilities, competences and tasks of the ECB during recent financial and economic crises shows the expansionist potential of such informal influence. Instead of ECB *independence* as the standard constitutional *Leitmotif* we are now witnessing ECB *intervention* into the economic policies of the Member States.[57] As Wilsher points out:

> [T]he ECB has been emerging as the most important creditor and, therefore, the actor with most de facto political power. Even though it has not directly provided funds to Member States, the ECB has become heavily involved in approving and monitoring the fiscal and socio-economic restructuring of debtor countries.[58]

Still other institutions and actors (the Commission, agencies) are explicitly established as 'independent' (from the Member States, from the Commission,

[53] ibid.

[54] Art 255 TFEU.

[55] JM Sauvé, 'Le rôle du comité 255 dans la sélection du juge de l'Union' in A Rosas, E Levits, and Y Bot (eds), *The Court of Justice and the Construction of Europe* (The Hague, Asser Press, 2013) 99–120.

[56] See further D Curtin, 'Accountable Independence of the European Central Bank' (2017) *European Law Journal*, forthcoming; C Zilioli, 'Accountability and Independence: Irreconcilable Values or Complementary Instruments for Democracy? The Specific Case of the European Central Bank' in G Vandersanden (ed), *Mélanges en hommage à Jean-Victor Louis* (Brussels, Editions de l'Universite de Bruxelles, 2003) 395–422; F Amtenbrink and K van Duin, 'The European Central Bank before the European Parliament: Theory and Practice after Ten Years of Monetary Dialogue' (2009) 34 *European Law Review* 561; S Collignon, 'Central Bank Accountability in Times of Crisis: The Monetary Dialogue 2009–2014' (2014) note prepared at the request of the EP Committee on Economic and Monetary Affairs.

[57] T Beukers, 'The New ECB and its Relationship with the Eurozone Member States: Between Central Bank Independence and Central Bank Intervention' (2013) 50 *Common Market Law Review* 1579.

[58] D Wilsher, 'Law and the Financial Crisis: Searching for Europe's New Gold Standard' (2014) 20 *European Law Journal* 241, 273.

from the Council) but with nascent webs of accountability being layered around them—some thin, some thicker. For example, the Commission is increasingly considered as a 'normalised' core executive[59] and its institutional separateness in the sense of a psychological 'independence' as the traditional 'motor' of the integration process is well established. This independence is mainly discussed in terms of its 'independence' from the Member States appointing Commissioners, but the Commission's institutional separation from the other institutions is also established (Article 17(3) TEU). However, it is similarly subject, both in law and in practice, to inter-institutional dialogic and accountability processes that can emerge either through formal or informal practices, eg, the recent EP influence on the selection of the Commission President.[60]

These examples illustrate that formal rules provide only one clue as to the likely influence of a body within the system's overall checks and balances. In none of the examples given above of independent or inter-linked institutions can the formal rules be said to provide a complete picture of how the institutions actually engage with or are influenced by each other. An institutional theory needs to be sensitive to these power dynamics if it is to offer any genuine descriptive or analytical insight.

B. The Impact of Informal Practices on Formal Checks

The previous section demonstrated that a formal system of separation can be effectively amended by the emergence of informal working practices. The same is also true of the kind of formal inter-institutional checks that are, perhaps, most commonly associated with the separation of powers. As this section shows, the way in which EU institutions actually exercise their formally separated powers can undermine the rule-of-law values which a system of separation should promote.

A notable example of this is the way that the transparency of EU law-making has been undermined in recent years by the informal use of so-called trilogues in practice.[61] Within these trilogues, delegations of Council and EP, with the Commission in a more coordinating role, meet behind closed doors to hammer out a compromise text on which the two institutions can reach early agreement. The advantages of trilogues are that they can much speed up the legislative process and

[59] A Wille, *The Normalization of the European Commission: Politics and Bureaucracy in the EU Executive* (Oxford, Oxford University Press, 2013).

[60] See Editorial Comments, 'After the European Elections: Parliamentary Games and Gambles' (2014) 51 *Common Market Law Review* 1047, at 1047–52; SB Hobolt, 'A Vote for the President? The Role of Spitzenkandidaten in the 2014 European Parliament Elections' (2014) 21 *Journal of European Public Policy* 1528, especially at 1532–33.

[61] R de Ruiter and C Neuhold, 'Why is Fast Track the Way to Go? Justifications for Early Agreement in the Co-decision Procedure and their Effects' (2012) 18 *European Law Journal* 536; C Reh, A Héritier, E Bressanelli, and C Koop, 'The Informal Politics of Legislation: Explaining Secluded Decision Making in the European Union' (2013) 46 *Comparative Political Studies* 1112.

avoid painful confrontations between the two institutions. Obviously, however, they come at the cost of some important aspects of democratic accountability as they fudge responsibility, move much of the decision-making process behind closed doors and prevent the full public presentation and elaboration of reasons for and against the decisions adopted. These are precisely the kind of process values which were identified in Section II as the core of the case for a 'new' separation of powers system for the EU.

This is part of a wider phenomenon of autonomous institutions informally developing working practices in a manner that excludes other institutions or the broader public. The conclusion by EU institutions of inter-institutional agreements is an early (and frequent) example of this tendency.[62] In the EU context this is especially pronounced in EU-level institutions and other actors composed of members of the national executive power (such as the European Council, the Council, the Euro summits and the Eurogroup). 'The response to the crisis has … undermined the concept of institutional balance by way of a power shift towards executive dominance'.[63] These institutions have in practice incrementally acquired more powers, and are de facto taking the most important decisions after the euro crisis in ways that are not evident from a reading of their formal (Treaty-based) tasks.[64] The introduction in 2008 of the position of full-time European Council President reinforces the autonomy of the European Council as an institution with 'non-legislative' powers.[65] This marked a change in the collective face of the European Council and its ability to interact as such with the other institutions and be included in existing inter-institutional accountability mechanisms (legal, financial).

In the meantime the European Council has gradually developed into a very significant agenda setter of the larger developments of the EU, in spite of the Commission's formal monopoly of legislative initiative.[66] Empirical evidence points to a 'progressive erosion' of the Commission's power of initiative and a much more pronounced role of the European Council in setting the legislative agenda despite its lack of formal legislative powers.[67] This contrasts unfavourably, for example, with the manner in which the Commission Work Programme is drafted, ie on the

[62] SP Riekmann, 'The Cocoon of Power: Democratic Implications of Inter-institutional Agreements' (2007) 13 *European Law Journal* 4.

[63] M Dawson and F de Witte, 'Self-determination in the Constitutional Future of the EU' (2015) 21 *European Law Journal* 371, 373.

[64] M Dawson and F de Witte, 'Constitutional Balance in the EU after the Euro-crisis' (2013) 76 *Modern Law Review* 817, 829–30; D Curtin, 'Challenging Executive Dominance in European Democracy' (2014) 77 *Modern Law Review* 1.

[65] HCFJA de Waele and JLW Broeksteeg, 'The Semi-permanent European Council Presidency: Some Reflections on the Law and Early Practice' (2012) 49 *Common Market Law Review* 1039.

[66] P Bocquillon and M Dobbels, 'An Elephant on the 13th Floor of the Berlaymont? European Council and Commission Relations in Legislative Agenda Setting' (2013) 21 *Journal of European Public Policy* 1.

[67] P Ponzano, C Hermanin and D Corona, 'The Power of Initiative of the European Commission: A Progressive Erosion?' (2012) Notre Europe, Studies and Research 89/2012.

basis of a dialogue between the Commission and the EP and with an opportunity for national parliaments to comment on it.[68] In terms of information provision, debate and accessibility of the system, this is reasonably well developed in the context of Commission activity, and political responsibility is clearly established under the Community method. The European Parliament feels excluded from any similar kind of dialogue with the European Council and fears a shift in the balance of legislative power in practice, despite the formal Treaty provisions that the European Council only has non-legislative powers. In a strongly worded resolution the EP stresses 'that any further initiative ... must imperatively be established in accordance with the Community method' and calls upon the European Council to 'stop instructing the Commission on the form and/or content of any further legislative initiative', emphasising in this respect that '[the European Council] does not have any Treaty-based prerogative of legislative initiative.'[69]

Institutions may in fact develop working methods that may mean that no effective accountability is possible or takes place. The European Council only relatively recently established its own rules of procedure and makes extensive use of informal working methods. These autonomous practices follow a conscious choice made by the first President and the institution as a whole[70] and inevitably influence the ability of other institutions and actors (especially the EP and the national parliaments) to exert the kind of check on its powers that would enhance the democratic or normative legitimacy of either the specific decision or the general system as a whole. As Puetter observed:

> Already in one of his first statements as new permanent president, Herman van Rompuy defined the adjustment of working methods as one of his main priorities. He called for more focussed sessions with fewer officials and a distinction between formal and informal meetings. He also suggested that there should be fewer written documents tabled for discussion, thus allowing more room for *open debates* between participants.[71]

The reference to 'open debates' points to debates that only involve the high-level Members of the European Council itself (without staff); take place behind closed doors; and are informed (as anticipated by Van Rompuy) by fewer documents.[72] These informal working methods hinder the already rather weak accountability relationships that have developed at the political level.[73]

This section highlights a particular problem with a formal account of inter-institutional checking at the EU level. The risk with any system of formal checks

[68] European Commission, Strategic Planning and Programming Cycle, http://ec.europa.eu/atwork/planning-and preparing/strategic-planning/index_en.htm.

[69] EP resolution of 12 June 2013 on strengthening European democracy in the future EMU (2013/2672 (RSP)), point 3.

[70] U Puetter, 'Europe's Deliberate Intergovernmentalism: The Role of the Council and the European Council in EU Economic Governance' (2012) 19 *Journal of European Public Policy* 161, 175.

[71] ibid, 174 (emphasis added).

[72] J Tallberg, 'Bargaining Power in the European Council' (2008) 46 *Journal of Common Market Studies* 685, 686.

[73] See further Bovens and Curtin, above n 14.

is that its efficacy may be reduced by informal practices that make rigorous inter-institutional enforcement less likely. This danger seems compounded in an EU context by the inherent potential for co-ordination between EU institutions on issues where they have an inherent commonality of incentives or interest (such as, for example, on the pursuit of EU rather than domestic interests). Furthermore, where such informal co-ordination occurs, the possibility of public or third party scrutiny is lessened by the complexity and impenetrability of EU measures as well, perhaps, by the distance from a *demos*. The trilogues are a reminder that institutional self-interest does not necessarily coincide with the satisfaction of public interest values or goals. Even the objections of the EP about the growing informal powers of the European Council can be characterised as bureaucratic self-interest which is open to accommodations that would not necessarily be in the public interest. This shows that it is not enough to establish a system of formal checks that trusts in the self-interest of the separated institutions to ensure normatively appropriate outcomes. Using separation to secure good governance requires attention on the processes through which these purportedly arms-length engagements occur.

C. The Potential of Informal Practices

The previous two sections have tended to show how informal practices can undermine the principles of autonomy and accountability that were claimed (in Section II) to be critical to an effective separation of powers system. On the other hand, the emergence of alternative forms of de facto engagement between institutions has obvious potential, in the abstract, to provide supplementary forms of accountability. For the reasons set out in Section II, dialogic inter-institutional processes have the potential to promote rule-of-law values wherever they occur.

This is very relevant in an EU context, given the involvement of non-core institutional actors operating outside of the Community method in its regulatory processes. Agencies, for example, clearly do not fit within the classic institutional framework of the EU despite now numbering well over 40. They do not fit with—and were traditionally regarded as threats to—the Union's formal structures. In reality, however, they can and do 'add value' to the EU's normative authority by providing opportunities for inter-institutional dialogue and debate and multiple accountability forums.[74]

The EU evolves in day-to-day policy-making practice and such practices are important in understanding the nature of the contemporary EU. A central role for peer review is, for example, built into the European Semester framework. Superordinate bodies (such as the Commission) set framework goals and measures for gauging their achievement. Then, lower-level units (such as national ministries or regulatory authorities and the actors with whom they collaborate) implement

[74] MLP Groenleer, *The Autonomy of European Union Agencies: A Comparative Study of Institutional Development*, dissertation (Delft, Eburon, 2009) 380.

these goals as they see fit. They are obliged to engage in a regular dialogic reporting process. In addition, they participate in a peer review process in which their results are compared with those of others and the various methods the same general ends compared.[75] Finally, 'the framework goals, performance measures, and decision-making procedures themselves are periodically revised by the actors, including new participants whose views come to be seen as indispensable to full and fair deliberation'.[76] More broadly, the accountability of various types of European governance mechanisms is frequently provided in apolitical arrangements (for example, management boards composed of technical experts rather than national representatives overseeing European agencies, peer review committees of experts overseeing comitology committees, or the more widespread use of benchmarking and visitation). Such processes can be considered part of a form of dynamic accountability 'that anticipates the transformation of rules in use'.[77] More fundamentally, for the purposes of the argument being made here, this is exactly the kind of rational, accountable, transparent and public goal-oriented process that a functioning system of separated institutions should ensure. This shows that separation of powers scholarship need not—and should not—focus on a small (tripartite) core of central institutions.

In the EU context, there are numerous examples of evolving, dynamic and non-centralised accountability processes. These processes 'routinely result either in revisions of EU directives, regulations, and administrative decisions, or in the elaboration of revisable standards mandated by law and the enunciation of new principles which may eventually be given binding force'.[78] In this process of continuous institutional revision, regulation 'increasingly takes the novel form of contestable rules to be understood as rebuttable guides to action even when they are also taken as enforceable sovereign commands'.[79] The entire process, Sabel and Zeitlin conclude, 'is a machine for learning from diversity'.[80] The very process of dynamic accountability, according to Mansbridge, probably helps create and support a selection- and trust-based accountability regime—one that, when achievable, is very probably more efficient than a regime predominantly based on sanctions.[81]

EU comitology committees can, in practice, be considered an example of this type of interactive accountability. This still today constitutes a not insignificant part of the 'backstage' of implementation of European law and technical standards and is powerful advice. Comitology is in fact: 'a huge system. It is composed

[75] See further, CF Sabel and J Zeitlin, 'Learning from Difference: The New Architecture of Experimentalist Governance in the EU' (2008) 14 *European Law Journal* 271.

[76] ibid, 271.

[77] ibid, 305.

[78] ibid, 276.

[79] ibid, 275.

[80] ibid, 276.

[81] J Mansbridge, 'A Contingency Theory of Accountability' in M Bovens, RE Goodin and T Schillemans (eds), *The Oxford Handbook of Public Accountability* (Oxford, Oxford University Press, 2014) 65.

of some 220 committees, which discuss and vote on up to half of all European decisions, directives and regulations. In this respect the system produces far more acts than the Council and the European Parliament do legislation'.[82] Comitology research has shown that members of these committees form epistemic communities and engage in deliberative type discourse with other members. This internal discourse is based on shared values and a common outlook, and there seems to be a high degree of autonomy of committee members (national civil servants) vis-a-vis their political principals (the Member States).[83] In the eyes of many participants, finding the best technical solution seems to take priority over their own individual national interests.[84]

There is undoubted normative potential in the interactive and deliberative character of peer review processes. However, the comitology example also shows that the internalised norms, complex subject-matter and limited practical visibility within the committees impose some limits on that potential. In the context of the broader argument being made, comitology demonstrates why it is misguided to ignore the informal realities of such sub-central processes in devising a separation of powers system. It also indicates, however, that these sub-central processes supplement rather than obviate the necessity for a clear and coherent separation of powers system that can be applied at higher institutional levels.

IV. A Procedural Model of Checks and Balances?

In keeping with much recent scholarship, we argue that the EU would benefit from developing a new understanding of its separation of powers. However, at a time when the traditional theory has been subject to much criticism in domestic constitutional theory,[85] we also believe that a turn to tripartism would be ill-advised and potentially counter-productive. A separation of powers model must be cognisant of the empirical power relations which it is supposed to regulate. As we have shown, the tripartite separation advocated by Conway and Lenaerts does

[82] GJ Brandsma, *Controlling Comitology. Accountability in a Multi-Level System* (Basingstoke, Palgrave Macmillan, 2013) 2.

[83] ibid and GJ Brandsma, 'Accountable Comitology?' in M Bovens, D Curtin and P 't Hart (eds), *The Real World of EU Accountability* (Oxford, Oxford University Press, 2010).

[84] Brandsma, above n 82, 8.

[85] For example, see G Marshall, *Constitutional Theory* (Gloucestershire, Clarendon Press, 1971); DJ Levinson and RH Pildes, 'Separation of Parties not Powers' (2006) 119 *Harvard Law Review* 2311; Carolan, above n 28; EA Posner and A Vermeule, *The Executive Unbound: After the Madisonian Republic* (Oxford, Oxford University Press, 2010); J Power, 'Fiducial Governance: Heads of State and Monitory Branches' (2012) 44 *Administration & Society* 30; B Ackerman, 'Goodbye Montesquieu' in S Rose-Ackerman and PL Lindseth (eds), *Comparative Administrative Law* (Cheltenham, Edward Elgar Publishing, 2010); NW Barber, 'The Separation of Powers in the British Constitution' [2012] *Law: The Journal of the Higher School of Economics* 3.

not correspond to the actual exercise of institutional influence within the EU. Any such model would, for the reasons outlined in Section II, be likely to fail.

This raises the question, however, of what form a 'new' separation of powers for the EU should take? This article cannot and does not answer that challenge. What it does provide, however, is an indication of the direction which we believe EU separation of powers scholarship might most fruitfully pursue. Several key insights emerge from the empirical overview of EU structures in Section III. The first is that informal practices can negate a separation of powers system based on formal rules or institutional self-interest. Even in combination, these two cornerstones of traditional separation of powers strategies may be circumvented by informal co-ordination between institutions with a commonality of interests or disparities in practical power or prestige. Second, the practices that have grown around the EU's central institutions have the potential to promote the kind of process values (arguably because their non-political mandate requires a more deliberative and reasoned form of decision-making) associated with rule-of-law accounts of the separation of powers. However, the transparency and publicity that such process values can provide is also, in practice, limited by the fact that these sub-central processes are so numerous, complex and epistemically closed.

This last point has particular relevance for the EU given the familiar concerns about the complexity and impenetrability of its institutional architecture. This may limit the potential for process alone to provide a normative model of checks and balance. As the persistence of the tripartite model—despite long-standing questions about its historical accuracy or contemporary relevance—suggests, there is considerable force in an allocation of authority that speaks to the democratic legitimacy of its constituent parts. The discussion of process here shows that it is fundamental to a functioning system of checks and balance to take account of *how* institutions interact. But this does not exclude the importance of also considering the *who* and *why* of such interaction. Where we disagree with Conway and other EU separation of powers advocates is not in the basic potential of an EU model of checks and balances but rather in their focus on powers as the organising principle. The better approach would seem to us to be one that connects the authority of an institution with the normative claims than can be made on its behalf. The question of how an institution's input might be legitimated is, of course, a much larger question. But work published previously provides one example of how a system of institutional separation between political, legal and administrative bodies could be normatively justified by reference to the (overlapping) claims of each body to representative authority and legitimacy.[86] That work argued for a triangular model of separation between constituent interests rather than functions. Under this separation of interests model, the political institutions represented collective interest; the courts represented the interests of the individual; with administrative agencies providing the site for a reconciliation of both interests in the light of the available evidence. While the specifics of that model may better fit domestic government

[86] Carolan, above n 28, 155–59.

(at least in Westminster systems), the basic strategy of a separation that tracks institutional claims to legitimacy seems more suited to the EU system—not least because of the multiple sites and sources of legitimacy claim within the Union. It may also be instructive to recall, in this regard, that the idea of a separation of constituencies or interests has a long pedigree in European constitutional thought.[87] In a Union facing renewed frictions between its supranational and intergovernmental elements, there may be merit in a model of separation which explicitly conceives of the Union's institutional arrangements in terms that can plausibly be connected to those constituent interests. This might not only present a more realistic picture of institutional engagement but could allow for the separation to be structured in a manner that better balances these enduring supranational-intergovernmental tensions.

Yet, for the reasons already given, the EU's multiplicity of institutional authority along both horizontal and vertical dimensions means any model of separation based around the Union's core institutions is likely to be, at best, partially effective. This underlines the importance of process as a core component of the project of recovering separation of powers for the EU. The Union's governing structures are too complicated to be exclusively regulated by a model of simple separation between a small number of institutions. The divergence between formal and informal realities—and the myriad means by which informal practices amend formal structures—further compounds the difficulty of trying to institute a normatively effective separation between such bodies. If the potential value of the separation of powers lies in its capacity to promote the process values identified in Section II, then it seems sensible to devise a system which takes direct account of the normative potential of those process values themselves. A system which laid down minimum procedural standards of, for example, publicity and transparency for *any form* of inter-institutional engagement (regardless of how it might be tripartitely characterised) would limit the scope for institutions to use informal means to avoid formal rules. Furthermore, a focus on process values would mean that the principles of separation would be capable of being applied to central and sub-central processes alike. By bringing in dynamic and non-centralised processes, this would present a more descriptively accurate template for reviewing—and improving—interactive forms of decision-making. As an approach, this might seem closer to low-level administrative principles rather than high-level constitutional concepts. However, in an EU system where abstract conceptualisation may prove empirically misleading and where there is a clear history of sub-central or informal processes and actors being used to circumvent more formal divisions of power, a system of checks and balances cannot hope to be effective if it does not take due account of the everyday realities of these multi-actor processes.

[87] See for example the discussions of the Venetian and Florentine republics in Q Skinner, *Machiavelli* (Oxford, Oxford University Press, 1981); and N McCormick, 'People and Elites in Republican Constitutions, Traditional and Modern' in N Walker and M Loughlin (eds), *The Paradox of Constitutionalism: Constituent Power and Constitutional Form* (Oxford, Oxford University Press, 2007).

4

Bolstering Authority by Enhancing Communication: How Checks and Balances and Feedback Loops can Strengthen the Authority of the European Court of Human Rights

MIKAEL RASK MADSEN*

It is hardly controversial to note that international courts ('ICs') exercise public authority.[1] Among the two dozen currently operational ICs, there are however very significant differences in this regard. ICs' exercise of public authority is highly uneven, ranging from being mere conflict resolution organs of treaty regimes to having a genuine influence on public policy. It is the latter that is in focus in this chapter as ICs exercising significant public authority have become increasingly contested in many places. For example the European Court of Human Rights (ECtHR or Court) has been the object of criticism, particularly with regard to the alleged democratic deficit of its power to influence public policy. Although criticism very often is based on single judgments turned into a general critique, there are good reasons not to write this off as only politically motivated interventions seeking short-term gains. As I will argue, there is a need to take seriously the interplay of law and politics and developing better ways of ensuring workable feedback mechanisms between international courts and particularly their political interlocutors. This can be seen as a concrete response to the inherent challenge of relative authority as conceptualised in this book.

* This research is funded by Danish National Research Foundation Grant No. DNRF105 and conducted under the auspices of iCourts. Special thanks to Joana Mendes and Ingo Venzke for excellent feedback on the chapter.

[1] For example A von Bogdandy and I Venzke, 'On the Functions of International Courts: An Appraisal in Light of Their Burgeoning Public Authority' (2013) 26 *Leiden Journal of International Law* 49; M Goldmann, *International öffentliche Gewalt* (Springer, Verlag, 2015).

As noted by Mendes and Venzke in their opening chapter of this volume, the division and allocation of authority between institutions is important in this regard. Yet, although foundational treaties in principle settle the division of labour and allocation of authority, the history of, for example, European law and its courts is above all marked by evolution and change. This is due to the fact that ICs like the ECtHR, as well as others, are not static institutions but have in practice developed their authority and power over time and oftentimes beyond the confines originally envisaged. What is moreover important in this regard is that governance systems like that of European law can hardly be made intelligible as simply treaty institutions. Although they are created as treaty mechanisms and, thus in principle established by public international law, such a contractual logic fails to fully accommodate the social and legal phenomenon at hand: in practice it consists of complex interfaces of international and national legal and political institutions. Agreeing on these points, the editors call for a reconstructive approach that highlights the legitimacy assets of the differentiated but related institutions of international governance systems. Relative authority is the product of the interrelations of these institutions; each of them more suited to particular tasks as a result of their particular assets: for example independence (courts), expertise (administrations) or representation (parliaments). The problem of relative authority connects to the broader question of the international separation of powers and its possible role for understanding global governance. In Mendes and Venzke's account, the separation of power can inspire but not solve the question of legitimate global governance; that is, it is helpful for thinking about the different roles, strengths and legitimacy assets of each of the involved institutions and their interdependences, but it does not provide a workable recipe for global governance.

This chapter addresses this book's central question of relative authority and separation of powers, but it takes a more sociological and empirical approach than the more functional-normative stance proposed by the editors. While agreeing on the preliminaries with regard to global legal governance put forward by the editors and briefly discussed above, this chapter puts emphasis not on the essential assets (legitimacy assets in the editors' account), but rather on the processes that might perpetuate and even bolster authority in complex regimes of global governance. Building on a previous work on the variable authority of ICs, and notably how contexts shape that authority,[2] the chapter is particularly interested in how inter-institutional processes and feedback mechanisms operate in practice and create workable ensembles of institutions exercising relative authority. The chapter's empirical demonstration is limited to an analysis of the evolution of the

[2] JK Alter, LR Helfer and MR Madsen, 'The Variable Authority of International Courts—Special Issue' (2016) 79 *Law & Contemporary Problems* 1; KJ Alter, LR Helfer and MR Madsen, 'How Context Shapes the Authority of International Courts' (2016) 79 *Law & Contemporary Problems* 1.

law-politics interface of the ECtHR.[3] It highlights particular moments in which the authority of the ECtHR has been challenged and how such challenges have been overcome or resulted in insolvable collusions between the Court and the Member States. These case studies and the conclusions that can be drawn from them are used in the subsequent section for suggesting institutional changes that might better these interactions and consolidate, even bolster, the authority of the ECtHR.

The chapter is structured as follows. It starts with a brief theoretical discussion that specifies and explains the particular approach of the chapter. It then moves on to discuss cases of authority challenges in different moments of the evolution of the ECtHR and European human rights more generally. Against the background of these case studies, the chapter develops new ideas for institutional reform that might help create better feedback loops in the area of European human rights. In conclusion, I return to some of the theoretical implications of such reforms.

I. Theoretical Framework: Public Authority as Object of Empirical Inquiry

Authority does not come with a readily available and generally agreed upon definition. In the introduction to this book, Mendes and Venzke define the exercise of public authority as 'acts based on law that have the capacity to impact the freedom of others'.[4] That said, they are focused on the different legitimacy assets of the involved institutions in this regard. For the purpose of this chapter, I measure authority following the theoretical framework recently developed by Alter, Helfer and Madsen.[5] This approach is centred on whether a given international court has de facto authority in society as measured by the reception of its decisions by specific audiences. They make a key distinction between de jure authority—the legal mandate of the institution allowing it to act within a relative defined space of law—and de facto authority—different audiences' actual acceptance of an IC and its rulings in terms of taking consequential steps triggered by these decisions. While de jure authority is obviously important, the key claim made by these scholars is that de facto authority is the benchmark for assessing whether ICs are paper tigers or legal institutions with real bite and societal impact.

The question of the legitimacy of ICs is less central in this approach. Although positive perceptions of ICs as being legitimate actors might well have an effect on

[3] The empirical demonstration is based on a set of previous publications that have presented an empirical account of the development of the ECtHR, most recently MR Madsen, 'The Challenging Authority of the European Court of Human Rights: From Cold War Legal Diplomacy to the Brighton Declaration and Backlash' (2016) 79 *Law & Contemporary Problems* 1.

[4] See J Mendes and I Venzke in their introduction to this book, fn 1.

[5] Alter, Helfer and Madsen, 'How Context Shapes the Authority', above n 2.

audiences' acceptance of ICs and their will to take consequential steps with regard to judgments, perceived (or sociological) legitimacy does not translate entirely into de facto authority. As they argue, there may well be discrepancies between actors' internal, subjective views of ICs and their decisions and the externally observable actions taken by, for example, government officials. Alter et al therefore focus on observable practices rather than subjective perceptions and motivations which cannot be directly observed.

More controversially, the authors argue that normative legitimacy alone is insufficient for de facto authority: '[W]e … recognize that a court can do everything normative theorists might expect of a legitimate international judicial body and still not have authority in fact. The converse scenario—authority in fact, without normative legitimacy—is also possible.'[6]

It follows from this that de facto authority is a capacity to rule and direct action—not merely a formal competence. This capacity might be considered legitimate or not according to certain normative criteria or the perceptions of the audiences, but this is not the central point.[7] The central point is instead whether the institution has the actual capacity to rule and direct action.[8] It thereby also differs from a more formalist (for example de jure) conception of authority that highlights not the actual capacity but the formal competence.

Rather than contributing to the burgeoning literature on both normative and sociological legitimacy of ICs, the theory is instead focused on a different and novel question, namely the variable authority of ICs. The authors argue that that the existence of authority of an institution cannot be answered in binaries. Instead, authority is often varied across different audiences. Their theory focuses particularly on three types of authority in fact, all of which are measured in different audiences: narrow, intermediate and extensive authority.[9] In all cases, the test for authority is the same, namely whether the specific audience accepts ICs' decisions as binding and takes consequential steps to implement those decisions. *Narrow authority* concerns the immediate parties of a given case. *Intermediate authority* concerns the larger group of actors similarly situated to the parties of a given case, such as potential litigants and government officials charged with implementing IC decisions. *Extensive authority* concerns the broader range of actors that engage

[6] ibid, 7.

[7] Similarly, J Mendes and I Venzke are also focused on the capacity to influence the freedom of others. However, they do not make the distinction between de jure and de facto authority.

[8] That said, at the legal level (de jure authority) ICs are generally considered legitimate. They usually have an express legal competence based on a consensual act of delegation from states. This also often makes their de jure authority less contentious than for example other international institutions exercising public authority. But as noted by the authors, de jure authority does not automatically translate into de facto authority.

[9] In addition, their framework considers two other types of authority in fact: no authority and popular authority. No authority in fact occurs when no audiences accept IC rulings and take consequential steps. Popular authority occurs when society at large accept IC decisions and take consequential steps.

with an IC, including legal professionals, academics and business actors. Hence, an IC with extensive authority will typically be a key institution in developing law and politics within its area of law. Importantly, the framework does not suggest that an IC necessarily broadens its authority from narrow, over intermediate, to extensive authority. There is in other words no teleology implied in this theory; rather, different types of authority can coexist. Moreover, the authority of an IC—and its various types of authority—might well vary across Member States.[10]

Although this model is developed with the objective of assessing authority, it also allows for disaggregating the audiences of ICs in order to identify when authority is challenged, even refused, by specific audiences. For the purpose of this paper, this model of authority is applied to assess when and by which audiences IC authority is not accepted. This chapter thus uses the analysis with the inverse objective, namely to identify those instances when the exercise of public authority by the ECtHR is challenged. This empirical determination of those instances is done by conducting case studies of controversial rulings by the ECtHR. Against this background, the analysis then connects back to the framework theory of the book by identifying where the public authority of the Court is hampered by such controversy. Moreover, in a subsequent section, it seeks to identify possible institutional amendments that can help better balance the system and allow each of the institutional actors to better use their assets and ensure the exercise of public authority.

This empirical and normative assessment of the interplay of law and politics takes its cue from the discussion of the separation of powers and its possible role for understanding global governance provided by Mendes and Venzke in their introduction. However, the chapter takes once again a more empirical direction. Rather than considering the different roles, strengths and legitimacy assets of different institutions and their relations at a more abstract level, the chapter seeks to pinpoint the precise challenges in these interactions and why they might have negative effects on authority. This part of the analysis is inspired by the work of Richard Bellamy who has theorised political constitutionalism and highlighted the necessary feedback mechanism between courts and politics for it to work. Contrary to many legal analyses of the ECtHR, which tend to focus exclusively on legality, judicial independence and proportionality, Bellamy does not shy away from pointing to the necessary feedback mechanism for ensuring workable law-politics interfaces. A key argument in Bellamy's political constitutionalist account is that institutions of democracy, including courts, have to be well-informed when making decisions.[11] While the legislature and the government

[10] For an analysis of how this has occurred with regard to the ECtHR, please see above, n 3.

[11] R Bellamy, *Political Constitutionalism: A Republican Defence of the Constitutionality of Democracy* (Cambridge, Cambridge University Press, 2007).

are checked periodically by popular vote, and therefore have to develop policies that align with the electorate, courts live more in isolation. This raises the central question of who checks the courts? And, linked to that, how are courts sure to receive the necessary information when casting judgment if they live in relative isolation?

In the classical doctrine of the separation of power, courts check the other branches of government. Courts are themselves limited by their constitutional mandate and checked by amendments to the applicable law. In this regard the system set up by the European Convention of Human Rights ('ECHR' or 'Convention') has a certain in-built risk of differentiating and even isolating the Court from the other relevant institutions. One of the key challenges is that the communication between the Court and national political and legal institutions takes place predominantly through final judgements against Member States in contentious cases. Moreover, the Court's review of national laws, policies and judicial decisions resembles, in function if not in name, that of a constitutional court, implying that the possibility of changing the underlying basic law—the Convention—is inherently difficult. It requires a form of constitutional politics by qualified majorities—in the case of the ECHR this requires unanimity of the Member States.[12] This situation sometimes creates frustration on the part of governments, civil society groups and national legal actors. It follows, conversely, that one way of improving this governance structure is to ensure feedback mechanism. Within the existing institutional framework this can be done by enhancing Member State participation, as well as bettering communication and dialogue between the Court and Member States. I will return to these questions in the normative discussion below.

II. Empirical Analysis: Instances of Controversy and Defiance of the ECtHR

This chapter analyses instances of controversy over the public authority of the ECtHR. The case selection has been organised with the goal of covering both different and similar situations across a number of dimensions. Generally, human rights provide a highly relevant object of inquiry for understanding the controversies surrounding contemporary judicialised global governance. Human rights

[12] The other option for the other branches of global governance to possibly influence ICs is by the appointment of new judges to these institutions. Different from national courts, judges at ICs typically have time-limited mandates and are replaced by the Member State nominating new judges. This mechanism of control is however not particularly efficient with regard to very large ICs such as the ECtHR which currently employs 47 judges. Individual states' impact on the court via nomination is in practice minimal.

are not just at the heart of the modern constitutional state and its international superstructure;[13] human rights are also common goods that 'involve considerations beyond the law in question and require a responsiveness to the consequences for the public at large'.[14] Put differently, human rights remain questions of public good and public policy, even when they are highly judicialised and legalised as is the case of the ECtHR and its case law.[15] This means that the adjudication of European human rights by the ECtHR is an emblematic example of the international exercise of public authority concerning public goods.

Second, but closely linked, international institutions exercising public authority in morally and politically contentious areas, such as the ECtHR, are prone to being challenged for either going beyond their formal mandates or being illegitimate decision-makers with regard to matters of public policy. For the purpose of this chapter and this book, this implies that we are likely to observe issues related to relative authority in terms of striking the right balance between the ECtHR and other institutions in the controversies over its decisions. In practice, other institutions will claim that they are better situated and more legitimate actors to make the decisions in question. This permanent challenge of striking the right balance has, since the very first cases were presented before the system, been articulated in the Court's margin of appreciation doctrine which can be viewed as a tool to deal with the complex institutional interfaces that the Convention triggers in this regard. The primary responsibility to protect the substantial rights of the Convention rests with the Member States (Article 1), but the Court monitors that obligation (Article 19). The subsidiary role of the Court is further cemented by the principle of exhaustion of local remedies (Article 35(1)) and the right to an effective remedy (Article 13). All of this allows for balancing the different legal and political levels of European human rights and has resulted in key jurisprudential innovations such as 'European consensus' and notably the doctrine of the margin of appreciation.

European human rights are in other words both likely to trigger questions related to relative authority and to articulate legal doctrines in this regard. In order to provide an analysis of a varied set of situations in this respect, the actual cases included have been selected using criteria that highlight how the institutional structure has changed over time and how the balancing act of European human rights involves different levels of interaction (European and national) and areas of law and politics. To address the historically different institutional structures of the ECHR system, cases are included from both before and after

[13] C Thornhill, 'The Formation of a European Constitution: an Approach from Historical-political Sociology' (2012) 8 *International Journal of Law in Context* 354.

[14] R Bellamy, 'Public Law as Democracy: The Case of Constitutional Rights' in CM Amhlaigh, C Michelin and N Walker (eds), *After Public Law* (After Public Law, Oxford University Press, 2013) 148.

[15] MR Madsen, 'Reflexivity and the Construction of the International Object: The Case of Human Rights' (2011) 5 *International Political Sociology* 259.

Protocol No 11 (1998), which changed the institutional structure of European human rights.[16] To address the different levels of interaction with the ECHR system, the cases selected involve both legal and legal-political interfaces.

The first case analysed is the *Cyprus* case,[17] which gave rise to both legal and political interfaces before the European Commission of Human Rights. The second case study from the early period (pre-Protocol No 11) concerns institutional reform of the French judiciary which was prompted by judgments by the ECtHR. With regard to the post-Protocol No 11 period, the chapter analyses the issues surrounding the *Hirst* case,[18] which has triggered both legal and political reactions over prisoners' right to vote. Finally, the chapter looks into the Brighton Declaration as an example of a mainly political interface.[19] As it appears from this selection, the chapter has opted for looking into cases concerning some of the large Member States with a so-called high reputation.[20] The assumption is that interfaces with those states are likely to trigger more reaction than would be the case with smaller Member States.

The case selection is illustrated in Figure 1.

National/European	**National law**	**National Politics**
European Law	Judicial reform in France	*Hirst* case
European Politics	*Cyprus* case	Brighton

Figure 1: Case Selection

III. Pathways to Legal Diplomacy: The *Cyprus* Case

The first case before the European human rights system was filed in 1955 before the European Commission of Human Rights. The case *Greece v United Kingdom*[21]

[16] Before Protocol No 11 a central institution in the broader system was the European Commission of Human Rights. Individuals (or states) could submit claims to the Commission. The recommendations of the Commission were however not legally binding unless the Committee of Ministers accepted them. Yet, the Commission was vested with the power to bring a case before the Court (if the state in question had accepted the Court's jurisdiction and the case could not be settled by conciliation). Importantly, individuals did not have that right, yet a state could refer a case to the Court. After Protocol No 11, the ECHR system was centred on a single permanent court and no intermediate institutions such as the European Commission. In the post- Protocol No 11 regime, individuals can appeal directly to the Court (if they had exhausted local remedies). The result of the reform was in other words a complete judicialisation and legalisation of the system. Thereby the political intermediary of the Commission and notably the Committee of Ministers was discontinued.

[17] *Greece v United Kingdom* no 176/56 (Commission decision of 2 June 1956).

[18] *Hirst v The United Kingdom* (no 2) App no 74025/01 (ECtHR, 6 October 2005).

[19] Brighton Declaration (adopted on 20 April 2012 at the High Level Conference on the Future of the European Court of Human Rights, 18–20 April 2012, Brighton, United Kingdom).

[20] S Dothan, *Reputation and Judicial Tactics: A Theory of National and International Courts* (Cambridge, Cambridge University Press, 2014).

[21] See generally *Greece v United Kingdom*, above n 17.

was launched as an interstate case by Greece against the United Kingdom and concerned the rights of Greek insurgents in Cyprus, at the time a British crown colony. The case was a serious test-case for the emerging and still fragile European human rights system. Not only did it involve a dispute between two North Atlantic Treaty Organization (NATO) allies, it was also filed at the height of the Cold War and concerned a particularly delicate issue, namely decolonisation. It immediately caused hectic activity at the British Foreign Office which had not foreseen such a case could reach the Commission; and they had not predicted that a NATO ally would retort to using the ECHR against the late empire.[22]

The United Kingdom had in practice extended the reach of the Convention to some colonial possessions, including Cyprus. But it was also assumed that by not yet ratifying the optional right for individuals to bring a case to the Commission this extension was mainly relevant at the level of symbolic politics.[23] Yet, by Greece opting to launch an inter-state complaint, it effectively evaded the Foreign Office's strategic plan to use the Convention as a means of symbolic politics. The United Kingdom then had to suddenly explain and defend its actions on the island of Cyprus—how it was necessary to use force as it was an allegedly emergency situation. This triggered a mission by the Commission that was sent to Cyprus to examine the alleged emergency situation and the possible violations of the ECHR.[24]

The case is emblematic of the status of the ECHR system in the eyes of the Member States and thus the de facto authority of the system in a narrow sense. The United Kingdom basically treated it as a political intervention in its domestic affairs. Revealing of this particular perception is the fact that a great deal of energy went into drawing up psychological portraits of the members of the Commission arriving in Cyprus in order to develop an effective response. The conclusion was hardly flattering and revealed a lack of recognition of the emergent European human rights system. Only Waldock of the United Kingdom and Professor Sørensen of Denmark were considered credible: 'the only members of real caliber'.[25] The other members were ridiculed in the internal assessments circulating between London and Cyprus.[26] The Italian Dominedo was considered a 'garrulous and rather ridiculous individual'; the French Pernot was a flip-flopper 'quite capable of supporting the British case in the morning, the Greek in the afternoon, and a compromise of his own making in the evening.'[27] The high political context of the case involving both decolonisation and Cold War politics was also reflected in these assessments. The portrait of Jonasson from Iceland is striking in

[22] AWB Simpson, *Human Rights and the End of Empire: Britain and the Genesis of the European Convention* (Oxford, Oxford University Press, 2004) 838–41.
[23] ibid, 838–41.
[24] ibid.
[25] ibid, 941.
[26] Simpson, above n 22, 941.
[27] ibid.

this regard and further revealing of the general perception of European human rights in the United Kingdom: 'NATO's enemy [number one]' and 'impetuous, obstinate, and ambitious. He is, like all Icelanders, an anti-colonialist and very idealistic about anything which does not concern him or Iceland. We fear he will vote for Human Rights.'[28]

In terms of the authority of the ECHR system as measured by acceptance and willingness to take consequential steps, the case is informative of the real difficulties facing early European human rights. When the delegation arrived, the United Kingdom was quick to use the gathered intelligence to sabotage the work of the Commission, restraining access to the essential information and facilities.[29] It would be wrong, however, simply to conclude that the ECHR system had no authority at this point. First the Foreign Office invested considerable energy in preparing the visit and its counter-strategies. Moreover, the Commission, regardless of the hostile reception in Cyprus, managed to collect evidence and prepare a report. The actual normative shadow of the system is further illustrated by the fact that when the situation was starting to clearly point towards a British embarrassment in Strasbourg, the diplomats decided to turn to a different venue and solution. The case was eventually solved with diplomacy—the London-Zürich Agreement on Cyprus.[30] The price was high for Britain: in 1959, it was officially the end of the empire as regards Cyprus as the United Kingdom gave up this possession. In terms of European human rights such a friendly settlement solved the situation and the case was thereby closed without further action.[31]

For the purpose of this book, some interesting conclusions can be drawn from this first European human rights case and its striking political solution. First, it is clear that the nascent ECHR system and its Commission actually had authority regardless of the strategies of sabotage employed by the British actors. Yet, the solution to the case appears at first glance to be in the periphery of the ECHR institutions and their authority. However, their mandate recognised the importance of relative authority, allowing a case to be solved by other or alternative means, including friendly settlement via diplomacy. Conversely, if the European Commission actually had had to pronounce violations and then bring the case before the Committee of Ministers, it is likely this would have had severe negative consequences for the system at large. But by allowing for a better situated institutional solution—a diplomatic agreement—the system at large maintained its authority. The case thereby moved out of the strictly speaking legal ambit, but the shadow of the law undoubtedly played a role in forging the diplomatic solution. Put differently, it is difficult to imagine that the United Kingdom would have accepted this solution without the normative force of the Strasbourg institutions.

[28] ibid.
[29] ibid, 991.
[30] ibid, 1049–52.
[31] GA Res 59/32 (Dec 1, 2004).

IV. Head-On Collisions: Judicial Adaptations in France

The Cyprus case suggests the importance of relative authority for the emerging ECHR system allowing for a political solution to a legal claim without putting the authority of the ECHR system in peril. The next case concerns a more direct legal-legal interface, namely a showdown between the French judiciary and the ECtHR, starting in the 1990s. The ECHR system generally changed during the 1990s—and also prior to Protocol No 11. What occurred was a process of increased embeddedness of the Convention in the Member States' legal and political systems, as well as a growing judicialisation of the system evidenced in a growing number of cases going before the Court and a resulting closer web of European human rights norms.[32] In 1990 the Court had delivered only 30 judgments; in 1999 the number was up to 177.[33] What was basically at stake in France in the 1990s, and in most of the other Member States, was the acceptance of a new, more embedded role of an expanding European human rights regime. Incorporating the Convention into national law had basically a broader effect that was different from the case-by-case logic of the previous period. Now the ECtHR was increasingly in a position to more generally change the interplay of European and national law and politics—and that typically in favour of European human rights law.

France's full participation in the ECHR system was late when compared to other Member States. The right to individual petition before the system was first accepted in 1981 and only in the mid-1980s were the first judgments delivered against France.[34] Scholarship suggests that the central institutions such as the the *Cour de Cassation*, the highest French court on civil and criminal matters, were generally receptive to the ECtHR jurisprudence and integrated it in their legal practices.[35] Equally important, scholars also suggest that the *Cour de Cassation* took consequential actions with regard to cases brought against France before the ECtHR.[36] In other words, when measured against the authority theory used in this

[32] See on embeddedness of the ECHR LR Helfer, 'Redesigning the European Court of Human Rights: Embeddedness as a Deep Structural Principle of the European Human Rights Regime' (2008) 19 *European Journal of International Law* 125.

[33] In the following decade it would climb to an average of some 1500 judgments per year—but that was not foreseeable prior to Protocol No 11 (1998).

[34] EL Abdelgawad and A Weber, 'The Reception Process in France and Germany' in H Keller and AS Sweet (eds), *A Europe of Rights: The Impact of the ECHR on National Legal Systems* (Oxford, Oxford University Press, 2008) 107 and 109.

[35] They estimate that some 700 French decisions referred to the ECHR in the period between 1987 and 1997. L Goldstein and C Ban, 'The Rule of Law and the European Human Rights Regime' (2003) Center for the Study of Law and Society Jurisprudence and Social Policy Program (University of California, Berkeley).

[36] ibid, 23.

chapter, the ECtHR had both narrow and intermediate authority—and possibly extensive authority as well.

The partnership with Strasbourg however came to a sudden halt when the ECtHR embarked on a critique of how the judicial system operated in France, notably at its highest level.[37] While critique of police practices and administrative practices had not caused consternation at the courts, the ECtHR clearly overstepped a fine line that was essential for the mutual recognition when it made the French courts object of its criticism. The key question was the impartiality of the general advocates working at the *Cour de Cassation*; the ECtHR would launch a comparative critique of the *Commissaires du gouvernement* of the *Conseil d'État*.[38] The reaction from the *Cour de Cassation* has been described as a rebellion by one scholar.[39] And this rebellion was precisely challenging the authority of the ECtHR: the two highest French courts started disregarding case law from the ECtHR, including cases that had found French violations of the ECHR.[40]

Interestingly, regardless of this judicial sabotage, the ECtHR's judgments opened up a formerly closed door. Lawyers suddenly eyed the chance for challenging more generally the ways in which justice was delivered in France by the highest courts. The negative reactions from the French courts only intensified the use of the ECtHR by French lawyers who also benefitted from the short physical distance to Strasbourg. Empirically, one can observe a significant growth in the number of cases brought against France, making it one of the top three most frequent Member States before the Court during the period. The French courts counter-attacked by portraying the ECtHR as the advocate of an idea of a uniform European legal system at odds with the in-built subsidiarity of the ECHR. But the strategy did not seem to work. Instead, one can observe a growing institutionalisation of European human rights law in France during the same period: in state departments, academic programmes, and the work of lawyers, integrating the ECHR into their general tools of public international and constitutional law.[41]

What can be concluded is that the counter-attack launched from the highest towers of the French judiciary increasingly was out of sync with the larger field of interlocking institutions involved in European human rights in France. That is, although the French highest courts challenged the narrow authority of the ECtHR, other central institutions of the French state were more receptive to the

[37] MR Madsen, 'France, the UK and "Boomerang" of the Internationalization of Human Rights (1945–2000)' in S Halliday and P Schmidt (eds), *Human Rights Brought Home: Socio-Legal Perspectives on Human Rights in the National Context* (Oxford, Hart Publishing, 2004) 78.

[38] JP Marguenaud, 'l'Effectivité des arrêts de la Cour européenne des droits de l'Homme en France' (2001) 24 *Journal des droits de l'Homme* 1. See more generally, D Kosař and L Lixinski, 'Domestic Judicial Design by International Human Rights Courts' (2015) 109 *American Journal of International Law* 713.

[39] Marguenaud, ibid.

[40] Abdelgawad and Weber, above n 34, 129.

[41] S Hennette-Vauchez and J-M Sorel (eds), *Les droits de l'homme ont-ils constitutionnalisé le monde?* (Brussels, Bruylant, 2011).

growing force of the Strasbourg institutions which helped establish intermediate authority and eventually extensive authority. The fundamental problem facing the French state was that it became increasingly difficult to write off the ECtHR when France was found in violation of the Convention in consecutive cases. And some of these cases were real embarrassments to the French state and its politico-administrative elites. In particular *Selmouni v France* of 1999,[42] finding France in violation of the prohibition of torture, made the Strasbourg Court known to a broader public which made it impossible to ignore it or write it off as a superficial technicality following the line of argument of the French courts. The authority of the ECtHR—and the relative authority of the broader system—was in other words 'rescued' by the way in which the human rights question was broadened to concern a more general problem of French *raison d'état*.[43] This demonstrates something that is well-known to scholars of the European human rights system, namely that the system and its relative authority is vulnerable to pointed attacks over singular judgments but it is generally more unwavering when it comes to the general question of the protection of human rights.

V. Irreconcilable Norms: Prison Votes and the Impossibility of Agreement

The third case study included in this chapter also concerns clashes over entrenched ideas, namely the struggle over the right of prisoners to vote in the United Kingdom. Different from the French case, which essentially concerned ideas about procedural fairness, the British case concerns a more moral-politico question: what happens to citizens when they go to prison? Are they only deprived of their liberty—or are they also deprived of their rights as citizens, for instance their right to vote?

The collision between the United Kingdom and the Court that was triggered by this fundamental question is in some ways surprising as it came at a time when Britain had relatively few cases in Strasbourg. Moreover, human rights had been integrated into the legal and even social fabric of British society. New Labour had put human rights at centre stage as the politico-normative response to modern-day multicultural and global Britain.[44] The centrepiece of that effort was the

[42] See *Selmouni v France* App no 25803/94 (ECtHR, 28 July 1999). For the first time the court found a respondent state to be guilty of torture, see Case of *Aksoy* v *Turkey* App no 21987/93 (ECtHR, 18 December 1996).

[43] Compare the analysis in M Delmas-Marty, *Raisonner la raison d'État: Vers une Europe des droits de l'homme* (Paris, Presses Universitaires de France, 1989).

[44] Madsen, above n 37.

Human Rights Act of 1998 which incorporated the ECHR (and other international human rights) into domestic law and created a new internationally-inspired bill of rights.[45] The change of direction came a few years after and was in many ways a reaction to the so-called War on Terror and New Labour's engagement in this regard. In this new political situation, it created indignation and even anger when the ECtHR blocked the deportation of radical Islamists associated with terrorism on human rights grounds.[46] Sparked by the outrage over these highly sensitive cases concerning deportation, cases that at first glance appeared more technical now also triggered political turbulence. This was the case with regard to *Vinters and Others v United Kingdom*,[47] concerning the blanket ban of appeals of whole life sentences, and then *Hirst (No II) v United Kingdom*,[48] concerning the lack of voting rights of British inmates, finding that a blanket ban on voting by British prisoners violated the Convention.

As it appears, the root problem was the lack of flexibility of the British administration, a question that has also been central to earlier cases against the United Kingdom, notably in the 1980s. In those instances such issues had been tackled by administrative reforms. But with *Vinters* and *Hirst* technical cases were now also high political cases and brought into the heart of national politics, indeed the very politics of the state and its sovereignty. Another major difference was the way in which all of this was turned into front-page news, notably in the tabloid press, which offered quick political gains for critics of the ECtHR. Most consequential in this regard were the ways in which the European system was projected as an external and illegitimate ruler clashing with the virtues of British democracy, in particular the notion of the supremacy of Parliament.[49]

More specifically with regard to the *Hirst* case, it created an ongoing struggle between Strasbourg and key state institutions in the United Kingdom, including politicians at the highest level. According to the Committee of Ministers, the body in charge of compliance at the Council of Europe,[50] there is to this day non-compliance with the decision as well as two dozen cases on similar issues. Adding fuel to the fire, politicians, including then Prime Ministers David Cameron and now Prime Minister Theresa May, publicly raised the question of Britain altogether pulling out of the ECHR system.

[45] C McCrudden, 'Common Law of Human Rights?: Transnational Judicial Conversations on Constitutional Rights' (2000) 20 *Oxford Journal of Legal Studies* 499.

[46] For an analysis, see C Gearty, '11 September 2001, Counter- terrorism, and the Human Rights Act' (2005) 32 *Journal of Law and Society* 18.

[47] Case of *Vinter and Others v The United Kingdom* App no 66069/09; 130/10; 3896/10 (ECtHR, 9 July 2013).

[48] *Hirst v The United Kingdom*, above n 18.

[49] See for example D Davis, 'Britain must Defy the European Court of Human Rights on Prisoner Voting as Strasbourg is Exceeding its Authority' in S Flogaitis, T Zwart and J Fraser (eds), *The European Court of Human Rights and its Discontents: Turning Criticism into Strength* (Cheltenham, Edward Elgar Publishing, 2013).

[50] See for instance, Council of Europe Committee of Ministers, Supervision of the Execution of Judgments and Decisions of the European Court of Human Rights (2013) 7 Annual Rep 1,100.

For the purpose of this analysis, what is interesting, besides the striking question of relative authority raised by Britain by publicly stating that domestic institutions are the most legitimate actors with regard to settling the issues at stake, is the fact that the ECtHR actually tried to respond to the British outcry and supply mediated solutions to the crisis. In the case *Scoppola v Italy*,[51] the Court introduced a way out for the United Kingdom by a slight retreat from the *Hirst* decision. According to the judgment, prisoners could be deprived of their voting rights under certain conditions: if there was legitimate aim and the deprivation of right was not just done automatically. Yet, at the same time, the Court maintained its position on blanket bans in *McHugh and Others v the United Kingdom*.[52] But the United Kingdom did not take the bait. When the Court retreated in *Scoppola*, Britain did not follow up on the offer but rather re-stated its unwavering position against *Hirst*.

The *Hirst* case is itself in a deadlock but the institutional politics it has triggered might well be playing out in new and different ways, which are instructive for understanding the dynamic relationships between institutions and relative authority. One apparent result, which is analysed below, was the Brighton Declaration. Here the united governments of the Council of Europe agreed on a new and greater subsidiarity in the European human rights system. Basically, it called for a new balance in the system more in favour of national politics and law. Another effect is more subtle. Linked to the Brighton Declaration, but initiated prior to it, the ECtHR has devised new legal approaches that seemingly grant certain Member States, including the United Kingdom, a wider margin of appreciation.[53] A Section President of the ECtHR has spelled this out in an article on the 'Age of Subsidiarity'.[54] According to the judge, the ECtHR will give more deference to national institutions if they can prove that they have conducted a thorough, transparent and inclusive review of relevant case law from Strasbourg. This obviously changes the focus from individual substantive justice to a new form of procedural justice. Unsurprisingly, this has already triggered critical comments from academics and the Court seems split on these issues.[55] With regard to the authority framework defined above, the general tendencies in the case law following *Hirst* suggest that the ECtHR is seeking to maintain its authority by rebalancing the institutional order, that is, by allowing more subsidiarity. This process has been

[51] *Scoppola v Italy* (no 3) App no 126/05 (EctHR, 22 May 2012).

[52] *McHugh and Others v the United Kingdom* App no 51987/08 and 1,014 others (ECtHR, 10 February 2015).

[53] *RMT v United Kingdom* App no 31045/10 (ECtHR, 8 April 2014); *Animal Defenders v United Kingdom* App no 48876/08 57 (ECtHR, 22 April 2013); and *A, B and C v Ireland* App no 25579/05 (ECtHR, 16 December 2010).

[54] R Spano, 'Universality or Diversity of Human Rights?: Strasbourg in the Age of Subsidiarity' (2014) 14 *Human Rights Law Review* 487.

[55] JP Rui, 'The Interlaken, Izmir and Brighton Declarations: Towards a Paradigm Shift in the Strasbourg Court's Interpretation of the European Convention of Human Rights' (2013) 31 *Nordic Journal of Human Rights* 28.

termed 'democracy-enhancing' by the above cited judge; from the perspective of this analysis, it might better be seen as authority-enhancing.

VI. 'Constitutional Politics': The Brighton Declaration and its Consequences

The politics of the *Hirst* case is revealing of the authority challenges that the ECtHR has faced in recent years. The finer details of the ECtHR's reactions to the pushback from Britain suggest that the Court is both receptive to critique from the Member States and that these interplays impact the institutional order. Other examples from the same period also illustrate how the Court is willing to retreat from an initial overreach. The most obvious example is the case *Lautsi v Italy* where the Grand Chamber of the ECtHR[56] overruled an earlier Chamber ruling that had caused uproar in Italy as well as a number of other countries, both at the government level and among many civil society institutions, notably Christian organisations. These cases illustrate how the institutional order is not written in stone but dynamic and involves some implicit checks and balances.

A different way of reallocating and redistributing authority in the European system is by treaty reform. This can be viewed as the equivalent to constitutional politics at the national level. Interestingly, this has not been used very much during the history of the ECtHR—at least not in terms of retaking power from the Court. On the contrary, the reform of the ECtHR in all of the additional protocols 1 to 14 has expanded the rights catalogue, the access points or generally rationalised the system to provide a swifter handling of cases.[57] The main driver of many of these reforms, at least since the 1980s, has been the fear of backlog in Strasbourg.[58] And when the British chairmanship of the Committee of Ministers of the Council of Europe started leaking its plans for an extensive reform package of the ECtHR in February 2012, it also did that against the backdrop of an all-time high in terms of a backlog of some 150,000 cases and a generally overburdened court. While this was used to justify the undertaking, what became the Brighton Declaration (2012) half a year later contained the first systematic critique of the Court, its judges and decisions. Its main message was that European human rights

[56] *Lautsi and others v Italy* App no 30814/06 (ECtHR, 18 March 2011).

[57] Only main exception to this is the introduction of a new access criterion of 'significant disadvantage' in Protocol No 14 (2004—in force 2010).

[58] R Harmsen, 'The Reform of the Convention System: Institutional Restructuring and the (Geo-)Politics of Human Rights' in J Christoffersen and MR Madsen (eds), *The European Court of Human Rights between Law and Politics* (Oxford, Oxford University Press, 2011).

had to be rebalanced in favour of national law and politics.[59] Put differently, if the Court was to maintain authority it was to have less power.

It is important to note that the Brighton Declaration was not simply a document exhibiting British exceptionalism but an international declaratory agreement signed by all 47 Member States of the Council of Europe. It is beyond the scope of this chapter to go into detail with regard to the drafting of the Declaration, but the main message of the Declaration as included in the two resulting Protocols No 15 and 16 have the following core elements:

— National courts' access to advisory opinions from the Court (Protocol No 16; Brighton, paragraph 12d);
— A reference to the principle of subsidiarity and the margin of appreciation in the Preamble (Protocol No 15, Article 1; Brighton, paragraph 12b);
— An age limit for the appointment of judges (Protocol No 15, Article 2; Brighton, paragraph 25f);
— Delete the parties' access to object to Chambers' relinquishment of jurisdiction to the Grand Chamber (Protocol No 15, Article 3; Brighton, paragraph 25d);
— Shorten the time bar for applications from six to four months (Protocol No 15, Article 4; Brighton, paragraph 15a);
— Extend the scope of the significant disadvantage admissibility provision (Protocol No 15, Article 5; Brighton, paragraph 15c).

There is no doubt that the Brighton Declaration sent a very robust message to the Member States in terms of a new balance of European human rights. However, the two Protocols No 15 and 16 have not yet entered into force as an insufficient number of Member States have ratified. This means that the Brighton showdown with the ECtHR remains political signalling—not binding law. For the purpose of this analysis, it is however interesting to assess whether the Brighton Declaration and resulting Protocols have engendered change at the Court. That is, whether the institutional balance has been altered as a result of the political messages and in the direction suggested by the Brighton Declaration.

A recent work has systematically examined whether the ECtHR is giving more deference to the Member States following the Brighton Declaration by comparing evolutions in the case law in the period before and after the Declaration.[60] The results of the inquiry are striking. Overall, the ECtHR provides more subsidiarity following the Brighton Declaration. The main legal tool used for

[59] For details, see L Helfer, 'The Burdens and Benefits of Brighton' (2012) 1 *ESIL Reflections* 1; J Christoffersen and MR Madsen, 'Postscript: Understanding the Past, Present and Future of the European Court of Human Rights' in J Christoffersen and MR Madsen (eds), *The European Court of Human Rights between Law and Politics* 2nd edn (Oxford, Oxford University Press, 2013).

[60] MR Madsen, 'Rebalancing European Human Rights: Has the Brighton Declaration Engendered a New Deal on Human Rights in Europe?' (forthcoming 2018) *Journal of International Dispute Settlement*.

prompting this change is an increase in use of the doctrine of 'margin of appreciation' and 'wider margin'. The increase in use of subsidiarity is found in particularly three areas of law: Article 8 on the right to privacy, Article 35 on access to the Court and, but less strikingly, Article 3 on the prohibition of torture and inhuman and degrading treatment.[61] The analysis essentially demonstrates that the ECtHR is receptive to the political signals sent at the occasion of the Brighton Declaration and associated Protocols, regardless of their current status as only soft law documents.

In the conjunction of this analysis, this suggests that the allocation and distribution of public authority in the European human rights system is subject to the international equivalent of constitutional politics. This implies that there are genuine checks-and-balances in the system—that the principals (the member states) have not left the building and left the agents alone. Moreover, the fact that the changes at the Court have been triggered without the relevant legal documents yet having entered into force further underlines that the checks-and-balances are not only a question of constitutional politics in a formal sense. They are the result of political communication and participation in the system in a larger sense.

VII. Strengthening Authority by Enhancing Communication and Participation

Regardless of their very different outcomes, the four case studies included in this analysis all suggest that the dynamics of relative authority of the European human rights system evolve around communication and participation. This is of course only an informal system of checks-and-balances, implying that the different institutions can push for their position and interests by formal and informal means of communication, ranging from judgments and amendments of the Convention to protests and political campaigns. The system plays out transnationally and cuts across the law-politics divide: it is national and European, as well as it is legal and political. It is centred on the fundamental differences in the roles played by law and politics and at both levels. The case studies however suggest that, on the one hand, there is a risk of overly differentiating the different branches of the system thereby making legal-political communication difficult, and, on the other, a risk of conflating the legal and political roles in the protection of European human

[61] For a qualitative legal analysis of these changes, see B Cali, 'Coping with Crisis: Towards a Variable Geometry in the Jurisprudence the European Court of Human Rights?' (forthcoming 2018) *Wisconsin Journal of International Law.*

rights. Part of the problem is that the idea of separation of powers contains somewhat of a paradox which is inherited in the European human rights system: the different branches of government are separate yet need to communicate and work together toward common aims. The challenge is therefore how different institutions can create a workable process of governance while maintaining their independence.

Generally the case studies suggest that the system has institutionally limited channels of communication that risk introducing frictions in the interactions between the different institutions of the system. More specifically, a key challenge in the European human rights system is that in its current set-up the communication between the Court and national political and legal institutions primarily occur through final judgments against Member States in contentious cases as well as through their participation before the Court in these cases. These are very uneven and institutionally hierarchised forms of communication that are hardly ideal for a workable process of governance. Of course, a conventional international law reading of the situation would argue that there is no such thing as separation of powers in the system: the role of the Court is simply to check whether the Member States live up to their obligation to respect the Convention. This is per definition a one-sided communication and a deliberately uneven playing field. While this is true from a formalist international legal viewpoint, the history of the system as illustrated in the four case studies clearly suggests that the authority of the system requires forms of feedback between the national and European levels and between law and politics. The case studies further suggest that although a form of constitutional politics is available as suggested by upheavals triggered by the Brighton Declaration, the general operation of the system and its effectiveness in terms of ensuring the authority of the Court depends on communication and participation.

This raises the basic question of whether the operation of the system could be improved by taking more seriously that communication and participation is fundamental for securing the authority of the Court across the different levels of audiences. And whether some of the frictions that have negatively impacted the system at certain moments of its evolution could, if not be avoided, then be diminished if the relevant parties were better informed, earlier informed and encouraged to participate in a more profound way throughout the proceedings in Strasbourg. In lieu of a conclusion, in what follows, three suggestions are made that all seek to improve communication and participation in the system. The assumption is not that this can solve all frictions in the system—some of them are intrinsic to the adjudication of human rights—but it can limit the negative effects of miscommunication and improve information flows and feedback mechanisms. If we take seriously the idea of relative authority, it is important that the institutions involved, and their different assets, are brought into the process in a more organised way that improves the dialogue between the judicial and political branches of European human rights governance.

A. Different Role for the Committee of Ministers

International courts like the ECtHR exercise public authority but they are not formally operating in a system of checks-and-balances where a legislator can continually check and seek to influence the course taken by the Court. As shown in the case studies, the system includes the option for constitutional politics, but this is a very heavy solution and one that risks upsetting the system at large as evidenced by the Brighton processes. In other words, there is arguably a need for a more pointed communication between the political and legal levels with regard to the understanding of the Convention and its evolution.

One solution to this problem could be to organise an annual meeting of the Committee of Ministers with the goal of reviewing developments in the jurisprudence of the Court. The debate should be limited to overall trends in the case law and should not be about singular judgments. The outcome of the meeting could be a set of comments on the developments in the law. These should not be recommendations or direct suggestions as this could upset the institutional order and possibly infringe on the judicial independence of the Court.[62]

Arguably, such an approach would help foster a new and more direct dialogue between the Court and the Member States. Importantly, it would allow for a clearer notion of what the consensus is among governments on certain areas of law. It could also provide a solution to the inherent problem of so-called 'treaties over time' and anchor the development of European human rights in a more democratic structure, namely the Committee of Ministers.[63] Critics will however be quick to point out the risks of such an approach. It might in practice be very difficult to find consensus among 47 governments. Moreover, it might be difficult to maintain the focus in such a forum as some states might seek to use it to discuss singular cases and delay implementation.

B. Increased Participation before the Court

As an alternative or supplement to the above, the communication and information between the legal and political levels could also be improved by increased participation of Member States and civil society before the Court. As the system operates right now it is at times difficult for the Member States and civil society organisations to identify when cases are before the Court in which they have

[62] It could also be contemplated to involve the Parliamentary Assembly of the Council of Europe in these assessments in a separate session in the Parliamentary Assembly. Having both the Committee of Ministers and the Parliamentary Assembly involved would produce a double-legitimation of the jurisprudence.

[63] On the question of treaties over time, please see G Nolte (ed), *Treaties and Subsequent Practice* (Oxford, Oxford University Press, 2013).

particular interest. One solution is that the Court develops better communication in terms of early notification of pending cases of particular relevance.[64] Closely linked, the system currently lacks transparency with regard to relevant materials in individual cases. To increase participation and communication between the stakeholders and the Court an important step would be to make publicly available via online access all amicus briefs and written observations lodged with the Court by the parties to the proceedings.

The underlying rationale of such a reform is that it is clearly in the interest of the involved parties that all relevant arguments are brought before the Court, particularly when more principled questions are at stake. There are a number of arguments in favour of such a solution, including that it is likely to increase dialogue and knowledge as well as better identify European consensus. It is also generally likely to enhance the authority of the Court. Counting against such a solution is that it requires more resources on the part of the participants in the system. And it presupposes that it is indeed possible to identify where different stakeholders have strategic interests.

C. Allowing for Appeals to the Grand Chamber

The case studies included in this study generally suggest that sustainable solutions to the legal questions brought before the Court can be achieved if there is some option of appealing controversial judgments. The *Lautsi* case stands out in this regard as a successful appeals case that closed what was likely to become a major crisis in a number of Member States. The *Hirst* decisions and resulting tug of war between the United Kingdom and the ECtHR is however indicative of the fact that some human rights questions can create deadlock, even if the Court retreats from its initial more principled stance in subsequent decisions on comparable matters. Linked to the question of increased participation and better information also discussed above, it might nevertheless be fruitful for the system to introduce new ways that allow for revisiting decisions, both by the immediate parties or other Member States or parties.

As regard the latter, one way of ensuring better input and participation from other Member States is by introducing a provision that allows a larger group of Member States to bring a Chamber Decision before the Grand Chamber. The requirements for such an appeal could be that the case in question seemingly deviates from established practice or introduces expansive interpretations. These states would then appear as third parties before the Grand Chamber. To protect against abuse, it should be required that the appeal was launched by more than, for example, 15 states. With regard to the immediate parties of a case, it could be

[64] It is within the rules that the Court can invite submission from the Member States in the relevant cases. This competence could be used more fully.

contemplated whether all cases should start in chambers in order to allow for possible appeals by the parties to the Grand Chamber. This means that the current system of relinquishing cases to the Grand Chamber would be discontinued.

Such an appeals system would introduce institutionalised means for allowing parties to challenge interpretations in concrete cases. Generally, this might increase dialogue and knowledge on European consensus and lead to better judgments. More significantly, such an institutionalised system of appeals would allow the parties to challenge concrete cases without challenging the authority of the Court as such and its final say on the law. Although it does not change the existing balance of power, it might be of significant symbolic value, notably with regard to the acceptance of judgments in relevant audiences. The latter is, as argued, fundamental for the authority of the Court. On the negative side it could be argued that such a system and procedure might politicise cases before the Court. This is questionable however. What is though not questionable is that such a system would be likely to require more resources from the Court.

VIII. Conclusion

The chapter has assessed how relative authority is exercised in practice in the European human rights system. Against the background of a new theory and empirical model of the de facto authority of international courts, the chapter has explored different instances of authority challenges and conflicts in the history of the European human rights system, involving different institutional players from national and European law and politics. Generally, it can be concluded that the European system has an informal system of checks-and-balances that for the most part functions. In addition, the system allows for constitutional politics in more extreme situations. The analysis has not considered structural challenges to the European human rights system,[65] but rather the pockets of resistance that can be found in otherwise well-functioning Member States.

The analysis further concludes that the current informal system in some cases is insufficient for avoiding clashes over the Court's interpretations of the ECHR. The chapter has consequently written up a set of recommendations that may improve the interplay of the relevant institutions and stakeholders and generally create a better participation and communication in the system. These include a different role for the Committee of Ministers, a greater participation and transparency with regard to proceedings before the Court, and the introduction of a form of appeals system. All of the suggested solutions can be introduced in the current system with only minor amendments to the existing framework.

[65] That raises very different problems which cannot be solved by improving the system of relative authority of European human rights.

5

Authority Monism in International Organisations: A Historical Sketch

JOCHEN VON BERNSTORFF

Allocating authority through concepts such as the separation or division of powers stands for the normative ideal of the legitimate distribution and control of authority within a given institutional setting. It traditionally differentiates at least between three different functional entities: the legislator, the executive and the judiciary. Only recently the claim for a stronger separation of powers or checks and balances in international organisations (IOs) has been more prominently advanced by the literature, predominantly in constitutionalist approaches to international law.[1]

Under the allocation of authority lens both the distribution and existing controls of authority matter.[2] Any such authority-configuration is the outcome of continuing political power-battles between various factions of a given society. Depending on its content and context, the call for normative concepts such as separation of powers or checks and balances can confirm or challenge a specific authority-configuration. As a legitimacy-yardstick for the exercise of public authority the separation of powers concept encapsulates a number of normative expectations depending on the various constitutional traditions.[3] I will mention only two aspirations commonly linked to this normative field, which are particularly relevant for my contribution: first and foremost the claim that executive authority is being delegated by a separate legislative organ, which represents the general or majority interests of a given society and second that the executive can be held accountable by separate judicial institutions for exceeding the legal limitations of its authority.

[1] AL Paulus, 'The International Legal System as a Constitution' in JL Dunhoff and JP Trachtmann (eds), *Ruling the World? Constitutionalism, International Law and Global Governance* (Cambridge, Cambridge University Press, 2009) 92–93; A Peters, 'Compensatory Constitutionalism: The Function and Potential of Fundamental International Norms and Structures' (2006) 19 *Leiden Journal of International Law* 579.

[2] Mendes and Venzke, in this volume.

[3] C Möllers, *Die Drei Gewalten: Legitimation der Gewaltengliederung in Verfassungsstaat, europäischer Integration und Internationalisierung* (Weilerswist, Velbrück, 2008) 19–55.

The editors to this volume more appropriately translate the separation of powers concept for the current transnational domain into 'legitimacy assets', such as inclusiveness, functional specialisation and human rights protection.[4]

If we ask for the relevance of the separation of powers concept for rule- and decision making in international organisations from a historical nineteenth century perspective, my thesis and starting point is that instead of a separation of powers, international institutions originally were constructed according to a principle of enhancing one single institutional entity: national administrations. Their functional raison-d'être originally was to exclusively empower national executives for specific tasks in an increasingly globalised economic and societal environment. Where there was an increased call for checks and balances on the domestic level in the nineteenth century European States, the move to institutions on the transnational level from the very beginning was built on the single premise of enhancing administrative capacities through international expertise-driven cooperation. Arguably, this is a deeply entrenched legacy in most international organisations until today. I will in the first part of my presentation describe the characteristics of this authority configuration in more detail (section I). As a second step I will then highlight elements of the evolution of this authority-configuration in the twentieth century (section II) followed by a conclusion discussing recent attempts to involve human beings 'affected' by IO policies (section III).

I. The Authority Configuration in the First International Organisations

The age of international organisation starts with the Vienna Congress in 1815. Two patterns of international organisation stem, even though then in embryonic form, from the first half of the nineteenth century: the so-called concert of Europe and the public international commissions and unions. Historical research on the concert seems to concur that the diplomatic conference system of the Great European Powers can hardly be called an international organisation or even a system of cooperation. In its ad hoc and reactive character it served as a high politics crisis management system for the Great Powers based on the balance of powers doctrine. It certainly left its mark on the structure of later international institutions through the Great Power privileges in Executive Councils such as the League of Nations Council and the UN Security Council, but it lacked the characteristics of continuous and systematic cooperation based on common institutional structures.[5]

[4] Mendes and Venzke, in this volume.

[5] J Osterhammel, *Die Verwandlung der Welt: Eine Geschichte des 19. Jahrhunderts* (München, CH Beck, 2013) 680.

What we are left with then are the numerous nineteenth century public international unions and commissions created by international treaty law, such as the World Telegraph Union, the World Postal Union or the river commissions for the navigation on the Danube and the Rhine but also the late nineteenth century international debt commissions which regulated the Egyptian, Turkish and Chinese debt restructuring programmes or the International Sugar Commission. In the field of institutionalised humanitarian and social regulation the Office for the Prevention of Maritime African Slave Trade and Liquor Traffic based in Zanzibar, the Institute for Agriculture in Rome, the International Labor Office in Basel and the International Committee of the Red Cross in Geneva could be mentioned as examples.[6] These entities are rightly being considered as precursors of the currently prevailing model of international organisation.[7] Many of these institutions still exist today as regulatory or standard-setting international institutions.

The original blueprint of these forms of cooperation is the unification of administrative action between European countries on certain issues, which by their very nature seemed to require international regulation. Particularly obvious was this need for coordinated administrative action in the field of new communication technologies, which had only been invented during that period. The International Telegraphic Union, which later became the International Telecommunications Union (ITU) is a case in point and served as a precedent for the subsequent creation of other permanent forms of administrative cooperation of States.[8] When major European powers, which were particularly advanced in the development of telegraphic technology, realised that the envisaged global expansion of this technology needed international cooperation, they invited 20 States to Paris in 1865 for a first international conference. States were represented diplomatically by their ambassadors in Paris and by expert delegates from the respective national administrations. The aim of the conference was a continuous harmonisation of telegraph administration in the respective countries. Negotiators in Paris differentiated between the Convention as a basis for further cooperation and specific harmonised regulations. Even though the Convention had to be signed by the ambassadors, the concrete regulations were negotiated by the experts from the national administrations.[9]

[6] For an overview see I Claude, *Swords into Plowshares: The Problems and Progress of International Organization* (New York, Random House, 1956).

[7] C Tietje, 'Towards "Open" Transnational Administrative Networks: Emerging Structural Features' in O Dilling, M Herberg and G Winter (eds), *Transnational Administrative Rule-Making—Performance, Legal Effects, and Legitimacy* (Oxford, Hart Publishing, 2011).

[8] PS Reinsch, 'International Institutions and Their Administration' (1907) 1 *American Journal of International Law* 579, 583; on Reinsch and functionalist thought J Klabbers, 'The Emergence of Functionalism in International Institutional Law: Colonial Inspirations' (2014) 25 *European Journal of International Law* 645, relativising the alleged role of a coherent theory of 'functionalism' in the foundational phase G Sinclair, 'The Original Sin (and Salvation) of Functionalism' (2016) 26 *European Journal of International Law* 965.

[9] A Peters and S Peter, 'International Organizations: Between Technocracy and Democracy' in B Fassbender and A Peters (eds), *The Oxford Handbook of the History of International Law* (Oxford, Oxford University Press, 2012) 183–84.

The initial Convention foresaw regular conferences of the parties to amend its rules and regulations. Conferences would be organised by national administrations on a rotating basis. This is comparable to the current G-8 or G-20 organisational structure, which is based on the idea of a network of administrative entities. Plenipotentiary and diplomatic conferences became the exception and technical conferences became more frequent. Only later was a permanent Secretariat added to the organisational structure of the International Telegraphic Union with the task to facilitate the application of the Convention by national administrations.[10] At an even later stage the organisation decided to establish an Executive Council, consisting of a limited number of Member State representatives with the task to represent the plenary organ between the regular plenary conferences.

With this final organisational setup, a model for international organisation had been created: the Convention usually establishes a main plenary organ, in which rule-making in form of resolutions and standard-setting can take place. The plenary organs usually decide on the basis of the one state one vote principle, hereby respecting the principle of sovereign equality. Voting under the unanimity rule was common but some unions in the nineteenth century already worked with majority voting procedures. The unions ('bureaux') also often established a permanent Secretariat as a facilitator of future conferences and for enhancing the implementation of standards. In more mature organisations we can then observe the creation of an Executive Board or Council as an executive supervisory organ usually consisting of a limited number of national representatives, representing the membership.[11] Interestingly, the Secretariat could historically also be located within or under direct supervision of a national administration of one of the Member States, like the Swiss Department of Post Offices and Railways in the cases of the Secretariat of the International Telegraphic Union and the Secretariat of the International Union of Railway Freight Transportation.[12] As a lucid commentator in 1975 put it pointedly 'some Bureaux were mere extensions of host countries' administration'.[13]

[10] Art 61 Convention télégraphique internationale de Paris, révisée à Vienne (1868): Une Administration télégraphique, désignée par la Conférence, prendra les mesures propres à faciliter, dans un intéret commun, l'exécution et application de la Convention. A cet effet elle organisera, sous le titre de 'Bureau international des Administrations télégraphiques', un service spécial qui fonctionnera sous sa direction, dont les frais seront supportés par toutes les Administrations des Etats; Peters and Peter seem to imply that the history of international institutionalisation goes from network-like government-cooperation to a phase of strong institutionalisation and more recently back to network-like governmental cooperation. In the remainder of this contribution I argue that these government-networks from a sociological perspective always formed the very heart of institutionalisation-processes on the international level.

[11] HG Schermers and NM Blokker, *International Institutional Law* 3rd edn (Leiden, Brill, 1995) § 409.

[12] Reinsch, above n 8, 592.

[13] V-Y Ghébali, 'The League of Nations and Functionalism' in AJR Groom and P Taylor (eds), *Functionalism: Theory and Practice in International Relations* (London, London University Press, 1975) 143.

Some administrative unions like the Universal Postal Union even foresaw a dispute settlement body to settle disputes between national administrations over the application of standards. But also here this was not seen as a separate or even juridical task but as a task that first and foremost required administrative and technical expertise. The arbitrators generally were civil servants from technically respected national administrations or, as in the case of the International Union of Railway Freight Transportation, the director of the permanent Secretariat of the Union himself.[14] The prevailing logic thus is not to control organs by a separate judicial organ of the institution but to facilitate transnational cooperation by settling disputes between States and the interpretation of standards. This supportive action comes from within the transnational administrative network and is provided by technical experts. Today we still find this approach in Article 29 of the current IMF Articles of Agreement, according to which, 'Any question of interpretation of the provisions of this Agreement arising between any Member and the Fund or between any Members of the Fund shall be submitted to the Executive Board for its decision'. Hence, the institution itself remains the final arbiter of its own competences and the obligations of the Member States. As far as judicial controls of international institutions are concerned we can thus speak of a legacy of 'auto-interpretation' through executive councils in international institutions.

Like other international unions and commissions, the permanent Secretariat of the Telegraphic Union from the very beginning involved private expertise in its publication and knowledge dissemination activities.[15] This is not only the case for unions dealing with technical innovations but was also very common in the financial, humanitarian and cultural field. Often private innovation and privately organised international conferences preceded international diplomatic conferences.[16] Those NGOs, scientific institutions and industry representatives thus usually remain an integral part of the knowledge and policy network, which was at the very heart of the respective international organisation. The Egyptian Debt Commission of 1880 for instance consisted of national representatives from the major European creditors, which were in constant contact with the involved banks and their national financial stakeholders. Without the consent of the representatives of the creditor nations in the Commission, the Egyptian government could not incur any expenditures not authorised under the Convention.[17]

[14] See for arbitrations in the Union, S Kneisel, *Schiedsgerichtsbarkeit in Internationalen Verwaltungsorganisationen: Die Verrechtlichung der zwischenstaatlichen Streitbeilegung*, Band 20 (Sinzheim, Nomos, 2009); Reinsch, above n 8, 592.

[15] Claude, above n 6, 39–40.

[16] M Vec, *Recht und Normierung in der Industriellen Revolution: Neue Strukturen der Normsetzung in Völkerrecht, staatlicher Gesetzgebung und gesellschaftlicher Selbstnormierung*, Studien zur europäischen Rechtsgeschichte Band 200 (Frankfurt, Klostermann, 2006) 31; Peters and Peter, above n 9, 186–88.

[17] Reinsch, above n 8, 620.

Which conclusions can be drawn for the authority configuration in international organisations from this rough sketch of early prototypes of international institutions and what does this mean for the perspective of the separation of powers? To begin with, international organisations in their initial setup adhered to a monist or unified authority configuration. The authority lies with a sectorial network of administrative and private experts, which dominates the organs of the organisation, be they plenary organs, Executive Councils or the Secretariat.[18] Diplomats or Heads of States are now and then needed to provide the necessary basic legitimacy allegedly derived from State sovereignty. Rule-making as such, however, be it hard or soft law, is in the hands of administrative experts from the given functional sector.[19] 'Functional specialisation' between rule-making organs and those implementing and administering rules thus is largely absent from the initial set up of international organisations.[20]

Those countries with strong administrative capacities in a particular sector and a specific interest in a transnational regulation are often more influential in the negotiations of new rules than other national administrations. Very often these countries had also been the driving forces in the establishment of the particular organisation and in a sociological perspective remain 'more equal' members of the institution for a long time. A particularly striking twentieth century example is the position of the US in NATO or within the World Bank. It is also not uncommon that these countries also enjoy legally formalised privileges, such as a permanent representation in Executive Councils or veto rights.

Interestingly, this observed monist authority structure was not even altered by the establishment of the first dispute settlement bodies. These institutions were created to settle disputes between Member States and to thereby protect and further the application of the rules of the organisation. Consequently, dispute settlement bodies often consisted of the same national or international experts that pulled the strings in the other organs of the institution. From this perspective, international organisations had initially not been constructed as an external superimposed structure, but as an organic extension of national administrative capacities of major European powers to the international level in order to solve sectorial problems through cooperation. Their initial nineteenth century setup and inherent logic is often much closer to the Basel Committee or the G-8 than Anne Marie Slaughter seemed to imply when she cherished government networks

[18] See for specific regime-biases today M Koskenniemi and P Leino, 'Fragmentation of International Law? Postmodern Anxieties' (2002) 15 *Leiden Journal of International Law* 553.

[19] See on transnational rule-making today Dilling, Herberg and Winter, above n 7 and, in particular, S Oeter, 'The Openness of International Organizations for Transnational Public Rule-Making' in Dilling, Herberg and Winter, ibid.

[20] On functional specialisation as a potential 'legitimacy asset' see Mendes and Venzke, in this volume.

as the 'New World Order' at the beginning of the new Millennium.[21] Formal legitimation is provided by sovereign consent and informally by a strong ideology of universal cooperation in the common interest.

European nineteenth century observers of this early phase of international organisation embraced this spirit of progress through technological cooperation waxing lyrical about these new organs, which are seen as an expression of the solidarity between 'civilised' nations in tackling practical questions raised by a rapidly advancing European civilisation. In the words of British Prime Minister Lord Salisbury the telegraph had 'assembled all mankind on a great plane, where they can see everything that is done and hear everything that is said and judge of every policy that is pursued at the very moment these events take place'.[22]

Contemporary legal literature abounded with the rhetoric of an 'international community' based on common interests.[23] In 1907 the influential American commentator of the move to institutionalised cooperation, Paul Reinsch, looking back to this first phase of institutionalisation, expressed this optimistic liberal sentiment in the AJIL in the following words:

> During the Middle Ages the unity of civilization rested largely upon a cultural and religious basis. In our own age, such bonds of union have been powerfully supplemented by the growing solidarity of the economic world, as well as by the need of experimental and applied science to utilize the experience and knowledge of all countries. The existence of such an underlying unity of the civilized world has been borne in upon the nations with greater force every succeeding year.[24]

It was not by accident that these first international organisations were being created in the high time of the so-called first economic globalisation and European expansion. And many of these cooperative endeavours became necessary in order to better administrate and enforce European economic and military expansion in what contemporaries called 'non-civilised' areas of the world. New inventions and their industrial reproduction in line with coordinated technical standards played not only an important role as a symbol of European superiority but were of utmost practical importance in the colonial endeavours. Without the steamboat and the telegraph the 'Scramble for Africa'[25] would not have been possible and the railroads stepped up European settlers' expansion in the New World with the associated massacres and displacements of Native Americans. It is one of the traditional and long-lived blind spots of international legal scholarship to portray

[21] AM Slaughter, *A New World Order* (Princeton, Princeton University Press, 2004).

[22] Quoted in M Mazower, *Governing the World: The History of an Idea* (London, Penguin Books, 2012) 26.

[23] G Jellinek, *Die Lehre von den Staatenverbindungen*, Reprint of the Edition Vienna 1882 (Aalen, Scienta Verlag, 1969).

[24] Reinsch, above n 8, 580, on Reinsch see Klabbers, above n 8.

[25] RA Packenham, *The Dependency Movement: Scholarship and Politics in Development Studies* (Cambridge, MA, Harvard University Press, 1992).

in the tradition of nineteenth century observers technological cooperation as an embodiment of 'progress'[26] or as innocent and non-political in nature.[27] Another closely connected feature of this early phase of international organisation is rule-making for all societies of the World without effective non-European or non-Western participation. Territorial expansion and economic exploitation as well as benevolent paternalism were at the very heart of the European 'civilising mission' in the colonies.[28]

Let me conclude from the separation of powers perspective that the original set up of international organisations was obviously not influenced by this concept. The original model is based on the enhancement of executive or administrative authority alone. For a successful identification of existing horizontal controls or checks and balances we would rather have to look into the clearly not always harmonious power relations between various national administrations within the organisation than into the relationship between the functionally differentiated organs of the respective institutions.

From a vertical perspective we would have to differentiate between the Member States of a particular organisation. Is it a democracy? Does the respective national Constitution provide for the involvement of the legislator in the implementation of international standards or are other constitutional organs involved in preparing and implementing new international standards? Could national courts effectively limit the implementation of international standards in the domestic realm? Given that many of the participating states in the second half of the nineteenth century were constitutional monarchies, we should, at least for continental Europe, not expect strong vertical checks and balances of the activities of national representatives in these early forms of institutionalised cooperation. At least for the German system it is probably fair to say that the prevailing idea that foreign policy and foreign administrative cooperation is an exclusive prerogative of the executive is a monarchical Prussian nineteenth century legacy.

II. The Evolution of the Authority-configuration in the Twentieth Century

But has the basic authority configuration, which I have characterised as empowering de-territorialised sectorial networks of national administrations and related

[26] See for the notion of progress in general T Skouteris, *The Notion of Progress in International Law Discourse* (The Hague, Asser, 2010); see for the theory of functionalism and its problematic legacy J Klabbers, 'The EJIL Foreword: The Transformation of International Organizations Law' (2015) 26 *European Journal of International Law* 9.

[27] J von Bernstorff, 'Procedures of Decision-Making and the Role of Law in International Organizations' (2008) 9 *German Law Journal* 1939; Klabbers, ibid.

[28] A Anghie, *Imperialism, Sovereignty and the Making of International Law* (Cambridge, Cambridge University Press, 2005); on Reinsch and Colonial Legacies, Klabbers, above n 8.

private stakeholders, changed through the evolution of international organisation in the twentieth century? There are three general developments in the evolution of international organisations in the twentieth century which deserve closer attention in this context.

First, the failed attempts to centralise existing institutions under the roof and political supervision of one world organisation in the Interwar period and the subsequent post-World War II trend of proliferation of independent and specialised institutions in loose coupling to the UN. Second, there is the evolutionary tendency in many international organisations to strengthen permanent Secretariats and to gain more autonomy vis-a-vis national executives.[29] The third development is the proliferation of international courts and tribunals in the last decades of the twentieth century, which at least in theory could have prompted the development of horizontal checks and balances within the respective international organisations.

Let me start with the attempt to unite the embryonic nineteenth century sectorial forms of international organisation under the political leadership of the League of Nations and its central organs. Already during World War I pacifist currents in the US and Europe merged the idea of functional sectorial cooperation with the normative ideal of world peace.[30] In what would later develop into a theory of functionalism, they saw in the constant development and expansion of pragmatic and sectorial cooperation a means to ensure peace among nations.[31] According to Article 24 of the League Covenant all existing international bureaus and commissions were supposed to be put under the direction of the League. The provision also foresaw a general responsibility of the Secretariat for all matters of international concern regulated by general conventions. Rather exceptional was the newly founded International Labour Organization (ILO), which was designed as a strong and institutionally independent organisation.

Eventually, the attempted complete centralisation of existing sectorial organisations under the directorate of the Council failed. In many of the already existing unions and commissions important Member States rejected the idea of being placed under League of Nations supervision. Moreover, in the late 1930s the influential Bruce-report, which had been mandated by the League's Secretary General Avenol, proposed a clear separation between cooperation on technical and social issues and cooperation in security related issues.[32] In more concrete terms, the report suggested the establishment of a separate council for economic and social issues. The reason for this proposal was that the ever more conflictual atmosphere

[29] Bernstorff, above n 27; I Venzke, 'International Bureaucracies from a Political Science Perspective—Agency, Authority and International Institutional Law' (2008) 9 *German Law Journal* 1401, www.germanlawjournal.com/index.php?pageID=11&artID=1026.

[30] D Kennedy, 'The Move to Institutions' (1987) 8 *Cardozo Law Review* 841.

[31] See on functionalism Claude, above n 6 at 385 et seq; Klabbers, above n 26.

[32] C Tietje, *Internationalisiertes Verwaltungshandeln* (Berlin, Duncker & Humblot, 2001) 134–35.

in the League Council was considered to be an obstacle for pragmatic functional cooperation in the economic, social and cultural field.

This proposal could only be realised after World War II in the new UN Charter, which foresaw the creation of the ECOSOC as a coordinating council for economic and social affairs. Leading US representatives in the drafting process of the Charter felt that it would be advisable to have a set of specialised and separate councils and to decentralise the various international cooperative endeavours. As a consequence, the new separate Economic and Social Council had to cope with the situation in which the most important institutionalised (League-) structures, such as the ones dealing with health or food and agriculture were given the status of specialised agencies based on separate conventions with only a loose connection to the ECOSOC. This post-war period sowed the seeds for the proliferation of largely independent sectorial international organisations. During the decolonisation period it seemed that the ECOSOC nonetheless would be able to assume a leading role in international economic and social cooperation, before it was completely sidelined by the industrial states of the West. As a result, the most important fields of international cooperation are dealt with by independent and largely uncoordinated sectorial international organisations.

This leads me to my second point: the evolutionary tendency in many international organisations to strengthen permanent Secretariats in order to gain more autonomy vis-a-vis national executives. Compared to the nineteenth century many Secretariats of international organisations have become important and partially autonomous actors in their field of cooperation. In particular, the concept of the international civil servant played an important role in the attempt of Secretariats to gain a certain level of independence from the will and control of Member States and their national representatives.[33] However, this autonomy should not be conceived of as clinical isolation. In fact, in most instances, smaller networks of national administrations or one hegemonic Member State still influence the Secretariat, at least indirectly, through their clearly articulated policy preferences. Moreover, strong Member States increasingly tend to replace general contributions by 'earmarked' funding of international organisations for projects in line with their interests. It seems therefore as if general funding for international organisations in the twenty-first century has become an endangered species.

Whenever these softer mechanisms of control of strong Secretariats by particular Member States fail, in particular in the economic field, a return to 'pure' transnational administrative cooperation again became an increasingly attractive option. The G-8, and to a certain extent also the Organisation for Economic Co-operation and Development (OECD), are good examples of the path dependencies in the evolution of international organisations. Here states with an assumed common economic interest enhance transnational administrative cooperation in close contact with influential private actors in a relatively homogenous group

[33] Bernstorff, above n 27; Venzke, above n 29.

of states in order to cement and secure their advanced economic position in the world, if possible through direct and relatively informal forms of cooperation.

The third development is the proliferation of international courts and tribunals in the last decades of the twentieth century, which at least in theory could have prompted the development of horizontal checks and balances within the respective international organisations. At closer inspection however, the increase of the authority of judicial institutions can be reduced to one particular aspect of international organisation: it is the development and enforcement of legal rules of the organisation vis-a-vis the Member States either through dispute settlement procedures (the World Trade Organization (WTO) is the prime example here) or through individual or collective claims procedures, such as in the human rights or international criminal law field. The function of these quasi-judicial institutions thus is law-making and implementation of the rules and standards within and between the Member States[34] and not horizontal checks and balances within the institutional setting of the organisation. In terms of the above-mentioned 'authority configuration' these new judicial institutions, like their nineteenth century predecessors, ultimately further strengthen, rather than control, the existing executive-based authority configuration. The International Court of Justice is a good example of a court that almost routinely shies away from delineating spheres of competence between the main organs of the United Nations. The so-called 'legalisation' or 'juridification' phenomena are predominantly of a vertical nature and often refrain from horizontally restraining or limiting the exercise of authority within and through international organisations.

III. Conclusion—Controls through those 'Affected' by IO Policies

The attempt to define normative standards for allocating authority through concepts such as the separation of powers comes with a bias against the uncontrolled accumulation of authority in the hands of a relatively small group of individuals or administrative units. Hence the main concern is that other societal interests are not being taken into consideration in rule-making and implementation and that the outcome serves primarily specific vested interests rather than being beneficial for the whole of a given society. In the history of international organisation since the nineteenth century we can find many examples which can prove that this concern is a well-founded one also for international and transnational institutions. The most well-known one of the late twentieth century is the Agreement

[34] A von Bogdandy and I Venzke, *In wessen Namen?: Internationale Gerichte in Zeiten globalen Regierens* (Berlin, Surhkamp, 2014).

on Trade-Related Aspects of Intellectual Property Rights (TRIPS), which at the high time of a global Aids pandemic was initiated and implemented by a network of powerful economic actors and a small number of national administrations without taking into account the vital interest of millions of people in access to affordable drugs on all continents.[35]

But what could after all this realistically be expected from attempts to implement effective controls on authority networks in international organisations? Let me briefly go through rather recent institutional innovations, which are often mentioned when it comes to enhancing horizontal controls within international institutions: the first one is the creation of Parliamentary Assemblies. International organisations in the twentieth century have introduced parliamentary bodies. The North Atlantic Treaty Organization (NATO), the Council of Europe and the WTO could be mentioned here. Parliamentarians are being elected by national Parliaments of Member States and thus form a Parliament of the national Parliaments of Member States. Usually these bodies have no concrete say in the rule and decision-making of these institutions, neither do they have any controlling function vis-a-vis the other organs of the respective institution.[36] In practice, parliamentarians often are being selected to become members of these bodies precisely because they share a strong identification and allegiance with the aims, rules, standards and policies of the particular institution.

Unless parliamentarians are being directly elected on the basis of a specific political agenda for the institution, which is only the case in the European Parliament, it seems unrealistic to expect these parliamentary bodies to exert a controlling influence on other organs of the institution. The only controlling influence these assemblies may have derives from their ability to communicate developments on the international level to national Parliaments, which then could attempt to hold their national representatives from the executive branch accountable for their actions in the other organs of the institution. The same holds true for NGO participation in international organisations. Decision-making powers for NGOs are rare or non-existent, however, participation and speaking rights for international NGOs in deliberations of plenary organs have become the rule. Co-option into the authority-network is a latent danger.[37] Through their power to work with national and international media self-mandated NGOs can potentially put pressure on government representatives to justify their concrete ways of participating in rule-making activities of international organisations vis-a-vis interested

[35] HP Hestermeyer, *Human Rights and the WTO, The Case of Patents and Access to Medicines* (Oxford, Oxford University Press, 2008).

[36] M Krajewski, 'International Organisations or Institutions, Democratic Legitimacy' in R Wolfrum (ed), *Max Planck Encyclopedia of Public International Law [MPEPIL]* (2008), www.mpepil.com.

[37] B Rajagopal, *International Law from below: Development, Social Movements and Third World Resistance* (Cambridge, Cambridge University Press, 2003); BS Chimni, 'Co-option and Resistance: Two Faces of Global Administrative Law' (2005) IILJ Working Paper 2005/16, www.iilj.org/gal/documents/co-optionandresistancetwofacesof.pdf.

national publics.[38] They thus help to politicise rule-making in international organisations.[39] In sum, both Parliamentary Assemblies and NGO participation can have a positive effect on vertical controls of the performance of national experts in international organisations through making their work more transparent for international and national publics. Their controlling or counterbalancing impact on the horizontal level, however, is often fairly limited.

The most recent trend in enhancing horizontal controls in international organisations is the involvement of social movements and affected segments of society in the deliberations and decision-making processes of international institutions. NGO participation in international organisations is in fact increasingly replaced by the participation of those segments of populations 'affected' by the policy decisions and rule-making efforts of international organisations.[40] Currently especially the CFS (the Committee on World Food Security in Rome) and United Nations Environment Programme (UNEP) are experimenting with the involvement of social movements in the work of the institution. While these reforms have not yet been formalised within UNEP, the CFS as an institution is already practising social movement involvement. The most recent reform attempted to address two major concerns related to the authority configuration in international organisations. The first concern is the fragmentation of the international institutional landscape dealing with food security on the UN level.[41] As an umbrella institution for two specialised agencies, the Food and Agricultural Organization and the International Fund for Agriculture, as well as for the World Food Program, the CFS was institutionalised after the world food crisis in 2008 in order to coordinate global policies and standard-setting in the field of food security.

The second aspect is the attempt by the CFS to become a globally inclusive institution which can give voice to all actors dealing with, as well as being affected by, global food security policies.[42] Through a radical reform of the so-called Civil Society Mechanism (CSM) of the CFS,[43] civil society representatives have the right to take part and to speak in all meetings of the CFS at all times. Furthermore, the Civil Society Mechanism, together with other UN institutions and specialised agencies such as the World Bank, forms one of the constituencies in the newly created Advisory Committee of the CFS, which is supposed to advise the Bureau and the Secretariat of the CFS in a transparent fashion. Most

[38] Bernstorff, above n 27.

[39] M Zürn, 'The Politicization of World Politics and its Effects: Eight Propositions' (2014) 6 *European Political Science Review* 47.

[40] In general demanding to facilitate the participation of those constituencies that are most directly affected are the 'Almaty Guidelines' of the Economic Commission for Europe 2005, Annex para 15.

[41] See on fragmentation in this field O de Schutter, 'The Reform of the Committee on World Food Security: The Quest for Coherence in Global Governance' in N Lambek et al (eds), *Rethinking Food Systems: Structural Challenges, New Strategies and the Law* (Berlin, Springer, 2014).

[42] M Fraundorfer, 'Experiments in Global Democracy: The Cases of UNITAID and the FAO Committee on World Food Security' (2015) 4 *Global Constitutionalism* 328.

[43] N McKeon, *Food Security: from Crisis to Global Governance* (London, Routledge, 2013).

importantly, and breaking with former NGO participation models, the new Civil Society Mechanism is primarily based on the involvement of those 'most affected' by global food security policies.[44] Out of 11 thematic constituencies in the CSM only one is given to NGOs. The other 10 constituencies belong to social movements, which co-ordinate their input to the relevant issues on the agenda. The currently existing 11 constituencies are as follows: Farmers, Fisherfolk, Landless, Indigenous Peoples, Pastoralists, Consumers, Agricultural Workers, Urban Poor, Women, Youth, and NGOs. Corporate interests are represented only in the NGO-constituency. Next to the representatives of these 11 thematic groups the CSM Coordination Committee foresees elected social movement representatives from 17 sub-regions of the world. Each sub-region consists of a network of social movements from various countries from the region. To include social movements from the 17 sub-regions of the world in the work of the CFS is an attempt to remedy another traditional weakness of established NGO-participation schemes in international organisations: the underrepresentation of the Global South. Interestingly, the internal organisation of the CSM is not regulated by rules of the institution as a whole—it is a self-governed body with its own autonomous rules of procedure.

The underlying rationale of this approach is not to replace rule-making of national representatives by decisions of self-appointed social movements. Activists do not want to exercise formalised decision-making powers. Rather the general idea behind this strategy is to influence the content of adopted standards[45] and to foster the transnational mobilisation of social resistance against the global network of powerful national administrations and highly influential corporate actors.[46] Indeed, the inclusion of individuals, who claim to speak for those who are directly affected by certain global policies, can change the atmosphere of the deliberations in international organisations. It can constitute a strong irritation for national experts and scientists and potentially modifies the authority configuration within an institution. The status of speaking for those who are being negatively affected by certain policy moves on the ground, if credible and well-coordinated, gives these voices a high moral- and sometimes also empirical persuasiveness.

But is the promotion of the co-operation with transnational resistance-networks really the right remedy for an assumed lack of control of monist authority-networks within international institutions? If the underlying rationale of this approach is to create and strengthen transnational resistance networks against powerful administrative and corporate entities, it almost seems as if civil society replicates the structures used by its adversaries: transnational networking through international institutions in a deformalised and rather unaccountable fashion in

[44] J Duncan, *Global Food Security Governance: Civil Society Engagement in the Reformed Committee on World Food Security* (London, Routledge, 2015) 103.

[45] See on their effectiveness N McKeon, *Food Security Governance, Empowering Communities, Regulating Corporations* (London, Routledge, 2015) 161.

[46] See on resistance Chimni, above n 37.

order to change or manipulate the rules of the game. It is moreover hard to deny that the problem of co-option and affirmation of IO-policies through institutional involvement raised in the context of NGOs remains a crucial one also for social movements. And is the price for this gain in authority and legitimacy for civil society the pseudo-democratic legitimisation of standards, which may not deserve that dignity? Are resistance and institutional cooperation not as such irreconcilable concepts? If we include the vertical dimension, the situation becomes even more complex. Is the integration of social movements from the Global South not de-legitimising Third World governments, who may have a democratic mandate to speak on behalf of their peoples?

From the viewpoint of the respective international institution, this progressive form of involvement of 'affected' segments of the population organised in social movements can increase the perceived legitimacy of its authority configuration through more 'inclusiveness',[47] but it is not without risks. The authority-exercising network of national administrations and private expertise may as a consequence of such an institutional reform turn its back on that international organisation. Like transnational capital these powerful networks are elusive and on the constant look-out for the best institutional setting for the advancement of their agenda.[48] And if no other international institution is available, within which external resistance can be channeled and marginalised, a new informal institutional setting will be set up. Again, the Committee on Food Security is a good example. As long as the World Bank in its powerful policies vis-a-vis developing countries ensures market access for investments of the agro-industry, voluntary CFS standards on 'landgrabbing' will not matter in practice. This is the prize for the post World War II-plurality and independence of international institutions. In a fragmented institutional setting, forum-shopping and contradictory international policies are inevitable. And, contrary to some voices in the literature, institutional fragmentation should not be cherished as an emerging proto-democratic pluralistic world order, which provides for effective inter-institutional controls of authority. Instead, this global constellation upholds an only slightly concealed cementation of the economic, technical and social status quo in an unequal world.

[47] On 'inclusiveness', see Mendes and Venzke, in this volume.

[48] E Benvenisti and GW Downs, 'The Empire's New Clothes: Political Economy and the Fragmentation of International Law' (2007) 60 *Stanford Law Review* 595.

6

No Institution is an Island: Checks and Balances in Global Governance

ANDREAS VON STADEN*

I. Introduction

Every system for governing large and complex political communities is effectively characterised by different sites of relative, rather than absolute, authority. The real question is not *whether* authority is relative, but rather *how relative* it is, with authority (and power) being more concentrated, or dispersed, in some systems than in others, both as a matter of their formal legal allocation and their factual exercise. This applies to domestic constitutional systems of government as well as to governance arrangements beyond the state.

As Joana Mendes and Ingo Venzke note in the introduction to this volume,[1] the functional logic underlying the doctrine of the 'separation of powers', developed in the context of traditional three-branch forms of government within nation-states, is of limited utility as an analytical or guiding principle with respect to the allocation of authority to regional and global institutions. The politico-legal characteristics of the international sphere and the manner in which regional and global governance[2] arrangements are usually created—responding to issue-specific needs as they arise across time and space, with different sets of states participating, and without regard necessarily for fitting new arrangements into

* I thank Joana Mendes and Ingo Venzke for helpful comments on an earlier draft of this chapter, with the usual disclaimers applying to the final version. I dedicate this contribution to the memory of my dog Jack who sadly passed away while I was attending the workshop that gave rise to this edited volume.

[1] J Mendes and I Venzke, in this volume.

[2] For the sake of linguistic economy, I will in the following mostly refer to 'global governance', it being understood that the arguments also apply to regional arrangements. Similarly, I more or less interchangeably use the terms '(international) organisations' (mostly), 'institutions', and '(governance) arrangements', well aware that these come with different definitional backgrounds, but for the question of checking and balancing it is usually secondary in which particular institutional form the authority to be checked and balanced is embedded.

an overall, coherent design—are not amenable to its principled operation. The 'normative programme' that underpins separation of powers thinking, by contrast, as Mendes and Venzke also note, remains applicable even where the allocation of 'powers'[3] does not occur along distinct lines of legislative, executive and judicial authority. This normative perspective foregrounds the different sources of legitimacy that specific (elements of) governance arrangements—and the outcomes they produce—(may) draw upon as well as the balances that are struck between the interests and constituencies represented by them.

The idea of 'checks and balances' plays a central role in this respect. While distinct from the doctrine of the separation of powers, its genesis and development has been so closely related to the latter that the two are frequently considered as being two sides of the same coin, or even synonymous.[4] For conceptual and analytical reasons, however, it is useful to keep them separate. Conceptually, the idea of the 'separation of powers' foregrounds the allocation, or distribution, of powers to different institutions or institutional bodies. The idea behind the notion of 'checks and balances', by contrast, emphasises the *relationship* between the institutions and bodies to which powers have been allocated: it comprises the politico-legal controls and counterweights intended to prevent sites of authority from being unconstrained and potentially becoming repressive and tyrannical. The institutionalisation of checks and balances thus ensures that the separation of powers is not absolute.[5] Also, understood as variables, the separation of powers and checks and balances need not co-vary, that is, comparable allocations of legislative, executive and judicial powers to a set of institutions do not necessarily require that all control and balancing functions are defined and distributed identically. The traditional field of application of the concept of checks and balances has been with respect to interactions of the three branches of domestic government, but its principal thrust of establishing direct or indirect controls over consequential decision-making does not require a neat differentiation along functional lines; instead, it can be applied to any site of politico-legal authority, and thus also to

[3] MJC Vile long ago noted the confusion in separation-of-powers thinking that results from the ambiguity of the term 'powers', see MJC Vile, *Constitutionalism and the Separation of Powers* 2nd edn (Indianapolis, Liberty Fund, 1967) 13–14. While I agree that the separation of powers might be more appropriately reconceived as 'separation of authority', I retain the traditional terminology because it remains the most widely recognised label for discussing the allocation of political and legal decision-making authority in complex governance arrangements.

[4] See C Möllers, *Die drei Gewalten: Legitimation der Gewaltengliederung in Verfassungsstaat, Europäischer Integration und Internationalisierung* (Weilerswist, Velbrück, 2008) 13 and 20.

[5] See E Carolan, *The New Separation of Powers: A Theory for the Modern State* (Oxford, Oxford University Press, 2009) 20 (quoting South African Constitutional Court's statement that 'in democratic systems of government in which checks and balances (exist) … there is no separation of powers that is absolute'); F Vibert, *The Rise of the Unelected: Democracy and the New Separation of Powers* (Cambridge, Cambridge University Press, 2007) 170 ('the idea of checks and balances significantly modifies any idea that complete separation should exist between the different branches of government'). The necessary interconnectedness of separated powers was already noted in the Federalist Papers; see I Kramnick (ed), J Madison, A Hamilton and J Jay, *The Federalist Papers* (London, Penguin, 1987) 308 (no 48).

governance arrangements beyond the state with their (usually) functionally mixed competences.

While true in theory, it is the case that, empirically, institutionalised checks and balances are rare internationally, apart from the special case of the European Union.[6] Ruth Grant and Robert Keohane, for example, have highlighted the absence in international relations of 'an effective constitutional system that constrains power in an institutionalized way, through mechanisms such as checks and balances',[7] and with respect to the inner workings of international organisations (IOs), Jan Klabbers has noted 'that there are few, if any, general rules in international institutional law concerning checks and balances'.[8] Similarly, Eyal Benvenisti and George Downs, linking checks and balances to accountability and the availability of review mechanisms, note that 'the multiple oversight mechanisms and supervisory processes that exist at the domestic level of developed democracies that can scrutinize intergovernmental regulatory decisions tend to be lacking'[9] in global governance.

And yet, instances of checks and balances within and between international institutions do exist. In addition, if we broaden the scope of the concept of checks and balances to include vertical checks and balances that exist as a background condition due to the nature of the international legal and political system within which international institutions are embedded, then the set of relevant control mechanisms becomes significantly larger. That these 'self-help' mechanisms privilege certain actors—usually executives—and through them certain constituencies to the exclusion of others, may be seen as normatively problematic and sub-optimal, and thus as diminishing a mechanism's overall legitimacy, but it does not detract from such controls' availability as checks on authority beyond the state.

In this chapter I address select conceptual issues concerning checks and balances in global governance and provide illustrative examples as to their operation in practice. In addition, I articulate conjectures as to why horizontal checks and balances are so much rarer in global than in domestic governance, arguing, inter alia, that the vertical checks available to states as a result of the principal-agent relationship between them and the IOs of which they are members, and the dependency of IOs on states for the implementation of their decisions, provide key explanations as to why additional horizontal checks are usually perceived as unnecessary. The conclusion summarises and points to the need to address the role of non-state

[6] For a brief overview of the principal checks and balances at work in the institutional architecture of the EU, see A Staab, *The European Union Explained: Institutions, Actors, Global Impact* (Bloomington, Indiana University Press, 2008) 75–80.

[7] RW Grant and RO Keohane, 'Accountability and Abuses of Power in World Politics' (2005) 99 *American Political Science Review* 30.

[8] J Klabbers, 'Check and Balances in the Law of International Organizations' in M Sellers (ed), *Autonomy in the Law* (Dordrecht, Springer, 2007) 161.

[9] E Benvenisti and GW Downs, 'Toward Global Checks and Balances' (2009) 20 *Constitutional Political Economy* 366.

actors in future research on relative authority and checks and balances beyond the state, an aspect that, due to length constraints, is not covered here.

II. Types of Checks and Balances in Global Governance

The purpose of checks and balances is often portrayed as being, ultimately, the prevention of domination, abuse and tyranny; in normal, everyday politics, however, their role is less dramatic: their function with respect to different sites of decision-making is, in James Madison's words, to 'keep[] each other in their proper places',[10] that is, to assure that decisions are being taken in line with an authority's competence and the applicable rules and procedures so as to prevent encroachments on the competences of others. Nor do the protections afforded by checks and balances solely serve more vulnerable political minorities; they may also protect the interests of political majorities by preventing the hijacking of institutions by powerful and influential minorities for narrow interest group purposes. In addition, checks and balances may be seen as increasing the overall quality of the decisions of public authorities, where higher quality implies fairer and less biased, but also factually more correct. The fact that other actors have some role to play in proceedings or outcomes forces the primary or co-decision-maker to take the interests, expertise and normative judgments of these actors and the constituencies they represent into account. While conditional on the strength of the applicable checks and balances, the outcome has at least the potential to be better informed, more inclusive, less divisive, and hence politically 'better' overall.

A. Conceptualising 'Checks' and 'Balances'

The phrase of 'checks and balances' combines two elements that are conceptually distinct. A 'check', as understood here, constitutes a form of control by one authority over the exercise of another authority's competence, usually 'by authorizing it to play a part, although only a limited part, in the exercise of the other's functions'.[11] This may be a formal veto right, a conditional right to overrule another actor's decision, or the ability to postpone or suspend a decision. For the idea of 'balancing', by contrast, it suffices to create a separate site of authority that provides a political counterweight to the actor that is to be balanced (while checks always also involve an element of balancing, the reverse is thus not necessarily the case). Such a balancing site may or may not have consequential decision-making power of its own. If it does not—having, for example, only the power to issue non-binding

[10] Madison, Hamilton and Jay, above n 5, 319 (no 51).
[11] Vile, above n 3, 20.

resolutions and recommendations—we may think of it as a form of 'opinion balancing', making sure that other voices can articulate a position of their own and have a chance of being heard before a final decision is being taken elsewhere, or to criticise it afterwards. Alternatively, where the decisions of a balancing site do have binding force for the same set of addressees and run counter to another authority's decision, the result is normative incongruity and conflict that may require resolution through an appropriate mechanism.

For both checks and balances to fulfil their functions meaningfully, the relevant institutions, or organs, must draw authority from different sources of legitimation. The notion of checks and balances would be rendered nugatory if all that were required is the multiplication of separate decision-making sites that could then, however, represent the same constituencies and whose members might be selected by the same method of appointment or election. But checks and balances imply variation, not redundancy. As Madison had noted, to limit the power of the 'legislative authority', it should be divided into separate branches 'and to render them, by different modes of election and different principles of action, as little connected with each other as the nature of their common functions and their common dependence on the society will admit'. In addition, 'the members of each [department] should have as little agency as possible in the appointment of the members of the others'.[12]

Domestically, we can frequently observe these principles at work: in federal states the legislative function is frequently divided between one body that represents the people as a whole and another that represents the political entities below the federation (such as states, *Länder*, cantons, regions or provinces) or a particular social group or estate (as in the case of the House of Lords in the United Kingdom). In parliamentary systems, the executive draws its legitimacy from having been elected by a parliamentary majority, while the parliamentary minority usually retains certain control rights over the majority. In presidential systems, both legislature and president are elected by the people as a whole, but in different ways, with the latter voting only for their district's or state's representative in parliament, depending on their place of residence, but all selecting the president from the same pool of candidates. Finally, the judiciary, which may exercise a check on both the executive and the legislative branches, while often being appointed by one, the other, or both of them acting together (as well as, less frequently, popular vote), draws its legitimacy from certain aspects of the judicial role, including independence and impartiality, legal expertise, and insulation from the vicissitudes of electoral politics.

Some forms of institutional relationships and interactions evince elements of both checking and balancing, without falling predominantly into either of the two categories. An example is when one organ has agenda-setting power with respect to another one. In such a case, the first organ exercises control over the issues with

[12] Madison, Hamilton and Jay, above n 5, 320 and 319 (no 51).

which the second organ has to concern itself and thus circumscribes the latter's freedom to choose not to do so. On the other hand, without more, the agenda-setter can neither control what that other organ will do with the agenda item, nor what substantive outcome will result. An illustrative example is provided by the role of the European Commission in the legislative process within the EU: the Commission holds the formal prerogative to initiate (most) EU legislation by submitting a legislative proposal, but it does not itself adopt legislation which is done by the Council and the European Parliament under the applicable ordinary or special legislative procedures.[13]

B. Different Types of Checks and Balances

The manner in which checks and balances operate in global governance can be categorised in terms of at least three contrasting characteristics: horizontal versus vertical; intra-organisational versus inter-organisational; and specific versus general checks and balances.

i. Horizontal versus Vertical Checks and Balances

The first characteristic concerns what may be called 'directionality': checks and balances in global governance can operate either horizontally or vertically. Horizontal checks and balances operate between sites of authority located at the same level of political organisation, in this case situated at the regional or the global level. Vertical checks, by contrast, operate between sites of authority located at different levels of political organisation, that is, between institutions at the regional and the global level, or between (Member) States and regional or global governance arrangements. Importantly, verticality is not equivalent to hierarchy: hierarchical relationships between institutions may operate both at the same level of political organisation (that is, horizontally) or across different levels (that is, vertically), in either direction. Hierarchy determines which institution's decision shall formally prevail (that is, trump those of other institutions) in case of substantive conflict and is not intrinsically tied to the level of political organisation at which these bodies are situated: sometimes hierarchy operates vertically, as, for example, when EU law has primacy over conflicting national law; sometimes it is horizontal in character, eg, when the Court of Justice of the EU (CJEU) declares EU acts to be invalid. By contrast, while the European Court of Human Rights (ECtHR) is situated at the 'higher' level of regional organisation, its judgments by themselves cannot invalidate or displace domestic law and policy.

[13] See Consolidated Version of the Treaty on European Union [2012] OJ C326/13, art 17(2), and Consolidated Version of the Treaty on the Functioning of the European Union [2012] OJ C326/47, art 294 (for the ordinary legislative procedure).

ii. Intra- versus Inter-organisational Checks and Balances

Checks and balances are often conceived of as operating between different types of institutions, that is, inter-organisationally, but they also have a role to play between different organs or subsets of actors that are part of the same institutions, that is, intra-organisationally. Domestically, for example, parliaments may be checked by the two other branches of government, but the design of the legislative process, at least in democracies, also usually provides for control functions, including veto points, for political minorities, legislative committees, or the legislature's or the represented political parties' leadership. Because international organisations are not embedded in a global governmental system organised along traditional three-branch lines, they may combine under a single institutional roof (quasi-) legislative, executive and judicial functions. As a result, some intra-organisational control devices in international organisations institutionalise what in domestic systems would be organised inter-organisationally.

iii. Specific versus General Checks and Balances

Last, but not least, a third characteristic in terms of which checks and balances may vary is their specificity, that is, the question whether they apply to well-circumscribed, discrete (classes of) decisions by another decision-making body or whether they apply across the board to all or most decisions within another body's ambit. The first type is usually a result of design decisions taken during the drafting of an organisation's constitutive instrument when control and balancing elements are negotiated together with the primary allocation of functions and responsibilities to its main organs. The second type, by contrast, usually derives from the background condition of the general legal and political system within which the organisation operates. In the international sphere, since states are sovereign and remain, at least formally, the masters of the treaties they sign and ratify, they retain, as principals, certain powers over the agents they have created which can be used to check or balance their authority. Like the specific variant, this second type will often also be an element affecting a new organisation's institutional design choices, usually by being deemed sufficient for exercising control over an institution and its decision-making and so obviating the need to institutionalise additional horizontal control devices.

III. Examples of Select Types of Checks and Balances in Global Governance

This section provides select examples of concrete arrangements through which sites of authority in global governance are, or can be, checked and balanced.

A. Horizontal Checks and Balances in Global Governance

i. Intra-organisational Arrangements

In terms of quantity, horizontal checks and balances operating within the same organisation are more frequent than inter-organisational ones. As noted, this is largely due to the manner in which global governance arrangements are created. In contrast to domestic contexts where the basic parameters of (most of) the principal government institutions and their relationships are jointly designed and laid down in a state's Constitution, internationally, governance arrangements emerge more haphazardly in response to crises or at other critical junctures, tend to be limited in scope to specific issue areas, and comprise different sets of countries as state parties. Incongruent memberships in particular will normally prevent, or at least impede, the formal establishment of inter-organisational checks and balances for political, but also for normative reasons.

With respect to the internal design of international organisations, this last obstacle is absent and we almost always find some, if often limited, forms of checks and balances between the different organs that constitute the institution as a whole. A typical organisational design includes a plenary assembly in which all Member States are represented, an executive-type decision-making organ often composed of a subset of the Member States, a secretariat offering administrative assistance, and possibly a court or other quasi-judicial body for the settlement of disputes, with or (more frequently) without compulsory jurisdiction. Although ostensibly mirroring the three branches of domestic government, with the secretariats playing the role of the administrative bureaucracy, the analogy is flawed: even where we can identify distinct legislative, executive and judicial competences at the international level, these are much more limited and circumscribed than their domestic counterparts.

Strong checks in the form of establishing veto points may be rare in institutional designs of global governance arrangements, but they do exist. A case in point is the judicial check on prosecutorial discretion at the International Criminal Court (ICC). Decisions by the prosecutor not to commence an investigation or to end it without prosecution, for example, are subject to review by a Pre-Trial Chamber, either upon request by the referrer or on its own motion;[14] so are requests for arrest warrants, summonses to appear, and the confirmation of charges before the trial begins, amongst other aspects of the proceedings.[15] The Pre-Trial Chamber is thus in a position to review and, if it sees fit, reject requests by the prosecutor which constitutes a strong check on the latter's authority.[16] On the other hand,

[14] Rome Statute of the International Criminal Court, 17 July 1998, 2187 UNTS 3, art 53(3).

[15] ibid, arts 57, 58 and 61.

[16] See also generally AM Danner, 'Enhancing the Legitimacy and Accountability of Prosecutorial Discretion at the International Criminal Court' (2003) 97 *American Journal of International Law* 510.

although the prosecutor and his or her deputies are elected by the ICC's Assembly of States Parties, there is, in contrast to some domestic systems, no formal oversight mechanism in place to review and, if need be, modify the office's general policies with respect to investigations and prosecutions.[17]

Elsewhere, in the World Trade Organization (WTO), the Dispute Settlement Body (DSB)—composed of Member State delegates—has the power to veto the adoption of the (quasi-)judicial panel and Appellate Body decisions, but the threshold for rejection (consensus) is so high that such veto would become relevant, if at all,[18] only in the most egregious cases of ultra vires decision-making or otherwise inappropriate conduct on the part of the (quasi-)judicial bodies (if not rejected, decisions are adopted by default).[19] The power of panels and the Appellate Body (AB) can also be checked by way of authoritative interpretations of WTO law which only the Ministerial Conference and the General Council are authorised to adopt, an authority which, when to be exercised with respect to several of the multilateral trade agreements, is in turn made conditional on a recommendation by one of the specialised councils overseeing the operation of the agreement in question.[20] Similarly, under the North American Free Trade Agreement (NAFTA), the Free Trade Commission (FTC) can override and circumscribe the interpretive freedom of investor-state arbitral tribunals by issuing 'interpretations' of its own which shall be binding on such tribunals.[21] Notably, in the WTO's first 20 years of existence, no panel or AB report has ever been rejected[22] and no authoritative interpretation been adopted,[23] while in NAFTA, the FTC has issued only a single 'interpretation'.[24]

[17] See D Raab and H Bevers, 'The International Criminal Court and the Separation of Powers' (2006) 3 *International Organizations Law Review* 93, 112 and 118–20.

[18] After all, there will usually be at least one state that benefits from adoption—the winning one—whose interest in vetoing adoption is not obvious; cp P van den Bossche, *The Law and Policy of the World Trade Organization: Text, Cases and Materials* 2nd edn (Cambridge, Cambridge University Press, 2008) 236.

[19] See DSU, Dispute Settlement Rules: Understanding on Rules and Procedures Governing the Settlement of Disputes, Marrakesh Agreement Establishing the World Trade Organization, Annex 2, 1869 UNTS 401 (1994) 33 ILM 1226, arts 16(4) and 17(14).

[20] See Marrakesh Agreement Establishing the World Trade Organization, 15 April 1994, 1867 UNTS 154 (1994) 33 ILM 1144, art IX(2); L Bartels, 'The Separation of Powers in the WTO: How to Avoid Judicial Activism' (2004) 53 *International and Comparative Law Quarterly* 861, 864; van den Bossche, above n 18, 125.

[21] See North American Free Trade Agreement, 17 December 1992 (1993) 32 ILM 289 and 605 (1993) art 1131(2).

[22] See G Shaffer, M Elsig and S Puig, 'The Law and Politics of WTO Dispute Settlement' (2016) UC Irvine School of Law Legal Studies Research Paper Series 10/2016, 10 <ssrn.com/abstract=2748883> accessed 12 January 2017.

[23] CD Creamer and Z Godzimirska, 'Deliberative Engagement within the World Trade Organization: A Functional Substitute for Authoritative Interpretations' (2015–16) 48 *NYU Journal of International Law & Politics* 428.

[24] NAFTA Free Trade Commission, Notes of Interpretation of Certain Chapter 11 Provisions, 31 July 2001, www.sice.oas.org/tpd/nafta/Commission/CH11understanding_e.asp.

Importantly, there is no generally available judicial review of the lawfulness of the acts of one organ by another. IO organs, if so authorised under the UN Charter,[25] are in principle able to request advisory opinions from the International Court of Justice (ICJ) on matters involving the rights and duties of other organs, but save for a few exceptions concerning mostly the relationship between IOs and Member States,[26] ICJ advisory opinions are not legally binding. Incidental review of the lawfulness of the decisions of international organisations as part of contentious proceedings is a possibility, but while such a pronouncement may not remain without political and legal effects, as a formal matter it is likewise not formally binding on the IO (which is not a party to the case). Empirically, the ICJ has in any event remained quite cautious with respect to addressing the legality of IO acts and the relationships between different IO organs.[27]

An alternative to allocating direct oversight and control functions to one organ with respect to another are variants of joint decisions by requiring bodies to act together—concurrently or sequentially—in order to produce a particular outcome. The decision on admitting new members to the United Nations is a case in point: admission is effected by a decision of the General Assembly (GA), but requires a preceding recommendation for admission by the Security Council,[28] which thus has the right of initiative and can, by withholding a recommendation, prevent an admission request from proceeding to a vote in the GA.[29] Similarly, the election of judges to the ICJ requires affirmative outcomes in both the Security Council and the General Assembly,[30] giving each veto power with respect to any candidate put forward.

Overall, explicit or implicit balancing between organs is more common than assigning formal checking power. In many institutional contexts, balancing occurs primarily by way of allocating different functions to different decision-making organs with different bases of legitimacy, or, where both may address (though not decide) the same types of issues, by providing for a sort of balancing of opinion between different sets of actors represented in those organs. This is the case in a number of institutional contexts in which one organ is composed of members of the national executives and another composed of national parliamentarians.

[25] The Charter directly authorises the UN General Assembly and the UN Security Council to request advisory opinions, whereas '[o]ther organs of the United Nations and specialized agencies may be authorized to do so by the General Assembly'; see UN Charter art 96(1) and (2).

[26] For example, see R Ago, '"Binding" Advisory Opinions of the International Court of Justice' (1991) 85 *American Journal of International Law* 439.

[27] See Klabbers, above n 8, 155–61.

[28] United Nations, Charter of the United Nations, 24 October 1945, 1 UNTS XVI, art 4(2).

[29] See U Fastenrath, 'Article 4' in B Simma, D-E Khan, G Nolte and A Paulus (eds), *The Charter of the United Nations: A Commentary* vol I, 3rd edn (Oxford, Oxford University Press, 2012) 350–51; *Competence of the General Assembly for the Admission of a State to the United Nations*, Advisory Opinion of 3 March 1950, ICJ Reports 1950. In the OAS, a similar admission procedure is in place; see Charter of the Organization of American States, 30 April 1948, 119 UNTS 3, www.oas.org/en/sla/dil/docs/inter_american_treaties_A-41_charter_OAS.pdf, art 7.

[30] United Nations, Statute of the International Court of Justice, 18 April 1946, legal.un.org/avl/pdf/ha/sicj/icj_statute_e.pdf, art 4(1).

Examples include the Council of Europe (COE),[31] the Organization for Security and Co-Operation in Europe (OSCE),[32] the Organization of the Black Sea Economic Cooperation,[33] and the North Atlantic Treaty Organization (NATO) (although here, the Parliamentary Assembly is not a body of NATO, but a separate organisation, albeit specifically created to interact with NATO).[34] In all of these cases the different sources of legitimation of these assemblies may provide counterweights in opinion-forming without either body having formal checking power over their respective counterpart.

In many IOs, however, the range of differentiated bases of legitimation tends to be more limited as many plenary fora and the executive or specialised decision-making bodies are both composed of delegates that are selected by (usually) the executive branch of government of their Member States. In such a case, different grounds of legitimation may be said to apply based on plenary representation in one body versus a mix of expertise, relative political and/or economic significance, efficiency, and effectiveness on the other (plus legitimation through election of non-permanent members by the plenary assembly). Arrangements like this can be found at the United Nations,[35] at the International Monetary Fund (IMF) and the World Bank/International Bank for Reconstruction and Development (IRBD),[36] and at the WTO.[37] Secretariats tend to draw legitimacy from the

[31] The COE's Committee of Ministers usually meets at the level of the ministers' deputies (that is, diplomats posted in Strasbourg), while the Parliamentary Assembly is composed of representatives that are delegated to it by the national parliaments of the 47 Member States.

[32] Since 1991, the OSCE (then still the CSCE) features a Parliamentary Assembly composed of national parliamentarians which has, however, no checking power over the organisation's main decision-making bodies (the Ministerial and Permanent Councils, plus the Forum for Security Co-Operation).

[33] See Charter of the Organization of the Black Sea Economic Cooperation, 5 June 1998, www.bsec-organization.org/documents/LegalDocuments/statutory/charter/Download/CHARTER%20web%20080630.pdf, and the Parliamentary Assembly of the Black Sea Economic Cooperation's webpage at www.pabsec.org/default.asp.

[34] The NATO Parliamentary Assembly, with origins dating back to 1955, is an international institution created independently from NATO (founded in 1949), but with membership limited to NATO countries. The relationship between the two organisations is limited to informational exchanges.

[35] The Charter provides that the UN's different bodies shall be composed of 'members' and 'representatives'—see UN Charter, arts 9 (GA), 23 (SC), 61 (ECOSOC) and 86 (Trusteeship Council [inactive since 1994])—which in practice means representation by a Member State's executive.

[36] Board of Governors and Executive Board in the case of the IMF (see Articles of Agreement of the International Monetary Fund, 27 December 1945, 2 UNTS 39, arts 12(2) and (3)), and Board of Governors and Executive Directors in the case of the IBRD, the institution of the World Bank group of organisations that is usually meant when referring to the 'World Bank' (see Articles of Agreement of the International Bank of Reconstruction and Development, 27 December 1945, 2 UNTS 13, arts V(2) and (4)); see also IMF Articles of Agreement, art 12(3)(b) (reserving five of the currently 24 Executive Director posts for the five members that have the largest quotas), and IBRD Articles of Agreement, art V(4)(b) (reserving five appointments among the currently 25 Executive Directors for the five Members with the largest shares).

[37] The Ministerial Conference, the General Council/Dispute Settlement Body/Trade Policy Review Body, and the Councils for Trade in Goods, for Trade in Services and for Trade-Related Aspects of Intellectual Property Rights, as well as any subsidiary bodies, are all composed of representatives of, or office-holders appointed by, the Member States; see Marrakesh Agreement Establishing the World Trade Organization, art 4.

expertise, impartiality and representativeness of their staff, and while they often contribute to shaping an IO's decisions, they generally have no authority to do so in a formally binding manner.

Some types of arrangements provide balancing and (informal) checking powers to 'downstream' decision-makers. An example is the division of labour between the European Court of Human Rights (ECtHR) and the Committee of Ministers in the context of supervising compliance with the European Convention on Human Rights (ECHR).[38] The ECtHR here performs the function of a judicial dispute settler by determining whether state conduct has violated one or more provisions of the Convention, but the supervision of the execution of its judgments by respondent states is not done by the Court,[39] but by the Committee of Ministers, the Council of Europe's executive organ.[40] This allocation of authority balances two types of decision-making in which legal and political considerations—or 'rationalities'—tend to be represented in different degrees. On the one hand, while courts are also always political institutions, they are subject to the strictures of legal logic and conventions when interpreting and applying the law. The Committee of Ministers, on the other hand, while also legally constrained, retains some latitude, if often marginally so, with respect to determining the specific requirements of compliance with an adverse ECtHR judgment, and it has taken advantage of that latitude on a number of occasions. The concrete implications and consequences of an adverse judgment thus emerge as a result of the balancing of legal and political reasoning.

Last but not least, it should be noted that even 'opinion-balancing' may occasionally be ruled out by an organisation's constitutive instrument, as it is in the United Nations where the General Assembly is prohibited from making recommendations 'in respect to any dispute or situation' that is actively being dealt with by the Security Council, unless the Council so requests (Article 12(1) UN Charter).

ii. Inter-organisational Arrangements

Formal inter-organisational checks and balances are extremely rare in global governance.[41] As noted, one major obstacle to their institutionalisation is the

[38] Convention for the Protection of Human Rights and Fundamental Freedoms (as amended by Protocols nos 11 and 14) 4 November 1950, ETS no 005, www.echr.coe.int/Documents/Convention_ENG.pdf.

[39] For exceptions to this rule, see H Keller and C Marti, 'Reconceptualizing Implementation: The Judicialization of the Execution of the European Court of Human Rights' Judgments' (2016) 26 *European Journal of International Law* 829.

[40] ibid, arts 32(1) and 46(2). Compare this allocation of competences, eg, with the human rights system in United States of America, where the Inter-American Court of Human Rights has taken it upon itself to monitor compliance with its judgments; see JM Pasqualucci, *The Practice and Procedure of the Inter-American Court of Human Rights* 2nd edn (Cambridge, Cambridge University Press, 2013) 303–06.

[41] Arrangements providing for consultation and coordination between IOs are, by contrast, quite common; see eg the ILO's and Council of Europe's lists of such agreements at www.ilo.org/global/about-the-ilo/how-the-ilo-works/departments-and-offices/jur/legal-instruments/WCMS_442247/lang--en/index.htm and <www.coe.int/de/web/conventions/bi-or-multilateral-agreements.

varying membership of different IOs, and so for inter-organisational checks and balances to be practically feasible, we should expect either identity of membership in the two IOs or the membership of one IO being a perfect subset of the membership of the other IO, with the latter being authorised to check and balance the former, but not vice versa.

One rare example of an inter-organisational check is provided by Article 16 of the Rome Statute of the International Criminal Court. This provision gives the UN Security Council, which also has the power to refer cases to the Court under Article 13(2) of the ICC Statute, the authority to suspend the initiation or continuation of an investigation or prosecution for renewable periods of up to 12 months through the adoption of a resolution to that effect under Chapter VII of the Charter. The Article recognises that the pursuit of peace and of justice may at times be in conflict, at least in the short run, and that it is the Security Council that according to Article 24 of the UN Charter bears the 'primary responsibility for the maintenance of international peace and security'. The relationship between the UN and the ICC has since been formalised by a treaty between the two organisations.[42] Given the near-comprehensive membership of currently existing states in the United Nations, the problem of the incongruity of memberships as an impediment to establishing formal checks and balances between different organisations is here minimised.[43]

Another example, although no longer available, was the (limited) review competence granted to the International Court of Justice with respect to decisions of the Administrative Tribunal of the International Labour Organization (ILO). Prior to recent amendments, the Tribunal's statute and its annex provided that organs of select international organisations 'challeng[ing] a decision of the Tribunal confirming its jurisdiction, or consider[ing] that a decision of the Tribunal is vitiated by a fundamental fault in the procedure followed' could submit 'the question of the validity of the decision given by the Tribunal … for an advisory opinion, to the International Court of Justice'[44] with the advisory opinion in these cases being accorded 'binding' effect.[45] The ICJ exercised that review competence with respect to a 2008 decision by the ILO Administrative Tribunal concerning an employment dispute where it found in favour of the validity of the

[42] Relationship Agreement between the United Nations and the International Criminal Court, 4 October 2004, 2283 UNTS 195.

[43] Only two participants in the 1998 Drafting Conference were not UN members at the time (counting 188 states in 1998): Switzerland (joined the UN in 2002) and the Holy See (an international legal subject in its own right effectively representing the state of Vatican City and since 1964 a UN permanent observer); see Final Act of the United Nations Diplomatic Conference of Plenipotentiaries on the Establishment of an International Criminal Court, 17 July 1998, UN Doc A/Conf.183/10, Annex II.

[44] Statute of the Administrative Tribunal of the International Labour Organization (amended as of 16 June 1998) 9 October 1946, www.wsi.uni-kiel.de/de/lehre/vorlesungen/archiv/ss-2008/giegerich/vr2/vrii/materialien/PubIntLIIILOAT.pdf, art XII(1) and Annex, art XII(1).

[45] ibid, art XII(2) and Annex, art XII(2).

Tribunal's decision.[46] The provision had been criticised as being unfair because only the respondent organisations were authorised to request a review, not the individual complainant, but instead of seeking to provide for the ability of the complainant to initiate such review, the relevant provisions were deleted from the Tribunal's Statute in June 2016.[47] The Statute of the UN Administrative Tribunal—now defunct and replaced by the two-tier system composed of the UN Dispute Tribunal and UN Appeals Tribunal[48]—had between 1955 and 1995 featured a similar option of review by the ICJ that had been invoked several times[49] and that could also be initiated by individuals.[50] Two more requests for advisory opinions regarding these two administrative tribunals had reached the ICJ in the 1950s.[51] Given that the ICJ's advisory jurisdiction has been noted to 'owe[] its existence precisely to the idea of a horizontal control of the exercise of authority',[52] it has not been used that much for that purpose, either inter- or intra-organisationally. Proposals to rein in the threat of 'fragmentation' posed to international law arising from the proliferation of international courts and tribunals by enabling the latter to request advisory opinions from the ICJ on important legal issues of principle have likewise remained without practical effects.[53]

While the provisions just discussed established rather specific checking devices, the 'supremacy clause' in Article 103 of the UN Charter is a provision that creates a general (at least potential) check, if indirectly so, with respect to acts of other international organisations. Article 103 provides that '[i]n the event of a conflict between the obligations of the members of the United Nations under the present Charter and their obligations under any other international agreement, their

[46] See *Judgment No 2867 of the Administrative Tribunal of the International Labour Organization upon a Complaint Filed Against the International Fund for Agricultural Development*, Advisory Opinion, 1 February 2012 (2012) ICJ Reports 10.

[47] See Amendments to the Statute of the ILO Administrative Tribunal Adopted, 14 June 2016, www.ilo.org/global/about-the-ilo/how-the-ilo-works/departments-and-offices/jur/legal-instruments/WCMS_498369/lang--en/index.htm. The tribunal's amended statute is available at www.ilo.org/tribunal/about-us/WCMS_249194/lang--en/index.htm.

[48] For information on the new system, consult the webpage at www.un.org/en/oaj.

[49] See *Application for Review of Judgment No 333 of the United Nations Administrative Tribunal*, Advisory Opinion, 27 May 1987 (1987) ICJ Reports 18; *Application for Review of Judgment No 273 of the United Nations Administrative Tribunal*, Advisory Opinion, 20 July 1982 (1982) ICJ Reports 325; *Application for Review of Judgment No 158 of the United Nations Administrative Tribunal*, Advisory Opinion, 12 July 1973 (1973) ICJ Reports 166.

[50] See UNGA Res 957 (X) 8 November 1955. In 1995, the review option was deleted due to its alleged lack of utility; see UNGA Res A/RES/50/54, 29 January 1995.

[51] *Effect of Awards of Compensation Made by the United Nations Administrative Tribunal*, Advisory Opinion, 13 July 1954 (1954) ICJ Reports 47 (requested by the General Assembly); *Judgments of the Administrative Tribunal of the ILO upon Complaints Made against UNESCO*, Advisory Opinion, 23 October 1956 (1956) ICJ Reports 77 (requested by UNESCO).

[52] A von Bogdandy and I Venzke, *In Whose Name? A Public Law Theory of International Adjudication* (T Dunlap trans, Oxford, Oxford University Press, 2014) 16.

[53] See the proposals discussed in T Treves, 'Advisory Opinions of the International Court of Justice on Questions Raised by Other International Tribunals' (2000) 4 *Max Planck Yearbook of United Nations Law* 215.

obligations under the present Charter shall prevail'. It is a general check because it relates to *any* other conflicting obligation under another regime, and it is an indirect one because it does not establish direct control over the activities of another organisation, as does Article 16 ICC Statute, but addresses the Member States which are to disregard other obligations in favour of the ones articulated by the UN. Still, when the UN—effectively the Security Council[54]—adopts binding decisions that create obligations which are in conflict with obligations arising under the decision(s) of another IO's organ, it effectively exerts a check on the latter's authority by trumping its effects.

At the regional level, inter-organisational checks and balances are equally rare. Among the most far-reaching, if only prospective at the moment, would be the long-discussed accession of the EU to the ECHR, making it subject to the ECtHR's contentious jurisdiction. The draft accession agreement[55] adopted in mid-2013 inter alia foresaw the EU and Member States acting as co-respondents and being jointly responsible in cases where a violation was due to domestic acts implementing EU law. An unfavourable advisory opinion by the CJEU which found the draft agreement to be incompatible with EU law[56] halted the accession process for the time being. The ECtHR, for its part, has repeatedly dealt with complaints in which the alleged human rights violations were linked to the implementation of IO decisions. In these cases, the Court has formally limited its review to Member State acts implementing the decisions and regulations in question,[57] and, under its *Bosphorus* doctrine, refrains from such review-by-proxy where the IO in question is seen as providing a level of human rights protection that is considered 'equivalent' to that under the ECHR.[58]

The CJEU's much-discussed *Kadi* judgment proceeded along the same lines. As the CJEU took pains to point out, it did not pass formal judgment on the human-rights-compatibility of the Security Council's anti-terrorism resolutions and listing procedures, but reviewed compliance by the EU implementing

[54] See generally R Liivoja, 'The Scope of the Supremacy Clause of the United Nations Charter' (2008) 57 *International & Comparative Law Quarterly* 583, 585–86.

[55] See Draft Revised Agreement on the Accession of the European Union to the Convention for the Protection of Human Rights and Fundamental Freedoms, in Fifth Negotiation Meeting between the CDDH Ad Hoc Negotiation Group and the European Commission on the Accession of the European Union to the European Convention on Human Rights: Final Report to the CDDH, 10 June 2013, COE Doc 47+1(2013)008rev2, appendix 1.

[56] See Opinion 2/13, 18 December 2014, EU:C:2014:2454. For analysis and commentary, see contributions to Special Section—'Opinion 2/13: The EU and the European Convention on Human Rights' (2015) 16 *German Law Journal* 105, www.germanlawjournal.com/volume-16-no-01.

[57] Where no such attribution is possible and the IO itself remains solely responsible for the relevant acts, applications have been declared inadmissible ratione personae; see *Behrami and Behrami v France* and *Saramati v France, Germany and Norway* A nos 71412/01 and 78166/01 (2007) paras 151–52.

[58] See *Bosphorus Hava Yolları Turizm ve Ticaret Anonim Şirketi v Ireland* A no 45036/98 (2005) paras 155-156; see generally C Ryngaert, 'The Responsibility of Member States in Connection with Acts of International Organizations: Assessing the Recent Case Law of the European Court of Human Rights' (2011) 60 *International & Comparative Law Quarterly* 997.

legislation with human rights guarantees, both of which were part of the legal order of the EU.[59] That the criticism of the EU's implementing legislation necessarily traced back to the Security Council's decisions without which there may not have been any such legislation, or legislation different in content, is a point well taken, but only goes to show that checking and balancing across organisational boundaries, where it happens, may occur factually in the absence of formally institutionalised procedures or linkages. While the CJEU has reaffirmed its position that 'European Union measures implementing restrictive measures decided at international level enjoy no immunity from jurisdiction' in subsequent cases,[60] in the absence of formal control rights vis-à-vis the international source, this is more appropriately viewed as an instance of balancing between two otherwise independent sites of authority.

Much more prevalent in regional and global governance than institutionalised 'hard' checks between distinct organisations is balancing across different sites of authority by way of functional separation and specialisation between organisations. The frequently lamented fragmentation of international law and of the global regulatory landscape may indeed be seen as a balancing strategy in its own right to prevent the dominance of, and domination by, a single institution across more than one issue area.[61] Such balancing-through-fragmentation, however, necessarily remains imperfect and lopsided when the different sites of authority are endowed with dissimilar means—resources, legal status, enforcement options etc—to pursue their respective objectives.

B. Vertical Checks and Balances

Vertical checks and balances operate between sites of authority located at different levels of politico-legal organisation. With respect to regional and global governance arrangements, this usually means between IOs and their members. The latter are mostly states, but occasionally IOs themselves may be members of other organisations (the EU, for example, is a member of the WTO). Vertical checks and balances are partly institutionally designed and partly derive from the

[59] See Joined Cases C-402/05 and C-415/05 P *Yassin Abdullah Kadi and Al Barakaat International Foundation v Council of the European Union and Commission of the European Communities* [2008] EU:C:2008:461, paras 284–87 and 326. The General Court had argued that judicial review of UN Security Council resolutions was permissible only where ius cogens was at issue, but otherwise precluded; see Case T-315/01 *Yassin Abdullah Kadi v Council of the European Union and Commission of the European Communities* [2005] EU:T:2005:332.

[60] See Joined Cases C-584/10 P, C-593/10 P and C-595/10 P *Commission of the European Communities, Council of the European Union, United Kingdom v Yassin Abdullah Kadi* [2013] EU:C:2013:518, para 67.

[61] Occasionally organisations with a near-identical remit are created in parallel, such as is the case with the Council of the Baltic Sea States and the Baltic Sea Parliamentary Conference, composed of members of the executive and of parliamentarians, respectively, but without any formal link between them; see their websites at www.cbss.org and www.bspc.net.

principal-agent relationships between IOs and Member States, as conditioned by the nature of the international legal and political system.

i. Veto Power

Key design elements through which Member States exercise control over the decisions of international organisations are the stipulated decision-making rules and majority requirements. The strongest checking power is provided by granting members veto power over the decisions of the organisation. The most prominent example is the veto power given to the five permanent members of the UN Security Council under Charter Article 28(3), but any arrangement that requires unanimity or consensus for the adoption of decisions effectively grants veto power to each Member State. While pooling of authority is not uncommon in global governance, in many organisations, unanimity or consensus remain the principal decision rules with regard to some, if not all, decisions, and the more so the larger the policy scope of the organisation.[62]

An attenuated veto exists where a qualified minority consisting of a specified number of states, or a minority of states but with a majority of weighted votes, can (threaten to) block a decision of an IO and thus force a different decision by way of continuing negotiations or the reconsideration of a failed decision. In the case of the IMF, for example, 10 countries have more than 50 per cent of the voting power and are thus able to block decisions that require a simple majority. In addition, important decisions require a 70 per cent or even 85 per cent supermajority, which allows the top four countries and, in the latter case, the country with the single largest quota share, the United States (voting share of 16.54 per cent), to block these if they disagree with them.[63] A similar situation obtains at the IBRD where 11 countries hold just above 50 per cent of voting power.[64]

ii. (Threatening) Exit

Exiting an IO as a check on international authority appears counterintuitive: after all, exiting severs the ties with the IO, usually with some delay after having given notice, so that the exiting state loses its ability to influence the IO, at least from within. To this extent, then, exiting represents not so much a check on IO authority, but a decision to end acceptance of the IO's authority altogether. At the same time, *threatening* exit may be employed strategically, not as the

[62] See L Hooghe and G Marks, 'Delegation and Pooling in International Organizations' (2015) 10 *Review of International Organizations* 305, 310 and 318.

[63] See MA Weiss, 'International Monetary Fund: Background and Issues for Congress' (2014) CRS Report R420192014, 7–9, www.fas.org/sgp/crs/misc/R42019.pdf. The current allocation of voting shares can be found at www.imf.org/external/np/sec/memdir/members.aspx.

[64] The current allocation of weighted votes in the different World Bank organisations can be found at www.worldbank.org/en/about/leadership/votingpowers.

expression of a genuine wish to fully disengage from an IO, but rather to signal to its decision-making bodies the existence of sufficiently severe disagreement as to certain legal and/or policy developments which the state, or states, in question would prefer to see changed. In such a scenario, as Laurence Helfer has written, invoking Albert O Hirschman's work, 'states pursue exit … as a strategy to increase their voice within an intergovernmental organization or treaty-based negotiating forum'.[65] Helfer provides a number of examples, such as the United States' threats of and/or actual exits from the UN Educational, Scientific and Cultural Organization (UNESCO) and the ILO, that illustrate the use of the exit option to influence an organisation's policy.[66]

For threats of exit to act as a check on law- and policy-making, the institution needs to be sufficiently sensitive to the exercise of the exit option. Because the loss of a Member State also means losing that State's material contributions to the institution's resources and its political support, signalling the willingness to exit will mostly have checking power where the exiting state is sufficiently powerful or otherwise important to the organisation in question. Also, depending on the circumstances, such signals need not be aimed at the organisation's decision-making bodies, but may rather be directed at the other Member States directly, in order to extract concessions in future (re-)negotiations.

iii. Treaty Amendment and Renegotiation

States create international organisations and define their powers in the organisation's constitutive instrument. By the same token, if they are dissatisfied with the way in which authority is being exercised, they may seek to amend the treaty and circumscribe or redefine the relevant decision-making body's competence. Such amendments, however, usually require ratification by all Member States. This is a very high hurdle when compared to the simple majorities—and even the supermajorities in cases of constitutional amendments—that normally suffice domestically to counteract and constrain disagreeable exercises of authority through the adoption of new, modifying legislation. This is especially so given the fact that the disliked decision(s) and its legal implications will in most cases benefit one or more of the other parties to the treaty in question whose support for change would thus either not be forthcoming or would need to be obtained through side-payments of some kind. Moreover, where the decision originates in any of the organisation's representative decision-making bodies, this means that a majority of other states apparently supports that decision, which makes efforts to change it by way of amendment rather futile. Amending a treaty as a way to check a treaty body's authority thus becomes a realistic option mostly when that body is not itself

[65] L Helfer, 'Exiting Treaties' (2005) 91 *Virginia Law Review* 1579, 1583–84 (footnote omitted).
[66] ibid, 1584.

composed of Member States, such as, for example, in the case of courts. Indeed, there have been a number of (partly successful) attempts to rein in, through treaty amendments, judicial authority of several regional courts in Africa.[67]

The utility of pursuing amendments as a checking device is further restricted as a result of the fact that requests for certain changes of the treaty by some states will often trigger wishes for additional changes by other states that may not be desired by the first set of states. As a result, amending a treaty will usually be ill-suited as a targeted response to exercises of authority with which an actor disagrees. Indeed, the difficulty of using amendments to check an institution's law- and policy-making becomes evident when one takes a look at one of the few institutional arrangements where a treaty can be amended by a majority decision binding on the minority: the United Nations. Under the Charter, an amendment requires acceptance by a two-thirds majority in the General Assembly and subsequent ratification by two-thirds of the Member States of the UN, including the P-5 which thus once more possess veto power.[68] Since 1945, however, there have only been three formal Charter amendments.[69]

iv. Non-compliance

Because exiting an IO represents a full-scale repudiation of the organisation's jurisdiction, including the loss of all benefits associated with membership, it will often be a disproportionate and thus undesired response where substantive disagreement only concerns particular aspects of IO decision-making. In such situations, exiting as a check would be tantamount to throwing out the baby with the bathwater. Non-compliance with particular rules and decisions provides a more targeted alternative because it does not affect the entire web of rights and obligations that form part of a particular governance arrangement but only those that raise objections. Another related and common means to exert pressure on an IO in an effort to check its decision-making is withholding a state's contributions to the IO's budget. But non-compliance may of course also generate costs of its own, triggering the state's state responsibility and possibly countermeasures/sanctions under either the treaty or general international law; at a minimum, it may damage a state's reputation for being a reliable partner. Of course, a state may decide that it is willing to bear those costs if non-compliance with the obligation in question is sufficiently valuable to it. Non-compliance might thus be characterised in effect as a kind of 'unlawful veto'.

[67] See only KJ Alter, JT Gathii and LR Helfer, 'Backlash against International Courts in West, East and Southern Africa: Causes and Consequences' (2016) 27 *European Journal of International Law* 293.

[68] UN Charter, art 108.

[69] See G Witschel, 'Article 108' in B Simma, D-E Khan, G Nolte and A Paulus, above n 29, 2217–20.

v. Minimalist Compliance

An alternative to outright non-compliance is for states to exploit the legal and/or policy options available to them with a view to achieving *formal* compliance with a rule or decision, but to do so on *minimalist* terms, that is, to contain a rule's or decision's scope and substantive impact by adopting implementing measures that reflect a restrictive interpretation of the state's obligation. This is not so much a check on the exercise of authority as such, but rather on its consequences. Its availability depends on the nature of the rule/decision in question: where it is so specific as to permit, on any reasonable reading, only one interpretation and outcome, then this will usually preclude pursuit of a strategy of minimalist compliance. By contrast, where the obligation is one of result only, allowing different means to achieve that outcome; where the obligation itself requires further interpretation because it is vaguely defined, or entails (or is based on) at least residually indeterminate legal terms (eg 'proportionality'); or where it is focused on a particular aspect of a broader issue cluster or arrangement, the other parts of which remain dispositive, states often retain some choice as to how to respond specifically to the normative stimulus with which they are presented. Where states disagree with a decision in part or in full, but are not prepared to choose outright non-compliance, they can thus seek to minimise its impact instead. This strategy of what I have elsewhere termed 'rational choice within normative constraints' is in abundant evidence, for example, in the context of compliance with ECtHR judgments[70] and with those of the CJEU.[71]

IV. Explaining the Scarcity of Horizontal Checks and Balances beyond the State

While part and parcel of domestic constitutional designs, international governance arrangements rarely feature horizontal checks and balances as part of their explicit institutional designs. Instead, in most cases, the principal check on IO authority is exercised by the Member States, that is, it is vertical in nature, and horizontal balancing, if at all, occurs as a by-product of the fragmented nature of international regulatory authority. At a basic, abstract level, the situation at both levels is comparable: A collective principal—domestically: the people, internationally: a group of states—delegates and authorises political and/or legal action

[70] See A von Staden, *Strategies of Compliance with the Judgments of the European Court of Human Rights: Rational Choice within Normative Constraints* (Philadelphia, University of Pennsylvania Press, forthcoming).

[71] See L Conant, *Justice Contained: Law and Politics in the European Union* (Ithaca, Cornell University Press, 2002).

by one or more agents acting on the principal's behalf. Why, then, are horizontal checks a common feature in the domestic context, but not internationally?

International organisations are purposefully created entities and so a reasonable assumption is that states design governance arrangements rationally with a view to addressing problems they cannot solve unilaterally, and that they do so in light of their own interests and preferences as well as their perception of the strategic environment within which the arrangement is expected to operate.[72] The absence of horizontal checks must thus be understood as being intentional. From a rational design perspective, three reasons appear to explain this absence: first, there is often simply no need for horizontal checks and balances because the IO in question serves primarily as a forum without any consequential decision-making authority of its own; second, even if decision-making authority is delegated to the IO, there is no incentive on the part of negotiating governments to include horizontal control devices given the existence of Member States' vertical checks; and third, the utility and necessity of horizontal checks varies with the characteristics of the different principals concerned.

A. Lack of Consequential Decision-making Authority

One key reason for the scarcity of horizontal checks and balances on the international plane is the absence of meaningful, independent decision-making power on the part of global governance arrangements that would require, or justify, institutionalised checking and balancing elements beyond the vertical ones that exist by default. As noted in the Federalist Papers, '[t]he provision for defense must in this, as in all other cases, be made commensurate to the danger of attack'.[73] When governance arrangements are set up as pure inter-governmental fora, rather than actors in their own rights, the 'danger of attack' has already been effectively eliminated by design.

The Council of Europe provides a fitting example. Neither its 'executive organ', the Committee of Ministers, nor its deliberative body, the Parliamentary Assembly, can regulate with binding power any aspects of the Council's Member States' activities beyond organisation-internal matters; their output takes the form of resolutions that articulate recommendations only.[74] Other examples of governance arrangements that serve primarily as inter-governmental or inter-parliamentary fora without regulatory powers of their own include the Organization of the Black Sea Economic Cooperation and the Parliamentary Assembly of the Black Sea

[72] cp B Koremenos, C Lipson and D Snidal, 'The Rational Design of International Institutions' in B Koremenos, C Lipson and D Snidal (eds), *The Rational Design of International Institutions* (Cambridge, Cambridge University Press, 2004) 8 (treating institutions as 'rational, negotiated responses to the problems international actors face').

[73] Madison, Hamilton and Jay, above n 5, 319 (no 51).

[74] See Statute of the Council of Europe, 5 May 1949, ETS no 001, arts 15, 16 and 23(1).

Economic Cooperation,[75] the Gulf Cooperation Council,[76] and the Asia-Pacific Economic Cooperation (APEC).[77] Because there is in these cases hardly any meaningful transfer of consequential decision-making authority through pooling or delegation, there is likewise little need to institutionalise horizontal checks and balances.

It is noteworthy in this respect that 'consequentiality' is not necessarily dependent on an organisation's authority to issue legally binding rules and decisions, as 'soft law' and other non-binding pronouncements may also articulate strong normative claims and can have tangible behavioural, legal and policy effects,[78] in part as input to and through reception by legally binding governance mechanisms and procedures.[79] Also, as is well known, international institutions often take on a life of their own and their organs may develop an understanding of their authority that exceeds the one envisioned by their makers at the moment of institutional creation. Foregoing the institutionalisation of effective checks and balances at the design stage of a governance arrangement because of its apparent inconsequentiality due to the non-binding legal status of its output or the absence of formal delegation might thus in hindsight be seen as a negligent omission.

B. Lack of Incentives for Executives to Install Horizontal Checks

But even where consequential decision-making authority is being delegated to an IO, horizontal checks remain rare. This absence can in many instances be explained by the presence of (what are at least perceived to be) sufficiently efficacious vertical checking and balancing devices, in the form of, first and foremost, voting rules that require unanimity or consensus for the adoption of decisions. Giving states under the authority of an IO veto power with regard to that IO's output formally assures that no decision can be imposed against a state's express objection. In those circumstances, adding horizontal checks would not offer additional control beyond that which is already available, at least not for the executive branch of government which usually represents the state in international institutions.

To the contrary, from the vantage point of the executive which generally negotiates the design of governance arrangements, the establishment of horizontal checks might result in a loss of control as a result of the fact that the establishment

[75] See n 3.

[76] See Charter of the Cooperation Council for the Arab States of the Gulf, 25 May 1981, 1288 UNTS 151, arts 7–8 and 11–12.

[77] In contrast to the other examples, APEC is not an organisation as such, although there is a Secretariat and several standing committees, but consists of a series of intergovernmental meetings; see generally the information provided at www.apec.org.

[78] See eg D Shelton (ed), *Commitment and Compliance: The Role of Non-Binding Norms in the International Legal System* (Oxford, Oxford University Press, 2000).

[79] For examples of formally non-binding output by international decision-making bodies being given effect in the institutional context of the EU, see J Mendes, 'EU Law and Global Regulatory Regimes: Hollowing Out Procedural Standards?' (2012) 10 *International Journal of Constitutional Law* 988.

of such a check would make the adoption of decisions conditional on the approval by another organ in which it will not be represented (eg a parliamentary assembly or courts). If the executive represents the state in both organs, on the other hand, then its position on the utility of a horizontal control mechanism can be expected to depend on how it assesses its relative position in these two bodies: if it has a privileged position in one of the decision-making bodies, it should be disinclined to prefer horizontal checks to apply to that body; if it does not hold a privileged position, then being able to exercise such a check over those that do would increase its control over decision-making as a whole and should therefore be preferred. At the same time, those states that have a privileged position due to their military, economic or political strength will likely oppose such a check, certainly in general form, so that it nonetheless only has a small probability of being implemented. The case of the Security Council provides a fitting example: because it consists of only 15 members and can take decisions that overwhelmingly affect states not involved in its decision-making would suggest, from the vantage point of the latter, the utility of added controls because the standard vertical checks do not apply, or only at a cost (in the case eg of non-compliance). For the governments of the permanent members, however, who possess veto power, no obvious benefit is to be had from agreeing to additional checks or controls—such as the recently proposed 'use of force committee' intended to monitor the implementation of authorisations to use force[80]—and the distribution of power among the P-5 and the other UN members has made sure that none have been added so far, or will likely be implemented in the foreseeable future.

Aside from these considerations, adding horizontal checks and balances, especially in the form of veto points but also where they are merely suspensive in character, would in any event prolong decision-making and make it potentially more complicated and cumbersome, with the need to coordinate requiring additional time and resources, possibly in the form of side-payments. Giving just one body within an IO the authority to make decisions in a given issue area, by contrast, makes for simpler procedures and allows states to focus on deliberating and building support for whatever their own preferred policy may be within that body (which, depending on the size of the organisation, may already be difficult enough). Shunning institutionalised horizontal checks may thus be viewed as serving the objective of designing comparatively more efficient decision-making procedures (even if less representative of the full spectrum of opinions and thus normatively less agreeable).

C. Different Characteristics of Principal

A further reason that argues in favour of creating horizontal relationships of checking and balancing in the domestic context, but not necessarily in the

[80] See T Hostovsky-Brandes and A Zemach, 'Controlling the Execution of a Security Council Mandate to Use Force: Does the Council Need a Lawyer?' (2013) 36 *Fordham International Law Journal* 657.

international one, lies in the different character of the principals that delegate authority in these two cases. Domestically, at least in democracies, it is ultimately the people—if often only as a politico-legal fiction—that delegate decision-making on their behalf to the government. The 'people', however, is a compound principal composed of, in most cases, millions of individuals with a myriad of different preferences and divergent opportunities and skills for exercising oversight and control of government activity on a day-to-day basis. As a result of sheer numbers, such a principal faces profound collective action problems that make it ill-suited to exercise direct and continuous control over governmental activity. During periods of normal politics, sufficient mobilisation to engage in oversight and assessment at best occurs rarely—such as during elections and referenda, and even there to widely varying extent—while most people largely tend to their private lives. The separation of powers with attendant checks and balances is thus a functionally rational response to the principal's own limitation with respect to directly checking government that delegates both the exercise of authority and significant parts of its control to bodies specifically designed for those purposes.

The principals of international organisations, on the other hand, while also of a compound nature, comprise actors that, as governmental actors and in contrast to the people, are specialised precisely in engaging in governing, including monitoring and checking other actors. As importantly, each state/government has checking powers in the form of vertical checks, as discussed above, that are comparatively much more powerful vis-à-vis international authority than those exercised by individuals against their domestic government. Again, from the vantage point of the government, its ability to check and balance IO decision-making would not necessarily be further facilitated, helped or otherwise improved by adding horizontal checks to governance arrangements beyond the state. The functional benefits of horizontal checks thus present themselves much more compellingly in the case of the people than with respect to the compound principals of international organisations.

V. Conclusion

The authority of regional and global governance arrangements is relative authority. It is relative because each arrangement has jurisdiction only over a specified issue area, or subset thereof, and only over those states that have voluntarily submitted to it, thus sharing the international regulatory landscape with other arrangements with which there may or may not be jurisdictional or substantive overlap. It is also relative because within the scope of their jurisdiction, the authority of each governance arrangement is subject to certain checks and balances. Vertical checks and balances with regard to their authority always exist as a consequence of the nature of the international legal and political system in which states, as the formal masters of the treaties, can exercise their own authority as principals, through lawful or, if need be, 'unlawful' vetos and some other strategies. Formal horizontal checks and balances, by contrast, are much rarer, for the reasons stated, and appear mostly as intra-organisational, rather than inter-organisational, control devices.

As suggested, the lack of horizontal checks in particular is partly a result of the traditional domestic separation of powers which entrusts the conduct of a state's external relations, including the negotiation of governance arrangements and the state's representation within them, primarily to the executive branch which, *ceteris paribus*, will usually have few incentives to demand and install additional horizontal checks, even less veto points, by organs not under its control. While this may serve the objective of efficient decision-making, its normative implications are not as satisfactory because it tends to preclude a fuller representation of the range of preferences and views on an issue that could be achieved by empowering parliamentary assemblies or international courts to check or balance decision-making of executive-dominated fora. Change in this respect will likely only occur when domestic constituencies begin to demand appropriate institutional changes in sufficient numbers and exercise political pressure on their governments that can no longer be ignored without incurring electoral costs. In the absence of such demands and pressure, horizontal checks and balances will continue to remain an occasional, rather than a general, phenomenon.

In closing, two comments relating to the scope conditions of this chapter are in order. First, I have focused in these remarks on the relative authority of state-created entities and sites of decision-making and on the role of checks and balances between them inter se and in relation to their principals, but of course governance beyond the state has long ceased to be an exclusive domain of states and of public, intergovernmental organisations. Adding to the relative nature of their authority as a result of dispersed decision-making sites and their vertical and horizontal interactions is the fact that there is today in global politics a plethora of non-state actors that also claim, and often possess and exercise, authority in their field of activity. This proliferation and diversification of decision-making sites further adds to the phenomenon of relative authority. Second, I have foregrounded formal, institutionalised types of checks and balances. It goes without saying, however, that there are manifold non-institutionalised ways through which stakeholders may seek to affect and constrain, and thereby to informally check or balance, decision-making in regional and global governance arrangements, such as through social mobilisation, strategic use of publicity and the media, and the threat or actual imposition of various types of audience costs. For reasons of space, these aspects have not been addressed here, but they would need to be included in order to obtain a more comprehensive picture of both relative authority in governance beyond the state and of the checks and balances that apply to specific institutional arrangements.

Part II

Iterations in Practice

7

The Role of the Court of Justice in Shaping the Institutional Balance in the EU

BRUNO DE WITTE

I. Introduction

The European Union is rather unique among international organisations in possessing a judicial institution, the Court of Justice of the European Union,[1] equipped with the necessary powers to keep the other institutions 'in their place'; that is, the Court can ensure that the allocation of powers among the various institutions and organs of the Union, as made by the Member States from time to time when they adjust the text of the European treaties, is respected in practice. This situation contrasts with the often lamented situation in the UN legal order, in which *ultra vires* actions by the Security Council cannot adequately be sanctioned by the International Court of Justice (ICJ)—not to mention many other international organisations where there is no judicial control whatsoever on the activity of their political organs.

The Court has strengthened the power granted to it by the Member States by insisting on the fact that the EU institutional order is entirely 'judicialised'. In the *Les Verts* judgment of 1986, it held that all acts of the Community institutions were, in principle, amenable to judicial review, and that the EEC Treaty had 'established a complete system of legal remedies and procedures designed to permit the Court of Justice to review the legality of measures adopted by the institutions', even though the Treaty text seemed to contain some lacunas in this respect.[2]

[1] Hereafter abbreviated either as 'the Court' or as 'the CJEU'. Note that the CJEU, as an institution, comprises two organs with different powers and roles, namely the Court of Justice and the General Court. Unless specified otherwise, all the judgments discussed in this chapter were given by the Court of Justice, ie the 'top court'.

[2] CJEU, Case 294/83 *Parti Ecologiste 'Les Verts' v European Parliament* EU:C:1986:166, point 23. The textual lacuna which was at stake in this case was the absence of judicial remedies against acts of the European Parliament. The Court filled that lacuna by reading into Art 173 EEC (the current Art 263 TFEU) an implied right to bring actions for annulment against binding acts of the EP.

The Court itself frequently highlights the emblematic nature of that judgment by repeating its key sentences again and again in later cases.[3] The main importance of this doctrine lies in the protection it offers to individuals and firms against unlawful acts of the EU institutions; but the same principle of full judicial review also constitutes a guarantee for each EU institution that the other institutions will not be able to disrupt the existing balance of powers between them. Indeed, the Court has had many occasions to decide disputes involving the respective roles and powers of the EU institutions. The overall approach taken by the Court in such disputes is that it seeks to preserve what it calls the *institutional balance* laid down in the text of the Treaties.

The CJEU mostly uses the term institutional balance as shorthand for the set of Treaty rules which happen to apply to the particular institutional dispute in front of it. Thus, the notion of the institutional balance does not, despite its frequent use, add much to the rule (which is now inscribed in Article 13(2) Treaty on European Union (TEU)) that 'each institution shall act within the limits of the powers conferred on it in the Treaties, and in conformity with the procedures, conditions and objectives set out in them.' Indeed, both norms (the written Treaty norm of limited powers, and the unwritten Court-coined norm of institutional balance) are often used in one breath and seemingly interchangeably in the Court's case law.[4] In view of this, one may question the added *legal* value of the notion of the institutional balance. Its main function may be a *symbolic* one: the use of this synthetic expression allows the Court to present the complex division of powers between the EU institutions, which varies wildly from one policy domain to another, as somehow corresponding to a rational design rendered by the words 'institutional balance'. This view of the institutional balance, as a court-made device to give a veneer of rationality to the often chaotic allocation of powers to institutions and organs laid down by the Treaty text, implies that the CJEU has by and large adopted a deferential attitude. It corresponds to the views proposed by Alan Dashwood when, in a piece dealing with the evolution of the institutional balance during the first 50 years of European integration, he hardly mentioned any Court cases—the paper was entirely devoted to treaty changes and institutional practice, with the Court being positioned as a passive bystander.[5]

[3] Writing in 2010, Alemanno found 50 judgments in which the *Les Verts* formula had been cited by the Court; A Alemanno, 'What Has Been, and What Could Be, Thirty Years after *Les Verts/European Parliament*', in M Poiares Maduro and L Azoulai (eds), *The Past and Future of EU Law—The Classics of EU Law Revisited on the 50th Anniversary of the Rome Treaty* (Oxford, Hart, 2010) 324, 326, fn 217.

[4] See for example in Case C-133/06 *European Parliament v Council* [2008] EU:C:2008:257, paras 44 and 57; and in Case C-660/13 *Council v Commission* [2016] EU:C:2016:616, para 46.

[5] A Dashwood, 'The Institutional Framework and the Institutional Balance' in M Dougan and S Currie (eds), *50 Years of the European Treaties* (Oxford, Hart Publishing, 2009) 1. Other discussions of the notion of institutional balance pay more attention to the case law of the Court of Justice, but their conclusions generally concur on the modest practical role played by the notion of institutional balance in that case law. See recently, with references to earlier writings by other authors: M Chamon, 'The Institutional Balance, an Ill-fated Principle of EU Law?' (2015) 21 *European Public Law* 370.

And yet, despite the respect thus demonstrated by the Court to the institutional choices made by the drafters of the EU Treaties, the Court of Justice has been able, arguably, to shape the institutional system of the European Union in a number of ways that have complemented or twisted the wording of the Treaties. In the following sections, I will discuss four different ways in which the Court has put its stamp on the EU's institutional landscape: it has justified and entrenched institutional variation across policy fields (section II); it has drawn a borderline between legislative and administrative action (section III); it has umpired disputes between the EU institutions on the interpretation of their respective powers (section IV); and it has legitimised 'creative' institutional practice when seen as functional to the European integration process (section V). I will not discuss the question whether the Court of Justice may have modified the institutional balance in a very different way, namely by extending its own role to the detriment of the EU legislative institutions. In this respect, the judicial activism critique often made of the CJEU may be more persuasive.[6]

When discussing this judicial role in shaping the institutional landscape of the European Union, one should be aware of a number of inherent limits to the Court's role. A first limit is the fact that the institutional balance has repeatedly been redesigned, in rather great detail, by the Member States in repeated instances of treaty revision, thereby also reducing the scope and need for judicial interpretation in between those treaty changes. A second limit is the habit of the EU's political institutions to agree on new institutional practices, sometimes formalised into inter-institutional agreements, without seeking the Court's approval. A third limit, which will become most visible in section V, is that the Member States have conserved the option, subject to certain conditions, to engage in cooperation outside the EU legal order, and thereby to 'escape' altogether from the legal constraints of the EU's institutional balance.

II. Justification of Institutional Variation: The Treaties and Nothing But the Treaties

In several cases, the CJEU firmly rejected arguments that the Treaty rules on the division of powers between the institutions should, if necessary, be disregarded

Among those earlier writings, some of the most influential (in English) are: S Prechal, 'Institutional Balance: A Fragile Principle with Uncertain Contents' in T Heukels, N Blokker and M Brus (eds), *The European Union after Amsterdam* (The Hague, Kluwer Law International, 1998) 273; and J-P Jacqué, 'The Principle of Institutional Balance' (2004) 41 *Common Market Law Review* 383.

[6] For a recent case study on this question, see V Velyvyte, 'The Power to Shape the Internal Market: Implications of CJEU Case Law for the EU's Institutional Balance' (2016) 12 *Croatian Yearbook of European Law & Policy* 25. For a general discussion, see M Höreth, 'The Least Dangerous Branch of European Governance? The European Court of Justice under the Checks and Balances Doctrine' in

in view of an unwritten higher principle of institutional balance. The manner in which the Treaty text allocates powers to the various institutions may sometimes seem strange or inconsistent, but the Court is not prepared to correct the choices made by the authors of the Treaties. This attitude was exemplified by a judgment from 1982 dealing with the Commission's power to adopt directives on the transparency of financial relations between the Member States and their public undertakings. In the course of the proceedings, the applicant governments had sought the annulment of the Commission's directive, arguing that the reference in Article 90 EEC (the predecessor of today's Article 106 Treaty on the Functioning of the European Union (TFEU)) to the adoption of directives by the Commission could not be interpreted as granting the Commission an autonomous legislative power, given the overall role of the Commission in the Community's institutional system, which was of an executive rather than a legislative nature. In response to that argument, the Court stated that

> the limits of the powers conferred on the Commission by a specific provision of the Treaty are to be inferred not from a general principle, but from an interpretation of the provision in question, in this case Article 90, analysed in the light of its purpose and its place in the scheme of the Treaty.[7]

As the Court observed in another of those inter-institutional disputes, 'the powers of the institutions … are not always based on consistent criteria',[8] and it refused to establish institutional consistency across policy sectors when the drafters of the Treaties had chosen not to be consistent.

Thereby, the Court accepted and approved the phenomenon of institutional variation across policy fields, which marked the European Community at that time and still marks the European Union today. Institutional variation means that the allocation of powers between the European institutions is not determined in sweeping terms (as is typically the case in national constitutions) but is determined in a piecemeal fashion and varies from one policy sector to the next. Within the EEC, different legal instruments and different decision-making rules were used in the main policy fields as they then were—agriculture, competition and harmonisation within the operation of the common market. The main embodiment of institutional variation was the central role played, in Community law, by the *legal basis* requirement. Whereas federal Constitutions usually list the broad policy domains attributed to either the federal or Member State level, the Community Treaties operated a much more detailed division of competences between the Communities and their Member States, by specifying at great length *what* the

M Dawson, B De Witte and E Muir (eds), *Judicial Activism at the European Court of Justice: Causes, Responses and Solutions* (Cheltenham, Edward Elgar, 2013) 32, and other contributions in the same volume.

[7] Joined Cases 188 to 190/80 *France, Italy and UK v Commission* [1982] EU:C:1982:257, para 6. See also Case C-58/94 *Netherlands v Council* [1996] EU:C:1996:171, paras 32 and 41.

[8] Case 242/87 *Commission v Council* [1989] EU:C:1989:217, para 13.

EC could do, and *how*. Each legal basis provision specified not only the domain within which the Community could act and/or the objectives it should set itself, but also the legal instruments that could be used for that purpose, the institution that could adopt those instruments, and the decision-making rules that should be followed. So, for example, the chapter on competition law specified from the start that both the Council and the Commission had a law-making role (although a different one), and that the legal instruments to be used in this area were to be, essentially, the regulation and the decision; whereas harmonisation of national laws, when needed for a better functioning of the common market, would have to be done by means of directives adopted by the Council or conventions concluded between the Member States.

Institutional variation has remained a defining feature of the EU until today. It received an important boost by the Maastricht Treaty. That Treaty added a large number of new policy domains to those which the European Communities had previously had, but also—and at the same time—strongly increased the existing institutional fragmentation. It organised three important new policy domains which were subject to wholly idiosyncratic institutional rules that had little or nothing to do with Community law as we knew it. One such domain, namely the Economic and Monetary Union, was encapsulated within the EC Treaty as an—institutionally speaking—alien object; whereas the other two domains, Common Foreign and Security Policy (CFSP) and Justice and Home Affairs, were conceived so differently from the rest—again, institutionally speaking—that the Member States decided to enact a wholly new Treaty and establish a new organisation (the European Union) to accommodate them, so as to emphasise that 'normal' Community law mechanisms should not apply to them. Those institutional 'bits and pieces' created by the Maastricht Treaty[9] have now been reformed into a relatively more coherent whole. In particular, the Lisbon Treaty led to the absorption of the former intergovernmental pillars into the common regime of competences, legal instruments, decision-making, judicial review and legal effect, but CFSP remains a very distinct institutional field which is, as Article 24(1) TEU quaintly states, 'subject to specific rules and procedures'.

In this new post-Lisbon context, the Court reaffirmed its 1982 judgment and reiterated that the Treaties continue to make different policy areas subject to different decision-making arrangements and that the Court would not attempt to second-guess the choices made by the Member States when enacting the latest version of the Treaties. The occasion for this confirmation was provided by one of the very first inter-institutional disputes arising after the entry into force of the Lisbon Treaty. The Council had adopted, in December 2009, a new version of the regulation setting out the mechanism for imposing sanctions against

[9] The reference here is to the well-known article of Deirdre Curtin describing the institutional reforms enacted by the Maastricht Treaty: D Curtin, 'The Constitutional Structure of the Union: A Europe of Bits and Pieces' (1993) 30 *Common Market Law Review* 17.

persons associated with terrorist organisations.[10] The Council had adopted this as a CFSP-related measure, based on Article 215(2) TFEU. The European Parliament, not having been involved in the process of adopting the regulation, challenged its validity by arguing that the proper legal basis for such a measure would have been Article 75 TFEU, within the Treaty chapter on justice and home affairs. If that legal basis would have been chosen, the European Parliament (EP) would have acted as a co-legislator together with the Council. The Court observed that

> the difference between Article 75 TFEU and Article 215 TFEU, so far as the Parliament's involvement is concerned, is the result of the choice made by the framers of the Treaty of Lisbon conferring a more limited role on the Parliament with regard to the Union's action under the CFSP.[11]

The EP had added an extra twist to its argument by stating that it 'would be contrary to European Union law for it to be possible to adopt measures having a direct impact on the fundamental rights of individuals and groups ... by means of a procedure which excludes the participation of the European Parliament',[12] to which the Court simply responded that 'the duty to respect fundamental rights is imposed ... on all the institutions and bodies of the Union'.[13] Thereby, the Court refused to construct an EU version of what is known in many constitutional systems as the principle of legality, whereby restrictions to fundamental rights may only be imposed by, or on the basis of, an act of Parliament.

More generally, the Court has resisted the calls from the European Parliament to strengthen its institutional position in the name of a particular conception of democratic rule. The then Vice-President of the Court Koen Lenaerts wrote that the judicial protection of the EP's prerogatives 'is of paramount importance for the purposes of complying not only with the principle of institutional balance but also with the principle of democracy',[14] but, in fact, there is not a single case in which the Court allowed the principle of democracy to trump the principle of institutional balance (ie the allocation of powers made by the drafters of the Treaties).

There is only one case in the Court's history in which it decided to 'supplement' the text of the Treaties by using the unwritten norm of institutional balance. This is the judgment of 1990 in the *Chernobyl* case, relating to the standing of the European Parliament to bring actions for annulment. The text of the then

[10] Council Reg 1286/2009 of 22 December 2009, [2009] OJ L346/42. The Regulation replaced an earlier regulation on the same subject which the Court of Justice had annulled in the famous *Kadi* judgment of 2008 for giving insufficient protection to the rights of defence of the listed persons.

[11] Case C-130/10 *European Parliament v Council* [2012] EU:C:2012:472, para 82.

[12] ibid, para 34.

[13] ibid, para 83.

[14] K Lenaerts, 'The Principle of Democracy in the Case Law of the European Court of Justice' (2013) 62 *International and Comparative Law Quarterly* 271, 282.

Article 173 EEC Treaty (the predecessor of Article 263 TFEU) did not provide for such a right, but the Court decided to read it in Article 173 in order to protect the institutional balance. The Court stated that

> the absence in the Treaties of any provisions giving the Parliament the right to bring an action for annulment may constitute a procedural gap, but it cannot prevail over the fundamental interest in the maintenance and observance of the institutional balance laid down in the Treaties establishing the European Communities.[15]

Although the Court refrained from calling the institutional balance a 'principle', this was a case where the use of that term would have been entirely appropriate, as the concept of institutional balance was used as the source of a specific legal norm which could not be found in the text of the EEC Treaty or in any other written legal document. The solution adopted by the Court, to grant the EP a 'check' in order to protect its place in the 'balance of powers', would seem fair, and in fact the governments of the Member States accepted this Treaty correction by codifying the new Court-given rule at the next round of Treaty revision, in Maastricht. After this one instance, the Court has never again overruled the text of the Treaties in the name of an overriding principle of institutional balance.

III. Drawing the Borderline between Legislative and Administrative Action

The most important contribution of the CJEU to shaping the EU's brand of separation of powers is, arguably, its long-standing but intermittent effort to delimit the legislative from the administrative domain in EU law. In the absence of any such delimitation in the original EEC Treaty, the Court stepped in early on, in 1970, and decided in its *Köster* judgment that the Community's law-making institutions (primarily, at that time, the Council) could delegate the non-essential aspects of the subject matter covered by their laws to other organs, and that the Council could devise a whole machinery for that purpose, namely the so-called comitology system.[16] The Court thereby approved an institutional practice (comitology), which had been developed in a piecemeal fashion during the 1960s. The distinction coined in *Köster* between essential and non-essential elements of a legal matter served, in that case, to *positively* justify the existence of EU administrative measures, but that same distinction has also acted, since then, as a *negative* limit

[15] Case C-70/88 *Parliament v Council* [1990] EU:C:1990:217, para 26.

[16] Case 25/70 *Einfuhr- und Vorratsstelle für Getreide und Futtermittel v Köster and Berodt* [1970] EU:C:1970:115.

to the kinds of measures that the EU administration can adopt. Given its vague nature, the criterion of the essential elements can give rise to disputes between the institutions on whether a rule is part of the essential elements, and must therefore be contained in the legislative act, or whether it is not essential and can therefore be left to the competent administrative organ, which might be the Commission or the Council, as the case may be. One such dispute was submitted to the CJEU in the *Border surveillance* case, decided in 2012. The Court sided with the European Parliament in deciding that implementing measures adopted by the Council had unduly regulated 'essential elements' of the EU's external borders policy. Yet, the Court was not really able in that case to give more general guidance on the application of the essential elements doctrine, which will therefore remain controversial also in the future.[17]

The relatively simple dual regime of legislative and administrative acts has now been complicated by the Treaty of Lisbon's creation of *delegated acts*, which occupy an intermediate position between *legislative acts* and *implementing acts*, thus giving rise to two different types of borderline disputes (between first level and second level acts; and between second and third level acts), in each of which the institutions have conflicting interests. The Court has been called to resolve the first disputes on the borderline between delegated and implementing act.[18] It took the view that the EU legislator (normally now the Council and the European Parliament acting together) has a large amount of discretion in deciding whether the legislative act requires to be supplemented or spelled out by means of delegated or implementing acts, or whether indeed its implementation can be entirely left to the Member States. One might argue that, by leaving so much discretion to the legislator in this matter, the Court may have tilted the institutional balance against the European Commission, whose preferences on whether to provide for delegated or implementation acts may rather easily be overruled by the Council and Parliament.[19] Yet, by effectively leaving the choice of the mode of implementation to the legislator, the Court may have wanted to curb the emergence of a new stream of litigation, as the choice of whether to insert a provision for delegation or implementation arises very often when EU legislative acts are being negotiated between the institutions.

[17] Case C-355/10 *European Parliament v Council* [2012] EU:C:2012:516. See the comment by M Chamon, 'How the Concept of Essential Elements of a Legislative Act Continues to Elude the Court. *Parliament v Council*' (2013) 50 *Common Market Law Review* 849.

[18] Case C-427/12 *European Commission v European Parliament and Council of the European Union* [2014] EU:C:2014:170 ('Biocides'); and Case C-88/14 *European Commission v European Parliament and Council of the European Union* [2015] EU:C:2015:499 ('Visa reciprocity').

[19] A point made by M Chamon, 'Institutional Balance and Community Method in the Implementation of EU Legislation Following the Lisbon Treaty' (2016) 53 *Common Market Law Review* 1501, 1542.

IV. Umpiring Disputes between the Political Institutions

To the extent that the text of the Treaties does not—and cannot—regulate in an exhaustive manner all the aspects of the institutional operation of the European Union, there are many occasions when the institutions discover to have divergent views on their proper role in the system, based on conflicting interpretations of what the Treaty text says or (more often) of what the Treaty text omits to say. In many such instances of 'gaps' in primary EU law, the institutions reach a common understanding so that the need to 'bother' the CJEU does not arise. Sometimes, though, the institutions decide to take their dispute to the Court. The Commission and especially the European Parliament have done so regularly,[20] and the Council has also started more recently and more reluctantly to resort to inter-institutional litigation. In doing so, all three institutions accept to consider the Court as an umpire who does not hold preconceived views in favour of strengthening one or other of the institutions. The institutions decide to bring cases before the Court when they hope that the outcome may support their own political preference in the case at hand or, maybe more often, when they hope that the outcome may give support to a broader institutional claim whose importance reaches beyond the individual case.

Apart from the disputes about the borderline between legislative and administrative acts, discussed above, there are several other examples of such inter-institutional battles brought before the CJEU. By umpiring those disputes, the Court necessarily favours the interpretation offered by one institution over that defended by another. A well-known historical example, from the pre-Maastricht era, is the Court's insistence that the European Parliament's right to be consulted about Community legislation had to be taken seriously by the Council, meaning that the Council could not proceed to the adoption of an act without having given the occasion to the EP to discuss its merits.[21] More recently, the Court ruled that the Council's long-standing practice of delegating legislative powers to itself, by means of the creation of a so-called 'secondary legal basis', was simply unlawful;[22] and, more trivially, it decided that the formal adoption of the EU budget should

[20] In particular the European Parliament has been shown to pursue true litigation strategies, harnessing Court cases to achieve some of its institutional goals; see M McCown, 'The European Parliament before the Bench: ECJ Precedent and EP Litigation Strategies' (2003) 10 *Journal of European Public Policy* 974.

[21] See discussion of those cases by K Bradley, 'Maintaining the Balance: The Role of the Court of Justice in Defining the Institutional Position of the European Parliament' (1987) 24 *Common Market Law Review* 41, 49 ff.

[22] Case C-133/06 *European Parliament v Council* [2008] EU:C:2008:257.

take the form of a unilateral declaration of the president of the EP rather than of a joint Council-EP act.[23] A recent example of a long-standing institutional dispute which was finally submitted for its resolution to the Court of Justice is whether the Commission's power to withdraw a draft legislative act (which is recognised in principle by the Treaty text) can still be exercised when the draft has reached the active co-decision stage between Council and Parliament.[24] The three institutions had held different views on this question ever since the co-decision procedure was created by the Maastricht Treaty, but it took some twenty years until the Council brought a case in which it asked the Court to decide this as a matter of principle. Although the Court came down in favour of the Commission, upholding its right to withdraw a piece of legislation as long as the Council and Parliament have not formally acted within the ordinary legislative procedure, it did so whilst emphasising that the Commission, when doing so, had to respect the principle of sincere cooperation towards the other institutions. Whereas the Court sought, in its usual fashion, to offer an interpretation that would not contradict the wording of the various relevant Treaty provisions, it was criticised by some commentators for failing to give precedence to the constitutional value of representative democracy because of its support for the position of the unelected EU institution.[25]

The most prominent, and ongoing, example, is the litigation on the *choice of the legal basis*, where the Court exercises rigorous scrutiny whenever the choice of one legal basis for the adoption of an EU act rather than another affects the respective roles of the institutions in the decision-making procedure. This is most clearly the case when one legal basis prescribes the use of the ordinary legislative procedure, giving full co-legislative powers to the European Parliament, and the alternative legal basis allows the Council to decide on its own or after merely consulting the EP. A typical example of this constellation was the seemingly technical dispute between the Council, on the one hand, and the Commission and Parliament, on the other, as to whether Article 43 (2) TFEU or Article 43 (3) TFEU should have been used as the legal basis for the adoption of a long-term plan for cod stocks.[26] Depending on that choice, the act should have been adopted under the ordinary legislative procedure or under a special procedure in which the Council decides on its own without the participation of the EP. This particular case was decided in favour of the European Parliament and the Commission. Yet, it would not be correct to depict the Court as a 'friend' of either Commission or Parliament as against the Council. The Court chooses the legal basis which is 'objectively' most appropriate, in view of the content and purpose of the measure, and its verdict

[23] Case C-77/11 *Council v European Parliament* [2013] EU:C:2013:559.

[24] Case C-409/13 *Council v Commission* [2015] EU:C:2015:217.

[25] D Ritleng, 'Does the European Court of Justice Take Democracy Seriously? Some Thoughts after the *Macro-Financial Assistance* Case' (2016) 53 *Common Market Law Review* 11.

[26] Joined cases C-124 and 125/13 *European Parliament and Commission v Council* [2015] EU:C:2015:790.

may satisfy now one institution, and then another,[27] and there is no evidence that the Court pursues a normative agenda inspired by a particular conception of the separation of powers.

V. Legitimising 'Creative' Institutional Practice

The picture that emerges from the preceding discussion is that the CJEU seeks to ensure the smooth functioning of the EU's institutional system, by enforcing the Treaty provisions with the interpretative aid of unwritten principles but without unduly constraining the room for manoeuvre of the institutions. Its acceptance of institutional 'creativity' is particularly visible in cases where all three institutions agree to engage in a new institutional practice that is then challenged before the Court by a Member State or by a private party, through an action for annulment or a preliminary reference on the validity of the act. Two examples from the case law illustrate the Court's flexible attitude in such situations.

In the *ESMA* judgment of January 2014, it accepted—against the view defended by the UK government—that the EU legislative organs could lawfully create forms of EU-level implementation beyond the regime of delegated and implementing acts mentioned in Articles 290 and 291 TFEU.[28] In the case at hand, the European Securities and Markets Authority, an EU agency, had been granted the power to adopt binding emergency measures under an EU regulation in the financial services sector. The text of the TFEU nowhere mentions the possibility to attribute administrative decision-making powers to EU agencies, but the CJEU considered this to be an oversight of the Treaty authors; since the Treaty authors had, elsewhere in the TFEU, stated that acts of agencies can form the object of an action for annulment, this presupposes that agencies (at least some of them) can adopt binding decisions. By allowing this practice, the Court may be said to have tinkered with the central administrative role of the Commission recognised by Articles 290 and 291 TFEU, leading to what has been termed 'a significant adaptation of the principle of the institutional balance to the new realities of European governance'.[29] This may appear as an exception to the argument, made in section II, that the Court scrupulously sticks to the allocation of powers resulting from

[27] See, for example, the defeat of the EP in the anti-terrorism legal basis dispute, Case C-130/10, discussed above.

[28] Case C-270/12 *United Kingdom v European Parliament and Council* [2014] EU:C:2014:18. See the case comment by C F Bergström, 'Shaping the New System for Delegation of Powers to EU Agencies: *United Kingdom v European Parliament and Council (Short selling)*' (2015) 52 *Common Market Law Review* 219.

[29] M Everson and E Vos, 'European Agencies: What About the Institutional Balance?' in A Lazowski and S Blockmans (eds), *Research Handbook on EU Institutional Law* (Cheltenham, Edward Elgar, 2016) 139, 148.

the Treaty text, even though the allocation may be dysfunctional or outdated. In fact, the context of the disputes may explain this discrepancy. Whereas in the cases discussed in section II, different EU institutions held opposed views, so that the Court sought to enforce a strict reading of the Treaty text without privileging one institution over the other, the *ESMA* case was one in which all EU institutions (including the Commission) positively supported the granting of decision-making rules to the agency, and the opposition came from one single Member State. In these circumstances, the Court may have felt less constrained to stick to a narrow reading of the Treaty text. Interestingly, the Court did not mention the words 'institutional balance' in this ruling.

A second example of the Court giving its blessing to unorthodox institutional practices is the *Pringle* case, decided in November 2012. In that well-known judgment, the CJEU accepted that the EU institutions can be 'borrowed' by the Member States when the latter conclude a separate international agreement on matters related to the functioning of the EU.[30] In this particular case, the Treaty establishing a European Stability Mechanism (ESM) provided that the Commission and the European Central Bank (ECB) were to play a role in the preparation, implementation and review of financial rescue decisions adopted by the ESM. Mr Pringle had invoked Article 13(2) TEU as an argument to challenge this arrangement. According to that Treaty provision, the EU institutions shall act within the limits of the powers given to them under 'the Treaties' (meaning: the TEU and the TFEU, and—arguably at least—no other treaties). On a literal interpretation, this could mean that it is not possible to give any additional functions to the Commission or the ECB (or indeed the Parliament and the Council) under separate international agreements such as the ESM treaty. Yet, the Court of Justice had accepted, in a couple of low profile judgments of the 1990s dealing with development aid, that the Commission could perform tasks entrusted to it by all the Member States under a separate international agreement. The EC Treaty, it held in the *Bangladesh* case, 'does not prevent the Member States from entrusting the Commission with the task of coordinating a collective action undertaken by them on the basis of an act of their representatives meeting in the Council.'[31] And it repeated shortly afterwards, in the *Lomé* case, that 'no provision of the Treaty prevents the Member State from using, outside its framework, procedural steps drawing on the rules applicable to Community expenditure and from associating the Community institutions with the procedure thus set up'.[32] The importance

[30] Case C-370/12 *Thomas Pringle v Government of Ireland et* al [2012] EU:C:2012:756, paras 153 to 177. See the detailed and contrasting examinations of this aspect of the judgment by S Peers, 'Towards a New Form of EU Law? The Use of EU Institutions outside the EU Legal Framework' (2013) 9 *European Constitutional Law Review* 37, and by P Craig, 'Pringle and Use of EU Institutions outside the EU Legal Framework: Foundations, Procedure and Substance' (2013) 9 *European Constitutional Law Review* 263.

[31] Joined Cases C-181/91 and C-248/91 *European Parliament v Council and European Parliament v Commission* [1993] EU:C:1993:271, para 20.

[32] Case C-316/91 *European Parliament v Council* [1994] EU:C:1994:76, para 41.

of the tasks entrusted to the Commission and the ECB in the ESM treaty, compared to the rather anodyne administrative tasks of the Commission which had been challenged in the *Bangladesh* and *Lomé* cases, prompted the Court to add an extra condition for any institutional borrowing; the extra tasks should not 'alter the essential character of the powers conferred on those institutions by the EU and FEU Treaties'.[33] This formula stems from some Opinions given by the Court in the context of the conclusion of international agreements by the EU, in which it had emphasised, by the use of that formula, that such agreements should not alter the institutional identity of the Union.[34] The formula is here transposed from the context of the EU's external relations to the context of *inter se* agreements between the Member States. In applying the test, the Court finds—without surprise—that the ESM tasks entrusted to the Commission and the ECB do not affect the essential character of those institutions' powers.

One way to understand and justify the Court's rather liberal attitude towards the ancillary use of EU institutions in an intergovernmental framework, despite the strict language used by Article 13 TEU, is to distinguish between 'powers' and 'tasks'. What Article 13 TEU arguably seeks to convey is that the nature of the powers of the institutions is fixed by the Treaties; it does not exclude that extra tasks may be given to the institutions as long as those tasks fit within their existing powers, and as long as all EU Member States agree to 'lend' the EU institutions. In the case at hand, the Court considered that the role awarded to the Commission and the ECB by Article 13 ESM treaty, namely to negotiate and monitor the Memorandum of Understanding with countries benefitting from financial support by the ESM, was modelled on the existing mode of operation under the EFSM Regulation, where the Commission and the ECB are called to coordinate the rescue operations, forming together with the IMF the so-called troika.

Crucially, the Court noted that the 'duties conferred on the Commission and ECB within the ESM Treaty, important as they are, do not entail any power to make decisions of their own. Further, the activities pursued by those two institutions within the ESM Treaty solely commit the ESM'.[35] Thus, the integrity of the EU legal and institutional order is preserved by the absence of decision-making powers under the ESM treaty; there is no danger that the Commission and ECB will resort to law-making outside the constitutional constraints imposed by EU law (such as transparency, democratic accountability and respect for fundamental rights).

More generally, the re-acquired habit of the EU Member States to negotiate international agreements outside the EU legal order has been viewed by many commentators as creating parallel institutional regimes, thereby undermining

[33] *Pringle* judgment, above n 30, para 158.

[34] Opinions 1/92, 1/00 and 1/09, referred to by the Court in the same para 158 of the *Pringle* judgment.

[35] *Pringle* judgment, above n 30, para 161.

and modifying the institutional balance of the EU. But this view was not shared by the CJEU. To the extent that the EU Member States have retained the right to conclude such satellite agreements (which depends on whether the policy domain has been 'occupied' by the EU or not), they operate outside the EU legal system and are therefore not bound to respect the institutional balance established by the TEU and TFEU. And yet, whenever the Member States make use of the EU institutions within such a satellite organisation (as they did in the ESM Treaty), they actually strengthen the powers of those EU institutions that are being 'borrowed', to the detriment of the ones (the EP, in this case) that are not borrowed. Also, one should note that the formal decision-making power relating to stability support schemes is held by the ESM's Board of Governors. The members of this Board are the very same persons who compose the Ecofin formation of the Council, but when acting within the ESM framework they are not subject to the normal constraints of EU law, such as the Commission's power of initiative, parliamentary control and judicial review. One might argue that the Member State representatives, by the simple device of changing hats and becoming members of the ESM's Board of Governors, can escape the supranational strictures on their powers resulting from the EU's institutional system. Thus, the Court's liberal attitude towards the operation of extra-EU institutional arrangements may well, in an indirect way, contradict its constant doctrine that it scrupulously protects the institutional balance as laid down by the Treaties. Yet, one might justify this very flexible attitude by the high stakes of this case and also by the fact that there were convincing legal and practical reasons why the national governments chose to set up an extra-EU financial mechanism but nevertheless wanted to tie that mechanism closely to the EU's institutional apparatus.

VI. Conclusion

In a co-authored piece published in 2002 (one of whose authors was and is a judge at the CJEU), it was argued that 'a proper understanding and due application of the notion of institutional balance may … lessen the democratic deficit from which the Union is perceived to suffer.'[36] It becomes clear, though, in the remainder of their lengthy article, that the authors advocate a particular *political conception* of the institutional balance that would lead to an improvement of the democratic quality of the European Union; they do not advocate the judicial use of that principle to achieve that goal. Indeed, the Court has, throughout its history,

[36] K Lenaerts and A Verhoeven, 'Institutional Balance as a Guarantee for Democracy in EU Governance' in C Joerges and R Dehousse (eds), *Good Governance in Europe's Integrated Market* (Oxford, Oxford University Press, 2002) 35.

refused to correct the institutional arrangements laid down by the Member States when adopting the original Community Treaties and their later revisions. It has rather defined its task, principally, as making sure that the various EU institutions remain within their roles and respect each other's powers and also, additionally, as interpreting the Treaty rules on the attribution of powers in a way that facilitates the smooth functioning of the institutional machinery and, more broadly, of the political process of European integration—even if this implies, occasionally, allowing the Member State governments to step out of the EU legal order so as to pursue the integration process in alternative institutional ways.

8

Refining Relative Authority: The Judicial Branch in the New Separation of Powers

JOSEPH CORKIN

This chapter considers the continuing relevance of separation of powers theory now that so much of the authority of national parliaments to enact, amend and repeal the law, of governments to execute and enforce the law, and even of the judiciary to interpret and apply the law, has passed to other institutions beyond this *trias politica*. Public authority is wielded by many means, but the focus here is on law-making and the special demands it makes of the legitimacy assets of those who do it. Law, ranging from the less 'concretised'[1] (abstract, general rules) to the more 'concretised' (detailed implementation and application) is now made beyond national elected hierarchies in a vastly extended executive branch; beyond the nation state in supranational institutions; and beyond state (as in public) institutions altogether through the self- and co-regulation of all manner of corporate, commercial and consumer transactions by particular groups that succeed in governing much wider groups.[2] Law is made then as much *between* institutions, as within and through them; a cooperative task, distributed across elected, bureaucratic, national, European, public and private institutions and all their hybrids that interact in intricate constellations, with flattened hierarchies and blurred boundaries. Reductive models of constitutional law that aspire only to constitute and

[1] The term 'concretised' is adopted from the German, '*Konkretisierung der Staatzwecke*' (H Peters, *Lehrbuch der Verwaltung* (Berlin, Springer, 1949)) to capture how even case-by-case enforcement decisions produce de facto rules over time, much in the same way as the gradual accumulation of precedents in common law systems generate legal principles. As Hans Kelsen put it in his *Pure Theory of Law* (M Knight trans, Berkeley, University of California Press, 1967) 234: 'Application of law is at the same time creation of law'. The difference between making, implementing and applying the law is then one of degree, not of kind, such that each represents a distinct region on a single continuum, the precise position of which is simply a function of how 'concretised' any particular instance of norm generation is.

[2] See, eg, H Schepel, *The Constitution of Private Governance: Product Standards in the Regulation of Integrating Markets* (Oxford, Hart Publishing, 2005).

legitimate the unified, hierarchically-layered and self-contained law-making systems of a simple polity (paradigmatically the nation state) struggle to address their irreducible plurality, interdependence and fragmentation. They can just about accommodate limited transfers of law-making to an extended executive branch and even to supranational institutions, by depicting national elected hierarchies as ill-equipped to fulfil all our ambitions for the law (given the complexities and cross-border dimensions of contemporary policy problems) and as recovering that capacity by delegating, always carefully-circumscribed law-making tasks to what are no more than administrative and supranational agents.[3] But law-making is now more profoundly dispersed than this, so radically diffusing the enterprise that it is simply not susceptible to such principal-agent modelling.

Given how far we have departed from the classic tripartite division of the functions of the state, separation of powers theory appears to be a strange place to look for a constitutional account of these new modes of making law and its functional equivalents. But while the theory is fundamentally about which institutions are constitutionally legitimated to do what, it does not concern this allocation alone, but also how the resulting interdependencies and mutual constraints that the allocation fosters contribute to the legitimacy of the whole. This 'checks and balances' dimension suggests we can down-play the requirement that all law is made by some idealised legislature and its formal (legal) agents—legitimacy contingent on the quality of particular links back to a particular *locus* or *loci* of legitimated authority—and instead focus on the idea that legitimacy is relational; the product of interactions between institutions and the different legitimacy assets that each brings to the party. If so, we might rethink 'checks and balances' as applying not just between institutions *within* the state, but also to those *beyond* it,[4] and not just between those in hierarchical relations, but also to those in heterarchical relations. A hierarchically-organised world of parliaments, statutes, government departments, administrative law, legal and constitutional formalism, judicial review and other assorted trappings of traditional democratic constitutionalism, which emphasise formal lines of legal and political accountability back to elected hierarchies and the judicial branch, has become ever more deeply enmeshed with a heterarchically-organised world of governance, institutionalised experimentation, reflexivity and proceduralisation, without (obvious) lines of legal and political accountability. These horizontal and vertical accountabilities complement one another; not in some trite triangulation, but in profound and complex ways, with much falling to the judicial branch to achieve that complementarity through an evolving, experimental case law whose incremental iterations are more likely to

[3] See, generally, D Kennedy, 'Three Globalizations of Law and Legal Thought: 1850-1968' in D Trubek and A Santos (eds), *The New Law and Economic Development: A Critical Appraisal* (Cambridge, Cambridge University Press, 2006) 19; P Lindseth, 'Equilibrium, Demoi-cracy, and Delegation in the Crisis of European Integration' (2014) 15 *German Law Journal* 529, 537 and 551.

[4] E Benvenisti and G Downs, 'Towards Global Checks and Balances' (2009) 20 *Constitutional Political Economy* 366.

succeed in refining their subtle interactions than any preconceived grand design. This chapter grounds this theory of the role of the judicial branch in the new separation of powers with critical reference to the actual practice of the Court of Justice.

I. Conceptualising Law-making's Diffusion

To fuse a horizontally-organised world and its accountabilities with the vertical accountability demands of democratic constitutionalism necessitates an appreciation of the subtleties of law-making's diffusion and the interdependencies and mutual constraints thereby generated. Perhaps the most thoroughgoing theoretical exposition of such new modes of law-making are theories of 'societal constitutionalism' and 'reflexive' or 'responsive' law.[5] Simplifying somewhat: to handle social and economic complexity, law-making is increasingly organised so that law's addressees are simultaneously its co-authors; no longer merely passive subjects of law made by another, but directly and systematically involved in the law-making enterprise via self-organising networks that operate in an amorphous space between society, the market and the state. This makes the law 'cognitively open' to the expertise and experience of those proximate to the policy problems it confronts. Although this plays down the supposedly inextricable association between law-making and the state—inextricable at least for classical ideas of democratic constitutionalism—the state still operates to attune these processes to the interests of society as a whole, only no longer as a principal to formal (legal) agents. Instead, it proceduralises these societal subsystems so they, in Gunther Teubner's terms, steer *themselves* in directions that are more broadly beneficial. Jody Freeman uses a 'contractual metaphor' to describe the relationship: a multi-faceted and negotiated partnership in which law-making is now decentred from the state and involves 'a variety of actors making collections of decisions in a web of relationships.'[6]

There are also 'experimental' variants of these reflexive models, aimed at policy problems that present 'persistent' or 'strategic' uncertainty.[7] Here, law or its

[5] P Nonet and P Selznick, *Law and Society in Transition: Towards Responsive Law* (New York, Harper and Row, 1978); G Teubner, 'Substantive and Reflexive Elements in Modern Law' (1983) 17 *Law and Society Review* 239, 274; G Teubner 'Autopoietic Law: A New Approach to Law and Society' in G Teubner (ed), *Juridification of Social Spheres: A Comparative Analysis in the Areas of Labor, Corporate, Antitrust and Social Welfare Law* (Berlin, Walter de Gruyter, 1987); D Sciulli, *Theory of Societal Constitutionalism* (Cambridge, Cambridge University Press, 1992); I Ayres and J Braithwaite, *Responsive Regulation: Transcending the Deregulation Debate* (New York, Oxford University Press, 1995).

[6] J Freeman, 'The Private Role in Public Governance' (2000) 75 *New York University Law Review* 543, especially 547–48, 572 and 673–75; See also D Feaver and B Sheehy, 'The Shifting Balance of Power in the Regulatory State: Structure, Strategy, and the Division of Labour' (2014) 41 *Journal of Law and Society* 203.

[7] C Sabel and J Zeitlin, 'Learning from Difference: The New Architecture of Experimentalist Governance in the EU' (2008) 14 *European Law Journal* 271.

functional equivalent is made in recursive processes that institutionalise experimentation. Local units responsible for enacting, implementing, administering and/or enforcing the law in one location, and typically belonging to the extended executive branch, are brought together with other such local units that perform the exact same tasks elsewhere, so they learn from one another in an open-ended, experimental exploration of their differing solutions to the policy problems that they have in common. They exchange knowledge, pool ideas and compare results *en route* to discovering new solutions, disturbing settled but sub-optimal practices and avoiding the repetition of one another's mistakes. Again, this mode of law-making—the antithesis of rule-following and strong political steering—is not susceptible to principal-agent modelling, above all because it requires the local units to be entrusted with significant discretion so that, through cooperative problem-solving, they re-conceptualise the problems and goals with which they were only ever loosely tasked, discover new ones and re-define the standards by which they measure each other's achievements, all the while softly disciplining one another via various mechanisms of peer review. The whole process is to remain provisional or truly experimental; open to continual revision via the experimental feedback loops of the network, which again precludes extensive pre-definition of its tasks by supposed political principals or the hardwiring of its soft disciplining into hard law. Whatever the formal position, the local units and the networks themselves simply no longer act, in any real sense, as the agents of their erstwhile political principals. The lines of vertical accountability are too attenuated to be characterised in this way. More significant are the horizontal accountabilities that link the local units to one another.

Reflexive law, institutionalised experimentation and similar accounts of the horizontalisation of law-making are not purely positivistic accounts of how law-making has adapted to modernity. There is a normative flavour to them that is scarcely avoided because they effectively declare the institutions of classical democratic constitutionalism no longer fit for purpose. David Harvey, for instance, claims a shrinking world of 'new organizational forms, new technologies, new lifestyles, new modalities of production and exploitation' and the ever-faster circulation of goods, people and information, make traditional institutions 'too rigid, clumsy and slow';[8] Martin Rhodes and Jelle Visser, that 'changes in industrial and economic organization—namely, the arrival of a service or knowledge economy, and the shift from Fordism to post-Fordism'—have necessitated 'new forms of flexible yet durable coordination under decentralised conditions, with only limited scope for the exercise of hierarchical power';[9] and Anne-Marie Slaughter, that

[8] D Harvey, *Justice, Nature and the Geography of Difference* (Oxford, Wiley-Blackwell, 1996) 240–41; cf W Scheuerman, 'Democratic Experimentalism or Capitalist Synchronization? Critical Reflections on Directly-deliberative Polyarchy' (2004) 17 *Canadian Journal of Law and Jurisprudence* 101.

[9] M Rhodes and J Visser, 'Seeking Commitment, Effectiveness and Legitimacy: New Modes of Socio-economic Governance in Europe' in A Héritier and M Rhodes (eds), *New Modes of Governance in Europe* (Basingstoke, Palgrave, 2011) 104, 105.

networks are the 'optimal form of organization for the Information Age' and the 'blueprint for the international architecture of the 21st century', capable of establishing a 'new world order' to perform legislative, administrative and adjudicative functions in the absence of world government.[10]

These are grand claims, but what of political self-determination? If law or its functional equivalent is made so remotely from elected hierarchies, where are the politics that underpin that law-making to take place? Have we simply traded the legitimacy of democratic constitutionalism for the increased efficacy of these new modes of law-making, which we should evaluate on the basis of their functional problem-solving qualities alone (a positivistic inquiry) and so avoid inquiring too deeply into their constitutional qualities (a normative inquiry)? Or might they lay claim to a legitimacy that is independent of any connection to an elected hierarchy and derives exclusively from their capacity, as Teubner puts it, to steer themselves?

The argument that these horizontal arrangements can stake an independent claim to legitimacy runs as follows: the diffusion of the law-making enterprise and the institutional resources necessary to do it effectively have resulted in interdependence and mutual constraint among all involved. And so it is to these horizontal accountabilities to one another—whether the self-referential (autopoietic) steering of reflexive law or the soft disciplining of institutionalised experimentation—that we should look for an account of their law-making legitimacy. So, for Collin Scott, legitimacy is a function of the overall equilibrium of the system: the 'dispersal of key resources of authority' (power, information, expertise and the capacity to bestow legitimacy) institutionalises tensions between all concerned to achieve an aggregate accountability; they constrain (or, in the language of separation of powers, 'check and balance') one another, to create a continuous reciprocal accountability that is 'not linear, but more like a servo-mechanism' that holds the whole system 'in a broadly acceptable place through the opposing tensions and forces generated'.[11] Each is forced 'constantly to account for at least some of its actions to others within the space', placing it under control even though no one (specifically) controls it.[12] This is similar to what John Keane calls a 'monitory democracy' in which concentrations of seemingly unaccountable power are in fact held to account through intricate (albeit opaque) webs of control, so law is more a series of flexible, dynamic responses to broad goals, themselves subject to continual re-definition, than a set of fixed rules issued from on high.[13]

[10] A-M Slaughter, 'The Real New World Order' (1997) 76 *Foreign Affairs* 183, 195–97; A-M Slaughter, 'Governing the Global Economy through Government Networks' in M Byers (ed), *The Role of Law in International Politics: Essays in International Relations and International Law* (New York, Oxford University Press, 2000) 204.

[11] C Scott, 'Accountability in the Regulatory State' (2000) 27 *Journal of Law and Society* 38, 50–52 and 60.

[12] G Majone, *Regulating Europe* (London, Routledge, 1996) 300.

[13] J Keane, *The Life and Death of Democracy* (London, Simon and Schuster, 2009).

These ideas challenge the vertical accountability demands of democratic constitutionalism, which require all law to be specifically enabled by the constitution, traceable back along an unbroken chain of formal (legal) delegations from all with a hand in making it to an elected hierarchy that stands in for the people. In these horizontal arrangements, legitimacy stems instead from a careful proceduralisation that ensures all involved act deliberatively and inclusively. Stakeholders are given the opportunity to participate directly and encouraged to interact non-strategically (in a principled way) so that each takes the others' distinct concerns, interests and contributions seriously. In this way, it is claimed, the public good can be legitimately defined at those locations where the law or its functional equivalent is given its final, concretised form, in collaboration with those on its receiving end. As such, the public good need not be articulated, as per classical democratic constitutionalism, by an elected hierarchy, before being transmitted along formal (vertical) lines of legal and political accountability to the remote agents that concretise the law or its functional equivalent, which are thereby bent to that hierarchy's will.

II. What of the Elected Hierarchy?

But these 'complex webs of extended accountability which spring up in practice'[14] cannot generate legitimacy out of nothing; their participants somehow pulling each other up by each other's bootstraps. Their self-referential steering remains just that, self-referential, ungrounded and necessitating some anchoring in vertical accountabilities back to an elected hierarchy that stands in for an absent people, thereby re-connecting their law-making, albeit at times tenuously, to *all* who are subject to it, and not just those select stakeholders who secured direct access to or even became part of these webs of horizontal accountability.

How law or its functional equivalent is made in networks designed to institutionalise experimentation among local units provides an instructive example of how horizontal accountabilities can fall short: these networks have ultimately to derive their legitimacy from that of the local units they bring together and, more particularly, their embedding in their respective national constitutional orders. Yet the very act of combining local units into transnational networks disturbs that embedding. The officials concerned are specialists, members of functionally specific units, and so limited in their breadth of vision. They rely on the generalists in the elected hierarchies to whom they must formally account to factor this breadth back in. But those elected hierarchies were already struggling to achieve this even before these units were incorporated into transnational networks. Forcing specialist national officials to account to one another in transnational networks that bring

[14] Scott, above n 11, 60.

them together with their equally specialised counterparts from other local units will neither scarcely broaden their vision nor, without careful design, make them more responsive to national elected hierarchies and thence to the public. Instead they will tend to orientate themselves towards their peers in the network and the soft discipline that flows from that orientation (those with whom they share discourses, a professional ethos and epistemic perspectives).[15] The result is that they collectively pull (further) away from their erstwhile political principals in favour of accounting to one another and to the select stakeholders with which they surround themselves.[16] Carol Harlow suggests such 'self-serving coteries' are 'blunted by mutual interest' and establish complacent, 'old boy'-style networks whose participants are reluctant to rock the boat because they are 'more concerned with policy input and long-term relationships than retrospective evaluation', even to the point of capturing their own stakeholders.[17] As such, the horizontal accountability achieved may be painfully thin, but worse, comes at the expense of vertical accountability; *politically* back to elected hierarchies and, given the emphasis on soft disciplining, *legally* back to courts that might otherwise have brought important rule of law values to bear.

The horizontal accountabilities that these networks institutionalise tend also to be insular and opaque. Transnational networks do not always publish agendas or minutes and commonly meet behind closed doors, excluding not only the public from their cycles of peer review, but also organised civil society that might (to an extent) have stood in for the public.[18] And when they *are* transparent and the participation of the public *is* somehow facilitated, even if only indirectly via organised civil society, they are only really accessed selectively, by those whose interests are sufficiently concentrated, or whose concerns are sufficiently specific, to motivate that participation, and who can simultaneously justify their input through reasoned, factual and 'decision-relevant' analysis as well as force the network to take that input seriously because they are 'blockage-capable'.[19] Excluded are what Everson and Joerges call the less well-organised and -articulated 'anxious and ethical … concerns of the concrete, "socialised" and often politically-motivated

[15] S Picciotto, 'Constitutionalizing Multilevel Governance?' (2008) 6 *International Journal of Constitutional Law* 457; MD Cross, *Security Integration in Europe: How Knowledge-based Networks are Transforming the European Union* (Ann Arbour MI, University of Michigan Press, 2011); M Barnett, 'Accountability and Global Governance: The View from Paternalism' (2016) 10 *Regulation and Governance* 134.

[16] J Corkin and N Boeger, 'Are Expert Networks Driving the Trend towards Soft Transnational Coordination?' in P Jurcys, P Kjaer and R Yatsunami (eds), *Regulatory Hybridisation in the Transnational Sphere: Developments in International Law* (Leiden, Brill, 2013) 149.

[17] C Harlow, 'Global Administrative Law: The Quest for Principles and Values' (2006) 17 *European Journal of International Law* 187, 212; C Harlow and R Rawlings, 'Promoting Accountability in Multilevel Governance: A Network Approach' (2007) 13 *European Law Journal* 542.

[18] M Dawson, *New Governance and the Transformation of European Law* (Cambridge, Cambridge University Press, 2011).

[19] B Eberlein and E Grande, 'Beyond Delegation: Transnational Regulatory Regimes and the EU Regulatory State' (2005) 12 *Journal of European Public Policy* 89, 106.

European citizens' whose political, social and ethical values are less readily integrated into a 'grammar of science and technology' that has currency in these functionally differentiated settings.[20]

The EU has attempted to surmount the problem, and the difficulty of establishing a genuine European public sphere, by encouraging the formation of a European civil society sector-by-sector; one capable of directly injecting the concerns and interests of particular constituencies into these law-making processes by articulating and filtering public concerns, to deliver neatly-packaged, scientifically-grounded but nonetheless public opinion into what would otherwise be purely technocratic settings. But this offers only an anaemic, apolitical imitation of democratic legitimacy. Though it is tempting to believe micro-deliberative strategies can offer a shortcut to realising deliberative democracy, circumventing the need to seek out actual public opinion, they are (at best) only a means to make public opinion more considered, informed and reflective and only then if they are set up to do just this; certainly not simply to bypass the need to transform public opinion.[21]

Mechanisms of horizontal accountability may now be a permanent feature of contemporary law-making, but we can avoid the familiar conclusion that we have traded legitimacy for effectiveness, or that we might secure both with a bit of proceduralist alchemy that combines 'deliberation' (that old favourite of democratic theory[22]) with a modicum of participation from organised civil society.[23] We ought instead to seek ways to expand opportunities for genuine political scrutiny and to contest expert claims, thereby breaking the mould of the various 'insider clubs' and opening up debates too often framed as purely technical.[24]

When making law in the context of divergent concerns and interests, any resulting conflicts have to be worked through *politically*. They cannot be settled through what Dawson calls 'the benevolent pursuit of an administrative "single right answer."'[25] The law-making process must be organised to provide for law's political renewal. While exposure to raw politics need not happen on a daily basis, the potential to revert to politicised law-making must always exist.[26] No amount of

[20] M Everson and C Joerges, 'Reconfiguring the Politics-Law Relationship in the Integration Project through Conflicts-Law Constitutionalism' (2012) 18 *European Law Journal* 644.

[21] C Lafont, 'Deliberation, Participation, and Democratic Legitimacy: Should Deliberative Mini-publics Shape Public Policy' (2015) 23 *The Journal of Political Philosophy* 40, 59–60.

[22] See, eg, J Elster (ed), *Deliberative Democracy* (Cambridge, Cambridge University Press, 1998); U Puetter, 'Europe's Deliberative Intergovernmentalism: The Role of the Council and the European Council in EU Economic Governance' (2012) 19 *Journal of European Public Policy* 161.

[23] Art 11 TEU; See, eg, C Hendriks, 'The Democratic Soup: Mixed Meanings of Political Representation in Governance Networks' (2009) 22 *Governance* 689.

[24] M Dawson, 'Transforming Into What? New Governance in the EU and the "Managerial Sensibility" in Modern Law' (2010) 2 *Wisconsin Law Review* 389, 393 and 409–10.

[25] ibid, 409.

[26] M Goldoni and C McCorkindale, 'Why We (Still) Need a Revolution' (2013) 14 *German Law Journal* 2197.

sophisticated proceduralisation—reflexivity, institutionalised experimentation, or otherwise—can substitute for the supposedly old-fashioned political contestation within an elected hierarchy that can stake a genuine claim to embody the will of the people and so anchor the politics inherent to the law-making task.[27] Ensuring remote law-makers account to one another and/or to selected stakeholders is no substitute for the crucial final connection that their having to account to an elected hierarchy makes back to the people *as a whole*, ensuring their law-making is nevertheless a collective endeavour.

Whenever elected hierarchies delegate forms of law-making to an extended executive branch, to EU institutions or to private actors, they provoke a 'dynamic of political and cultural contestation over legitimacy'[28] because the people struggle to experience these delegations as democratic and contest their proper limits (as incessant newspaper campaigns against 'pen-pushing' bureaucrats and Eurocrats, or the shortcomings of self-regulation, attest). The evolution of contemporary administrative governance has always been dogged by this conflict and it is not specific to delegations to the EU (even if their scale brings it into sharper relief). The result is an ever-changing constitutional settlement in which the people reluctantly consent to diffused and fragmented forms of administrative governance, out of functional necessity, yet continue to dispute the extent of that necessity. So, for instance, the equilibrium position within the nation state that has shifted power to 'an increasingly complex and variegated administrative sphere' is tolerated as long as the transfer remains within broad limits, linked, at least in law, to historically-constituted and strongly-legitimated elected hierarchies.[29]

Ultimately then, while the intricate institutional constellations in which law is now made may have shifted law-making away from elected hierarchies, these constellations have always still to be situated in relation to them because they remain the base constitutional unit as a matter of sociological fact; what Peter Lindseth calls the 'historically grounded condition of democracy'.[30] This is so simply on the basis that the people continue to see them as guaranteeing their political self-determination. While it might be constitutionally convenient to dismiss the people's attachment as an old-fashioned and parochial constitutional relic, for as long as these hierarchies retain this totemic status, they must remain the focal point of any serious constitutional theory, regardless of the strength of countervailing functional necessities that make remote law-making inevitable.

None of this should be taken to mean that we have to rely exclusively on *national* elected hierarchies to anchor all law-making in Europe or, given the

[27] R Bellamy, 'Democracy as Public Law: The Case of Constitutional Rights' (2013) 14 *German Law Journal* 1017, 1018.

[28] Lindseth, above n 3, 542 and 555–56.

[29] P Lindseth, *Power and Legitimacy: Reconciling Europe and the Nation-state* (New York, Oxford University Press, 2010) 38.

[30] P Lindseth, 'Delegation is Dead, Long Live Delegation: Managing the Democratic Disconnect in the European Market Polity' in C Joerges and R Dehousse (eds), *Good Governance in Europe's Integrated Market* (New York, Oxford University Press, 2002) 142.

external effects of national law, that those hierarchies are even capable, unilaterally, of legitimately anchoring all law-making within the state itself.[31] The EU's own representative institutions, the European Parliament and the Council, are now in a position to carry some of that weight themselves, with relevant vertical accountabilities extending also back to them. They may not be able to lay claim (as a matter of sociological fact) to democratic credentials as strong as those of national elected hierarchies, but nor are they, as Lindseth suggests,[32] mere administrative agents of the Member States, but are rather linked back to the peoples of Europe via sufficient direct and indirect mechanisms of democratic accountability to give them a mandate (again assessed as a matter of sociological fact) that places them sui generis somewhere between a traditional legislature and some sort of shared/extended supranational executive/administrative branch.

III. Blending Horizontal and Vertical Accountabilities

Separation of powers theory, indeed constitutional theory generally, must acknowledge real world understandings of legitimate law-making as well as the weight of functional necessity. While the public may yearn for legitimacy founded on national elected hierarchies, this is only realisable to the extent that they possess the necessary law-making capacity; a capacity that is severely diminished by social and economic complexity and cross-border interdependence. Law-making beyond them and sometimes scarcely even within their sphere of influence is inevitable.

Separation of powers theory is about who ought to do what and the normative criteria for that allocation, which might still offer useful insights into how public (and especially law-making) power is now wielded, provided this goes beyond simplistic calls to revert back to an idealised tripartite division that would return all law-making to its 'rightful' place with (or at least closely controlled by) a traditional legislature. However, while we ought not to critique contemporary modes of law-making simply for departing from the narrow understandings of constitutional legitimacy that we inherited from the truly sovereign nation states of yesteryear, nor should we continually play functional necessity as a trump card to justify dismantling all manner of democratic constitutional guarantees.

Jürgen Habermas's theory of 'popular sovereignty as procedure' may offer some way out of the impasse.[33] Importantly, it is not about developing ever more

[31] C Joerges, 'Europe's Economic Constitution in Crisis and the Emergence of a New Constitutional Constellation' (2014) 15 *German Law Journal* 985, 1026.

[32] Lindseth, above n 3, 533–34 and 566.

[33] J Habermas, *Between Facts and Norms: Contributions to a Discourse Theory of Law and Democracy* (W Reghs trans, Cambridge MA, MIT Press, 1996) 441 and 463–90.

sophisticated modes of proceduralisation as an alternative to an elected hierarchy, but rather about enabling an elected hierarchy to be more effective as 'an intelligent adviser or supervisor who makes procedural law available', so that, instead of making law directly, it deploys 'post-interventionist' alternatives to command-and-control law; smarter instruments of control and persuasion that prompt, facilitate and coordinate others. Crucially, any such proceduralisation, including the exploitation of horizontal accountabilities, is about ensuring that the 'institutionally structured political will-formation' of all who make the law (or its functional equivalent) is 'coupled' with the non-institutionalised deliberation of the public. Or, as Habermas put it, the political sphere must be 'porous' to (as in steered, but not captured by) the issues, value orientations and contributions that circulate in the unstructured public sphere of 'spontaneous, unsubverted circuits of communication'.[34] In the final instance, this would seem to require an elected hierarchy whose self-evident accountability to the public encourages its competing political elites to discern and articulate the inchoate concerns and diffuse interests of the silent majority and to ensure law-making bends to their will. The all-important semi-autonomous political sphere is achieved because the requirement to submit to regular elections attunes it to the public sphere, whereas the periods between elections leave it sufficiently autonomous to avoid having mechanically to aggregate the bare preferences it discerns among the public.

The normative impulse that underpins the distinction between powers justifiably exercised by unelected institutions, vis-à-vis those exercised by elected hierarchies, is not asserted here as some transcendental, a priori truth, but rather based on the same contingent sociological observation outlined above: that of the continuing symbolic importance of electing our law-makers. The idea that those who make the law ought to serve at the pleasure of the rest of us who must live our lives within its bounds—support that we renew or withdraw at every election—is as elegant as it is a treasured term of our social contract. Elections affirm that, ultimately, we are the masters of our collective destiny, even when we submit to laws made by others. For as long as a law-maker's authority is open to our electoral challenge, *their* laws can be seen, without too much artifice, as *our* laws; an expression of our collective self-determination, because law is not just something done *to* us, but also something *we* do. That is so even if our authorship passes through a long chain of delegations and our influence is diluted by millions of co-authors.

Democratic constitutionalism has to be re-imagined and updated for dramatically-changed law-making conditions, but remains relevant as long as we accept it is no longer realistic for all law to be *specifically* enabled by the constitution, so that the power to make it is always traceable along an unbroken chain of formal (legal) delegations to an elected hierarchy that stands in for the people, to

[34] J Habermas, 'Reply to Symposium Participants, Benjamin N Cardozo School of Law' (1996) 17 *Cardozo Law Review* 1477, 1541.

make all law-makers, no matter how remote, that hierarchy's formal agents. It is enough that remote law-makers, as not-quite-agents, operate in the shadow of our elected hierarchies, subordinated to their never fully supplanted *Gewaltmonopol*, which they now assert less directly and generally only in extremis. Its latent presence—the mere possibility of its exercise—may generate sufficient (informal) vertical accountability to ensure the inchoate concerns and diffuse interests of the silent majority count for something in the more rarefied (functionally specific) deliberations of remote law-makers, while still ensuring they have sufficient space in which to operate so as to secure the benefits of various experimental and reflexive institutionalisations and their horizontal accountabilities.

Charles Sabel once implied institutionalised experimentation might serve as an alternative to democratic constitutionalism; that, combined with 'direct deliberativeness', it amounted to nothing less than a 'Constitution of Democratic Experimentalism'.[35] He has subsequently rowed back from such ambitious claims and now uses the altogether less assuming term 'experimentalist governance' that depicts institutionalised experimentation as merely complementing elected hierarchies, through the 'democratising effects' of its 'dynamic', 'forward-looking' accountability.[36] For Sabel, forcing local units to justify themselves publicly, against the comparable decisions and criticisms of other such units, renders them more accountable to elected hierarchies through a 'democratising destabilisation' that combines mutual learning and self-government with heightened political accountability:[37] their open critique of one another undermines any pretension they might otherwise have cultivated to possess incontrovertible technocratic authority, so the elected hierarchies that anchor their horizontal accountabilities gain access to richer, properly contested (and therefore tested) information. This chapter locates its own constitutional theory (to be operationalised by the judicial branch) in just such a blend of horizontal and vertical accountabilities.

IV. The Role of the Judicial Branch

If we are to rely on a subtle blend of horizontal and vertical accountabilities to stem a seemingly inexorable drift towards de-politicisation and, at least in the

[35] M Dorf and C Sabel, 'A Constitution of Democratic Experimentalism' (1998) 98 *Columbia Law Review* 267.

[36] C Sabel and W Simon, 'Destabilization Rights: How Public Law Litigation Succeeds' (2004) 11 *Harvard Law Review* 1015.

[37] C Sabel and J Zeitlin, 'Learning from Difference: The New Architecture of Experimentalist Governance in the EU' (2008) 14 *European Law Journal* 271, 277 and 313. Similarly, Frank Vibert argues in his *The Rise of the Unelected: Democracy and the New Separation of Powers* (Cambridge, Cambridge University Press, 2007) that unelected bodies represent a new branch of government and are held to account through a new separation of powers that promotes democracy by providing the public with more trustworthy and reliable information.

case of institutionalised experimentation, de-legalisation, we must recognise how immense and delicate that task is. For instance, we risk destroying all the reflexive, experimental and deliberative benefits of these horizontal arrangements if we embed them too crudely into a vertical hierarchy of recognisable, democratic constitutional institutions, which we then insist are realised through formal lines of legal and political accountability to courts and elected hierarchies. But while the horizontal-vertical framing provides some conceptual clarity in how we might go about such blending, it ultimately offers little prospect of a comprehensive set of procedural rules and principles that might serve as a blueprint for organising the enterprise as a whole, not least because we are dealing with a moving target. So, instead of relying on big, set-piece Administrative Procedure Acts[38] that may cause more problems than they solve—being based on particular, highly contested, constitutional understandings—we are better off relying on incremental change in the form of gradual, experimental iterations that the judicial branch is well-placed to effect.

As the executive branch extends in size, power, complexity and reach, including supranationally, so too does administrative law and the regularity with which the judicial branch gets to review its concretised law-making (standing rules, litigant resources etc permitting). This puts it in a position to refine the legitimacy of the procedures that the branch follows. Continually supplied with new cases from which it can set precedents, and blessed with security of tenure, it can develop long-term, yet experimental, strategies that direct its traditional concern for constitutional principle towards developing an ambitious process-perfecting case law, as well as fine-tuning, rescinding or expanding the same in future jurisprudence, as and when necessary.[39] The judicial branch might thereby attend to the mutual (horizontal) 'checks and balances' between remote law-makers, as well as to their (vertical) lines of legal and political accountability back to itself and to elected hierarchies, inculcating both with important constitutional values. It can, for example, enforce commitments to the rule of law, to according due process before burdens are imposed, to democratic participation, to administrative rationality and to fundamental rights protection.

Judicial review is fundamentally about 'bounded government'[40] and subjecting officialdom to the rule of law. The struggle to ground this task theoretically is as old as administrative law itself.[41] Traditional models of administrative law, based on a principal-agent understanding of the relations between political principals

[38] See, eg, European Parliament resolution of 15 January 2013 with recommendations to the Commission on a Law of Administrative Procedure of the European Union, 2012/2024 (INL).

[39] M Dawson, 'How Does the European Court of Justice Reason? A Review Essay on the Legal Reasoning of the European Court of Justice' (2014) 20 *European Law Journal* 423, 428.

[40] M Shapiro, 'Administrative Law Unbounded: Reflections on Government and Governance' (2001) 8 *Indiana Journal of Global Legal Studies* 369.

[41] SA Shapiro and R Levy, 'Heightened Scrutiny of the Fourth Branch: Separation of Powers and the Requirement of Adequate Reasons for Agency Decisions' (1987) 3 *Duke Law Journal* 440.

and their administrative agents, depict delegations as detailed and comprehensive and favour robust review to discipline agents' inclination to act independently of (or even to subvert) the will of their principals. Then there are what Harlow and Rawlings call 'red light' models that they associate with a libertarian tradition that views *all* state interventions as prima facie unjustified intrusions into individual liberty—an aberration from the natural order of the free market—and suitably checked by a vigilant judiciary.[42] They contrast this Hayekian understanding of judicial review, concerned primarily with controlling the excesses of the state per se (not just those of its extended executive branch) with what they call 'green light' models that demand judicial deference towards administrative action, to avoid an elite judiciary, imbued with legalistic, rights-based ideologies and an eccentric (typically conservative) vision of the public good, exerting too much control over the state's administrative apparatus and thwarting its capacity to use that apparatus to solve social problems progressively.

While the red light-green light dichotomy focuses on the impact of judicial review on the substantive plane—contrasting activist red light models that prevent the state from interfering in individual liberty with deferential green light models that leave the political organs of the state to determine what interference will further the public good—the model proposed here operates on the procedural plane. The idea that judicial review might perform a process-perfecting function focuses on the capacity of the judicial branch to structure and systematise the law-making process in all its institutional complexity, rather than on its restraint per se.[43] This demands substantive deference, as per green light theory, combined with procedural activism; not this time to protect individual liberty, as per red light theory, but rather with the aim of rendering remote law-making more legitimate. The judicial branch defers substantively to the rights and obligations defined through the law-making process and confines itself instead to scrutinising whether that process respected what Habermas calls the 'logic of argumentation' by following procedures that enabled 'better arguments to come into play in various forms of deliberation.'[44] Of course this neat conceptual distinction between substantive and procedural review is more easily maintained in theory than in practice, but that does not render it irrelevant if it still usefully informs judicial practice.

This process-perfecting case law operates in what Joerges calls that 'legally undefined space that is located somewhere between administrative and constitutional reform'.[45] And with no bright line separating the two, nor any pressing need to do so—for each speaks to the same constitutional concern of defining the appropriate relationship between the public, elected hierarchies and remote

[42] C Harlow and R Rawlings, *Law and Administration* 2nd edn (London, Butterworths, 1997) 67.

[43] See, eg, J Ely, *Democracy and Distrust: A Theory of Judicial Review* (Cambridge MA, Harvard University Press, 1980).

[44] Habermas, above n 33, 278–79.

[45] C Joerges, 'Guest Editorial: The Commission's White Paper on Governance—A Symptom of Crisis?' (2002) 39 *Common Market Law Review* 441; C Joerges and M Everson, 'Challenging the Bureaucratic Challenge' in E Eriksen and J Fossum (eds), *Democracy in the European Union: Integration through Deliberation?* (London, Routledge, 2000) 184.

law-makers—this chapter simply refers to it as 'administrative constitutional' law.[46] In effect, the judicial branch referees the law-making process, not only by enforcing the administrative constitutional rules and principles that it finds dispersed throughout the body of existing law, ensuring they bite in judicial review proceedings, but also by using its interpretive freedom to subtly change those rules and principles; glossing them so as to perfect the imperfections that it finds in them.[47]

The process-perfecting perspective focuses on the prospective effects of judicial review: the precedents that the judicial branch sets out, and how they combine, to proceduralise future law-making by upholding key democratic constitutional values. It is concerned less with judicial review as a direct means of upholding individual rights, even if the two are linked (eg when the judicial branch liberalises standing requirements, it enables individuals to challenge decisions of the other branches to uphold their individual (legal) rights, which simultaneously enhances their voice, and the voice of other similar individuals, in future law-making processes of the same type).

Case-by-case, orientated by a democratic constitutional theory that allows for the difficulties of making law and its functional equivalent under conditions of social and economic complexity and cross-border interdependence, the judicial branch fashions a body of administrative constitutional law, the contours of which are necessarily internalised by those it addresses to avoid future legal challenges to what they do. This judicial shadow thereby channels them through more legitimate modes of law-making, influencing the division of power between institutions, how they organise their internal processes and how they interact with (and are rendered accountable to) one another, as well as to the public (directly or via elected hierarchies).

At the same time, separation of powers theory also requires that the judicial branch show particular restraint when reviewing the decisions of institutions better suited than it to balance the competing concerns and interests at stake when law is made. That restraint must, in the final instance, come from the judicial branch itself; a self-restraint in which it determines the limits of its own competencies through an internalised sense of its proper constitutional role.[48] This is

[46] Similarly, a former President of Germany's Federal Administrative Court, Fritz Werner, once described administrative law as 'materialised constitutional law' (F Werner, 'Verwaltungsrecht als konkretisierendes Verfassungsrecht' (1959) 74 *Deutsches Verwaltungsblatt* 527).

[47] Here it is instructive to read the abundant literature on how American courts have been active in this regard. See, eg, M Garland, 'Delegation and Judicial Review' (1985) 98 *Harvard Law Review* 505, 529; M Asimow, 'Delegated Legislation: United States and United Kingdom' (1983) *3 Oxford Journal of Legal Studies* 253, 256; A Scalia, 'Vermont Yankee: The APA, the DC Circuit, and the Supreme Court' (1978) *The Supreme Court Review* 345, 348; M Shapiro, 'Judicial Delegation Doctrines: The US, Britain and France' (2002) 25 *Western European Politics* 173, 182–83.

[48] There is some (limited) external check on the judicial branch, in that it cannot work too hard against the grain because its judgements are not self-enforcing, for which it relies, ultimately, on the political support of the other branches (in another instance of the 'check and balances' of a separation of powers).

particularly important when it calibrates the intensity with which it reviews the other branches. But, though mindful of the limits of its proper constitutional role, it ought also to take seriously the possibilities of that role because it is, as Scott and Sturm point out, well equipped 'to listen to, and evaluate, diverse explanations as to why any given political process is, or is not, such as to satisfy core constitutional requirements, including that of democracy'.[49] It can then articulate the origin and scope of these requirements and determine how they ought to be implemented through frameworks that respond to imperfections in existing processes by adjusting the capacities and incentives of the various protagonists.

As Mendes and Venzke note in their introductory chapter, determining *how* to strike sensitive balances between competing policy goals, that are then concretised in the law, is no substitute for determining *who* should strike them and *how*, so the balance is continually re-struck in institutions that possess the appropriate legitimacy assets (relative to what Neil Komesar calls their more 'imperfect alternatives'[50]). Separation of powers theory, and the 'checks and balances' that flow from the separation, is about ensuring that decisions are, in the words of the German Constitutional Court, 'taken by those institutions, which, according to their organization, composition, function, and procedure, are best suited for taking them'.[51] This depends on what Habermas calls the 'distribution of the possibilities for access to different sorts of reasons'.[52] While elected hierarchies can legitimately engage in discourses of norm justification, enjoying unrestricted access to the widest range of reasons with which to determine abstract, general law, the extended executive and especially the judicial branches may engage only in discourses of norm application, constrained by what is permitted in legal discourse.[53] The judicial branch should refrain from resolving unresolved political and social conflicts, deferring to the substantive solutions offered by those better placed that it to do so, including the extended executive branch. At the same time, it *is* well placed to apply constitutional theory to develop and apply rules and principles that improve how that extended executive branch goes about its law-making; that determine process rather than substance (albeit recognising the distinction is more easily made conceptually than in practice). Indeed, the more successfully the judicial branch perfects remote law-making processes through its procedural activism, the more deferential it ought to be towards the substantive outputs of those processes.

[49] J Scott and S Sturm, 'Courts as Catalysts: Re-thinking the Judicial Role in New Governance' (2006) 13 *Columbia Journal of European Law* 565, 590–93.

[50] NK Komesar, *Imperfect Alternatives: Choosing Institutions in Law, Economics, and Public Policy* (Chicago, Chicago University Press, 1997); NK Komesar, *Law's Limits* (Cambridge, Cambridge University Press, 2001) 151.

[51] BVerfG, 68 BvR I, 86; BVerfG, 98 BvR 218, 251–2.

[52] Habermas, above n 33, 192–93 and 229–37.

[53] See also N Luhmann, '*Quod Omnes Tangit*: Remarks on Jürgen Habermas's Legal Theory' (1996) 17 *Cardozo Law Review* 883.

The term 'judicial activism' is usually associated with the claim that the judiciary over-reaches its legitimate authority and undermines the separation of powers, but oriented procedurally, judicial activism may well improve the legitimacy of remote law-making because the judicial branch does not thereby assume law-making authority, but rather directs its concern for constitutional principle towards legitimating the processes through which *others* exercise *their* law-making authority. It demands they are properly accountable, both legally and politically; transparent in their dealings; open to full and fair participation; responsive; informed; inclusive; appropriately deliberative; and so on.[54] In this way, it attends to, or process-perfects, the vertical lines of legal and political accountability between remote law-makers and elected hierarchies, the horizontal accountabilities of remote law-makers to one another and the interrelations between these various vertical and horizontal accountabilities.

V. As Operationalised by the Court of Justice

The judicial branch and particularly dedicated administrative and constitutional courts have long performed a process-perfecting function at the national level that responds to legitimacy imperfections in national bureaucratisation patterns, but the impact of the Court of Justice on EU law-making is potentially more dramatic. The Court of Justice oversees an emerging constitutional order that calls for special attention. Absent the orientation of an uncontested constitutional end-point, or seemingly even the remotest possibility of one in the near future, institutional reform in the EU, whether driven incrementally from within or engineered and written into the treaties by the Member States, has largely involved a pragmatic search for problem-solving capacities in specific fields. Reforms have then tended to neglect a systematic consideration of underlying constitutional principle, which has placed considerable responsibility on the Court of Justice to steer the resulting institutions—a product of pragmatic compromise and disjointed reform (or, perhaps more significantly, inertia)—onto more coherent paths by offering continuity in the articulation of the administrative constitutional values at play.

The Court of Justice has certainly built a powerful base from which it might fashion such process-perfecting law. It was creative in setting up and rigorously enforcing a legal regime that ensured the Member States honoured the integration commitments they had originally struck. And once it started out along this constitutionalisation path, declaring that sufficiently precise EU law has 'direct effects'

[54] E Jordão and S Rose-Ackerman, 'Judicial Review of Executive Policymaking in Advanced Democracies: Beyond Rights Review' (2014) 66 *Administrative Law Review* 1, 39; M Ioannidis, 'A Procedural Approach to the Legitimacy of International Adjudication: Developing Standards of Participation in WTO Law' (2011) 12 *German Law Journal* 1175, 1181–82.

and so created rights that individuals could rely on in national courts,[55] each of its constitutional innovations thereafter, including supremacy,[56] have built more or less logically upon the last. Initially, the Court of Justice directed its attention to the EU's integration deficit, enforcing an economic constitution that aimed at keeping the Member States to the particular (economic) path of integration they had committed to in 1957, but were making slow progress along. This centred on imposing a duty to 'mutually recognise' the efficacy of one another's legal standards, rather than insist on applying their own in a way that hindered free movement.[57] More recently, however, the economic integration project having progressed so far, there is more call on it to assume a similar responsibility for the EU's democratic deficit.

Where the Court of Justice was once largely indifferent to the democratic credentials of the institutions that were necessary to enable economic integration, accepting their functional (output) legitimacy as part of the genetic code of the EU, to which the peoples of Europe had at least tacitly consented, such indifference is no longer tenable. The more that law-making power has shifted to EU institutions, largely in the form of powers to initiate vast programmes of regulatory harmonisation, the more that permissive consensus has broken down and the greater the need to render that power democratically accountable. This is especially so given the strong rule of law established by the Court's direct effect and supremacy jurisprudence, which makes the effects of that power so non-negotiable. The Court of Justice ought then to re-orientate its jurisprudence, away from purely integration-producing (economic constitutional) case law, towards developing more legitimacy-producing (administrative constitutional) case law, thereby demonstrating its concern for the legitimacy of the economic constitutional order it was so instrumental in establishing, but whose democratic constitutional foundations have become so obviously thin the more that has been built upon them.

The EU is a unique legal paradigm in which the Court of Justice does not derive its authority from any classic theory of the separation of powers and can be bolder in identifying the constitutional values that will 'civilise' EU law-making and render its institutions more accountable to one another and to the peoples of Europe than was perhaps envisaged when they were created.[58] The role it thereby assumes is well captured by Ronald Dworkin's theory of 'law as integrity':[59] the Court's avowedly teleological approach, with liberal reference to the 'spirit' of the treaties and to 'inspirations' drawn from national legal traditions,[60] respects the limits of

[55] Case 26/62 *Van Gend en Loos v Netherlands Inland Revenue Administration* [1963] EU:C:1963:1.

[56] Case 6/64 *Flaminio Costa v E.N.E.L.* [1964] EU:C:1964:66.

[57] Case C-120/78 *Rewe-Zentrale AG v Bundesmonopolverwaltung für Brandwein (Cassis de Dijon)* [1979] EU:C:1979:42.

[58] M Everson, 'Administering Europe?' (1998) 36 *Common Market Law Review* 195, 197; C Harlow, *Accountability in the European Union* (New York, Oxford University Press, 2002) 190; Dawson, above n 24, 420; Jordão and Rose-Ackerman, above n 54,1, 9 and 69.

[59] R Dworkin, *Law's Empire* (Cambridge MA, Harvard University Press, 1986).

[60] G Beck, *The Legal Reasoning of the Court of Justice of the EU* (Oxford, Hart Publishing, 2013).

its interpretive freedom ('fit' in Dworkin's terms) even while it uses that leeway it *does* enjoy to make EU law-making processes the best they can be ('justification' in his terms). This is made all the easier by the fact that the EU is a relatively new legal order, in a more or less permanent state of flux, with little weight of precedent to have to manoeuvre into new positions.

So the Court of Justice gradually unfolds a constitutional theory of the EU, its 'constitutional charter',[61] in ever more intricate case law that builds incrementally on a series of broad administrative constitutional principles that it locates in the treaties and some secondary legislation. It has, for instance, developed a 'right to information' that it describes as a 'cornerstone' of the EU that strengthens the democratic character of its institutions and the trust the public can place in them.[62] It requires that those whose interests are perceptibly affected by an EU decision are given a fair hearing.[63] It insists that, when the complexity of a decision so demands, the EU consults relevant experts, notwithstanding the absence of any formal requirement to do so.[64] It requires that the EU clearly and unequivocally disclose the reasoning and factual basis of decisions, which must also withstand that closer scrutiny.[65] And so on.

The Court of Justice can also enhance national law-making processes. As Chantal Mak illustrates in this volume: its intervention in *Aziz*[66] opened up deliberation over the fairness of a Spanish law that permitted mortgage contracts with seriously detrimental terms for borrowers, feeding into and enriching a wider public debate about the problems of the Spanish housing market and their connection to the Eurozone crisis. Private legal relations between banks and their customers are governed by laws/rules made in national and EU legal systems, as well as in contract, which puts the Court of Justice in a unique position, at the interface of all three types of law/rule, able to transmit and translate arguments for legal change between them and thereby to pressure each to justify itself in relation to the other two.

There is of course always the danger that legal scholars, blessed with hindsight and eager to join the dots, impose patterns and coherence on a jumbled case law that in fact follows little more than the accidents of litigation, but this is to ignore the fact that there are judges of the Court of Justice who claim it is more

[61] Case 294/83 *Parti écologiste 'Les Verts' v Parliament* [1986] EU:C:1986:166, para 23.

[62] Case T-14/98 *Heidi Hautala v Council of the European Union* [1999] EU:T:1999:157, paras 82–84, citing Case C-58/94 *Kingdom of the Netherlands v Council of the European Union* [1996] EU:C:1996:171, Opinion of AG Tesauro, para 19.

[63] Case 17/74 *Transocean Marine Paint Association v Commission of the European Union* [1974] EU:C:1974:106, para 15.

[64] Case C-269/90 *Technische Universität München v Hauptzollamt München-Mitte* [1991] EU:C:1991:438 and Case C-212/91 *Angelopharm GmbH v Freie Hansestadt Hamburg* [1994] EU:C:1994:21.

[65] Case 203/85 *Nicolet Instrument GmbH v Hauptzollamt Frankfurt am Main-Flughafen* [1986] EU:C:1986:269.

[66] Case C-415/11 *Mohamed Aziz v Caixa d'Estalvis de Catalunya, Terragona i Manresa (Catalunyacaixa)* [2013] EU:C:2012:700.

deliberate in its jurisprudence than this. Writing extra-judicially, the now President of the Court, Judge Lenaerts, praises it for unfolding administrative constitutional principles from 'minimal guarantees of fairness' scattered throughout existing EU law, which it deems manifestations of 'meta-fundamental rights of due process', to be fixed as 'substantial democratic obligations' that reinforce the accountability of EU institutions to EU citizens who rely on their restraining power to compel prudent, diligent law-making.[67] And in a line of reasoning that coincides closely with Dworkin's theory of 'law as integrity', Judge Mancini (also writing extra-judicially[68]) describes how the Court of Justice could not have invented a European Parliament had the Treaty not provided for one (Dworkin's 'fit'), but precisely because there was some, if limited, provision for such a representative institution to participate in EU law-making, the Court was able to emphasise Parliament's role in holding the Council to a strict duty to consult it on the basis inter alia of a fundamental democratic principle (Dworkin's 'justification').[69] He also claims that when the Court of Justice rules on the extent of EU competencies in legal base cases, it systematically favours the base that gives Parliament the greatest influence over the law-making process.[70]

While we ought to take these judicial claims seriously—they are, after all, insights from inside the Court itself[71]—we should not take them at face value, without subjecting them to serious scrutiny; asking whether the actual practice of the Court measures up, or whether, in fact, these insights are just a little too self-justificatory. Certainly, its case law does not always process-perfect and sometimes does quite the reverse. If we consider its jurisprudence on the role of the European Parliament alone, as praised by Judge Mancini: Bruno de Witte, writing in this volume, can detect no such systematic bias towards any one institution in the many cases in which it has been called upon to referee inter-institutional disputes. Recent examples include its *Biocides* judgment[72] and its endorsement of the EU's intergovernmental management of the Eurozone crisis that side-lines the European Parliament.[73]

[67] K Lenaerts, '"In the Union we Trust": Trust-enhancing Principles of Community Law' (2004) 41 *Common Market Law Review* 317, 343.

[68] F Mancini and D Keeling, 'Democracy and the European Court of Justice' (1994) 57 *Modern Law Review* 175, 179.

[69] Case C-138/79 *SA Roquette Frères v Council of the European Communities* [1980] EU:C:1980:249.

[70] See, eg, Case C-300/89 *Commission of the European Communities v Council of the European Communities (Titanium Dioxide)* [1991] EU:C:1991:244.

[71] A Vauchez, 'The Transnational Politics of Judicialization: *Van Gend en Loos* and the Making of EU Polity' (2010) 16 *European Law Journal* 1.

[72] Case C-427/12 *European Commission v Parliament and Council of the European Union (Biocides)* EU:C:2014:170; See commentary by D Ritleng, 'The Dividing Line between Delegated and Implementing Acts: The Court of Justice Sidesteps the Difficulty in *Commission v Parliament and Council (Biocides)*' (2015) 52 *Common Market Law Review* 243.

[73] Case C-370/12 *Thomas Pringle v Government of Ireland, Ireland and The Attorney General* [2012] EU:C:2012:756 and C-62/14 *Peter Gauweiler and Others v Deutscher Bundestag* [2015] EU:C:2015:400.

On the other hand, there are also cases in which the Court of Justice has demonstrated a subtle understanding of the interaction between vertical and horizontal accountabilities. A good example lies in its jurisprudence on law-making in the context of scientifically uncertain risk that is paradigmatic of the sort of policy problems that arise out of 'social practices and the dynamic interaction between culture, cognition, and context', demanding situated knowledge that combines scientific and political judgment.[74] Not only this, but the mixed questions of law and fact that arise when gaps in expert evidence meet claims based on the protection of rights and/or democratic legitimacy, do not lend themselves to clear substance-process distinctions either, which all puts the Court at the very limits of its authority, yet on which it has demonstrated considerable self-awareness. Reluctant to superimpose outcomes, even if only by enforcing the fundamental rule of law principle that institutions ought to publish reasons to justify their exercise of public power (almost impossible without shading into substantive review by inquiring into the adequacy of those reasons) its review is deferential, yet it does not shy away from considering procedural imperfections. When asked to review such law, it is effectively invited to reach a different conclusion to that which emerged through the machinations of a law-making process that comprises institutions better placed than it (by their various horizontal and vertical accountabilities) to answer the difficult questions that surround law-making in this context. Those institutions were designed (perhaps imperfectly, but nonetheless more appropriately than it) to respond to and to mediate between a range of relevant lay and scientific voices. But while it rightly acknowledges its own lack of epistemic capacity to review the substance of their decisions in depth (to which it then defers, refusing to assess the scientific evidence de novo by comparing what they did to what it would have done with the same) it does not defer uncritically, but rather considers whether the procedures they followed were capable of generating the kind and quality of information necessary for decisions of the type they took.

Instead of assuming direct responsibility for imposing a legal standard in the face of normative or scientific uncertainty, the Court of Justice prompts others to engage in appropriate problem-solving modes *themselves*; demanding only that they take proper account of the available scientific evidence. It also applies the precautionary principle to widen their margin of appreciation when the evidence fails to resolve the uncertainty, yet still clears the threshold of at least 'reasonably raising doubts'.[75] So, although the Court affords them room to respond to the heightened politics of making law in the context of scientifically uncertain risks, opening up space for elected hierarchies to respond to public concerns, it does not permit them to ignore the available scientific evidence altogether, but obliges

[74] Scott and Sturm, above n 49, 570–71; J Corkin, 'Science, Legitimacy and the Law: Regulating Risk Regulation Judiciously in the European Community' (2008) 33 *European Law Journal* 359.

[75] Cases T-74, 76, 83–85, 132, 137 and 141/00 *Artegodan GmbH and Others v Commission of the European Communities* [2002] EU:T:2002:283, para 192.

them to be explicit about the objectives and informational base of their decisions; to demonstrate how they considered the full range of relevant voices (lay and scientific) and how they mediated between them. It thereby reaches into the EU's scientific committees to review their proper functioning, the internal consistency of their opinions and the adequacy of their statements of reasons, while permitting them to enlarge their discretion, with reference to the precautionary principle, if triggered by the specter of a risk established by 'solid and convincing evidence' that is founded on the principles of excellence, transparency and independence. The Court thereby acknowledges their, its and science's appropriate place in the EU's constitutional order. Effectively, it insists the EU draws on evidence derived from scientists who themselves relied on replicable methodologies that receive review and validation within their own epistemic community.[76]

This monitoring of the adequacy of the EU's epistemic or information base, as a processual rather than a substantive matter, does not wholly exclude substantive review, only requires that it is deferential. Moreover, such review is assisted by a rich informational record that is directly attributable to procedural requirements developed in the process-perfecting case law and particularly the need for a record that enables legal and political accountability. When reviewing substantively, the Court of Justice tests for abuse of discretion, which essentially involves determining whether an outcome was within the range of outcomes an institution might reasonably have reached on the basis of the informational record before it. The purpose of the inquiry is to allocate primary decisional authority, and its outer limits, and thereafter to defer to that institution.

VI. Concluding Remarks

Those who celebrate reflexivity and institutionalised experimentation can be too quick to dismiss democratic constitutionalism as an outdated theoretical ideal, only really applicable to a bygone era of truly sovereign states, long since disempowered by social and economic complexity and cross-border interdependence. But, as William Scheuerman puts it, democratic constitutionalism 'hardly depends on liberal nostalgia or a romanticized account of a mythical nineteenth-century "golden age"'.[77] We still cleave to national elected hierarchies as the principal guardians of our political self-determination. While social and economic complexity and cross-border interdependence have inevitably shifted law-making somewhat away from them and their sphere of influence in search of the necessary capacity, we can still pay homage to their totemic status, even while creatively rethinking

[76] Scott and Sturm, above n 49, 567 and 574.
[77] Scheuerman, above n 8.

'checks and balances' in horizontal and vertical terms to establish new legitimating connections to, and importantly also between, these increasingly powerful, remote law-makers.

The same story of a rapidly expanding executive branch that triggers an expansion in administrative law can be told of all developed constitutional orders. While it may resemble one long exercise in inventing mechanisms of legal accountability to plug gaps in political accountability, left by increasingly emasculated elected hierarchies, those mechanisms do not necessarily substitute for a loss in political control, but in fact re-establish or reinforce it. In developing that administrative law, the judicial branch draws, explicitly or otherwise, on the rich theoretical tradition of the separation of powers and its normative criteria for allocating different types of public authority, depending on the legitimacy assets of those concerned. The judiciary can thereby refine (process-perfect) the respective contributions (and interactions) of elected and unelected institutions in what are now fiendishly complex transnational processes.

The judicial branch is, of course, not alone in grappling with these questions, but it appropriately makes a significant contribution. At the same time, theories of legitimate law-making beyond the state are highly contested, so it would be inappropriate for the judicial branch to single out one and to further it alone. There are, however, sufficient overlaps between the competing theories for it to further a conception of legitimacy that is common to all, or, at the very least, to avoid running counter to any one of them. But are we not asking too much of it or even of constructing an empire of law? This depends on how the judiciary goes about the task. The approach of the Court of Justice is instructive. As long as its interventions remain properly directed and carefully weighted—broadly speaking, procedurally activist and substantively deferential—there is every reason to expect that its increased activism might make a significant contribution to the evolution of the EU into a more democratic constitutional order than was envisaged in 1957, or indeed that piecemeal administrative constitutional reforms have managed to achieve since. But nor should we get carried away. There is a danger of over-optimism if we cherry-pick from the case law and highlight only those cases in which the Court has successfully process-perfected. Were we to survey its case law more comprehensively, we might be left more sceptical, or even find that we are expecting it to perfect the imperfectable (on the basis that EU law-making processes are so removed from the requirements of democratic constitutionalism that no mere judicial tweaks can rescue them).

And so to end on a sobering note. The Court of Justice can only process-perfect at the margins. The administrative constitutional rules and principles that are dispersed throughout the treaties, and some secondary EU law, are more significant in determining how EU institutions make law or its functional equivalent than are the precedents of the Court, that can do no more than refine those rules and principles. That does not mean those precedents do not make a real contribution, or that there is no cause for optimism in some of the jurisprudence outlined above. However, on the basis that a primary duty of the legal scholar is to keep the judicial branch honest, this chapter concludes with three notable failures: first, although there is limited scope for judicial enforcement of the normative output of so-called institutionalised experimentation which relies on softer modes of disciplining and disrupts the institutional balance and the separation of powers by significantly empowering national executive branches, the Court of Justice has also done little to engage with its development by entertaining challenges to its precise form or to the enforceability of its soft disciplining. Second, the Court's subsidiarity jurisprudence ignores all calls for more vigorous enforcement of the principle that might have kept law-making closer to relevant elected hierarchies.[78] And, finally and most recently, the Court was unwilling to subject the EU's handling of the Eurozone crisis to the same level of scrutiny as that to which it subjects fundamental rights (on which it insists that wherever the EU goes, so too must fundamental rights[79]) even though the EU is founded just as explicitly on the 'rule of law' and 'representative democracy',[80] neither of which were much in evidence in the EU's prioritisation of the survival of the euro as a 'European raison d'état',[81] so meekly endorsed by the Court.

[78] Lindseth, above n 3, 558.

[79] Joined Cases C-402/05 P & C-415/05 P *Yassin Abdullah Kadi and Al Barakaat v Council of the European Union and Commission of the European Communities* [2008] EU:C:2008:461.

[80] Arts 2 and 10 TEU; C Kilpatrick, 'On the Rule of Law and Economic Emergency: The Degradation of Basic Legal Values in Europe's Bailouts' (2015) 35 *Oxford Journal of Legal Studies* 325, 352.

[81] D Chalmers, 'European Restatements of Sovereignty' (2013) 10 LSE Society and Economy Working Papers, 26.

9

Judicial Review of EU Administrative Discretion: How Far Does the Separation of Powers Matter?

DOMINIQUE RITLENG

Pursuant to the dominant reading of the separation of powers, public authority is distributed and public functions are allocated among the different institutions in relation to the legitimacy assets each of them relies on.[1] The legitimacy assets they avail themselves of are connected to their organisation, composition, function and procedure.[2] To reflect on the possible influence of the separation of powers on judicial review of EU administrative discretion amounts thus to ask whether the leeway the judiciary leaves to the EU administration—and inside it to the different EU administrative bodies—and the intensity of review it consequently exerts on their acts are proportionate to the legitimacy which they bring into EU decision-making via their organisation, composition, function and procedure. In other words, the question is whether the legitimacy one administrative body may claim to ground its authority on translates into the scope of discretion the reviewing court allows it to have and into the ensuing intensity of review of its action. In particular, assuming that, thanks to its composition, function and procedure, the legislature enjoys a higher level of legitimacy than the administration—something which remains to be ascertained in the EU institutional system—do EU Courts pay heed to the separation of powers between these two branches of government by granting a broader discretion to the EU legislature than to the EU administration and accordingly subjecting legislative acts to a looser scrutiny compared to the review performed over administrative acts? Further, do EU courts make a difference in the scope of discretion left to the different EU administrative bodies and

[1] For a reminder, see C Möllers, *The Three Branches: A Comparative Model of Separation of Powers* (Oxford, Oxford Univeristy Press, 2013).

[2] See 68 Bundesverfassungsgericht (BVerfG) I, 86; 98 BVerfG 218, 251–52: the 'institutional and functional differentiation and separation of powers serves the distribution of political authority and responsibility as well as the control of those in power. It pursues the aim that, as much as possible, decisions are right. This means that they be taken by those institutions, which, according to their organization, composition, function, and procedure, are best suited for taking them'.

in the intensity of review of their acts in accordance with the different legitimacy assets each of them may rely on?

These are the questions to which this chapter will attempt to respond. For that purpose, three preliminary observations should nonetheless be made aiming at delimiting the realm of the administration, specifying how discretion will be understood and ascertaining the relevance of the separation of powers principle within the specific framework of the EU institutional system.

Concerning first the scope of the EU's administrative activity and of the respective legal acts, this chapter takes as a starting point that the administrative activity relates to the executive function, executive and administration remaining largely undifferentiated in constitutional theory.[3] In the multi-level system of the European Union, this function is primarily carried out by the Member States[4] in accordance with the executive federalism model[5] and it is only by way of exception that the administrative activity is performed directly by EU bodies.[6] Nevertheless, since this chapter aims at assessing the extent to which the trias politica doctrine influences judicial review of administrative discretion, it will focus on the 'direct administration' of the European Union. Indeed, the trias politica doctrine relates to the horizontal allocation of authority. It will be showed below that the difficulty before the Lisbon Treaty to identify and isolate administrative acts among all EU legal acts—in particular to distinguish them from legislative acts—had a bearing on the way the Court of Justice envisaged administrative discretion and reviewed its exercise. For current purposes, administrative acts are understood to be all measures of individual application, be they based directly on the Treaty or on another EU legal act and all secondary measures of general application, ie measures of general application adopted on the basis of another EU legal act.[7]

Second, discretion can be defined as the freedom of action which the holder of public authority enjoys in its decision-making or rule-making activity. It is the part of its activity that falls outside the ambit of judicial review. Some legal scholars have thus endeavoured to conceive of a notion of discretion as something that the judiciary must acknowledge and that limits its supervision.[8] But administrative

[3] But not entirely: some acts of the executive, such as acts relating to foreign affairs, may be viewed as pertaining to the governmental function considered as distinct from the administrative function.

[4] See Arts 4(3) TEU and 291 TFEU.

[5] Or, to put it differently, in accordance with the principle of indirect administration (see B Dubey, 'Administration indirecte et fédéralisme d'exécution en Europe' (2003) 39 *Cahiers de droit européen* 87.

[6] For an attempt to identify the EU executive function, see D Ritleng, 'L'identification de la fonction exécutive dans l'Union' in D de la Rochère (ed), *L'exécution du droit de l'Union, entre mécanismes communautaires et droits nationaux* (Brussels, Bruylant, 2009) 27.

[7] See to that effect, Case 16/88 *Commission/Council* [1989] EU:C:1989:397, para 11: 'The concept of implementation ... comprises both the drawing up of implementing rules and the application of rules to specific cases by means of acts of individual application'. However, it will be shown below that under the Lisbon Treaty, the category of 'non-legislative' acts includes also some primary acts of general application.

[8] See especially in French administrative law, A Hauriou, 'Le pouvoir discrétionnaire et sa justification' (Sirey, Mélanges Carré de Malberg, 1933) 233; JC Venezia, *Le pouvoir discretionnaire* (Paris, LGDJ, 1959); in public international law, G Cahin, 'La notion de pouvoir discrétionnaire

or legislative discretion is not something that would be imposed on the judiciary from the outside. It is the leeway left by the judge to the holder of public authority. Indeed, every court being judge of its own jurisdiction, it must set the boundary between what will fall under its control and what will remain within the ambit of the discretionary power of the author of the legal act. As the judge is the master of the intensity of his review, he is ultimately the master of the extent of administrative or legislative discretion.[9] It is therefore pointless to want to impose a priori theoretical frontiers on judicial review.[10] In particular, in order to decide whether or not to leave the holder of public authority a margin of discretion and to determine consequently the level of scrutiny, the EU judicature does not consider itself bound by the wording and the texture of the enabling legal text but takes also into account other elements.[11] However, even if viewed from a judicial perspective, the extent of administrative or legislative discretion is contingent upon the level of scrutiny freely determined and carried out by the judge, administrative or legislative discretion cannot be removed. As Rivero put it, 'à tout moment, [le pouvoir discrétionnaire] est ce que le juge veut qu'il soit, étant entendu que le juge ne peut vouloir qu'il ne soit plus'.[12]

Third, the reason why the reviewing court must leave a margin of discretion to the holder of public authority lies primarily in the separation of powers doctrine, according to which the court must stay within the limits of its judicial activity and cannot interfere in what is considered to be the province of the executive or of the legislative.[13] The granting of a margin of discretion is the necessary corollary

appliquée aux organisations internationales' (2003) 107 *Revue générale de droit international public* 535; in European law, A Bouveresse, *Le pouvoir discrétionnaire dans l'ordre juridique communautaire* (Brussels, Bruylant, 2010).

[9] See D Galligan, *Discretionary Powers, A Legal Study of Official Discretion* (Oxford, Oxford University Press, 1986) 24: 'It is the courts that finally determine from a legal point of view whether an official has discretion, and, if so, how much.'

[10] As Judge Pescatore asserted, 'la solution du problème de justiciabilité relève du seul pouvoir judiciaire. La Cour … détermine elle-même l'étendue et les limites de sa compétence. Il apparaît donc vain de vouloir lui tracer a priori des frontières théoriques' ('Commentaire de l'article 164' in V Constantinesco et al (eds), *Le Traité instituant la CEE, commentaire article par article* (Paris, Economica, 1992), 941, para 73): 'the solution to the problem of justiciability is a matter for the judiciary alone. The Court determines itself the extent and the limits of its jurisdiction. It seems therefore vain to want to draw a priori theoretical frontiers' (our translation). See also C Harlow and R Rawlings, *Process and Procedure in EU Administration* (Oxford, Hart Publishing, 2014) 71: 'how far a judge will wish to go in scrutinising administrative decision-making is essentially a discretion matter'.

[11] See D Ritleng, 'Le juge communautaire de la légalité et le pouvoir discrétionnaire des institutions communautaires' (1999) *Actualité juridique du droit administratif* 645. See also A Fritzsche, 'Discretion, Scope of Judicial Review and Institutional Balance' (2010) 47 *Common Market Law Review* 361, 362–63.

[12] 'Discretion is what the judge at any moment wants it to be, on the understanding that he cannot want it not to exist anymore' (our translation) (Preface on Venezia, *Le pouvoir discretionnaire* (1959)).

[13] See C Baron de Montesquieu, *The spirit of Laws*: 'there is no liberty, if the judiciary power be not separated from, the legislative and executive. Were it joined with the legislative, the life and liberty of the subject would be exposed to arbitrary control; for the judge would be then the legislator. Were it

of the specific tasks entrusted to the executive and the legislative in correlation with the amount of legitimacy those two branches of government bring into the process of governance, without which the latter would not be able to fulfil them.[14] In that regard, it has been sometimes contended that the separation of powers is—or at least was—a principle unknown to the EU institutional system. In saying so, it was meant that public authority has not been distributed among the institutions so as to entrust each function (legislative, executive, judicial) to a different institution. Apart from the fact that this is far less true since the Lisbon Treaty, the absence of such an organic understanding of the separation of powers does however not mean that the structuring of the EU system of exercise of public authority did not follow from the outset the rationale of the separation of powers doctrine,[15] which is to avoid concentration of all power in a single body.[16] Indeed, the distribution of public authority between the various institutions of the European Union has been designed to set up an institutional balance, assigning each institution its own role in the institutional structure of the Union and the accomplishment of the tasks entrusted to the Union, and whose observance compels each of the institutions to exercise its powers with due regard for the powers of the other institutions.[17] Under the aegis of the principle of institutional balance, it was in fact nothing else than the separation of powers principle that

joined to the executive power, the judge might behave with violence and oppression' (English translation available at www.constitution.org/cm/sol.htm, of C Baron de Montesquieu, *De l'esprit des lois*, Ch VI, Livre XI (Gallimard, Bibliothèque de la Pléiade, 1951): 'Il n'y a point encore de liberté si la puissance de juger n'est pas séparée de la puissance législative et de l'exécutrice. Si elle était jointe à la puissance législative, le pouvoir sur la vie et la liberté des citoyens serait arbitraire: car le juge serait législateur. Si elle était jointe à la puissance exécutrice, le juge pourrait avoir la force d'un oppresseur'; see also J Madison, *The Federalist Papers* no 47: Madison says of 'the political maxim, that the legislative, executive, and judiciary departments ought to be separate and distinct', that 'accumulation of all powers, legislative, executive, and judiciary, in the same hands, whether of one, a few, or many, and whether hereditary, self-appointed, or elective, may justly be pronounced the very definition of tyranny' (text available at www.congress.gov/resources/display/content/The+Federalist+Papers).

[14] See Möllers, above n 1; A Fritzsche, 'Discretion, Scope of Judicial Review and Institutional Balance' (2010) 47 *Common Market Law Review* 361.

[15] On the different meanings of the separation of powers doctrine, see J Waldron, 'Separation of Powers in Thought and Practice' (2013) 54 *Boston College Law Review* 433; M Barberis, 'Le futur passé de la séparation des pouvoirs' (2012) 143 *Pouvoirs* 515.

[16] See C Baron de Montesquieu, *The Spirit of Laws*: 'When the legislative and executive powers are united in the same person,or in the same body of magistrates, there can be no liberty; because apprehensions may arise, lest the same monarch or senate should enact tyrannical laws, to execute them in a tyrannical manner.' (English translation available at www.constitution.org/cm/sol.htm, of Montesquieu, *De l'esprit des lois*, Chapitre VI, Livre XI, Gallimard, Bibliothèque de la Pléiade, (1951): 'Lorsque, dans la même personne ou dans le même corps de magistrature, la puissance législative est réunie à la puissance exécutrice, il n'y a point de liberté; parce qu'on peut craindre que le même monarque ou le même sénat ne fasse des lois tyranniques pour les exécuter tyranniquement'.)

[17] See Case C-70/88 *European Parliament/Council* [2017] EU:C:1990:217, paras 21–22. See also, J-P Jacqué, 'The Principle of Institutional Balance' (2004) 41 *Common Market Law Review* 387; K Lenaerts and A Verhoeven, 'Institutional Balance as a Guarantee for Democracy in EU Governance' in C Joerges and R Dehousse (eds), *Good Governance in Europe's Integrated Market* (Oxford, Oxford University Press, 2002) 35.

was guaranteed,[18] which the Court of justice has ended up acknowledging. It has explicitly held that the principle of separation of powers governing the relationship between the different institutions characterises the EU as a Union based on the rule of law and has given that principle the same meaning as that of the principle of institutional balance.[19] And the Court of Justice is, as every institution of the Union, also bound by the principle of separation of powers. This too is a relevant point to understand the scope of judicial review of administrative discretion. As prescribed in Article 13(2) Treaty on European Union (TEU), it 'shall act within the limits of the powers conferred on it in the Treaties', and hence may not disregard the nature of its judicial function[20] by impinging on the powers of the other institutions. In response to a request for a preliminary ruling, the Court of Justice thus ruled that its alleged creative interpretation of a regulation had not violated the principle of separation of powers, given that the Court had been seized on the basis of Article 267 Treaty on the Functioning of the European Union (TFEU) and made a proper use of the methods of interpretation.[21] With respect to the legality review of EU legal acts, the requirements of the separation of powers forbid the Court of Justice to conceive it so broadly as to encroach on the specific prerogatives of the legislative and the executive. That is why Article 33 of the European Coal and Steel Community (ECSC) Treaty explicitly excluded from the supervision of the Court of Justice the evaluation of the situation resulting from the economic facts or circumstances in the light of which the High Authority took its decisions, except where the High Authority was alleged to have misused its powers or to have manifestly failed to observe the provisions of the Treaty.[22] This limit put on the Court's powers of review was clearly intended to avoid a 'complete confusion of powers'.[23]

[18] See K Lenaerts, 'Some Reflections on the Separation of Powers in the European Community' (1991) 28 *Common Market Law Review* (1991) 11; C Blumann, 'Equilibre institutionel et séparation des pouvoirs en droit communautaire' in Université Panthéon-Assas (Paris II) *Clés pour le siècle* (Paris, Dalloz, 2000) 1639; S Rolland, *Le triangle institutionnel communautaire à l'aune de la théorie de la séparation des pouvoirs* (Brussels, Bruylant, 2008).

[19] Case C-413/11 *Germanwings* [2013] EU:C:2013:246, para 16.

[20] As it is defined in Art 19(1) TEU: the Court of justice of the European Union 'shall ensure that in the interpretation and application of the Treaties the law is observed'.

[21] See Case C-413/11 *Germanwings* [2013] EU:C:2013:246. For a confirmation that the EU courts consider themselves bound by the separation of powers, see Case C-246/11P *Portugal/Commission* [2013] EU:C:2013:118, para 80.

[22] For an application of that provision, see Case 6/54 *Kingdom of the Netherlands/High Authority* [1955] EU:C:1955:5.

[23] Opinion of AG Roemer in Case 6/54 *Kingdom of the Netherlands/High Authority* [1955] EU:C:1955:1, 126, quoting the Report of the French delegation on the ECSC Treaty. AG Roemer went on, quoting also the statement of reasons by the German government for the draft law auhorising the ratification of the Treaty: 'The principle of the separation of powers prevailing in the provisions of the Treaty relating to institutions required that the judicial control by the Court should not make it the supreme body representing the will of the Community in economic questions in place of the High Authority. Therefore in general terms the Court can only extend its examination to the situation arising out of the economic facts or circumstances when the High Authority is charged with misuse of powers or where it has manifestly failed to observe the provisions of the Treaty'.

Thus, in line with the separation of powers thinking, the Court of Justice avoids interfering too much in the administrative activity by granting a margin of discretion to EU administrative bodies and hence subjecting the legal acts they adopt only to light touch review. In so doing, the Court of Justice more accurately abides by the division of powers between the judiciary and the executive. This is a first manifestation of the separation of powers' influence on judicial review of administrative discretion. Whether the Court of Justice also differentiates the measure of discretion allowed to the different administrative bodies in correlation with the distinct legitimacy assets they may claim and accordingly varies the intensity of review of their respective acts remains, however, to be checked (section II below). The relationship between separation of powers and judicial review of administrative discretion raises, further, another issue: does the separation of powers between the legislature and the executive have a bearing on the way in which the Court of Justice reviews the exercise of administrative discretion that may contrast with its review of legislative discretion? More precisely, the question is whether the separation of powers between the legislative and the executive, which the Court of Justice must uphold, leads to a difference in the extent of discretion granted to the administration and the legislature respectively and, accordingly, whether there is a different degree of scrutiny depending on whether administrative or legislative acts are challenged (section I below).

I. Judicial Review of Administrative Discretion and Separation of Powers Between the Legislature and the Executive

The point here is to ascertain if the Court of Justice when wielding its power of review takes account of the separation of powers between the legislature and the executive, or even contributes to separating the legislative and the executive power by controlling the use of administrative discretion more thoroughfully than the exercise of legislative discretion.

When reflecting on a possible difference in the intensity of the judicial review of administrative acts and of legislative acts, the first element that comes to mind pertains to the legal framework which is imposed on the legal act concerned. Indeed, the more an act is located down in the hierarchy of norms, the more the density of the legal framework the enacting authority is bound to respect increases. This is also valid in EU law. As a consequence, it may be assumed that the extent of administrative discretion will, in principle, be smaller than that of legislative discretion, at least insofar as administration is viewed as an activity of implementation, which still remains the main part of the administrative activity. If this were empirically confirmed, it would however have little to do with the separation of powers principle.

Yet, it might be expected that, to be in keeping with the separation of powers doctrine, the Court of Justice differentiates legislative discretion from administrative discretion and the control thereof. Indeed, lessons drawn from national constitutional laws teach us that, whereas the need for judicial control of administrative acts is not disputed, the democratic legitimacy of judicial review of legislative acts is still today often challenged.[24] The critique is grounded on the comparative legitimacy assets the administration and the legislature may rely on to justify their authority. Democracy having become in modern states the chief source of legitimation of political authority, the power to pass legislative acts is in principle vested in parliament, a representative assembly whose members are elected by direct and universal franchise. Moreover, the already big amount of legitimacy that the legislative act draws from its adoption by the directly elected body is still increased by the participation of other institutions, with different interests and loyalties, in the legislative procedure. The legislative act is thus endowed with a very high level of legitimacy, even if ultimately the will of the majority prevails. Given that Courts lack the legitimacy conferred by an electoral mandate and are not politically accountable, their power to oppose the will of the sovereign people uttered by their representatives in legislative acts is therefore disputed. If today this 'countermajoritarian difficulty'[25] seldom leads to call into question the very existence of judicial review of legislative acts,[26] the concern not to exacerbate the ceaseless democratic challenge to its legitimacy prompts to grant the legislature a certain protection against judicial control over its acts. Such a protection may be ensured through limited access to judicial review, restrictive regime under which the state may be held liable for the damages caused by its legislative activity or

[24] For recent renewed criticism, see especially J Waldron, 'The Core of the Case Against Judicial Review' (2006) 115 *Yale Law Journal* 1346; id, *Law and Disagreement* (Oxford, Oxford University Press, 1999); R Bellamy, *Political Constitutionalism: A Republican Defence of the Constitutionality of Democracy* (Cambridge, Cambridge University Press, 2007); ibid, 'The Democratic Constitution: Why Europeans should Avoid American Style Constitutional Judicial Review' (2008) 7 *European Political Science* 9; M Tushnet, *Taking the Constitution Away from the Courts* (New Jersey, Princeton University Press, 2000); L Kramer, *The People Themselves: Popular Constitutionalism and Judicial Review* (Oxford, Oxford University Press, 2005). For a very recent attempt to defend the democratic character of judicial review of legislation, see J Mendes, *Constitutional Courts and Deliberative Democracy* (Oxford, Oxford University Press, 2015).

[25] As is very often called the issue of the democratic legitimacy of judicial review of legislative acts especially in the United States. For an account of this issue in the United States, see AM Bickel, *The Least Dangerous Branch: The Supreme Court at the Bar of Politics* 2nd edn (Literary Licensing LLC, 1986); B Friedman, 'The History of the Countermajoritarian Difficulty, Part One: The Road to Judicial Supremacy' (1998) 73 *New York University Law Review* (1998) 333; ibid, 'The History of the Countermajoritarian Difficulty, Part Four: Law's Politics' (2000) 148 *University of Pennsylvania Law Review* 971; ibid, 'The History of the Countermajoritarian Difficulty, Part Three: The Lesson of Lochner' (2001) 76 *New York University Law Review* 1383; ibid, 'The History of the Countermajoritarian Difficulty, Part Two: Reconstruction's Political Court' (2002) 91 *Georgetown Law Journal* 1; ibid, 'The Birth of an Academic Obsession: The History of the Countermajoritarian Difficulty, Part Five' (2002) 112 *Yale Law Journal* 153.

[26] See however, Waldron, above n 24, Bellamy, 'Political Constitutionalism' above n 24, Tushnet, above n 24 and Kramer, above n 24.

through the observance by adjudicators of a certain self-restraint.[27] One of the kind of self-restraint adjudicators are often called on to observe is to leave the legislature some leeway in the performance of its activity by not to subjecting legislative acts to too strict scrutiny.

Needless to say, the administration cannot avail itself of the same democratic credentials as the legislature. Therefore, the legitimate reach of the judicature's authority is in principle greater towards the administration, and hence one may expect that the reviewing court makes a difference in the nature and/or the extent of the discretion granted to the legislature and the administration. It might be all the more expected so that, because of the different levels of legitimacy that the two categories of acts draw from their author and procedure of adoption, in principle legislative acts are destined to entail political choices whereas administrative acts are confined to make, if any, choices of barely technical nature or, at least, less politically loaded.

In order to verify whether these assumptions match the reality of the European legal order, only the case of measures of general application will be analysed, as it is the sole case where the comparison makes sense. Indeed, the making of individual decisions does, in principle, not fall within the ambit of the legislator; it is a matter for the administration only. Conversely, both the legislator and the administration are empowered to enact measures of general application.

As will be shown below, it transpires from the case law that under the pre-Lisbon era the Court of Justice did not distinguish between administrative and legislative discretion and accordingly between the intensity of review exercised over legislative and administrative acts. Moreover, it turns out that, despite the separation of powers rationale informing the new typology of legal acts introduced by the Lisbon Treaty, the Court of Justice still does not make any difference between administrative and legislative discretion nor in the level of scrutiny performed over legislative and administrative acts.

A. Before Lisbon: Administrative Discretion Equated with Legislative Discretion

As is widely known, there was no organic separation of powers in the pre-Lisbon institutional system of the European Union. It proved impossible to identify among the various institutions of the European Union the ones which were the holders of the executive or the legislative power, and hence to separate the executive from the legislative branch of EU government. The Council, in particular, had been conferred the legislative function (although it increasingly had to

[27] On the meaning of judicial self-restraint as a means to pay heed to the separation of powers by defering to legislature and executive and leaving policy-making to their initiative, see RA Posner, 'The Meaning of Judicial Self-Restraint' (1983) 59 *Indiana Law Journal* 1.

share it with the European Parliament) and had also been vested with the EU executive power, even though it had in principle to delegate its exercise to the Commission.[28] Nevertheless, the legal scholarship deduced from the distinction made by the *Köster* case law[29] between the measures directly based on the Treaty itself, on the one hand, and derived law intended to ensure their implementation that primary acts of general application, on the other, mirrored the distinction between legislative acts[30] in the substantive sense[31] and executive acts. Accordingly, it was considered that there existed at least a functional separation of powers in the EU institutional system.[32]

Furthermore, legislative acts had been allocated a reserved domain. Pursuant to the non-delegation doctrine set out by the *Köster* jurisprudence, which has been taken over by the Lisbon Treaty in Article 290 TFEU, the essential elements of an area must be drawn up by the legislature itself (ie primary acts) and cannot be delegated to the administration (ie cannot be regulated through secondary acts). On essential elements, the Court of Justice specified that 'provisions which, in order to be adopted, require political choices falling within the responsibilities of the European Union legislature' must be regarded as the essential rules governing the matter in question and cannot, therefore, be delegated.[33] The making of political choices obviously implies the granting of a degree of discretion to the legislature and in addition, since the making of such choices is, in view of the above, the legislature's prerogative, it could have meant that the discretion granted to the legislature is different in nature and/or in extent from the discretion granted to the administration and that this difference leads to a difference in the intensity of judicial review.

Yet, despite the *Köster* distinction between primary and secondary acts and the definition of an exclusive sphere for the benefit of the former, the analysis of the case law pre-Lisbon reveals that the intensity of review of discretionary legislative acts did not differ from the intensity of review of discretionary administrative acts. The same formulae defining the margin of discretion and the intensity of review were used with respect to both legislative and administrative acts. It was in particular repeatedly held that the Commission may be vested with 'wide

[28] See Arts 202 and 211 EC.

[29] See Case 25/70 *Köster* [1970] EU:C:1970:115.

[30] See C Blumann, *La fonction législative communautaire* (Paris, LGDJ, 1995); J Rideau, 'La fonction législative dans les Communautés européennes' (1995) 1 *Revue des Affaires Européennes* 63; P-Y Monjal, 'Remarques sur l'emploi de la notion de fonction législative en droit communautaire' (1998) *Revue de Recherche Juridique* 1117.

[31] Formal elements of distinction were not totally absent, since the distinction between primary and secondary acts led to a hierarchy between the two types of act.

[32] K Lenaerts, 'Some Reflections on the Separation of Powers in the European Community' (1991) 28 *Common Market Law Review* 11.

[33] Case C-355/10 *Parliament/Council (Schengen Borders Case)* [2012] EU:C:2012:516, paras 64–65. For a recent confirmation, see Case C-363/14 *Parliament/Council* [2015] EU:C:2015:579, para 46.

powers of discretion and action'[34] and that the discretionary powers thus delegated on it—like the discretion allowed for the making of basic acts[35]—'correspond to the political responsibilities' of the European legislature.[36] Conversely, the then Court of First Instance ruled that the wide discretion enjoyed by the Community legislature to adopt and amend basic regulations in the common commercial policy area 'corresponds to the latitude which the Community institutions have when adopting specific anti-dumping measures pursuant to basic regulations'.[37] Furthermore, when the Court of Justice was asked to rule simultaneously on the legality of basic and implementing regulations in the field of common agricultural policy, it resorted to a syncretic formula to recall the wide discretion enjoyed by the 'Community institutions'[38] or by the 'Community legislature'.[39] Irrespective of whether legislative acts or administrative acts were concerned, the Court of Justice ruled also that the European authorities must be allowed a broad discretion whenever they are called upon to make social, political or economical choices and/or to undertake complex assessments.[40] As a result of the broad discretion enjoyed by the European authorities, administrative acts were subject to the same light touch review as legislative acts. Indeed, in both cases, judicial review was said to be limited to examining whether the exercise of that discretion 'had been vitiated by manifest error or misuse of powers, or whether the institution concerned has manifestly exceeded the limits

[34] See, on agricultural markets, Case 23/75 *Rey Soda* [1975] EU:C:1975:142, paras 10–11; Joined cases 279 280, 285 and 286/84 *Rau c/Commission* [1987] EU:C:1987:119, para 14; Case 167/88 *Association générale des producteurs de blé* [1989] EU:C:1989:234, para 15; Case C-478/93 *Netherlands/Commission* [1955] EU:C:1995:324, para 30; Case C-285/94 *Italy/Commission* [1997] EU:C:1997:313, para 22; Case C-241/95 *Accrington Beef* [1996] EU:C:1996:496, para 20; Joined Cases C-9/95, C-23/95 and C-156/95 *Belgium and Germany v Commission* [1997] EU:C:1997:50, para 36; on foreign trade, Case C-159/96 *Portugal v Commission* [1998] EU:C:1998:550, paras 40–41.

[35] See Case C-280/93 *Germany/Council* [1994] EU:C:1994:367, para 89.

[36] See Case C-221/09 *AJD Tuna Ltd* [2011] EU:C:2011:153, para 80; Case T-367/10 *Bloufin Touna Ellas Naftiki Etaireia* [2013] EU:T:2013:97, para 64; Case 265/87 *Schräder* [1989] EU:C:1989:303, para 22; Joined Cases C-254, 255 et 269/94 *Fattoria Autonoma Tabacchi* [1996] EU:C:1996:320, para 56; Case C-171/03 *Toeters et Verbek* [2004] EU:C:2004:714, para 52; Case C-94/05 *Emsland-Stärke* [2006] EU:C:2006:185, para 54; Joined Cases C-37 and 58/06 *Viamex Agrar Handels* [2008] EU:C:2008:18, para 34.

[37] Case T-162/94, *NMB France* [1996] EU:T:1996:71, para 72.

[38] Joined Cases 197 to 200, 243, 245 and 247/80 *Ludwigshafener Walzmühle* [1981] EU:C:1981:311, para 37.

[39] Case 84/87 *Erpelding* [1988] EU:C:1988:245, para 27; Case C-8/89 *Zardi* [1990] EU:C:1990:260, para 11.

[40] See, regarding legislative acts, Case C-84/94 *United Kingdom/Council* [1996] EU:C:1996:431, para 58; Case C-150/94 *United Kingdom/Council* [1998] EU:C:1998:547, paras 53–54; Case C-491/01 *British American Tobacco*, para 123; Case C-210/03 *Swedish Match* [2004] EU:C:2004:802, para 48; Case C-154/04 *Alliance for Natural Health* [2005] EU:C:2005:449, para 52; Case C-344/04, *IATA et ELFAA* [2006] EU:C:2006:10, para 80; Case C-127/07 *Arcelor* [2008] EU:C:2008:728; Case C-58/08 *Vodafone* [2010] EU:C:2010:321, para 52; regarding administrative acts, Case C-425/08 *Enviro Tech* [2009] EU:C:2009:635, para 47; Case C-326/05P *Industrias Químicas del Vallés* [2007] EU:C:2007:443, para 75; Case T-285/03 *Agraz and others/Commission* [2005] EU:T:2005:109, para 42; Case T-13/99 *Pfizer Animal Health* [2002] EU:T:2002:209, para 166.

of its discretion'.[41] Review of the application of the principle of proportionality was confined to checking whether the impugned measure had been 'manifestly inappropriate having regard to the objective which the competent institution was seeking to pursue'.[42] And that limitation of judicial review was explicitly intended to avoid reviewing the expediency of the challenged measure or substituting the competent authorities' assessment with the own assessment of the Court;[43] otherwise, the Court would usurp their role by imposing its own views of the policies to be pursued by the European Union, thereby violating the separation of powers.[44]

So the *Köster* distinction between primary (ie legislative) acts and secondary (ie administrative) acts did not translate into the intensity of the legality review exerted over both categories of act. Nor did it lead to a distinction between the two types of act in the establishment or the assessment of the conditions under which the European Union may incur non-contractual liability—the criticisms of the doctrine[45] and the suggestions of the Advocate-Generals[46] notwithstanding. Admittedly, in its early case law, the Court of Justice had set forth different conditions according to the nature of the legal act at issue. Whereas the sole unlawfulness of the damaging administrative act was needed for the non-contractual liability to arise, a sufficiently serious breach of a superior rule of law intended to confer rights on individuals was requested when the damaging measure was of 'legislative' character.[47] However, the criterion of distinction

[41] See for instance, regarding legislative acts, Case C-84/94 *United Kingdom/Council*, para 58; Joined Cases C-248/95 et C-249/95 *SAM Schiffhart* [1977] EU:C:1997:377, para 24; regarding administrative acts, Joined Cases C-254, 255 et 269/94 *Fattoria Autonoma Tabacchi* [1996] EU:C:1996:320, para 56; Case C-375/05 *Geuting* [2007]EU:C:2007:574, para 44; Case C-425/08 *Enviro Tech*, para 47.

[42] See for instance, regarding legislative acts, Case C-491/01 *British American Tobacco*, para 123; Case C-210/03 *Swedish Match*, para 48; C-154/04 *Alliance for Natural Health*, para 52; C-344/04 *IATA et ELFAA*, para 80; regarding administrative acts, Case C-265/87 Schräder [1989] EU:C:1989:303, 22; Case C-171/03*Toeters et Verbek* [2004] ECLI:EU:C:2004:714, para 52; Case C-535/03 *Unitymark* [2006] EU:C:2006:193, para 57; Case C-174/05 *Natuur en Milieu* [2006] EU:C:2006:170, para 29; Joined Cases C-37 and 58/06 *Viamex Agrar Handels* [2008] ECLI:EU:C:2008:18, para 36.

[43] See for instance, regarding legislative acts, Case C-84/94 *United Kingdom/Council* [1996] ECLI:EU:C:1996:431, para 23; Case C-233/94 *Germany/Parliament and Council* [1977] EU:C:1997:231, para 56; regarding administrative acts, Case 57/72 *Westzucker* [1973] EU:C:1973:30, para 14; Case C- 425/08 *Enviro Tech* [2009] ECLI:EU:C:2009:635, para 47; Joined Cases T-332 and 350/00 *Rica Foods* [2002] EU:T:2002:274, para 155.

[44] See Opinion of AG Jacobs in Case C-248/95 *SAM Schiffhart* [1997] EU:C:1997:92, paras 23–24; see also Opinion of AG Léger in Joined Cases C-317 and 318/04 *Parliament/Council* [2005] EU:C:2005:710, paras 232–33; Opinion of AG Poares Maduro in Case C-127/07 *Arcelor* [2008] EU:C:2008:292, para 35; Opinion of AG Bot in Case C-274/11 *Spain and Italy/Council* [2012] EU:C:2012:782, para 27.

[45] See for instance, A Barav, 'Injustice normative et fondement de la responsabilité non contractuelle de la CEE' (1977) 13 *Cahiers de Droit Européen* 439, 454.

[46] In his Opinion delivered on 18 June 1991 in the *Cato* case (Case C-55/90 [1992] EU:C:1992:52, paras 37–39) Advocate-General Darmon proposed to distinguish between the discretion allowed to the Commission within the framework of its administrative activity and the discretion enjoyed by the Council in its legislative activity, and hence to confine the restrictive regime of non-contractual liability to basic acts.

[47] For the explicit affirmation of this dual regime of liability, see Case T-390/94 *Schröder* [1997] EU:T:1997:51, paras 51 and 52. See also, Joined Cases T-79/96, 260/97 and 117/98, *Camar* [2000] EU:T:2000:147, para 205. It is however to be noticed that in the French version of the rulings, it was not spoken of 'acte législatif', the translation of 'legislative measure' was 'acte normatif'.

between legislative and administrative measures was that of their individual or general nature.[48] As a result, the conditions for legislative acts to give rise to the non-contractual liability of the Community were applied as well to secondary acts of general application.[49] Moreover, as is well known, the *Bergaderm* jurisprudence[50] put an end to the dual regime of non-contractual liability of the European Union. Since *Bergaderm*, a sufficiently serious breach of a rule of law intended to confer rights on individuals is a condition of non-contractual liability whatever the nature of the damaging measure at issue.[51] True, the assessment of this condition depended on the discretion enjoyed by the institution concerned, not on the general or individual nature of the measure at issue. It was only if the institution concerned had no discretion that the mere infringement of EU law might be sufficient to establish the existence of a sufficiently serious breach; otherwise for this condition to be met, the institution concerned must have manifestly and gravely disregarded the limits on its discretion.[52] However, here as well, the existence, nature or extent of the discretion available to the institution concerned did not depend on whether the damaging measure was a primary or an implementing act. Not only primary acts but also implementing measures could be deemed to 'involve economic policy choices'—thus to be the expression of a wide discretion—and hence could give rise to the non-contractual liability of the Community only if the institution concerned had manifestly and gravely disregarded the limits on its discretion.[53]

In sum, judicial review of administrative discretion did not differ from judicial review of legislative discretion. Though efforts had been deployed to distinguish legislative acts from administrative acts—as seen with the *Köster* case law—they did not lead to a differentiation in the intensity of the review of the two types of act. The Court of Justice applied the same rules on judicial remedies to both. More accurately, administrative acts were given the limited justiciability which ought to be reserved to legislative acts: the same limited intensity of legality review, the same restrictive conditions under which they may give rise to the non-contractual liability of the European Union and even the same limited standing granted to

[48] See for instance, Case T-390/94 *Schröder* [1988] ECLI:EU:C:1998:597, paras 53–57; Joined Cases T-481 to 484/93 *Vereniging Van Exporteurs* [1995] EU:T:1995:209, paras 81–88; Joined Cases T-79/96, 260/97 and 117/98, *Camar* ECLI:EU:T:2000:147, para 206.

[49] See for instance, Case 59/83 *Biovilac* [1984] EU:C:1984:380, para 10; Case C-152/88 *Sofrimport* [1990] EU:C:1990:259; Joined Cases T-480 and 483/93 *Antillean Rice Mills* [1995] EU:T:1995:162, paras 177–80; Joined Cases T-481 et 484/93 *Vereniging Van Exporteurs* [1995] EU:T:1995:209, paras 91–96.

[50] Case C-352/98P *Bergaderm and Goupil* [2000] EU:C:2000:361. For a confirmation, see Case C-312/00P *Camar* [2002] EU:C:2002:736; Case C-472/00P *Fresh Marine* [2003] EU:C:2003:399; Case C-234/02P *European Ombudsman c/Franck Lamberts* [2004] EU:C:2004:174, para 49.

[51] See to that effect explicitly, Case C-282/05P *Holcim* [2007] EU:C:2007:226, para 49.

[52] See Case C-352/98P *Bergaderm and Goupil* [2000] ECLI:EU:C:2000:361 paras 43–46; Case C-282/05P *Holcim v Commission* [2007] ECLI:EU:C:2007:226, paras 47–48.

[53] See Case C-312/00P *Commission/Camar and Tico* [2002] EU:C:2002:736, paras 54–61; Case C-198/03P *Commission/CEVA Santé Animale* [2005] EU:C:2005:445; Case T-429/05 *Artedogan* [2010] EU:T:2010:60, paras 52–56.

individuals to challenge their legality before the Court. Indeed, given the strict interpretation of the condition of individual concern,[54] private applicants could not seek the annulment of measures of general application,[55] be they of legislative or administrative nature.[56]

The reason for such an undifferentiated judicial treatment is to be looked for in the impossibility to make a clear-cut distinction between the two categories of act. Substantive criteria relating to the preserve of legislative acts could not be of real help. Not only the essential elements of an area whose drawing up falls within the purview of primary acts remains an indeterminate notion[57] but also the legislature can go beyond the boundaries of its reserved field and regulate all the points it wants. Above all, in the absence of an organic separation of powers, it remained impossible to distinguish formally legislative from administrative acts, and hence to associate each category with different levels and assets of legitimacy.

If it is therefore understandable that administrative and legislative acts were applied the same judicial treatment, the choice to grant all of them the protection against judicial review which in national laws is only afforded to legislative acts was nevertheless more disputable. It could be argued that the two categories of act should, on the contrary, have been given the judicial status which, in national laws, administrative acts are endowed with.[58] Indeed, the relative judicial immunity enjoyed by legislative acts in national legal orders is justified by the democratic legitimacy they draw from their adoption by the representatives of the sovereign people, something which could not be said about European legislative acts.[59]

Be that as it may, the establishment by the Lisbon Treaty of a formal distinction between the two types of act has offered an opportunity to put an end to this anomaly.

[54] Unchanged since the ruling in the *Plaumann* case (see Case 25/62 *Plaumann v Commission* [1963] EU:C:1963:17).

[55] As the Court of justice acknowledged it: under Art 230 EC, 'a regulation, as a measure of general application, cannot be challenged by natural or legal persons other than the institutions, the European Central Bank and the Member States' (Case C-50/00P *Union de Pequenos Agricultores* [2002] EU:C:2002:462, para 35).

[56] To mention but one example where the measure of general application which the individual could not challenge directly before the Court was an implementing regulation, see Case C-263/02P *Commission/Jego-Quéré* [2004] EU:C:2004:210.

[57] For an attempt to specify the content and the scope of this notion, see D Ritleng, 'The Reserved Domain of the Legislature: the Notion of the "Essential Elements of an Area"' in CF Bergström and D Ritleng (eds), *Rule-making by the European Commission : the New System* (Oxford, Oxford University Press, 2016) 133.

[58] See Opinion of AG Jacobs in Case C-50/00P *Union de Pequenos Agricultores* [2002] EU:C:2002:197, paras 87–90 (as regards locus standi under Art 230 EC); as regards the regime of non-contractual liability of the Community, see Opinion of AG Capotorti in Joined Cases 83 and 94/76, 4, 15 et 40/77 *Bayerische HNL* [1978] EU:C:1978:40, 2. See also R Joliet, *Le droit institutionnel des Communautés européennes—le contentieux* (Liège, Presses Universitaires de Liège, 1981) 269–70.

[59] See D Ritleng, 'La loi' in Auby (ed), *L'influence du droit européen sur les catégories du droit public* (Paris, Dalloz, 2010) 215, 239–42.

B. After Lisbon: Nothing New Under the Sun

The Lisbon Treaty has introduced a new categorisation of EU legal acts alongside the old distinction between regulation, directive and decision which remains. The treaty-makers have attempted to design this new categorisation in pursuance of the separation of powers doctrine. Expectations could be nourished that such a change would entail legal consequences on the respective judicial status of administrative and legislative acts. But for the moment the judicial developments have not come up to expectations. Administrative discretion is still subject to the same judicial control as legislative discretion.

i. Incentive to Differentiated Judicial Review

The Lisbon Treaty in Articles 288 to 291 TFEU has set up a new typology of legal acts, taken over from the Treaty establishing a Constitution for Europe.[60] One of the major changes introduced by the new classification is to differentiate legislative from non-legislative acts on the basis of organic and procedural considerations. Article 289(3) TFEU defines 'legislative acts' as 'legal acts adopted by legislative procedure'. And a 'legislative procedure' may be either the 'ordinary legislative procedure' which, according to Article 289(1) TFEU, consists in the joint adoption by the European Parliament and the Council of a legal act on a proposal from the Commission; or a 'special legislative procedure' which, pursuant to Article 289(2) TFEU, consists in the adoption of a legal act by the European Parliament with the participation of the Council, or by the latter with the participation of the European Parliament. In other words, a legislative act is a legal act whose passage requires the association on an equal or unequal footing of the Council and the European Parliament. A formal notion of EU legislation is thereby enshrined for the first time in primary law, which transcribes in normative terms the advent of a separation of powers. Indeed, while the exercise of the legislative function is jointly assigned to the Parliament and to the Council (as Articles 14 and 16 TEU explicitly stipulate), the executive function, which includes the adoption of secondary acts as well as basic acts, is not in principle within the ambit of the couple Parliament-Council and results at EU level in the enactment of 'non-legislative acts'.[61]

[60] For an analysis, see especially C Blumann, 'Actes législatifs et mesures d'exécution dans le projet de Constitution pour l'Europe' in *Mélanges Jean-Claude Gautron* (Paris, Pedone, 2004) 249; J Roux, 'Les actes: un désordre ordonné?' (2008) *Revue Europe*, Chron no 9; D David and D Ritleng, 'Les actes de l'Union' in V Constantinesco, Y Gautier and V Michel (eds), *Le traité établissant une Constitution pour l'Europe. Analyses et commentaires* (Strasbourg, Presses Universitaires de Strasbourg, 2005) 203; K Lenaerts and M Desomer, 'Towards a Hierarchy of Legal Acts in the European Union? Simplification of Legal Instruments and Procedures' (2005) 11 *European Law Journal* 744; J Bast, 'New Categories of Acts after the Lisbon Reform: Dynamics of Parliamentarization in EU Law' (2012) 49 *Common Market Law Review* 885; H Hofmann, 'Legislation, Delegation and Implementation under the Treaty of Lisbon: Typology Meets Reality' (2009) 15 *Europaen Law Journal* 482.

[61] See D Ritleng, 'L'identification de la fonction exécutive dans l'Union' in J Dutheil de la Rochère' (ed), *L'exécution du droit de l'Union, entre mécanismes communautaires et droits nationaux* (Brussels, Bruylant, 2009) 27.

Even the new category of delegated acts (Article 290 TFEU) does not call into question this separation-of-powers-based classification. True, from a substantive point of view, they may be equated to legislative acts: as they aim at supplementing or amending a legislative provision, they are quasi-legislative in nature although they cannot intrude into the reserved legislative domain. But viewed formally, they are authored by the Commission, and therefore named 'non-legislative acts'. This new system of legal instruments provides strong arguments to differentiate the judicial status of legislative acts from that of administrative acts.

First, there is now in principle a clear delineation between the two species of act. Second, the formal definition given to EU legislative acts ensures that they always will enjoy the double legitimacy on which the European Union as a Union of states and citizens rests.[62] And the democratic character of the two sources of legitimacy of the European Union is henceforth emphasised: whereas the European Parliament accounts for the voice of the European citizens,[63] it emerges from Article 10(2) TEU, by virtue of which 'Member States are represented … in the Council by their governments, themselves democratically accountable either to their national Parliaments, or to their citizens' that the Council is to be regarded as representing not only the Member States but also, or even above all, the national communities of the Member States. Third, the democratic legitimacy of EU legislative acts stems not only from the representativeness of their authors. What singles out the law-making process of EU legislative acts is openness, deliberative quality and enhanced public and national parliamentary scrutiny:[64] by virtue of Articles 16(8) TEU and 15(2) TFEU, not only the Parliament but also the Council shall meet in public when deliberating and voting on a draft legislative act; where the Council is acting in its legislative capacity, wider access to its documents must be granted to the citizens, with a view to strengthening democracy by enabling them to scrutinise all the information which has formed the basis for a legislative act;[65] under the Protocol no 1 on the role of national parliaments in the European Union, any draft legislative act shall be forwarded to the national parliaments; pursuant to the Protocol no 2 on the application of the principles of subsidiarity and proportionality, the Commission is obliged to consult widely before proposing legislative acts and national parliaments are given a prominent role in the oversight of the respect of the subsidiarity principle by legislative acts. A broad

[62] And that was one of the aim of the reform of the typology of legal acts. See Final Report of Working Group IX on Simplification, CONV 424/02, 2: 'The democratic legitimacy of the Union is founded on its States and peoples, and consequently an act of a legislative nature must always come from the bodies which represent those States and peoples, namely the Council and the Parliament'.

[63] See Art 10(2) TEU: 'Citizens are directly represented at Union level in the European Parliament'. See also Art 14(2) TEU: 'The European Parliament shall be composed of representatives of the Union's citizens'.

[64] See, insisting on that point, J Bast, 'New Categories of Acts after the Lisbon Reform: Dynamics of Parliamentarization in EU Law' (2012) 49 *Common Market Law Review* 885, 893–94; ibid, 'Legal Instruments and Judicial Protection' in A von Bogdandy and J Bast (eds), *Principles of European Constitutional Law* 2nd edn (Oxford, Hart Publishing, 2011) 392–93.

[65] See Case C-280/11P *Council/Access Info Europe* [2013] EU:C:2013:671, para 33.

spectrum of loyalties and interests is thus allowed to participate in the passage of a legislative act and, hence, to scrutinise and influence its content.

Considering the dialectical relationship between democratic control and judicial review, it could be argued that EU legislative acts henceforth really deserve the protective judicial status they are benefitting from, since legislative acts are now clearly singled out as legal acts emanating from the legislative power embodied by the couple Parliament-Council and provided with a high degree of democratic legitimacy both in its representative and deliberative dimensions.[66] Above all, it could be argued that from the entry into force of the Lisbon Treaty onwards this protective judicial status should be reserved to them. Administrative acts do not reflect the Union's two sources of democratic legitimacy and their decision-making process is not, at least to the same extent, characterised by enhanced transparency, intense public scrutiny and deliberation. Besides, suggestions in that direction have already been made or expectations expressed by the legal scholarship. Some have wondered about the introduction of a difference in the intensity of review between administrative and legislative acts.[67] Others have advocated for limiting the restrictive non-contractual liability regime to legislative acts.[68]

ii. Disappointment

The case law of the Court of Justice has so far not met those expectations. Yet, in one aspect the separation of powers logic underpinning the new categorisation of legal instruments has influenced the case law: the relaxed rules on standing for individuals to bring actions of annulment before the Court of Justice laid down in Article 263(4) TFEU. In its famous *Inuit* judgment,[69] the Court interpreted the notion of 'regulatory act'—the legality of which natural and legal persons may now challenge directly before the Court without having to prove that this act is of individual concern to them—as covering all acts of general application other than legislative acts.[70] The Court took into account the new organic and procedural distinction between legislative and administrative acts and reserved the privileged

[66] On the virtues of deliberative and procedural democracy, see among many others, J Elster (ed), *Deliberative Democracy* (Cambridge, Cambridge University Press 1998); J Habermas, *Between Facts and Norms* (Cambridge, MIT Press, 1996).

[67] See PP Craig, 'Accountability and Judicial Review in the UK and EU' in N Barnforth and P Leyland (eds), *Accountability in the Contemporary Constitution* (Oxford, Oxford University Press, 2013) 197–98; AH Türk, 'The Concept of the "Legislative" Act in the Constitutional Treaty' (2005) 6 *German Law Journal* 1555, 1568.

[68] See, in particular, the suggestion already made in the follow-up of the introduction of the codecision procedure by F Capelli and M Migliazza, 'Recours en indemnité et protection des intérêts individuels: quels sont les changements possibles et souhaitables?' (1995) *Cahiers De Droit Européen* 585. See also, D Ritleng, 'De l'irresponsabilité extracontractuelle de la Communauté' in *Mélanges Philippe Manin* (Paris, Pedone, 2010) 921.

[69] Case C-583/11P *Inuit Tapiriit Kanatami* [2013] EU:C:2013:625.

[70] For an extensive comment, see CF Bergström, 'Defending Restricted Standing for Individuals to Bring Direct Actions Against "Legislative" Measures' (2014) *European Constitutional Law Review* 481.

position in relation to the admissibility of an action of annulment to the sole acts whose legitimacy may now be compared with national parliamentary laws.[71]

It might have been expected that the Court would stand by this line of reasoning and likewise cease to equate administrative acts with legislative acts in relation to the intensity of the legality review and to the conditions of the non-contractual liability of the European Union. But this has hitherto not been the case. Whether the administrative act at issue has been adopted before or after the entry into force of the Lisbon Treaty, which in my view is anyway not decisive,[72] the Court carries on ascribing all of them equally to the will of the 'EU legislature' and subjecting them to the same legality review limited to the search of manifest errors, in order not to interfere with the 'political responsibilities' of the former.[73] One of the standard formulae used in that respect is the following:

> The European Union legislature enjoys a wide discretionary power …, corresponding to the political responsibilities given to it by [the Treaty]. Consequently, judicial review by the Court must be limited to verifying that the measure in question is not vitiated by any manifest error or misuse of powers and that the authority concerned has not manifestly exceeded the limits of its discretionary power.[74]

When recalling the broad discretion which the EU legislature enjoys to adopt legislative acts in a given policy area and the resulting limited intensity of the judicial review, the Court has even referred to previous case law relating to the legality review of implementing measures.[75]

Also on the terrain of the EU's non-contractual liability continues administrative discretion to be likened to legislative discretion.[76] Sometimes, the assimilation is explicit, the Court characterising the discretion granted to the administrative authority as the 'broad discretion enjoyed by the EU legislature'.[77] More often,

[71] See Opinion of AG Kokott in the *Inuit Tapiriit Kanatami* Case [2013] EU:C:2013:21, para 38. See also A Bouveresse, 'De l'incidence des considérations organiques dans le contentieux de la légalité' (2015) *Revue Trimestrielle de Droit Europeen* 63.

[72] An evidence that it is not decisive is given by the *Inuit* case, where the impugned measure was a regulation of the European Parliament and the Council adopted on the 16th September 2009, when the Lisbon Treaty was not applicable yet.

[73] See for instance, concerning implementing measures adopted before the entry into force of the Lisbon Treaty, Case C-213/09 *Barsoum Chabo* [2010] EU:C:2010:716, para 18; Case C-221/09 *AJD Tuna Ltd* [2011] EU:C:2011:153, para 80; and, regarding implementing measures enacted after the entry into force of the Lisbon Treaty, Case T-367/10 *Bloufin Touna Ellas Naftiki Etaireia* [2013] EU:T:2013:97, para 64; Joined Cases T-178, 263 and 265/10 *Spain/Commission* [2012] EU:T:2012:314, para 100.

[74] Case C-221/09 *AJD Tuna Ltd* [2011] EU:C:2011:153, para 80; see also Case T-367/10 *Bloufin Touna Ellas Naftiki Etaireia* [2013] EU:T:2013:97, para 64.

[75] See Case C-343/09 *Afton Chemical Limited* [2010] EU:C:2010:419, para 28, referring to Case C-425/08 *Enviro Tech (Europe)* [2009] ECLI:EU:C:2009:635, para 47.

[76] On the absence of any specificity of the non-contractual liability of the EU for administrative acts as compared with the non-contractual liability of the EU for legislative acts, see L Coutron and F Picod, 'La responsabilité de l'Union européenne du fait de son activité administrative' in J-B Auby and J Dutheil de la Rochère (eds), *Traité de droit administratif européen* 2nd edn (Brussels, Bruylant, 2014) 229.

[77] See Case T-333/10 *ATC/Commission* [2013] EU:T:2013:451, para 64, where a decision and a regulation of the Commission were concerned.

it is implicit and ensues from the fact that the mere unlawfulness of the damaging administrative act, even of individual application, does still not suffice to hold that the condition of a sufficiently serious breach is satisfied. Like in the case of legislative acts, if the author of the damaging administrative act enjoyed a discretionary power, it would be requested that he has manifestly and gravely disregarded the limits on its discretion. This is patent in the case law about administrative measures, most of them enacted after the entry into force of the Lisbon Treaty, emanating from the Commission[78] as well as from the Council,[79] the European Ombudsman,[80] the European Central Bank[81] or the Court of Auditors.[82] As explained by the Court, the requirement of a manifest and grave disregard of the limits on discretion when the author of the damaging administrative act has been conferred a discretionary power

> is intended, whatever the nature of the unlawful act at issue, to avoid the risk of having to bear the losses claimed by the persons concerned obstructing the ability of the institution concerned to exercise to the full its powers in the general interest, whether that be in its legislative activity or in that involving choices of economic policy or in the sphere of its administrative competence.[83]

Or as held by the Court in another instance,

> as regards the legislative activity of the institutions, including the adoption by the ECB of measures of general application, …, it has been held that the strict approach taken towards the liability of the European Union in the exercise of those legislative activities is attributable to two considerations. First, even where the legality of the measures is subject to judicial review, exercise of the legislative function must not be hindered by the prospect of actions for damages whenever the general interest of the European Union requires the adoption of legislative measures that may adversely affect individual interests. Second, in a legislative context characterised by the exercise of a wide discretion, which is essential for implementing an EU policy, the European Union cannot incur liability unless the institution concerned has manifestly and gravely disregarded the limits on the exercise of its powers.[84]

[78] See Case T-45/13 *Rose Vision SL* [2015] EU:T:2015:138, paras 116–17; Joined Cases T-539/12 and 150/13, *Ziegler SA* [2015] EU:T:2015:15, para 94; Case T-317/12 *Holcim (Romania)* [2014] EU:T:2014:782, para 87.

[79] See, regarding implementing regulations of the Council in the CFSP area, Case T-384/11 *Safa Nicu Sepahan* [2014] EU:T:2014:986, paras 49–52; about decisions and regulations of the Council concerning restrictive measures against Iran, Case T-328/14 *Mahmoud Jannatian* [2016] EU:T:2016:86, paras 42–43.

[80] See Case T-217/11 *Claire Staelen* [2015] EU:T:2015:238, paras 70–72.

[81] See, about a decision of the ECB of 2004 refusing to grant access to documents, Case T-436/09 *Julien Dufour* [2011] EU:T:2011:634, para 190; about the decision of the ECB issued in 2012 on the eligibility of marketable debt instruments issued or fully guaranteed by the Hellenic Republic in the context of the Hellenic Republic's debt exchange offer, Case T-79/13 *Accorinti/ECB* [2015] EU:T:2015:756, paras 67–69.

[82] See Case C-220/13P *Kalliopi Nikolaou* [2014] EU:C:2014:2057, para 53.

[83] Case T-384/11 *Safa Nicu Sepahan* [2011] ECLI:EU:T:2011:545, para 51. See also, with a slightly different formulation, Case T-429/05 *Artedogan* [2010] ECLI:EU:T:2010:60, para 55; Case T-333/10 *ATC/Commission* [2014]ECLI:EU:T:2014:842, para 65.

[84] Case T-79/13 *Accorinti/ECB* [2015] ECLI:EU:T:2015:756, para 69.

In conclusion, the setting up by the Lisbon Treaty of a new typology of legal acts based on separation of powers considerations has so far not led to any change in the judicial review of administrative discretion. Administrative discretion continues to be equated with legislative discretion as regards its justification as well as its nature/extent and the intensity of review of its exercise.

C. Should There Be Any Difference at All?

A provocative question could be asked: should ultimately the continuing assimilation of administrative discretion to legislative discretion regarding judicial review of EU legal acts be deplored?

Some authors could certainly put forward good reasons for such a persistent undifferentiated treatment. First, not all legislative acts enjoy genuine parliamentary legitimacy, since some special legislative procedures require only the consultation of the Parliament.[85] Second and more importantly, as pointed out by many commentators,[86] the treaty-makers have not been consistent in their endeavour, inspired by separation of powers considerations, to define what legislation is as opposed to executive action. There are, indeed, procedures laid down in the Treaties that do not constitute special legislative procedures although, like the latter, they associate the Council and the Parliament on an unequal footing with regards to the passage of primary acts. A careful reading of Article 289(2) TFEU reveals that not every procedure which provides for the adoption of a legal act 'by the European Parliament with the participation of the Council, or by the latter with the participation of the European Parliament, shall constitute a special legislative procedure'; it is so only 'in the specific cases provided for by the Treaties'. In other words, if a Treaty provision that provides for the participation of the Parliament and the Council on an unequal footing in the adoption of a legal act does not term this procedure a special legislative procedure, it is not such a procedure and, accordingly, pursuant to Article 289(3) TFEU, the legal act passed on this basis does not constitute a legislative act.[87] Yet, non-legislative procedures providing for the participation of the Parliament and the Council in the adoption of

[85] See for instance, Arts 21(3), 22, 23, 77(3) and 87(3) TFEU.

[86] See especially, P Craig, *The Lisbon Treaty. Law, Politics and Treaty Reform* (Oxford, Oxford University Press, 2010) 256–60; B de Witte, 'Legal Instruments and Law-Making in the Lisbon Treaty' in S Griller and J Ziller (eds), *The Lisbon Treaty—EU Constitutionalism without Constitutional Treaty*, (Vienna, Springer, 2008) 79, 100–01; K Lenaerts and M Desomer, 'Towards a Hierarchy of Legal Acts in the European Union? Simplification of Legal Instruments and Procedures' (2005) 11 *European Law Journal* 744, 753–54 and 764; J Bast, 'New Categories of Acts after the Lisbon Reform: Dynamics of Parliamentarization in EU Law' (2012) 49 *Common Market Law Review* 885, 895–98; D Ritleng, 'Les catégories des actes de l'Union. Réflexions à partir de la catégorie de l'acte législatif de l'Union' in B Bertrand (ed), *Les catégories juridiques du droit de l'Union européenne* (Brussels, Bruylant 2016) 155, at 169–70; D Ritleng, 'La nouvelle typologie des actes de l'Union. Un premier bilan critique de son application' (2015) *Revue Trimestrielle de Droit Europeen* 7, 13–15.

[87] To mention only few examples, see Arts 95(3), 103 and 109 TFEU.

non-legislative primary acts set the same institutional balance as corresponding special legislative procedures do and endow non-legislative primary acts with the same legitimacy as special legislative procedures do for legislative acts. The Council may sometimes even choose to pass under the same procedure either a legislative or a non-legislative act.[88] There need not be any difference between a legislative and an administrative act but legal nominalism.

Those reasons are however not entirely compelling. The formal definition given to legislative acts in the Lisbon Treaty indeed lacks coherence. But why then did the Court take account of it with respect to relaxed rules on standing for individuals to seek the annulment of EU legal measures? It seems here that it is the case law of the Court which falls short of consistence. The Court should have instead built on the efforts made by the treaty-makers to establish a typology of legal acts based on organic and procedural considerations by introducing a distinction between judicial review of administrative discretion and judicial review of legislative discretion. It is all the more so that, as noticed before, only legislative acts are subject to enhanced transparency and increased national parliamentary oversight. Legislative acts present thus in any case a distinctive procedural character, even if its importance may be disputed. That provides arguments for claiming that, in any case, legislative acts bring stronger legitimacy into the process of governance than administrative acts, which should have a bearing on judicial review of both types of act.

To be sure, even if the test for review of legislative and administrative acts is said to be the same, even if the formulae used to define it are identical, the intensity of control may in reality vary. The manifest error is a vague notion under the guise of which the Court of Justice can perform a more or less thorough scrutiny. And it has been contended that judicial review is 'less exhaustive' when the institutions legislate in a given field than when they act in their capacity as administrative authorities.[89] It may be so. That would however not mean that the Court takes sufficient account of the separation of powers absent any difference displayed in the standard of judicial review. The separation of powers requires making visible that the three functions of government in which the exercise of power is divided are distinct in character so as to safeguard the integrity of each.[90] It is all the more so if those functions have been assigned to different authorities or are performed according to different procedures, each of them providing different legitimacy assets. The Court of Justice should therefore show that it pays more deference to legislative action given the greater legitimacy the EU legislature enjoys.

[88] See Arts 349 and 352 TFEU.

[89] See Opinion of AG Léger in Case C-40/03P *Rica Foods* [2005] EU:C:2005:93, paras 44–49; see also his Opinion in Case C-26/00 *Netherlands/Commission* [2005] EU:C:2005:90, paras 44–48. It is however to be noticed that by 'legislation' Advocate General Léger obviously refers to all acts of general application and by 'administration', he means individual measures.

[90] See J Waldron, above n 15.

It might be replied that the higher level of legitimacy enjoyed by legislative acts is already taken into account by the different terms of direct access to EU courts and that, on the other hand, it ought not necessarily be a difference in terms of intensity of review since administrative discretion is as much warranted as legislative discretion. It remains indeed to be ascertained whether in domestic law the protection allowed to legislative acts against judicial control translates always into a difference in the amount of discretion granted and hence in the intensity of review in comparison with administrative acts.[91] Granted, but that administrative discretion is given the same definition and vindication as legislative discretion proves at any rate hard to reconcile with the separation of powers doctrine. The granting of administrative discretion should at least be grounded more on the technical expertise owned by the administration whereas legislative discretion is justified by the political responsibilities and the democratic legitimacy of the legislature. Moreover, this desirable difference in the nature and justification, if not in the amount, of both types of discretion should also lead if not to different conditions for the incurring of the non-contractual liability of the European Union then to a difference in the assessment of those conditions.

II. Judicial Review of Administrative Discretion and Separation of Powers Between the Judge and the Administration

According to settled case law, the European Union judicature allows the enacting authority a margin of discretion when the making of an administrative measure involves complex scientific[92] or economic[93] assessments. As a consequence, the exercise of that discretion is subject to only limited review. Judicial control is thus confined to verifying 'whether the rules on procedure and on the statement of reasons have been complied with, whether the facts have been accurately stated, and, whether there has been any manifest error of assessment or misuse of powers'[94]

[91] See, arguing that there is not any big difference in France, G Vedel, 'Excès de pouvoir administratif et excès de pouvoir législatif' (1997) 1 and 2 *Cahiers du Conseil constitutionnel.*

[92] See for instance, Case C-77/09 *Gowan* [2010] EU:C:2010:803, para 55; Case C-326/05P *Industrias Químicas del Vallés* [2007] EU:C:2007:443, para 75; Case T-326/07 *Cheminova A/S* [2009] EU:T:2009:299, para 106.

[93] See for instance, Case C-62/14 *Gauweiler* [2015] EU:C:2015:400, para 68; Case C-290/07P *Commission/Scott SA* [2010] EU:C:2010:480, para 64; Case C-525/04P *Spain/Commission* [2007] EU:C:2007:698, para 56; Case C-68/94 *France/Commission* [1998] EU:C:1998:148, para 223.

[94] See eg Case 42/84, *Remia* [1985] EU:C:1985:327, para 34; Case C-77/09 *Gowan* [2010] EU:C:2010:803, para 56; Case T-44/90, *La Cinq SA* [1992] EU:T:1992:5, para 85; Case T-413/03 *Shandong Reipu Biochemicals* [2006] EU:T:2006:211, para 62; Case T-541/13 *Albertis Telecom* [2015] EU:T:2015:898, para 122.

or 'whether there has been a manifest error of appraisal or a misuse of powers, or whether [the administrative authorities] have manifestly exceeded the limits of their discretion'.[95] The justification explicitly put forward for the granting of a discretion to the administrative authority and for the consequent limitation of the intensity of the review relates to the separation of powers.[96] It is meant to prevent any encroachment on the province of the administration, which would occur if the judge were to substitute its own appraisal to that of the appointed authority. As repeatedly stated, 'the European Union judicature must not substitute its own [economic] assessment for that of the Commission'.[97] Because it is the 'sole responsibility'[98] of the administrative authority to undertake such complex assessments, it must be afforded a margin of discretion 'to be able to fulfil its tasks'.[99] In other words, the recognition of administrative discretion and the ensuing restriction of the power of review serve the duty, imposed by the separation of powers principle, not to trespass the limits of the judicial mandate and interfere with the tasks entrusted by law to the administration on account of the legitimacy assets (competence, commitment to the general interest) that the latter feeds into governance by examining the merits of the impugned administrative measure.

Set up by the early case law, this stance has since remained unchanged. True, it is often contended that from the 1990s the EU judicature has deepened its intensity of review of administrative discretionary measures.[100] However, it never overtly deviated from the standard of review. Even in cases where the EU Courts performed a more rigorous substantive control, the scrutiny remained always cast in terms of manifest error.[101]

A more in-depth survey of the case law nevertheless reveals that this jurisprudential stance hides differences in the intensity of the control exerted over

[95] See eg Case C-425/08 *Enviro Tech* [2009] EU:C:2009:635, para 47; Case C-14/01 *Molkerei Wagenfeld Karl Niemann* [2003] EU:C:2003:128, para 39; Case C-157/96 *National Farmers' Union* [1998] EU:C:1998:191, para 39; Case T-13/99 *Pfizer Animal Health* [2002] EU:T:2002:209, para 166.

[96] For a thorough account, see Bouveresse, above n 8, 385–400.

[97] See eg Case C-73/11P *Frucona Košice* [2013] EU:C:2013:32, para 75; Case C-290/07P *Commission/Scott SA*, para 66; Case C-525/04P *Spain/Commission*, para 57; Case C-425/08 *Enviro Tech*, para 47; Case T-541/13 *Albertis Telecom* [2015] ECLI:EU:T:2015:898, para 123; T-44/02 OP and alii, *Dresdner Bank* [2006] EU:T:2006:271, para 67.

[98] Case T-13/99 *Pfizer Animal Health* [2002] ECLI:EU:T:2002:209, para 169.

[99] See Case C-269/90 *Technische Universität München* [1991] EU:C:1991:438, para 13; Case T-109/02 *Bolloré SA* [2007] EU:T:2007:115, para 92. Or 'to enable it to accomplish effectively the task entrusted to it' (Case C-77/09 *Gowan* [2010] EU:C:2010:803, para 55).

[100] See notably, P Craig, *EU Administrative Law* 2nd edn (Oxford, Oxford University Press, 2012) 408–39; E. Vos, 'The European Court of Justice in the Face of Scientific Uncertainty and Complexity' in B de Witte and E Muir (eds), *Judicial Activism at the European Court of Justice* (Cheltenham, Edward Elgar Publishing, 2013) 142; C Harlow and R Rawlings, *Process and Procedure in EU Administration* (Oxford, Hart Publishing, 2014) 72.

[101] See eg, regarding merger control decisions, Case T-5/02 *Tetra Laval* [2002] EU:T:2002:264, upheld on appeal in Case C-12/03P *Tetra Laval* [2005] EU:C:2005:87; Case T-342/99 *Airtourss* [2002] EU:T:2002:146. See also, concerning risk regulation about the use of additives in feedingstuffs, Case T-13/99 *Pfizer Animal Health* [2002] ECLI:EU:T:2002:209.

administrative discretionary measures, according to whether they are of general or individual scope (subsection A below). In addition, it is to be questioned if there are, or should be, any differences depending on the holder of administrative discretion and the procedures under which he or she adopts legal acts (subsection B).

A. General or Individual Acts and Judicial Review of Administrative Discretion

The jurisprudential stance recalled above roughly holds true whether administrative adjudication or administrative rule-making is concerned. Under that unique veil are however concealed some differences.

A first difference pertains to the legitimacy assets the European judiciary attributes to the author of the challenged act to justify the recognition of a measure of discretion and the limitation of judicial review. It is only in case of administrative acts of general application that the Court often refers to the 'political responsibilities'[102] conferred on the enacting authority by the Treaties.

A second difference concerns the relationship between formal and procedural requirements and substantive review. To counterbalance administrative discretion whose exercise is not fully reviewable, the EU judicature has subjected the adoption of the act to more stringent formal and procedural constraints. Pursuant to a jurisprudence inaugurated by the *Technische Universität München* judgment, where the administration has a margin of discretion and accordingly the substantive legality of the acts adopted in the exercise of that discretion is subject to only limited review,

> respect for the rights guaranteed by the Community legal order in administrative procedures is of even more fundamental importance. Those guarantees include, in particular, the duty of the competent institution to examine carefully and impartially all the relevant aspects of the individual case, the right of the person concerned to make his views known and to have an adequately reasoned decision.[103]

The reason for such a dialectical relationship resides in the aim of formal and procedural rules, which is to enable the administration to make the best possible discretionary assessments and thus to ensure the substantive legality and, beyond, the merits of its measures.[104] Extended procedural guarantees mainly govern the adoption of individual administrative acts. They have been imposed in particular

[102] See eg Case 265/87 *Schräder* [1989] EU:C:1989:303, para 22; Joined Cases C-254, 255 and 269/94 *Fattoria Autonoma Tabacchi* [1996] EU:C:1996:320, para 56; Joined Cases C-37 and 58/06 *Viamex Agrar Handels* [2008] EU:C:2008:18, para 34; Case C-221/09 *AJD Tuna Ltd* [2011] EU:C:2011:153, para 80; Case T-367/10 *Bloufin Touna Ellas Naftiki Etaireia* [2013] EU:T:2013:97, para 64; Joined Cases T-178, 263 and 265/10 *Spain/Commission* [2012] EU:T:2012:314, para 100.

[103] Case C-269/90 *Technische Universität München* [1991] ECLI:EU:C:1991:438, para 14.

[104] For a reminder of that rationale, see Opinion of AG Bot in Case C-584/10P *Kadi II* [2013] EU:C:2013:176, para 97.

on discretionary decisions relating to duty-free imports,[105] competition,[106] state aids[107] or antidumping duties.[108]

A third difference relates to the intensity of substantive review. Though in both cases the test used for review of discretion remains formally the same, namely a review confined to manifest error, the Courts are said to carry out a looser substantive review of administrative rule-making than of administrative acts of individual application.[109]

Viewed in the light of the separation of powers principle, those differences appear hard to justify. As already pointed out, the reference made to its 'political responsibilities' to warrant the grant of a discretion to the enacting authority in case of administrative rule-making is due to an assimilation of the latter to proper legislation, which is fallacious from an organic and procedural point of view and hence in terms of the level of legitimacy enjoyed by administrative acts of general application and legislative acts respectively. Furthermore, whether they act in their adjudicative capacity or in their rule-making capacity, administrative bodies usually draw on the same legitimacy bases. In particular, the legitimacy inputs provided by the decision-making process under which the European Commission adopts administrative acts of individual application or administrative rules are the same (with the exception of delegated acts since the entry into force of the Lisbon Treaty). The adoption of both types of act is governed by the principle of collegiality and subject to the comitology system. It is indeed established case law that the concept of implementation to which the comitology system applies 'comprises both the drawing-up of implementing rules and the application of rules to specific cases by means of acts of individual application'.[110] As an example, the merger control decisions are to be adopted by the Commission after consultation of an Advisory Committee on concentrations composed of representatives of the competent authorities of the Member States and likewise implementing provisions of

[105] See Case C-269/90 *Technische Universität München* [1991] ECLI:EU:C:1991:438, para 14; Case T-346/94 *France-Aviation* [1995] EU:T:1995:187, paras 32–34.

[106] See eg Case T-44/90 *La Cinq SA* [1992] EU:T:1992:5, para 86; Case T-109/02 *Bolloré SA* [2007] EU:T:2007:115, para 92.

[107] See eg Case C-525/04P *Spain/Commission* [2007] EU:C:2007:698, para 58; Case T-541/13 *Albertis Telecom* [2015] EU:T:2015:898, para 123.

[108] As is well known, antidumping duties are imposed by regulations which at the same time concern individually the persons affected: see eg Case T-167/94 *Nölle* [1995] EU:T:1995:169, para 73; Case T-413/03*Shandong Reipu Biochemicals* [2006] EU:T:2006:211, para 63.

[109] See AH Türk, 'Oversight of Administrative Rulemaking: Judicial Review' (2013) 19 *European Law Journal* 126, 136–41. See also Case C-150/94 *United Kingdom/Council* [1998] EU:C:1998:547, para 54, in which the Court of Justice stated that limited judicial review of discretion is all the more required in instances where the act concerned is of general application. See also Opinions of AG Léger in Case C-40/03P *Rica Foods* [2005] ECLI:EU:C:2005:455, paras 44–49, and in Case C-26/00 *Netherlands/Commission*, paras 44–48.

[110] Case 16/88 *Commission/Council* [1989] EU:C:1989:397, para 11; Case C-440/14P *NIOC/Council* [2016] EU:C:2016:128, para 36.

the merger control regulation must be passed after consultation of an Advisory Committee composed of representatives of the Member States.[111]

That is why it is to rejoice that those differences in the breadth of discretion and in the judicial review between individual and general administrative acts tend to narrow in the recent case law. First, the regime of non-contractual liability of the European Union does not differ depending on whether the damaging administrative act is of individual or general application. In both cases the condition of a sufficiently serious breach of a rule of law intended to confer rights on individuals is required and, for that condition to be met, the decisive criterion is whether the EU institution concerned manifestly and gravely disregarded the limits on its discretion, in the cases in which the author of the act has discretion.[112] Second, the case law on the strengthening of the procedural guarantees in return for the grant of a discretionary power to the administration has been extended to administrative rule-making. EU Courts have thus shown no reluctance to apply the duty of careful and impartial examination of all the relevant factual elements also in procedures leading to the adoption of administrative discretionary acts of general application. This principle has been applied in administrative proceedings dealing with risk regulation concerning additives in feedingsstuff,[113] plantprotection products,[114] as well as classification, packaging and labelling of dangerous substances[115] and the regulation of the common agricultural policy[116] or the implementation of the monetary policy.[117] Admittedly, not all procedural requirements governing the passage of discretionary decisions have been extended to administrative rule-making. The EU courts have refused to transpose the right to a fair hearing to the context of proceedings leading to the adoption of discretionary acts of general application, be they of legislative[118] or administrative[119] nature. But this is because that rights-based procedural standard appears impractical in a procedure culminating in the enactment of administrative rules, which are not based on individual determinations and affect a large number of people.[120]

[111] See respectively, Arts 19 and 23 of Council Reg (EC) no 139/2004 of 20 January 2004 on the control of concentrations between undertakings.

[112] See for instance, Case T-351/03 *Schneider Electric* [2007] ECLI:EU:T:2007:212, paras 113–26, concerning a procedure for examination of the compatibility with the common market of a concentration.

[113] See Case T-13/99 *Pfizer Animal Health* [2002] ECLI:EU:T:2002:209, para 171.

[114] See Case C-326/05P *Industrias Químicas del Vallés* [2007] EU:C:2007:443, para 77; Case T-326/07 *Cheminova A/S* [2009] EU:T:2009:299, para 228; Case C-77/09 *Gowan* [2010] EU:C:2010:803, para 57.

[115] See Case T-369/03 *Arizona Chemical* [2005] EU:T:2005:458, para 85; Case C-425/08 *Enviro Tech* [2009] EU:C:2009:635, para 62.

[116] See Case T-285/03 *Agraz and others v Commission* [2005] EU:T:2005:109, paras 49–50.

[117] See Case C-62/14 *Gauweiler* [2015] EU:C:2015:400, para 69.

[118] See Case T-521/93 *Atlanta* [1996] EU:T:1996:184, paras 70–71. On appeal the Court of Justice upheld the position of the General Court (see Case C-104/97P *Atlanta* [1999] EU:C:1999:498, paras 37–38).

[119] See Case T-13/99 *Pfizer Animal Health* [2002] ECLI:EU:T:2002:209, para 487; Case T-369/03, *Arizona Chemical* [2005] ECLI:EU:T:2005:458, paras 51 and 73.

[120] See AH Türk, above n 109, 128–32.

Unsurprisingly therefore, this jurisprudential stance is supported by Article 41(2) of the Charter of Fundamental Rights, which confines the right to a fair hearing to individual measures. Third, the intensity of the substantive review performed over discretionary acts of general scope has increased, at least when the protection of fundamental rights is at stake. The Court of Justice has indeed given up the deference traditionally observed in this regard.[121] It has ruled that, 'where interferences with fundamental rights are at issue', discretion is reduced, 'with the result that review of that discretion should be strict'.[122] As a result, the standard of review has changed: the scrutiny of compliance with fundamental rights is not confined anymore to the search of manifest errors but tends henceforth to detect any error of appraisal, irrespective of whether the challenged general measure is of administrative[123] or legislative[124] nature.

B. Decision-maker, Enactment Procedures and Judicial Review of Administrative Discretion

If taking the separation of powers doctrine seriously, any effort to draw the line between what falls in the realm of judicial review and what comes under administrative discretion leads to query whether the frontier is or should be the same whoever is the holder of administrative authority. Indeed, as already recalled, according to the separation of powers doctrine, public authority is to be distributed among the different institutions in connection to their legitimacy assets.[125] In that regard, it is usually taken for granted that expertise and competence legitimate the authority of the administration. But beyond that, as democracy is today the main source of legitimacy, it could be assumed that the extent of the discretionary power granted to an administrative body correlates with the level of democratic legitimacy it may also claim. More precisely, as democratic legitimacy should lead to a differentiation in the amount of discretion allowed to the legislature and the administration respectively, the amount of administrative discretion and the

[121] Which had aroused harsh criticisms: see in particular, U Everling, 'Will Europe Slip on Bananas? The Bananas Judgment of the Court of Justice and National Courts' (1996) 33 *Common Market Law Review* 401.

[122] Joined Cases C-293/12 and C-594/12 *Digital Rights Ireland* [2014] EU:C:2014:238, paras 47–48. For a comment, see MP Granger and K Irion, 'The Court of Justice and the Data Retention Directive in Digital Rights Ireland: Telling Off the EU Legislator and Teaching a Lesson in Privacy and Data Protection' (2014) *European Law Review* 835.

[123] See eg Case C-362/14, *Schrems* [2015] EU:C:2015:650, paras 67–106; see already, for another example of strict scrutiny, Joined Cases C-92 and 93/09 *Volker* [2010] EU:C:2010:662, in which both the enabling provisions of a basic Council regulation and the Commission implementing regulation were challenged.

[124] See Joined Cases C-293/12 and C-594/12 *Digital Rights Ireland* [2014] ECLI:EU:C:2014:238; for previous examples of review not limited to the search of manifest errors, see Case C-236/09 *Test-Achats* [2011] EU:C:2011:100; Case C-291/12 *Schwarz* [2013] EU:C:2013:670.

[125] See Möllers, above n 1.

ensuing limitation of judicial review should vary in accord with the link of the authority of the administrative body concerned to the people's will in whose name it is exercised. To put it differently, the extent of discretion allowed to an administrative body ought to be commensurate to the level of democratic legitimacy given to it by its mode of appointment, the extent of its political accountability and the procedures according to which it makes decisions.

i. Delegated and Implementing Acts

To assess whether this is the case, let us focus first on the divide introduced by the Lisbon Treaty between two categories of non-legislative acts, the delegated and implementing acts.[126] Pursuant to Article 290 TFEU, the EU legislator may delegate to the Commission the power 'to supplement or amend certain non-essential elements of the legislative act' whereas, by virtue of Article 291(2) TFEU, 'where uniform conditions for implementing legally binding Union acts are needed, those acts shall confer implementing powers on the Commission, or, in duly justified specific cases ..., on the Council'. The difficulty of the distinction between the two species of act was said to reside in the difference between 'supplementing' and 'implementing' a legislative act.[127] Implementation is, indeed, meant to be a normative activity, that is an activity consisting of the passage of legally binding acts. It is therefore very difficult to conceive of any implementing act that does not entail some addition to the normative framework defined by the legislative act and hence that does not in some manner supplement that legislative act. A consensus had nonetheless emerged, according to which a legislative delegation was supposed to leave a greater margin of discretion to the Commission than a conferral of implementing powers.[128] Such a criterion presents the advantage to be in line with the democratic legitimacy bases on which delegated and implementing acts respectively rest. Indeed, delegated acts remain within the sphere of EU legislation and still benefit, albeit to a lesser extent, from the democratic legitimacy conveyed by EU legislation. For their part, implementing acts belong to the area of execution and enjoy only the legitimacy attached to the exercise of that function. That is what transpires from the different supervision and accountability mechanisms which operate in relation to the two types of acts. Whereas only the EU legislator may give a legislative delegation whose exercise will be subject

[126] For an analysis, see Bergström and Ritleng (eds), above n 57.

[127] See P Craig, 'Delegated Acts, Implementing Acts and the New Comitology Regulation' (2011) 36 *European Law Review* 671, 672–74.

[128] See Commission Communication of 9 December 2009, 'Implementation of Article 290 of the Treaty on the Functioning of the European Union' COM (2009) 673 final, 3; European Parliament's Report on follow-up on the delegation of legislative powers and control by Member States of the Commission's exercise of implementing powers, 4 December 2013, A7-0435/2013, point 1; Opinion of AG Cruz Villalón in Case C-427/12 *Commission/Parliament and Council (Biocides)* [2013] EU:C:2013:871, para 62; J-P Jacqué, 'Introduction: Pouvoir Législatif et Pouvoir Exécutif dans l'Union européenne' in J-B Auby and J Dutheil de la Rochère (eds), *Traité de droit administratif européen* 2nd edn (Brussels, Bruylant, 2007) 19, 36–37.

to its control specified in Article 290 TFEU,[129] implementing powers may be conferred even by non-legislative acts and Article 291(2) TFEU provides for supervision, *via* the comitology system,[130] of the adoption of implementing measures by the Member States, which are normally responsible for implementation (Article 291(1) TFEU). So while the compared levels of democratic legitimacy plead in favour of the recognition of a greater margin of discretion in case of a legislative delegation, it could conversely be argued that oversight by the legislature of the Commission's measures through the mechanisms provided in Article 290 TFEU is only meaningful—and hence recourse to legislative delegation lawful—where the Commission exercises a wide margin of discretion.[131]

Were it only for those legitimacy considerations, expectations could be nourished that the margin of appreciation would be judicially endorsed as the dividing criterion between delegated and implementing measures. But the Court of Justice did not fulfil these expectations. When it first ruled on this issue, the Court of Justice did not explicitly provide for a criterion distinguishing between supplementation and implementation. It limited itself to noting that implementing acts tend 'to provide further detail in relation to the content of a legislative act' whereas a delegated act aims at setting up 'rules coming within the regulatory framework as defined by the … legislative act'.[132] That is of very little help, for a measure which provides further detail to the content of a legislative act sets up rules completing the regulatory framework defined by the legislative act. It had, however, been argued that the application of those elusive formulae made by the Court of Justice in the *Biocides* case amounted in some manner to look for the degree of discretion left to the Commission.[133] Whether that reading could be reasonably sustained or not, it was in any event overruled less than one year later. In the *Visa Reciprocity* case, the Court of Justice specified that 'neither the existence nor the extent of the discretion conferred on it by the legislative act is relevant for determining whether

[129] So as to ensure respect of the principle of democracy: see Opinion of AG Mengozzi in Case C-88/14 *Commission/Parliament and Council* [2015] EU:C:2015:304, para 45, which noticed that supervision by the legislature of the exercise of a legislative delegation tends to 'counterbalance the derogation from the principle of the separation of powers … inherent in the legislative act providing for the delegation, and thus to ensure strict observance of the principle of democracy affirmed in EU law'.

[130] See, adopted on the legal basis of Art 291(3) TFEU, Reg 182/2011 of the European Parliament and of the Council of 16 February 2011 laying down the rules and general principles concerning mechanisms for control by Member States of the Commission's exercise of implementing powers [2011] OJ L55/13.

[131] See Opinion of AG Mengozzi in Case C-88/14 *Commission/Parliament and Council* [2015] ECLI:EU:C:2015:499, para 45.

[132] Case C-427/12 *Commission/Parliament and Council (Biocides)* [2014] EU:C:2014:170, paras 38–39. For a comment, see D Ritleng, 'The Dividing Line between Delegated and Implementing Acts: The Court of justice Sidesteps the Difficulty' (2015) 52 *Commnon Market Law Review* 243; M Chamon, 'Clarifying the Divide between Delegated and Implementing Acts?' (2015) 42 *Legal Issues of Economic Integration* 175.

[133] Ritleng ibid, 252; Opinion of AG Mengozzi in Case C-88/14 *Commission/Parliament and Council* [2015] ECLI:EU:C:2015:499, paras 25–26.

the act to be adopted by the Commission comes under Article 290 TFEU or Article 291 TFEU'.[134]

ii. Legal Acts of EU Agencies

How much discretion may be granted to EU decentralised agencies? This issue has become a critical and much debated one as the EU institutional system has experienced an impressive process of agencification. Not only their number but also the policy fields wherein they operate and the tasks and powers they are entrusted with have markedly increased and diversified. The arguments for recourse to those non-majoritarian bodies lie in the conviction that, given their insulation from partisan politics and electoral concerns, they are better able to carry out tasks requiring expertise in highly complex and technical matters. The legitimacy of EU agencies is thus output-oriented, it rests in their problem-solving capacity.[135] At the same time, at least two reasons would militate against the transfer of important decision-making powers to their benefit: the creation and the delegation of powers to those non-majoritarian bodies cannot be relied on an explicit provision in the founding Treaties and thus are not constitutionally legitimised; while power shall go hand in hand with responsibility, the EU agencies are neither democratically elected nor politically accountable.[136]

It may therefore be deemed right that the Court of Justice originally denied agencies discretionary decision-making powers. They can only, ruled the Court, be vested with 'clearly defined executive powers the exercise of which can, therefore, be subject to strict review in the light of the objective criteria determined by the delegating authority'.[137] And the Court grounded this limit put to delegation of powers to agencies on the principle of institutional balance, which would be distorted by the granting of discretionary powers since it would replace the choices of the delegator by the choices of the delegate and thus bring about an actual transfer of responsibility.[138] The understanding of the *Meroni* doctrine[139] commonly spread was that 'agencies cannot be given the power to adopt general regulatory measures. They are limited to taking individual decisions in specific areas where a defined technical expertise is required, under clearly and precisely defined conditions and without genuine discretionary power'.[140]

[134] Case C-88/14 *Commission/Parliament and Council* [2015] EU:C:2015:499, para 32. For a comment, see M Chamon, 'The Dividing Line between Delegated and Implementing Acts, Part Two: The Court of Justice Settles the Issue in Commission v Parliament and Council (Visa reciprocity)' (2015) 52 *Common Market Law Review* 1617; ARS van der Mei, 'Delegation of Rulemaking Powers to the European Commission post-Lisbon' (2016) 12 *European Competition Law Review* 538.

[135] See G Majone, *Regulating Europe* (London, Routledge, 1996).

[136] See for an in-depth assessment of the accountability of EU agencies, M Busuioc, *European Agencies: Law and Practices of Accountability* (Oxford, Oxford University Press, 2013).

[137] Case 9/56 *Meroni* [1958] EU:C:1958:7, 152.

[138] ibid.

[139] Supplemented by the *Romano* ruling (see Case 98/80 {1981] EU:C:1981:104).

[140] Communication from the Commission to the European Parliament and the Council 'European agencies—The way forward' COM (2008) 135 final, 5.

In recent years however, the *Meroni* doctrine has been increasingly seen as a hindrance to the needs of EU governance, in particular the exigencies of regulating complex matters. Pleas have been advanced to give it up or at least to relax it.[141]

In the *ESMA* case,[142] the Court of Justice for the first time allowed the EU legislature to endow EU agencies with rule-making powers. It held that the system for delegation of powers set out in Articles 290 and 291 TFEU must not be seen as 'a single legal framework under which certain delegated and executive powers may be attributed solely to the Commission'; 'other systems for the delegation of such powers to Union bodies, offices or agencies may be contemplated by the Union legislature'.[143] Admittedly, the Court still subjected the delegation of powers to EU agencies to the respect of the *Meroni* doctrine but the reading of it was much less constraining. Indeed, the Court acknowledged that the ESMA (European Securities and Markets Authority) has been granted a 'margin of discretion' for the purposes of the exercise of its rule-making powers; it however found that that margin of discretion is limited by the conditions and criteria laid down by the enabling legislative provision supplemented by a delegated act, so that the rule-making powers available to ESMA are 'precisely delineated and amenable to judicial review in the light of the objectives established by the delegating authority'.[144] Nevertheless, it follows from the recognition of a margin of discretion that, as a matter of principle, only limited judicial review should be performed.[145]

The granting of such a margin of discretion to the ESMA is explicitly legitimised by the 'high degree'[146] of technical and professional expertise possessed by that body, whose deployment is required to take the measures necessary to cope with adverse developments which threaten financial stability within the Union and market confidence. It may however be questioned whether those legitimacy

[141] See especially, S Griller and A Orator, 'Everything Under Control? The "Way Forward" for European Agencies in the Footsteps of the Meroni Doctrine' (2010) 35 *European Law Review* 3; T Zwart, 'La poursuite du Père Meroni ou pourquoi les agences pourraient jouer un rôle plus en vue dans l'Union européenne' in J Dutheil de la Rochère (ed), *L'exécution du droit de l'Union, entre mécanismes communautaires et droits nationaux* (Brussels, Bruylant, 2009) 159. For an extensive account of the debate, see M Chamon, *EU Agencies. Legal and Political Limits to the Transformation of the EU Administration* (Oxford, Oxford University Press, 2016) 192–207.

[142] Case C-270/12 *United Kingdom/Parliament and Council (ESMA)* [2014] EU:C:2014:18. For a comment, see CF Bergström, 'Shaping the New System for Delegation of Powers to EU Agencies' (2015) 52 *Common Market Law Review* 219; B Bertrand, 'La compétence des agences pour prendre des actes normatifs: le dualisme des pouvoirs d'exécution' (2015) *Revue Trimestrielle de Droit Europeen* 21.

[143] Case C-270/12 *United Kingdom/Parliament and Council* [2014] ECLI:EU:C:2014:18, paras 78–83.

[144] ibid, paras 45–53.

[145] See Case T-187/06 *Schräder/CPVO* [2008] EU:T:2008:511, paras 60–62, concerning the intensity of review of the acts of the Community Plant Variety Office.

[146] Case C-270/12 *United Kingdom/Parliament and Council* [2014] ECLI:EU:C:2014:18, para 85. See also Opinion of AG Jääskinen in Case C-270/12 *United Kingdom/Parliament and Council* [2013] ECLI:EU:C:2013:562, para 99: 'the need to make such technically difficult assessments on an objective and non-political basis is an argument in support of conferral of the powers concerned on an expert agency rather than on the Commission'.

assets are sufficient to that effect. The discretionary powers attributed to the ESMA are actually far-reaching. They entail not only complex technical and factual assessments but also policy considerations in that they prompt the ESMA to balance competing public interests,[147] while in *Meroni* the Court ruled that the task of reconciling conflicting objectives implied discretionary powers which could not be delegated.[148] As Advocate General Jääskinen noticed,

> the closest analogy in EU law to the ESMA's powers under Article 28 of Regulation 236/2012 is provided by the Commission intervention powers in the field of agriculture and anti-dumping, that is in areas where the Commission implements a common EU policy.[149]

Yet, in view of the modes of appointment and the political answerability, Union agencies obviously enjoy less legitimacy than the Commission.[150] Moreover, the delegation of powers they may be recipients of 'does not correspond to any of the situations defined in Articles 290 TFEU and 291 TFEU'[151] and its exercise is therefore not subject to the supervision mechanisms provided for in those provisions. To be sure, Advocate General Jääskinen was of the view that a legislative delegation may not be lawfully accorded to EU agencies on the account of the principle of democracy, which

> necessarily dictates that any power to adopt an EU measure that can alter the non-essential elements of an EU legislative act must be exercised by an EU institution that is democratically accountable, in other words by the Commission, which is ultimately accountable to the European Parliament.[152]

And it is to be underscored that, in the case at hand, the conditions and criteria imposed by the enabling legislative provision on the exercise of the rule-making powers delegated to the ESMA had been further elaborated by a delegated act. But the Court of Justice seems to have not excluded it: 'such powers' which, according to the Court, may be delegated by the Union legislature to agencies referred to 'delegated and executive powers'.[153] In any event, the Union legislature is entitled to vest agencies with at least implementing powers of the same extent as those which may be conferred on the Commission under Article 291 TFEU, whose exercise will not fall under the control of the Member States performed in keeping with the comitology system.

[147] See J Mendes, 'Discretion, Care and Public Interests in the EU Administration: Probing the Limits of Law' (2016) 53 *Common Market Law Review* 419.

[148] See Case 9/56 *Meroni* [1958] ECLI:EU:C:1958:7, 152.

[149] Opinion in Case C-270/12 *United Kingdom/Parliament and Council* [2014] ECLI:EU:C:2014:18, para 45.

[150] See, regarding the Commission, Art 17(7) and (8) TEU.

[151] Case C-270/12 *United Kingdom/Parliament and Council* [2014] ECLI:EU:C:2014:18, para 83.

[152] ibid, para 85.

[153] ibid, para 78.

iii. Legal Acts of the European Central Bank

The European Central Bank (ECB) has been recognised a 'broad discretion' since, according to the EU Courts, the fulfilment of the tasks assigned to it for the purposes of framing and implementing the EU monetary policy compels the ECB to undertake 'complex evaluations of an economic and social nature and of rapidly-changing situations, which must be carried out in the context of the Eurosystem, or even of the European Union as a whole'[154] or 'to make choices of a technical nature and to undertake forecasts and complex assessments'.[155]

As a consequence, the Court of Justice exerted only a limited review of the proportionality of the bond-buying programme called the Outright Monetary Transactions (OMT) programme to the objectives of the monetary policy. The Court limited itself to verifying that the analysis of the economic situation on the basis of which the ECB estimated the OMT programme appropriate was not 'vitiated by a manifest error of assessment' and that, considering that economic situation, the ECB 'could legitimately take the view' that the OMT programme was appropriate for the purposes of contributing to the European System of Central Bank (ESCB)'s objectives and, therefore, to maintaining price stability. It checked, then, whether such a programme 'does not go manifestly beyond what is necessary to achieve those objectives' and whether the disadvantages which the implementation of the programme might involve are 'manifestly disproportionate' to the programme's objectives.[156]

The grant of a 'broad discretion' to the ECB also has consequences in terms of liability of the Union. A sufficiently serious breach of a superior rule of law intended to confer rights on individuals, which is required for the Union to incur liability, is considered to be established only if the ECB has manifestly and seriously disregarded the limits on its discretion, that is has committed a 'manifest and serious failure'.[157] That is, observed the General Court,

> even more true because the exercise of that discretion implies the need for the ECB to foresee and evaluate complex and uncertain economic developments, such as the development of capital markets, the monetary mass and the rate of inflation, which affect the proper functioning of the Eurosystem and payment and credit systems, and also to make political, economic and social choices in which it is required to weigh up and decide between the different objectives referred to in Article 127(1) TFEU, the main objective of which is the maintenance of price stability.[158]

[154] Case T-79/13 *Accorinti/ECB* [2015] EU:T:2015:756, para 68.
[155] Case C-62/14 *Gauweiler* [2015] EU:C:2015:400, para 68.
[156] ibid, paras 72–92.
[157] Case T-79/13 *Accorinti/ECB* [2015]EU:T:2015:756, para 68.
[158] ibid.

How may that protection against judicial review, which is tantamount to that accorded to legislative acts, be warranted? The vindication resides in the complexity of the task of framing and implementing the monetary policy assigned to the ECB, which requires a high level of technical expertise. The same justification holds for the status of independence constitutionally granted to the ECB (Article 130 TFEU): independence is meant to enable the ECB to use its expertise free from political pressure with a view to achieving more effectively the primary objective of maintaining price stability.[159] Moreover, the ECB draws democratic legitimacy from the fact that its mandate is conferred by the Treaty, which has been democratically ratified by all Member States. Yet, at the same time, the independence of the ECB removes the policy-making in the area falling under its jurisdiction from democratic legitimation. Broad discretion should therefore only be allowed to the ECB with the aim of fulfilling a narrowly defined mandate,[160] normally related to technical competencies and clearly stated objectives. Nevertheless, in the *Gauweiler* case, the Court of Justice endorsed the extensive interpretation of its mandate, developed by the ECB itself; gave the latter broad discretion for the needs of the exercise of its widely defined mandate; and, accordingly, upheld the legality of the OMT decision after having performed only light touch review. At the same time, the Court neglected to give any reply to the democratic argument that had been raised by the German Constitutional Court in its preliminary reference.[161]

III. Conclusion

The separation of powers thinking clearly leads EU Courts to observe a certain self-restraint. With a view to remaining within the boundaries of its judicial mandate (ie ensuring that 'the law is observed' (Article 19 TEU)) and to avoid encroaching on the domains of the legislature and of the administration reserved to them on account of their specific legitimacy assets, the Court of Justice leaves both a margin of discretion and accordingly exerts only limited review of legislative and administrative acts.

The influence of the separation of powers on judicial review of administrative discretion does however not extend beyond this first observation. The Court of

[159] See Case C-11/00 *Commission/ECB* [2003] EU:C:2003:395, para 134; Case C-62/14 *Gauweiler* [2015] ECLI:EU:C:2015:400 para 40; Opinion of AG Cruz Villalón in Case C-62/14 *Gauweiler* [2015] EU:C:2015:7, paras 108–11.

[160] See the argumentation of the German constitutional Court (FCC, Case 2 BvR 2728/13, 14 janv 2014, *OMT*, judgment of 14 January 2014).

[161] Something which has been explicitly deplored by the German constitutional Court (see FCC, Case 2 BvR 2728/13, *OMT*, judgment, of 21 June 2016, paras 187–90).

Justice does not correlate the amount of discretion recognised to the legislature and to the administration, respectively, with the distinct legitimacy assets that each of them may claim. Nor does it do so with regard to the discretion allowed to the different EU administrative bodies. More precisely, although representative democracy is today viewed as the main source of legitimation of the European Union,[162] the democratic legitimacy the holders of public authority draw from their composition, organisation and procedures does not translate into differences in the extent of discretion granted to them and in the intensity of judicial review of their acts.

[162] See art 10(1) TEU: 'The functioning of the Union shall be founded on representative democracy'.

10

First or Second Best? Judicial Law-making in European Private Law

CHANTAL MAK*

'It is true that we cannot be visionaries until we become realists. It is also true that to become realists we must make ourselves into visionaries.'
Roberto Mangabeira Unger[1]

I. European Courts in Times of Societal Change

Is it possible to imagine a constellation in which courts sometimes are in a better position than legislatures to contribute to the democratic legitimation of new rules of private law? How can, for instance, the interaction of national courts and the Court of Justice of the European Union (CJEU) in the continuing series of Spanish mortgage cases be explained and maybe justified? In theoretical models of a constitutional division of powers, courts perform different functions. Courts are, in the first place, responsible for the interpretation and application of the law, especially in the civil law tradition of the European continent.[2] In the second place, the judiciary may have a certain role in processes of shaping new rules. The question is, however, what this law-making role is or should be in a democratic legal system. The task of defining policy objectives and translating these to the

* I wish to thank Laura Burgers, Anna van Duin, Joasia Luzak and the participants to the workshops organised within the framework of the project 'The architecture of post-national rulemaking' for their comments on earlier versions of this paper. All remaining errors are of course mine.

[1] RM Unger, 'Legal Analysis as Institutional Imagination' (1996) 59 *The Modern Law Review* 1, 23.

[2] J Habermas, *Between Facts and Norms* (Cambridge, Polity Press, 1996) 172–73, distinguishes discourses of justification (in legislative processes) from discourses of application (in adjudication); A Stone Sweet, *Governing with Judges* (Oxford, Oxford University Press, 2000); Compare C Möllers, *The Three Branches: A Comparative Model of Separation of Powers* (Oxford, Oxford University Press, 2013) 130–31.

legal framework is primarily assigned to the legislature, which assesses societal needs and develops longer-term programmes rather than case-by-case solutions. The legislature thus provides democratic legitimacy to law-making, since the legislative process involves representative bodies (such as a Parliament) that give a voice to and are accountable to those who will be governed by the rules coming out of this process.[3] The judiciary, on the other hand, would not be able to rely on such legitimacy and should, therefore, in principle not enter into the consideration of policy argumentation and the making of new rules.[4] Any legal system exclusively assigning certain law-making tasks to the judiciary would, from such a theoretical perspective, offer a second-best solution in terms of democratic legitimacy.

In this chapter, the contribution that the judiciary can make to the democratic legitimacy of rules of European private law will be assessed from three perspectives: reconstructive theory, legal realism and democratic experimentalism. It will be argued that a reconstructive theoretical model of constitutionalism does not seem to be able to fully explain nor normatively guide the current interaction among legal institutions in the field of European private law, understood as comprising the interplay of national and supranational rules governing legal relations among private actors in the European Union (EU). Especially in times of societal change, such as the handling of the economic crisis that the EU is going through, courts assume a different type of legal-political role, which places them in a position to sometimes respond to developments in a more effective manner than the legislature. Paradoxically, as I will demonstrate, this does not necessarily diminish the democratic legitimacy of rule-making in European private law, and may even enhance it. The empowerment of national judiciaries in respect to legislatures opens new possibilities for citizens' access to the deliberation of value and policy choices and the translation of these choices into new rules of European private law, as a legal-realist assessment will show. Judicial interaction in private law then provides opportunities for democratic experimentalism. Under these circumstances, the judiciary's second-best position in terms of democratic legitimacy may be the least imperfect or even best option available in a multi-level institutional constellation. Still, this type of experimentalism has certain drawbacks, as its procedural nature does not guarantee that outcomes will comply with more substantive notions of justice. Accordingly, the conception of democratic legitimacy in European private law requires rethinking.

[3] FW Scharpf, 'Economic Integration, Democracy and the Welfare State' (1997) 4 *Journal of European Public Policy* 18, 19.

[4] In this sense, R Dworkin, *Taking Rights Seriously* (London, Duckworth, 1977; fourth impression with a Reply to Critics, London, Duckworth, 1984); R Dworkin, *Law's Empire* (Cambridge, MA, Belknap Press, 1986).

II. Institutional Constraints: Dividing Powers among Legislatures and Judiciaries

A. Constitutionalism and Private Law in Europe

European private law involves a variety of actors on different levels of governance, who together define the legal framework within which private actors (individuals and businesses) interact. At EU level, legislative tasks have been assigned to the European Commission, European Parliament and Council, whereas questions regarding the interpretation and application of EU law are to be addressed to the Court of Justice of the EU. At the national level of the Member States, rules of private law are enacted in legislation and enforced through court systems, where common law countries traditionally leave courts in civil cases more leeway to develop new rules than civil law countries. Together, these bodies form the institutional structure within which private law develops.

Apart from the mandatory and default rules provided by EU Treaty provisions, Regulations and Directives and Member States' private laws, private actors have, moreover, an important role in setting the rules governing their relationships, in particular insofar as they contractually establish the terms of their engagement. On this point, questions of European private law are distinct from those in (institutional) European public law. While private law relies on the institutional framework defined in public law for its enactment and enforcement, it is also concerned with the outcomes of cases in light of party autonomy. It matters whether a certain contract is considered to be valid or not, how its terms are interpreted and which remedies are available upon non-performance. Respect for the autonomy of private actors requires careful consideration of the substantive boundaries to their interactions that are determined in the legal rules that govern their relationships. Law-making in the field of European private law, thus, has to take into account both public and private autonomy. Public autonomy, in a Habermasian sense, concerns the idea of self-legislation by citizens, according to which those who are subject to certain rules (as addressees) also participate in their enactment (as authors).[5] Private autonomy regards the sphere within which legal subjects are free to make their own choices, without having to justify their decisions to others or give publicly acceptable reasons for their action plans.[6] The question then is how—substantively and procedurally—and by which institutions—national and European—the borderlines to private autonomy are determined in a process that allows private actors to participate in the development of the rules of European private law that define those boundaries.

[5] Habermas, above n 2, 120–21, 123.
[6] ibid, 120.

Constitutional theory has sought to make sense of the interaction among legal institutions in Europe by exploring the monistic and pluralistic features of the EU's multi-level legal order. Some constitutional models aspire to relate all rule-solutions within the scope of EU law to one overarching set of values or principles, which would, thus, indicate a hierarchy among EU and national legislatures and courts.[7] Other models accommodate the plurality of values and principles underlying legal rules by either accepting the incommensurability or irreconcilability of these values and principles (and shifting the choice to the political process),[8] or trying to define meta-principles that determine which value or principle and which institution should decide a specific case.[9]

Private law theory is exploring similar themes, especially in light of the principle of freedom of contract that underlies national and supranational rules of contract law.[10] This investigation relates to the constitutional debate, in particular insofar as the CJEU has included freedom of contract in the scope of the freedom to conduct a business safeguarded by Article 16 of the EU Charter of Fundamental Rights (eg CJEU *Sky Österreich*[11] and CJEU *Alemo-Herron*[12]). A constitutional analysis of the place of private law in the EU's legal order advocates the importance of not only looking into procedural principles indicating which institution ultimately decides a case, eg the CJEU or a national court.[13] In addition, in this type of (re)constructive theory, there is a need for considering the outcomes of

[7] eg Möllers, above n 2.

[8] G Itzcovich, 'Legal Order, Legal Pluralism, Fundamental Principles. Europe and Its Law in Three Concepts' (2012) 18 *European Law Journal* 358, 366: '[E]xternal conflicts between legal orders are unsolvable or irrelevant because, by virtue of the autonomy and authority of the legal order, the norms belonging to different legal orders are incommensurable. This is the principle of the relativity of legal values, which is the logical consequence of the closure of the legal order.' His addition of a theory of 'authoritativeness' of legal orders, however, seems to correspond to constitutional pluralist views on the European legal order. On institutional choice, see also NK Komesar, *Imperfect Alternatives. Choosing Institutions in Law, Economics and Public Policy* (Chicago, University of Chicago Press, 1994).

[9] eg N Walker, 'The Idea of Constitutional Pluralism' (2002) 65 *Modern Law Review* 317; MP Maduro, 'Contrapunctual Law: Europe's Constitutional Pluralism in Action' in N Walker (ed), *Sovereignty in Action* (Oxford, Hart Publishing, 2003) 501–37; M Kumm, 'Who is the Final Arbiter of Constitutionality in Europe? Three Conceptions of the Relationship between the German Federal Constitutional Court and the European Court of Justice' (1999) 36 *Common Market Law Review* 351; N Krisch, *Beyond Constitutionalism* (Oxford, Oxford University Press, 2010).

[10] eg R Brownsword, H-W Micklitz, L Niglia and S Weatherill (eds), *The Foundations of European Private Law* (Oxford, Hart Publishing, 2011); L Niglia, *Pluralism and European Private Law* (Oxford, Hart Publishing, 2013).

[11] Case C-283/11 *Sky Österreich GmbH v Österreichischer Rundfunk* [2013] EU:C:2013:28.

[12] Case C-426/11 *Alemo-Herron and others v Parkwood Leisure Ltd* [2013] EU:C:2013:521; See J Prassl, 'Freedom of Contract as a General Principle of EU Law? Transfers of Undertakings and the Protection of Employer Rights in EU Labour Law. Case C-426/11 Alemo-Herron and others v Parkwood Leisure Ltd' (2013) 42 *Industrial Law Journal* 434; M Bartl and C Leone, 'Minimum Harmonisation after *Alemo-Herron*: The Janus Face of EU Fundamental Rights Review' (2015) 11 *European Constitutional Law Review* 140; MW Hesselink, 'The Justice Dimensions of the Relationship between Fundamental Rights and Private Law' (2016) 24 *European Review of Private Law* 425.

[13] C Mak, 'The One and the Many. Translating Insights from Constitutional Pluralism to European Contract Law Theory' (2013) 21 *European Review of Private Law* 1189.

such processes, eg the validity of a contract in light of conceptions of morality. Theoretical views based on substantive conceptions of justice, moreover, look into the possibility of defining substantive principles that can guide the decision-making process, taking into account the existence of varying limits to freedom of contract on different levels of governance.[14]

These views, in particular the monistic and moderately pluralistic ones, present a coherent picture of the division of powers among legislative and judicial institutions in Europe, including both EU and national bodies. They resonate with the description of the task of the judiciary as it is perceived by some judges themselves. Koen Lenaerts, vice-president of the CJEU, has for instance asserted that:

> [N]ational diversity and EU legislative consensus must both comply with values which are regarded as all-European, ie those that are the object of a constitutional consensus at EU level. It is this latter consensus that guarantees that the forces that bring Europeans together are stronger than those that pull them apart.[15]

Broadly speaking, the type of conceptualisation of the division of powers described here emphasises institutional constraints on judicial law-making. Both in a descriptive and in a normative sense, a primary site for legitimate rule-making is found in the legislative processes involving deliberations in representative institutions, ie national parliaments and the European Parliament. The judiciary's main role is to interpret and apply rules enacted through such processes, respecting a principle of democracy that divides authority to make and to apply laws into two branches of government.[16] Moreover, the legislature retains the power to reverse or confirm judicial decisions.

B. Democratic Legitimacy in a Multi-level Order

Since the division of powers in the EU's multi-level setting concerns two levels of governance, reference must be made to a principle of dual democracy.[17] While respecting national constitutional arrangements, EU governance has added a supranational layer of democratic decision-making, reflecting the idea that

[14] eg I Benöhr, *EU Consumer Law and Human Rights* (Oxford, Oxford University Press, 2013); J Klijnsma, *Contract Law as Fairness. A Rawlsian Perspective on the Position of SMEs in European Contract Law* (PhD thesis Amsterdam UvA, on file with author, 2014).

[15] K Lenaerts, 'Upholding Union Values in Times of Societal Change: The Role of the Court of Justice of the European Union', annual lecture, Durham European Law Institute, 17 February 2014, available at www.dur.ac.uk/resources/deli/events/annual%20lecture%202014/Lenaerts_2014_Durham.pdf. Note that the reference to 'values' raises further questions on the way in which Lenaerts conceptualises the relationship between the EU legal order and national legal orders; MW Hesselink, 'Private Law and the European Constitutionalisation of Values' (2016) CSECL Working Paper Series 2016/07 http://ssrn.com/abstract=2785536. A further elaboration of this dimension, however, lies beyond the scope of this chapter.

[16] Habermas, above n 2, 172.

[17] J Habermas, *Zur Verfassung Europas* (Berlin, Suhrkamp Verlag, 2011) 67.

citizens in Europe must be able to participate and be represented in the policy decisions affecting their rights under EU law.[18] Being simultaneously citizens of their respective Member States as well as EU citizens, people in Europe can take part in law-making processes at the national level and at the European level.

The democratic legitimacy of the rules of private law that make up a composite order of European private law in the interplay of national and EU law, accordingly, depends on the process of the coming into being of these rules. Four categories may be distinguished.

In the first place, the democratic legitimacy of a new rule of private law, eg a rule of a Civil Code, may be assessed at the national level, looking into the legislative procedure through which it was enacted. The application of the rule by the national judge then guarantees legal protection in individual cases. Judicial application may also affirm the legitimacy of the democratic process, insofar as (constitutional) courts provide for the judicial enforcement of a certain democratic ideal.[19] To the extent that the rule falls outside of the scope of EU law, the national democratic process alone determines to what extent its enactment was legitimate.

In the second place, in case a rule derives from the EU level, its democratic legitimacy will be assessed in light of the EU's legislative process. The dynamics in principle are similar to those at the national level: the legislature guarantees that new rules are generated through participatory procedures, whereas the judiciary is responsible for the application of the rules resulting from deliberation. An important difference, nevertheless, concerns the extent to which judicial decisions can be reversed. Given the complexity of amending EU legislation, a decision of the CJEU cannot easily be overturned by changing applicable provisions in the Treaties or secondary legislation.[20]

In the third place, insofar as rules of EU law have to be implemented in national laws, as is the case with rules adopted in EU Directives, these rules also go through a democratic legislative process at the national level. They are doubly legitimised, though by two constituencies that only party overlap—EU citizens and national citizens.

In the fourth place, a rule of private law may be democratically legitimate according to EU law, while its legitimacy is contested from the perspective of one or more Member States. This type of situation may occur if a rule of national private law is found to be non-compliant with EU law, in particular in a preliminary ruling of the CJEU. The implication of this assertion of non-compliance may be that national law must be changed, irrespective of the authentic preferences of national citizens as these are usually taken into account in national processes of law-making.

[18] K Lenaerts, 'The Principle of Democracy in the Case Law of the European Court of Justice' (2013) 62 *International and Comparative Law Quarterly* 271.

[19] Möllers, above n 2, 130–31.

[20] FW Scharpf, 'Legitimacy in the Multilevel European Polity' (2009) 1 *European Political Science Review* 173, 183.

It is particularly the latter category that is of importance for the present analysis. It raises questions regarding the role of the judiciary, since the CJEU is in principle engaged on the initiative of a national judge who refers a preliminary question. While the national judge, thus, performs her role as a European judge by safeguarding EU law (cf Article 19 Treaty on European Union (TEU)), she may create tensions in respect to courts of higher instance that seek to uphold national private law.[21] The involvement of the CJEU in law-making processes, moreover, is likely to affect national legislatures' power to reverse judgments. As will become clear in the discussion of Spanish mortgage cases in the following part of this paper, national legislatures may be required to amend national legislation on the basis of a CJEU judgment establishing non-compliance of national law with European law. The question arises to what extent such types of reforms of national laws can be considered to be democratically legitimised on the national level.

C. Input and Output Legitimacy

In terms of democratic legitimacy, the view described here on the division of powers between legislature and judiciary underlines the political system's assignment and responsibility to guarantee output as well as input legitimacy, based on the idea of collective self-determination. I borrow the distinction made by Fritz Scharpf here:

> Democracy aims at collective self-determination. It must thus be understood as a two-dimensional concept, relating to the *inputs* and to the *outputs* of the political system at the same time. On the input side, self-determination requires that political choices should be derived, directly or indirectly, from the *authentic preferences* of citizens and that, for that reason, governments must be held accountable to the governed. On the output side, however, self-determination implies *effective fate control*.[22]

Input-oriented authenticity and output-oriented effectiveness, thus, are both necessary to guarantee democratic self-determination. This insight informs Scharpf's analysis of the division of powers between EU and Member States. He convincingly demonstrates that issues of legitimacy do not affect European decision-making in its entirety, but only policy areas that are characterised by conflicts of interests and ideological disagreements.[23] In these areas, law-making

[21] eg the French Cour de Cassation's objections against courts ex officio testing the unfairness of standard terms in consumer credit contracts; Case C-473/00 *Cofidis SA v Jean-Louis Fredout* [2002] EU:C:2002:705. An insightful account of the referring judges' struggles with the Cour de Cassation's approach, and their recourse to the CJEU, can be found in Emmanuel Carrère's novel 'D'autres vies que la mienne' (Folio, POL éditeur, 2009).

[22] Scharpf, above n 3, 19.

[23] ibid, 22: 'In other words, it is incorrect to discuss the democratic deficit as if it were a general problem. It does not affect European decision-making across the board, but only certain types of policy area in which conflicts of interest and of ideology are endemic.'

competences should in principle be left to the Member States insofar as no consensus representing citizens' authentic preferences can be identified at EU level. As Sharpf points out, however, output legitimacy might be endangered in case the policies concerned cannot be effectively realised at the nation-state level anymore as a result of European integration.[24]

The extent to which rules may be seen as democratically legitimate is dependent on law-making institutions' explanations and justifications for policies and rules. Input-oriented legitimacy requires for institutions to justify their decisions in communicative discourses in which they seek to persuade the constituency of the necessity and appropriateness of their choices.[25] This is particularly significant in cases in which EU and national objectives diverge. As Scharpf observes, the approach that has been adopted by the Court of Justice of the EU is problematic in this regard:

> In the framework developed by the ECJ, the European concerns that might justifiably override democratically legitimated national institutions and policy legacies are defined as subjective rights of individuals and firms, rather than as substantive requirements on which the viability of the European community of nations, or the internal market, for that matter, would depend. … Subjective rights derived from (the interpretation of) European law may, in principle, override all countervailing national objectives, *regardless of their salience as manifestations of democratic self-determination*.[26]

Here, a beginning of an explanation can be found for the discomfort with judicial law-making in civil cases where EU and national laws differ.[27] In particular, a disconnect between coordinating constitutional principles and substantive private legal outcomes may result from the CJEU's supremacy-based approach. The CJEU's *Viking* and *Laval* judgments form notorious examples, insofar as they inserted national social rights (the right to take collective action) in the framework of the EU's economically oriented free movement law.[28] Such cases challenge both public and private autonomy, since those legal subjects who were affected by the rulings, especially workers in multinational companies, had very limited possibilities to contest the redefinition of their legal positions in the European market. National governments' objections against a codification of the CJEU's case law seemed to be the most that could be attained.[29]

[24] ibid, 22–23.

[25] Scharpf, above n 20, 189.

[26] ibid, 193. Emphasis added.

[27] The fourth category described in s II.B.

[28] Mak, above n 13, 1202–03; Scharpf, above n 20, 191–92; H Schepel, 'Constitutionalising the Market, Marketising the Constitution, and to Tell the Difference: On the Horizontal Application of the Free Movement Provisions in EU Law' (2012) 18 *European Law Journal* 177; N Reich, 'Free Movement v Social Rights in an Enlarged Union—the *Laval* and *Viking* Cases before the ECJ' (2008) 9 *German Law Journal* 125.

[29] The European Commission's Proposal for a Council Regulation on the exercise of the right to take collective action within the context of the freedom of establishment and the freedom to provide services [2012] COM 2012/130 was withdrawn after Member States had objected against it in a 'yellow card' procedure. See www.ipex.eu/IPEXL-WEB/dossier/document/COM20120130.do.

Yet, does the difficulty of politically justifying such case solutions imply that judicial law-making is always incompatible with democracy in European private law? The claim made in this paper is that a strong focus on the legislature and CJEU leaves out of the picture what is and what should be the contribution of judicial interaction to legitimate law-making in a multi-level European private legal order. How do national courts in their interaction with the CJEU and European and national legislatures handle cases in which input legitimacy (authenticity) or output legitimacy (effectiveness) of rules of private law are at stake? Can the judiciary make up for a lack of democratic legitimacy in the legislative process and, thus, sometimes offer a best, rather than a second-best, solution? In what type of cases and under which circumstances would this apply? In the following, it is submitted that the reality of case law shows that courts seem inclined to stretch the division of lawmaking powers in certain ideologically charged areas of private law, especially in times of societal change (section III). Such developments call for a further exploration of the concept of democratic legitimacy in European private law, for which theories of democratic experimentalism may offer inspiration (section IV).

III. Institutional Realism: Judicial Law-making in European Private Law

A. On Spanish Mortgages

Observing recent case law in the area of European private law, it appears that both the CJEU and national courts have under certain circumstances deviated from (ideal) theories of justice that assign a primary role to legislatures. The economic crisis in the EU has induced courts to more openly engage with policy argumentation going beyond the individual case at hand. This has even resulted in legislative reforms at the national level.

The interaction of domestic judges and the CJEU in the development of the legal framework for the assessment of mortgage contracts under Spanish law may serve as an illustration.[30] A first, ground-breaking judgment, in the *Aziz* case,[31]

[30] See also H-W Micklitz, 'Unfair Contract Terms—Public Interest Litigation before European Courts Case C-415/11 *Mohamed Aziz*' in V Colaert and E Terryn (eds), *Landmark Cases of EU Consumer Law—in Honour of Jules Stuyck* (Cambridge, Intersentia, 2013) 615.

[31] Case C-415/11 *Mohamed Aziz v Caixa d'Estalvis de Catalunya, Tarragona i Manresa (Catalunyacaixa)* [2012] EU:C:2012:700. On the implications of this judgment for the conceptualisation of a European private legal order, see also my contribution to the liber amicorum for Hans Micklitz: C Mak, 'On Beauty and Being Fair. The Interaction of National and Supranational Judiciaries in the Development of a European Law on Remedies' in K Purnhagen and P Rott (eds), *Varieties of European Economic Law and Regulation* (Springer, Springer, 2014) 823–34.

set in motion a process of legal reform. Subsequently, further judicial intervention was required to fine-tune the new rules (eg CJEU *Sánchez Morcillo* and *Unicaja Banco*).[32] In all decisions, the courts assessing the cases made specific reference to the socio-economic circumstances in which the disputes arose, which related to the problems on the Spanish housing market resulting from the European economic crisis. Furthermore, the judgments inspired public debate on the protection of home-owners and their families.[33] Judicial interaction, thus, created a space for public deliberation of the rules that should govern mortgage contracts and their enforcement.

The *Aziz* saga concerns the implications of EU Directive 93/13 on unfair terms in consumer contracts (hereafter: Unfair Terms Directive) for the assessment of standard terms relating to the enforcement of a mortgage contract under Spanish law. The CJEU's judgment in the pioneer case, sought by a national judge who was well aware of the societal impact of such enforcement proceedings, contributed to the initiation of a reform of Spanish procedural law. Subsequent cases concern complications arising in the application of the new rules.

B. *Aziz*

The facts of the *Aziz* case go back to July 2007, when Mr Mohamed Aziz concluded a loan agreement with the Catalunyacaixa bank in Barcelona. Security for the loan was provided by a mortgage on his family home. About a year later, at the time the economic crisis hit European markets, Aziz lost his job, got into financial problems and failed to pay several of the monthly instalments of the loan. The bank then invoked its contractual option to terminate the contract earlier (a so-called 'acceleration clause') and claim back the total amount of the loan. Furthermore, the bank started mortgage foreclosure proceedings regarding Aziz's property. Under Spanish law only limited grounds for objection against the foreclosure were available, none of which was applicable in this case. Furthermore, Aziz did not appear in these proceedings nor did he manage to prevent the public sale of the house by paying the remaining amount of the loan plus interest and costs. Following a

[32] Case C-169/14 *Juan Sánchez Morcillo and Maria del Carmen Abril García v Banco Bilbao Vizcaya Argentaria SA* [2014] EU:C:2014:2099; Joined Cases C-482/13, C-484/13, C-485/13 and C-487/13, *Unicaja Banco, SA v José Hidalgo Rueda and Others and Caixabank SA v Manuel María Rueda Ledesma and Rosario Mesa Mesa, José Labella Crespo and Others and Alberto Galán Luna* [2015] EU:C:2015:21. For an analysis of the case law, see F Gómez-Pomar and K Lyczkowska, 'Spanish Courts, the Court of Justice of the EU, and Consumer Law. A Theoretical Model of their Interaction' [2014] *InDret: Revista para el Análisis del Derecho* 4/2014.

[33] eg 'Más de 300 reclamaciones por las cláusulas abusivas hipotecarias' *El País* (Cataluña, 5 May 2013) http://ccaa.elpais.com/ccaa/2013/05/05/catalunya/1367767343_786819.html; 'El juez declara abusiva la hipoteca del "caso Aziz"' *El País* (Cataluña, 3 May 2013) http://ccaa.elpais.com/ccaa/2013/05/02/catalunya/1367520137_907887.html; 'La trastienda de los jueces estrella' *El País* (Cataluña, 2 April 2016) http://politica.elpais.com/politica/2016/04/02/actualidad/1459589958_048547.html.

public sale that attracted no bidders, the bank obtained property of the house for 50 per cent of its contractually established value. Aziz lost ownership of the house and was left with a remaining debt to the bank amounting to 40,000 euro. In order to put the bank in possession of the house, finally, the Aziz family was evicted from the property.

The national judge handling the case, José María Fernández Seijo (Juzgado de lo Mercantil no 3 de Barcelona), was in doubt as to Spanish law's compliance with EU consumer protection law, insofar as it offered no possibility to bring mortgage enforcement proceedings to a halt while judgment on the fairness of the contract terms was pending. He therefore referred a preliminary question to the CJEU concerning Spanish law's compliance with EU standards of consumer protection as reflected in the Unfair Terms Directive. An interview with the judge reveals that the reasons for involving the CJEU surpassed the individual case: first, according to the judge, between 2000 and 2009 banks did not sufficiently inform clients of the terms of mortgage contracts. Second, unlike many other European countries, Spanish law did not offer debtors any opportunities to redress their debts and return to a normal financial situation.[34]

The CJEU confirmed that Spanish law infringed the Unfair Terms Directive, since it did not guarantee effective consumer protection. In particular, rules of procedural law precluded the court assessing the fairness of the bank's general terms and conditions from *staying the mortgage enforcement proceedings* that had been initiated separately. In its judgment of 14 March 2013, the Court held:

> 60 As also observed by the Advocate General in point 50 of her Opinion, without that possibility, where, as in the main proceedings, enforcement in respect of the mortgaged immovable property took place before the judgment of the court in the declaratory proceedings declaring unfair the contractual term on which the mortgage is based and annulling the enforcement proceedings, that judgment would enable that consumer to obtain only subsequent protection of a purely compensatory nature, which would be incomplete and insufficient and would not constitute either an adequate or effective means of preventing the continued use of that term, contrary to Article 7(1) of Directive 93/13.
>
> 61 That applies all the more strongly where, as in the main proceedings, the mortgaged property is the family home of the consumer whose rights have been infringed, since that means of consumer protection is limited to payment of damages and interest and does not make it possible to prevent the definitive and irreversible loss of that dwelling.

In the national judgment following the CJEU's decision, the Spanish judge concluded that the general terms and conditions imposed on Aziz had to be declared null and void.[35] As a consequence, the contract did not allow the Catalunyacaixa

[34] 'Más de 300 reclamaciones por las cláusulas abusivas hipotecarias' *El País* (Cataluña, 5 May 2013) http://ccaa.elpais.com/ccaa/2013/05/05/catalunya/1367767343_786819.html.

[35] Juzgado de lo Mercantil no 3 de Barcelona, 2 May 2013, SJM B 21/2013, under the heading 'Consideraciones previas a las alegaciones de las partes' www.poderjudicial.es/stfls/SALA_DE_PRENSA/NOVEDADES/J.Mercantil_3_Barcelona.pdf.

bank to claim the full amount of the mortgage, but only the unpaid instalments plus interest.

In the observations leading to this conclusion, the national judge emphasised that his task was to assess the *Aziz* case on its legal merits—a view that is in line with the institutional constraints indicated in the previous section. Still, the judge was well aware of the economic, social and political context of the dispute:

> From the beginning of the proceedings both the plaintiff and the defendant in their briefs—writ of summons and defence—have introduced elements of an economic, social and legal-political nature that transcend the strictly legal scope of the dispute and of the parties' claims.
>
> These factors intensified from November 2012 onwards, when the Opinion of the Advocate General at the Court of Justice of the European Union (CJEU) was published, in which she answered the questions referred to the CJEU from the perspective of Community law.
>
> Without a doubt, the dissemination of this Opinion and the CJEU's judgment of 14 March 2013 have given the proceedings a dimension that by far exceeds the scope of the present case insofar as it coincided with an intense public debate—of a political, legislative, social and economic nature—that has prompted a process of legislative reform that has not yet come to an end.
>
> Regardless of these factors, the truth is that also the parties themselves have brought to the fore those meta-legal elements that without a doubt serve to understand the dispute—it is not without reason that the judiciary's function is to apply and interpret the laws in the context and reality in which they take effect, as is established in Article 3 of the [Spanish] Civil Code: 'Legal provisions are to be interpreted according to the proper meaning of their words, in relation to the context, the historical and legislative background and the social reality at the time of their application, serving primarily the spirit and finality of those' ....[36]

As indicated by the judge, the European intervention in Spanish law speeded up the reform of the relevant rules of procedural law. On 15 May 2013, just two months after the CJEU's *Aziz* judgment, Ley 1/2013[37] entered into force. Among other remedies for home-owners in financial difficulties, it introduced a possibility to stay mortgage enforcement proceedings upon a debtor's request to the competent court to assess the fairness of the standards terms and conditions applying to the mortgage contract.

[36] ibid. Translation by author. Note that the judgment was reversed in appeal: https://alonsocuevillas.files.wordpress.com/2014/12/sap-bcn-ejec-hipotec.pdf. At the time of finalisation of this paper, the case was pending at the Spanish Supreme Court, the Tribunal Supremo.

[37] BOE No 116, of 15 May 2013, p 36373. The preamble of Ley 1/2013 extensively refers to the socio-economic context in which the law was passed and the need to avoid social exclusion of citizens. Furthermore, it specifically mentions the CJEU's *Aziz* judgment.

C. *Sánchez Morcillo*

The Spanish legislature's response to *Aziz* was soon followed by new questions. In the case of *Sánchez Morcillo and Abril García v Banco Bilbao*,[38] the referring judge particularly questioned the (in)equality of procedural defence mechanisms available to the parties involved in mortgage enforcement proceedings. Article 695(4) of the Spanish Law on Civil Procedure stipulated that in such cases appeals could only be brought against a judicial order staying the proceedings or displaying an unfair contract term. This effectively offered the bank a possibility to immediately appeal against the sustenance of a home-owner's objection to enforcement, whereas the party against whom enforcement was sought (the owner of the house) could not appeal if his or her objection was dismissed. The national judge in the present case doubted whether this was in line with the consumer protection offered under the Unfair Terms Directive, read in combination with Article 47 of the EU Charter of Fundamental Rights. According to the CJEU, the relevant provisions of EU law indeed precluded a rule such as Article 695(4) of the Spanish Procedural Code, which gave the bank (creditor) an unjustified advantage in respect to the home-owner (debtor). The Court considered that the Spanish system of mortgage enforcement did neither offer adequate nor effective protection (in the sense of Article 7 of the Unfair Terms Directive) to home-owners, insofar as it still did not effectively prevent unjustified evictions: a judge in enforcement proceedings could assess the unfairness of contract terms, but this assessment was not mandatory and bound by time restrictions. Furthermore, in case home-owners started parallel proceedings regarding the unfairness of the contract terms and the judge in those proceedings eventually established that the terms of the mortgage contract were unfair, the consumer could only claim monetary compensation[39]—this is what happened in *Aziz*. In addition, the procedural defences available to the consumer were of a much weaker nature than those available to the bank—Spanish law did, thus, not respect the principle of equality of arms or procedural equality, safeguarded by Article 47 of the Charter.[40]

Again, the national court's recourse to the CJEU seemed to have, at least in part, been inspired by the context in which the case evolved. The referring judge's request for an accelerated procedure before the EU Court underscores this, insofar as it was motivated by the observations 'that the answer provided by the Court could have significant consequences for litigation in Spain given that, in the light of the economic crisis experienced by that Member State, a large number of natural persons are subject to mortgage enforcement measures in respect of their

[38] Case C-169/14 *Juan Carlos Sánchez Morcillo and María del Carmen Abril García v Banco Bilbao Vizcaya Argentaria, SA* [2014] EU:C:2015:508.
[39] ibid, para 43.
[40] ibid, paras 48–51.

dwellings' and 'the proceedings that may be affected by the Court's answer also concern the main dwelling of debtors', which 'would be liable to be sold at auction before the Court even handed down its ruling'.[41]

D. *Unicaja Banco* and *Caixabank*

A number of joined cases of consumers against the Unicaja Bank and Caixabank[42] focused on another provision resulting from the Spanish law reform, which imposes a ceiling (at three times the statutory interest rate) on the default interest that may be recovered through the enforcement of a mortgage. If that ceiling is exceeded, courts should give creditors (in this case: banks) the possibility to adjust the default interest rate so as to make it comply with the statutory limit. In the contracts at issue default interest rates ranged from 18 per cent to 22.5 per cent. The referring courts in essence asked whether they, in case they found these clauses to be unfair in light of Directive 93/13, should declare the clauses to be void and not binding or rather should mitigate the interest clauses. Furthermore, the national judges questioned the compatibility of the reform law with the Unfair Terms Directive.

The CJEU ruled that in this case the Spanish rules did not come into conflict with EU law, since they did not prevent national judges from assessing the fairness of default interest clauses and, in case of unfairness, declare them null and void.[43] A default rate of less than three times the statutory interest rate is not automatically deemed to be fair and may still be scrutinised,[44] whereas a higher default rate may, depending on the circumstances, either be mitigated under Ley 1/2013 or be declared unfair under the Directive.

Although in this case the CJEU's decision did not directly alter domestic law, the preliminary reference procedure did provide space for deliberation of the manner in which the objectives of EU law and their articulation (consumer protection by holding unfair terms non-binding) affected national goals and their expression in law (protection of debtors by mitigating excessively high default interest rates). Moreover, it induced the Spanish Supreme Court to develop general principles on the unfairness of general clauses regarding interest on late payments, making ample reference to the CJEU's case law.[45]

[41] Case C-169/14 *Juan Carlos Sánchez Morcillo and María del Carmen Abril García v Banco Bilbao Vizcaya Argentaria SA*, Order of the President of the Court of 5 June 2014 [2014] paras 7–8.

[42] Joined Cases *Unicaja Banco and Caixabank*, above n 32.

[43] ibid, para 36.

[44] ibid, para 40.

[45] Tribunal Supremo (Sala de lo Civil) 22 April 2015, no 2351/2012, www.poderjudicial.es/stfls/SALA_DE_PRENSA/NOTAS_DE_PRENSA/TS_Civil_22-04-2015.pdf.

E. Social Reality and Democratic Ideals

From the perspective outlined in section II of this chapter, the question arises if the Spanish judge in the *Aziz* case may only have been paying lip-service to established ideas of the division of powers between legislature and judiciary, while effectively having used the opening provided by the reference to 'the social reality at the time of application' in Article 3 of the Spanish Civil Code to redirect the outcome of the case. This form of interaction between national and supranational legislative and judicial institutions may raise criticism for not sufficiently respecting the principle of democracy underlying European (private) law-making. Rather than awaiting legislative intervention, the European and domestic judiciaries intervened in the Spanish national law of civil procedure and even provoked its reform. This may seem to be at odds with the idea of democratic legitimacy according to which EU citizens' voice in EU and national law-making processes is primarily guaranteed through the legislative process, not the judicial process.[46]

In the remaining part of this chapter, I will defend that the democratic legitimacy of rules of European private law is not necessarily diminished by the expansion of the judiciary's role in law-making processes. In particular under circumstances of societal change, access to judicial institutions may offer better means of democratic legitimisation than legislative processes, especially in a multi-level order such as that of European private law. Moreover, the role and function of the concept of democratic legitimacy itself needs to be reassessed in light of ideas of justice in the EU.

IV. Institutional Imagination: Rethinking the Role of the Judiciary

A. Democracy and European Private Law Adjudication

'The task of democratic government is not to maximize change. It is to balance order and change, and the scholarly challenge is to account for how and why institutions remain stable as well as how and why they change', Johan Olsen states in relation to institutional sources of democratic change and continuity.[47] It might

[46] S II above.

[47] JP Olsen, 'Change and Continuity: an Institutional Approach to Institutions of Democratic Government' (2009) 1 *European Political Science Review* 3, 4.

be argued that the CJEU's and national courts' far-reaching intervention in the legal framework for standard terms in (Spanish) mortgage contracts signifies a change in the division of powers between legislature and judiciary in Europe, even a *coup d'état*.[48] This leads back to the question how this case law can be understood from the point of view of democratic legitimacy.

The shift may be explained, and partly justified, in light of an emphasis on output legitimacy.[49] Judges sometimes find themselves in a better position than legislators to effectively achieve certain EU policy goals—in this case, protection of consumers who were about to lose their family homes.

Yet, is this what courts are supposed to do? In terms of input legitimacy the question arises if authentic preferences of European citizens, in their dual roles as national and EU citizens, are fully respected in the process of judicial interaction.[50] Are their voices heard in the development of rules of European private law through judicial law-making?[51] In other words, does judicial involvement in law-making processes endanger democratic input-oriented legitimacy? Several arguments support the view that this is not necessarily the case and that judicial deliberations of policy questions may even enhance the democratic nature of European private law.

In the first place, European citizens' access to law-making processes in the field of private law can be served by involving the judiciary. European citizens' involvement in preliminary reference procedures may substantively affect the outcomes of private legal disputes. The *Aziz* saga illustrates the point, insofar as the interaction of Spanish and European judiciaries influenced and informed the reform of national rules on mortgage contracts. Litigation here provided an accessible means[52] of contesting the legal framework that kept in place contractual terms detrimental to weaker parties.[53]

In the second place, judicial reference to EU rights can open up deliberative processes in (national) private law. The enforcement of EU law through national legal procedures (cf Article 19 TEU) requires national courts to consider the

[48] From a constitutional perspective, A Stone Sweet, 'The Juridical *Coup d'État* and the Problem of Authority' (2007) 8 *German Law Journal* 915, defines a '*coup d'état*' as 'a fundamental transformation in the normative foundations of a legal system through the constitutional lawmaking of a court'.

[49] S II above.

[50] FW Scharpf, 'After the Crash: A Perspective on Multilevel European Democracy' (2015) 21 *European Law Journal* 384, 398.

[51] Note that under emergency laws exceptions may be made to rules of democratic law-making. These situations fall beyond the scope of this chapter, since *Aziz* and similar cases were not adjudicated under laws applying to a state of emergency. The focus here lies on courts' powers in the default setting of democratic law-making processes.

[52] Litigation is in principle open to all. It should be noted, though, that accessibility is affected by other factors, such as financial resources. See further s IV.D below.

[53] Compare, for US law, WH Simon, 'Justice and Accountability: Activist Judging in the Light of Democratic Constitutionalism and Democratic Experimentalism' (2016) *Law, Culture and the Humanities* 6–7.

policy questions underlying private legal cases.[54] Again, the Spanish mortgage cases may serve as an illustration. In the absence of EU laws on housing and tenancy contracts, recourse to the judicial interpretation of the Unfair Terms Directive offered access to the deliberation of the compliance of Spanish law with (European) ideas of social justice. Moreover, the judicial deliberation of the fairness of Spanish mortgage contracts for consumers tapped into the public debate on the problems on the housing market and their relation to Europe's economic crisis.

In the third place, courts' roles in multiple regulatory environments sometimes put them in a better position to represent citizens' interests than other institutions. Rules governing private legal relations in the EU are generated in at least three environments: national legal systems, EU law and contractual negotiations between private parties. The judiciary is the only legal institution to play a role in all these environments:[55] it interprets and applies national and EU rules of private law and assesses the validity and implications of parties' contracts. The judiciary is represented on the supranational and national level and its decision-making is relatively easily accessible[56] to the everyday citizenry. It is, thus, in the position to transmit and translate arguments for normative changes among different regulatory environments.

These considerations raise questions concerning the conceptions of democracy and democratic legitimacy in European private law. On the one hand, the central ideas remain participation and representation in law-making processes by those who will be governed by the resulting rules. On the other hand, it seems that the manner in which these ideals are realised in the multi-level sphere of European private law does not necessarily have to take the same institutional shape as in national constitutional orders, in particular as regards the division of powers between legislature and judiciary.[57] A one-on-one translation of a conception of

[54] An analogy may be made to the 'constitutionalisation of private law', which makes explicit legal-political stakes in private legal disputes; Stone Sweet, above n 2, 129; C Mak, *Fundamental Rights in European Contract Law* (Alphen a/d Rijn, Kluwer Law International, 2008). See also Möllers, above n 2, 141: 'If civil and criminal law courts are obliged to implement a basic rights jurisprudence by a constitutional court, they are asked to apply constitutional law; a kind of legal reasoning that is less formalist, less textual, less technical, closer to political theory, and therefore in a certain sense more political and more general. The constitutionalization of the court system is then also a form of politicization of the judiciary.'

[55] Compare Dowdle on similar regulatory dynamics in Chinese constitutional developments: MW Dowdle, 'On the Regulatory Dynamics of Judicialization. The Promise and Perils of Exploring "Judicialization" in East and Southeast Asia' in T Ginsburg and AHY Chen (eds), *Administrative Law and Governance in Asia* (London, Routledge, 2008) 23–37.

[56] In some Member States, such as Poland and Croatia, however, only a selected number of judgments of the Supreme Court are made public, which limits the opportunities for public debate on civil cases. Thanks to Joasia Luzak and Mia Junuzovic for bringing this point to my attention.

[57] Compare H Collins, 'Cosmopolitanism and Transnational Private Law' (2012) 8 *European Review of Contract Law* 311, 324: 'What is needed is sometimes described paradoxically as the constitutionalization of transnational commercial law, though what is really needed is not subordination to any particular national constitution but rather the construction of a transnational economic constitution

democracy from the nation-state level to the EU encounters difficulties—while the underlying ideas of participation and representation retain their importance, part of their meaning may be lost in translation if the division of powers in European private law is based on existing divisions of tasks among national legislatures and judiciaries.

Consequently, the idea of dual democracy, referring to the engagement of EU citizens in both national and supranational democratic processes, does not automatically imply that citizens' democratic involvement should take the same institutional shape on both levels of governance. In particular in regard to the development of rules governing private-legal relationships, judiciaries involved in the integration of EU Regulations and Directives in national systems provide important opportunities for democratic deliberation of the reconciliation of the plurality of values that delimitates freedom of contract—and, thus, for input legitimacy (inclusion of European citizens' authentic preferences) as well as output legitimacy (effective realisation of European policies, eg consumer protection). Judicial actors may, thus, from the democratic perspective, deserve a greater role in law-making processes on the interface of national and supranational law than they do in the national setting, especially in times of societal change—or at least they should not be reproached for assuming that role.

B. Democratic Experimentalism

Is it possible to imagine an institutional constellation in which courts sometimes are in a better position than legislatures to contribute to the democratic legitimation of new rules of private law? A point of reference for a re-imagination of the judiciary's role in the communicative process of generating legal normativity in European private law may be found in theories on democratic experimentalism. In Roberto Unger's words, ideas on democratic experimentalism refer to a practice of 'existential bootstrapping', ie 'using the smaller variations that are at hand to produce the bigger variations that do not yet exist'.[58] Democratic experimentalism has been proposed as a counterpoint to critique of judicial activism, since it challenges the premise that judgments on substantive justice are incompatible with democracy.[59] While not aiming at presenting a full-fledged theory on democratic experimentalism in European private law here, an exploration of the judiciary's contribution to the democratic legitimacy of new rule-solutions in civil cases

or rules ensuring compatibility with other normative legal orders that protect public policy and external interests', referring also to G Teubner's, *Constitutional Fragments: Societal Constitutionalism and Globalization* (Oxford, Oxford University Press, 2012).

[58] RM Unger, *The Self Awakened. Pragmatism Unbound* (Cambridge, MA, Harvard University Press, 2007) 43.

[59] Simon, above n 53.

in Europe may indicate how this type of institutional imagination[60] can contribute to the debate. In particular, the focus here will be on the question in which situations judicial law-making can provide a first-best democratically legitimate solution rather than a second-best one in comparison to the legislative process.

In the work of Roberto Unger, Charles Sabel and other authors, democratic experimentalism distinguishes itself from monist and pluralist theories[61] particularly by challenging the ideas of necessity and indivisibility of systems of social organisation.[62] It adheres to the pragmatist view that 'the objectives presumed in the guiding understandings of theories, strategies, or ideals of justice are transformed in the light of the experience of their pursuit, and these transformations in turn redefine what counts as a means to a guiding end'.[63] The pervasiveness of unintended consequences is, accordingly, seen as constitutive of thought and action, rather than as a side-effect of the division of powers in political systems.[64] Democratic deliberation offers a means for identifying and correcting unintended consequences of coordination among private actors.[65]

In theories of democratic experimentalism, judicial law-making is not inconsistent with democracy. Typically, a central institution provides a framework for experimentation with different solutions at a decentralised level, while local units report back to this central institution.[66] Stakeholders take part in deliberative processes in which new solutions are formulated. Whereas general principles are, thus, developed locally, they may gain recognition and be adopted more widely. The role of courts, in the first place, is to ensure that experimentation falls within the scope of mandates given and that citizens' rights are respected.[67] In the second place, courts may contribute to the development of new solutions and the formation of consensus on substantive rules.[68] The legitimacy of courts' judgments, then, does not have an immediate democratic basis. Rather, democratic experimentalism 'suggest[s] that it rests on the potential contribution of such judgments to the processes of democratic decision-making and consensus formation'.[69]

C. Experiments in European Private Law

To what extent can democratic experimentalism justify judicial law-making in European private law? What smaller variations can be found in case law, which

[60] Unger, above n 1.
[61] See s II.A above.
[62] Unger, above n 58, 185.
[63] M Dorf and C Sabel, 'A Constitution of Democratic Experimentalism' (1998) 98 *Columbia Law Review* 267, 285.
[64] ibid, 285.
[65] ibid, 286.
[66] Simon, above n 53, 11.
[67] ibid, 28.
[68] ibid, 13.
[69] ibid, 20.

may produce bigger, democratically legitimate variations in the rules that govern private legal relationships in the EU? And what do they say about the division of powers between legislatures and judiciaries? The *Aziz* saga offers further inspiration.

A framework for the experimentation with new rule-solutions can be found in Article 47 of the EU Charter of Fundamental Rights, which safeguards the right to an effective judicial remedy in case of a violation of rights under EU law. Some judgments in the Spanish series contain references to this provision, sometimes in combination with other fundamental rights, such as Article 38 of the Charter, which ensures a high level of consumer protection. In the *Sánchez Morcillo* judgment, for instance, Article 47 substantiated the conclusion that Spanish law did not respect the principle of equality of arms insofar as banks could appeal a decision on unfair terms control at an earlier stage in legal proceedings than consumers could.[70] To the extent that the interaction of the CJEU with national courts within the framework of the Charter explores which substantive forms of consumer protection can be offered in national legal orders, it appears to comply with the basic features of democratic experimentalism.[71]

Furthermore, as Hans Micklitz has observed, the *Aziz* judgment itself may be deemed to have added a layer of 'hidden' constitutionalisation to European private law: while neither Advocate General Kokott nor the CJEU explicitly mentioned the Charter (in particular Article 34(3) on housing), the fundamental rights dimension does shine through in their considerations on the mortgage credit's purpose to provide Aziz and his family with a home.[72] This again suggests that the European judiciary seeks to place the preliminary reference procedure in a broader constitutional framework. The interaction of national courts with the CJEU through this procedure could be seen as a form of democratic experimentalism in which EU law provides the space within which alternative rule-solutions may be considered on the initiative of national civil courts raising preliminary questions.

Oliver Gerstenberg submits that from an experimentalist view, the Court would have 'a democracy-sustaining, collaborative role in a broader, EU-wide process of public opinion formation'.[73] The interaction of the CJEU with national courts may strengthen democratic legitimacy rather than undermine it, since '[t]he EU multilevel system enables consumers to put national law and politics under pressure to reform and overcome insularity'.[74] This is not a one-way process in which the

[70] See s III.C above.

[71] In a similar vein, from a public law perspective, O Gerstenberg, '(The Failure of) Public Law and the Deliberative Turn' in C MacAmhlaigh, C Michelon and N Walker (eds), *After Public Law* (Oxford, Oxford University Press, 2013) 219: 'Thus, the role of courts in this proceduralist model, including the ECtHR or the CJEU, lies in mobilizing other actors, namely national courts, through the formulation of a broad framework of principles.'

[72] Micklitz, above n 30, 649–50.

[73] O Gerstenberg, 'Constitutional Reasoning in Private Law: The Role of the CJEU in Adjudicating Unfair Terms in Consumer Contracts' (2015) 21 *European Law Journal* 599, 620.

[74] ibid, 620.

European Court imposes its views on national legal orders. Experimentalism supports a mutual learning process, or 'hybridisation', in which national courts apply general criteria to specific cases, while creating possibilities for the CJEU to revise these general criteria in light of their unintended consequences.[75]

From a democratic-experimentalist perspective, therefore, the interaction of the CJEU and national civil courts in *Aziz* and similar cases is certainly not undemocratic. It opens up a deliberative space for looking into different alternatives and urges courts to make explicit the reasons for their support of a certain rule-solution. This may contribute to the finding of a new consensus on where to define boundaries to private autonomy, as well as means to protect and support autonomous decision-making of private actors.

D. First or Second Best?

The question remains whether judicial law-making in European private law should be considered a first-best or a second-best solution in terms of democratic legitimacy. Theories of democratic experimentalism offer a justification for the development of new rules of private law through the judicial process. Still, they have drawbacks. Whether judicial law-making should be preferred over alternative ways of ensuring democratic legitimacy depends on its potential to give European citizens a real and better opportunity to author new rules of private law that affect them than other (legislative) processes do.[76] Moreover, it depends on the relation between pragmatic and principled approaches to European private law: is it possible to reconcile instances of experimentalist judicial law-making with principled views on the nature and desirable development of European private law? Specifically, attention needs to be paid to the tension between, on the one hand, national civil courts that refer politically sensitive questions to the CJEU and, on the other hand, the legislature and higher courts in their domestic legal orders that hold different opinions.

If the hypothesis that judicial law-making can offer a first-best solution is taken as a starting point, several objections present themselves. A first, radical argument concerns the critique that these types of deliberative processes may merely mirror existing distributions of power and can, thus, not improve the democratic legitimacy of rules of European private law. As Di Robilant observed in her evaluation of democratic experimentalism in property law, new deliberative forms 'may fail to involve, and may actually exclude, potential participants, such as those least able to participate on account of resources or education, those marginalized on account

[75] ibid. On hybridisation, see also N Reich, *General Principles of EU Law* (Antwerp, Intersentia, 2014) 98.

[76] Ss II.C and IV.A above.

of race, gender or sexuality, or those with ideologically radical views'.[77] Similar concerns may be expressed on the potential of deliberative processes originating in judicial interaction to involve European citizens affected by the outcomes of these processes. Judgments in civil cases in principle only regard the parties to the dispute. Since civil litigation is not equally accessible to all because of social and economic factors, deliberation through adjudication cannot include all affected parties and, therefore, cannot contribute to democratic legitimacy, the argument would be. If this line of reasoning were followed, judicial interactions in European private law would offer no advantages or first-best solutions. If, on the other hand, emphasis is put on judicial law-making's *contribution* to democratic legitimacy rather than its competition with or complete *substitution* of legislative processes, a different picture emerges. While judicial law-making may not directly rest on democratic principles, it can contribute to the formation of public consensus and democratic decision-making.[78] The public debate concerning, for instance, *Aziz* and other Spanish mortgage cases involved the Spanish population as a whole and even transcended national borders, as it drew Europe-wide attention.[79] Although differences in terms of education and background may still lead to some people being more involved than others, the deliberative space that is opened up through judicial interaction in civil cases in principle includes all affected by European private law. It may, thus, contribute to the democratic legitimation of rules of private law by providing an additional space for deliberation on alternative rule-solutions and consensus formation.[80]

A second objection relates to the limitations on input-oriented legitimacy that result from the CJEU interfering in areas of private law regardless of the effects of its interventions on national policies and laws. The CJEU's subjective rights approach may endanger national rules of private law that form expressions of democratic self-determination on the national level.[81] To the extent that this indeed can be a(n unintended) consequence of judicial law-making, input-oriented legitimacy might be at risk. Since national legislatures will have to adjust to the CJEU's evaluation of the compliance of national law with EU law, as happened in the Spanish reform of procedural law after *Aziz*, the national constituency's preferences will only play a marginal role in the reform of rules of national private law through the preliminary reference procedure. Still, as said, these types of judicial interactions may bring to light societal problems and expand the deliberative space in which

[77] A di Robilant, 'Property and Democratic Deliberation: The *Numerus Clausus* Principle and Democratic Experimentalism in Property Law' (2014) 62 *The American Journal of Comparative Law* 367, 414.

[78] Simon, above n 53, 20. See also s IV.B above.

[79] eg 'Spain's evicted fight back' *Euronews* (Spain, 11 April 2013), www.euronews.com/2013/04/11/spain-s-evicted- fight-back.

[80] The possibilities for this type of deliberative space to open up are highly dependent on the extent to which case law is published. See the reservations made in n 56 above. Still, other factors, such as the easy distribution of information through the Internet may facilitate access to a larger public.

[81] See s II.C above.

these can be discussed. Whether this places the judiciary in the first-best position to address such societal problems is likely to differ from case to case, eg depending on national legislatures' resistance to address certain issues, as in the Spanish mortgage cases. The possibility for judicial law-making to offer a best solution, or least imperfect alternative,[82] is, however, not ruled out.

A third and fundamental objection concerns the pragmatic background to democratic experimentalism. Pragmatism supposes the impossibility of defining first principles that will survive the efforts made to realise them.[83] It seeks to find ways to respond to unexpected circumstances rather than define ideal principles for the organisation of a political community. As such, it may fail to deliver just outcomes: Focussing on experimentalist deliberative procedures may lead to results that are democratically legitimate, but do not comply with substantive notions of justice.[84] This does not necessarily imply that judicial law-making cannot yield a best solution in terms of a proceduralist conception of democratic legitimacy. Yet, it does raise the question if judicial interaction in the EU's preliminary reference procedure can sufficiently take into account the different conceptions of social justice[85] reflected in national and EU laws. National rules of private law that express the national constituency's view on social justice may be 'overruled' by a decision of the CJEU, which can be conceived of as reflecting a European conception of social justice. Whilst judicial interaction may, thus, lead to a democratically legitimate best solution from an EU perspective, it does not solve the conflict between diverging conceptions of social justice in the EU and the Member State involved.

While it is, thus, not unlikely that judicial interaction in civil cases can offer first-best democratically legitimate solution in some disputes, the consideration of the merits of procedural theories of democratic experimentalism underscores the substantive 'justice deficit' in EU law.[86] A more substantive idea of deliberative democracy would be needed, emphasising the involvement of free and equal citizens in democratic law-making processes, to respond to the objections against pragmatic approaches.[87] Alternatively, evidence would have to be presented for the assertion that this type of democratic deliberation usually provides the least imperfect way to reach just outcomes.[88] In private law, pressing issues are to what extent judges in civil cases have to take into account the moral dimension of a dispute and how they should handle varying conceptions of social justice (eg concerning a right to housing) in determining the boundaries to party autonomy

[82] cf Komesar, above n 8.

[83] Dorf and Sabel, above n 63, 285.

[84] Compare Di Robilant, above n 77, 410–11.

[85] H-W Micklitz (ed), *The Many Concepts of Social Justice in European Private Law* (Cheltenham, Edward Elgar Publishing, 2011); D Kochenov, G de Búrca and A Williams (eds), *Europe's Justice Deficit?* (Oxford, Hart Publishing, 2015).

[86] ibid.

[87] Di Robilant, above n 77, 411.

[88] ibid.

in a multi-layered European legal order.[89] From that perspective, *Aziz* is not just an example of judicial action in times of societal change, but also a manifestation of persistent foundational questions of European private law. Experimentalist judicial law-making may, therefore, not unequivocally be deemed to offer the best solution for addressing societal problems. Still, looking at *Aziz*-type of cases from an experimentalist perspective can clarify and, to a certain extent, justify the role that courts can play in the democratic legitimation of rules of European private law.

V. Realists and Visionaries

Reconstruction, realism and experimentalism were the three lenses through which judicial interaction in European private law was explored in this chapter. Each of these three views provides different insights in the interaction of courts in this field of law, which is composed of rules of private law deriving from the EU level and the national level. A reconstructive approach offers an account of the institutional setting in which European private law is shaped, paying attention to public autonomy as well as private autonomy in democratic processes. A realist perspective highlights the contextual factors that can explain a certain judicial approach to a dispute among private actors in an asymmetrical contractual relationship. An experimentalist approach, finally, offers a justification for national judges referring a civil case to the CJEU in order to create space for a fundamental deliberation of the rule-solution provided in national law and possible alternatives deriving from an EU conception of social justice.

The Spanish mortgage cases arose against the background of a national crisis on the housing market, which was strongly connected to the economic crisis in the EU. A more fundamental dimension of European private law that is highlighted in this case law concerns the judiciary's position on the interface of national and EU laws that endorse different conceptions of social justice. Can democratic experimentalism in European private law find a place in a (partial) theory of adjudication that goes beyond crisis management? To the extent that judicial law-making in European private law can offer a first rather than second-best solution in terms of democratic legitimacy, by shaping a space for new consensus formation, *Aziz* is just a beginning.

[89] C Mak, *Justice through European Private Law* (inaugural lecture, Amsterdam UvA, 2016) www.oratiereeks.nl/upload/pdf/PDF-5662weboratie_Mak_-_DEF.pdf.

11

Relative Authority in Global and EU Financial Regulation: Linking the Legitimacy Debates

MAURIZIA DE BELLIS

I. Global Regulation, the EU, and the New Separation of Powers

Global financial regulation appears as a polycentric, highly fragmented regime.[1] Transnational regulatory networks ('TRN') such as the Basel Committee on Banking Supervision ('BCBS'), the International Organization for Securities Commissioners ('IOSCO') and the International Association of Insurance Supervisors ('IAIS'), started setting standards for banking, securities and insurance in the 1980s.[2] The number of global regulators intervening in global regulation increased over time. As a response to the global financial crisis, the G20 started meeting as a summit of the heads of State or government in 2008, setting the agenda of financial reforms. At the same time, a second, powerful actor was established: the Financial Stability Board ('FSB'), a 'network of networks' bringing together the TRNs for banking, securities and insurance as well as national authorities from the G20 countries, not only representatives of regulatory agencies, but also financial ministers.[3]

[1] Fragmentation is a feature common to many global regulatory regimes: see S Cassese, *The Global Polity. Global Dimensions of Democracy and the Rule of Law* (Sevilla, Global Law Press/ Editorial Derecho Global, 2012).

[2] The BCBS, established in 1974, started setting the first standards on banking at the end of the decade: see EB Kapstein, *Governing the Global Economy. International Finance and the State* (Cambridge, Harvard University Press, 1994). The IOSCO and IAIS were set up in 1983 and in 1994, respectively.

[3] For an analysis of global financial regulators, see M De Bellis, *La regolazione dei mercati finanziari* (Milan, Giuffrè, 2012).

The legitimacy concerns connected with the activity of these bodies became more pressing and were exacerbated with the global financial crisis.[4] Research perspectives have focused on each of these actors. A decade ago, Anne-Marie Slaughter identified transgovernmental networks as the key feature of the new financial architecture.[5] Ngaire Woods emphasised the role that the IMF and the World Bank play within the new international financial architecture.[6] More recently, analysis focused on the leading role of the G20[7] and of the FSB,[8] arguing that, because of their composition (purely political for the first body, and hybrid for the second one), they lead to a politicisation of global financial regulation.[9] Given this fragmentation of powers in financial regulation, however, the perspective of relative authority appears better suited to properly assess the impact of each global regulator. It investigates precisely how powers are distributed between the different actors and what are the connections and relationships of the different entities. That is essential in order to fully understand the respective role of the many different actors engaged in financial regulation.

The analysis will show that before the crisis there was a roughly tripartite separation of powers in global financial architecture: technical bodies (transnational regulatory networks such as the BCBS and the IOSCO) were the key standards setters, while a political body like the G7 attempted to set the agenda of financial reforms. In addition, intergovernmental organisations, such as the International Monetary Fund (IMF) and the World Bank, put in place powerful institutional mechanisms in order to foster the implementation of standards. After the crisis, a tectonic shift can be observed in global regulation.[10] On the one hand,

[4] See, among many, C Brummer, 'How International Financial Law Works (and How it Doesn't)' (2011) 99 *Georgetown Law* 257 and M Goldmann and S Steininger (eds), 'Democracy and Financial Order—Legal Perspectives Special Issue' (2016) 17 *German Law Journal* 705. The debate is widespread well beyond the world of legal scholars. For a sociological (and critical) perspective, see S Sassen, 'Global Finance and Its Institutional Spaces' in K Knorr and A Preda (eds), *The Oxford Handbook of the Sociology of Finance* (Oxford, Oxford University Press, 2012).

[5] A-M Slaughter, 'The Real New World Order' (1997) 76 *Foreign Affairs* 183.

[6] See N Woods, *The Globalizers. The IMF, the World Bank, and Their Borrowers* (Ithaca, Cornell University Press, 2006) and DD Bradlow and DB Hunter (eds), *International Institutions and International Law* (Alphen a/d Rijn, Wolters Kluwer, 2010).

[7] S Cho and CR Kelly, 'Promises and Perils of New Global Governance: A Case of the G20' (2012) 12 *Chicago Journal of International Law* 491, 507; and AC Eernisse, 'Banking on Cooperation: The Role of the G-20 in Improving the International Financial Architecture' (2012) 22 *Duke Journal of Comparative & International Law* 239.

[8] S Griffith-Jones, E Helleiner and N Woods (eds), 'The Financial Stability Board: An Effective Fourth Pillar of Global Economic Governance?, Centre for International Governance Innovation Special Report' (2010) Centre for International Governance Innovation, 32, www.cigionline.org/sites/default/files/g20_no_3_0.pdf; and DW Arner and MW Taylor, 'The Global Financial Crisis and the Financial Stability Board: Hardening the Soft Law of International Financial Regulation' (2009) 32 *University of New South Wales Law Journal* 488 and DW Arner and MW Taylor, 'The Global Financial Crisis and the Financial Stability Board: Hardening the Soft Law of International Financial Regulation' (2009) 32 *UNSW Law Journal* 488, 488.

[9] D Zaring, 'International Institutional Performance in Time of Crisis' (2010) 10 *Chicago Journal of International Law* 475.

[10] J Black, 'Restructuring Global and EU Financial Regulation: Character, Capacities and Learning' in E Wymeersch, KJ Hopt, and G Ferrarini (eds), *Financial Regulation and Supervision: a Post-Crisis Analysis* (Oxford, OxfordUniversity Press, 2012) 23.

the G20 took over and reinforced, in unprecedented ways, the agenda-setting function. On the other hand, a significant re-centralisation took place as the FSB moved beyond a purely coordination role, taking over new powers, ranging from setting its own standards to conducting peer reviews. As a result, the current regulatory landscape does not correspond to a logic of separation of powers, but it may well be grasped through the lens of a division of relative authority.[11]

This perspective is all the more relevant since the purpose of this chapter is not merely descriptive, but includes a normative dimension. The different actors engaging in financial regulation do not differ only because of their structure, but also due to their grounds of legitimation.[12] While the TRNs, made up of regulatory authorities, are technical bodies with a high level of expertise, the G20 constitutes a political body. The FSB—as will be further discussed—is a hybrid body, where both political and technical components are represented. Should these differences be reflected in the type of tasks these actors exercise and the standard used to assess their legitimacy? The analysis will show that efforts directed toward a clearer articulation of powers encounter many limits, stemming both from the practical unfeasibility of reforms and from the type of powers exercised. This suggests that the legitimacy of bodies involved in the exercise of public authority should be grounded on different sources.

Public authority is relative also in the context of EU financial regulation. In the aftermath of the crisis, the EU established a complex financial regulatory architecture, as a result of two major reforms. In 2010, three new agencies were set up: the European Banking Authority ('EBA'), the European Securities and Markets Authority ('ESMA') and the European Insurance and Occupational Pensions Authority ('EIOPA'), collectively known as the European Supervisory Authorities ('ESAs'), which, together with the competent national authorities, form the European System of Financial Supervision ('ESFS').[13] The building of the ESFS was followed by the European Banking Union ('EBU'), comprising the Single Supervisory Mechanism ('SSM')[14] and the Single Resolution Mechanism ('SRM').[15] Within the SRM, another new agency was established (the Single Resolution Board ('SRB')). Within the SSM, the European Central Bank ('ECB') was entrusted with new supervisory competences. As the analysis will show, a proper understanding of

[11] See J Mendes and I Venzke, 'Introduction: The Idea of Relative Authority in European and International Law' (this volume).

[12] See S Rose-Ackerman, *Democractic Legitimacy and Executive Rulemaking: Positive Political Theory in Comparative Public Law* (this volume).

[13] The regulations setting up the ESAs are: Reg of 24 November 2010 no 1093/2010, establishing a European Banking Authority; no 1094/2010 establishing a European Insurance and Occupational Pensions Authority; no 1095/2010 establishing a European Securities and Markets Authority.

[14] See Council Reg (EU) no 1024/2013 of 15 October 2013 conferring specific tasks on the European Central Bank concerning policies relating to the prudential supervision of credit institutions.

[15] Reg (EU) no 806/2014 of the European Parliament and of the Council of 15 July 2014 establishing uniform rules and a uniform procedure for the resolution of credit institutions and certain investment firms within the framework of a Single Resolution Mechanism and a Single Resolution Fund and amending Regulation (EU) no 1093/2010.

how authority is divided in this domain at the EU level should not underestimate the role of the Commission and of the Council. Moreover, the analysis of interactions between different actors must take into account the type of functional division that the new legal framework tentatively put in place: the distinction between regulation, supervision and resolution. This distinction does not focus on the type of power, but on the phase of financial regulation in which an agency intervenes. This paper will speak of a 'division of functions' only to refer to this specific differentiation, the fruit of EU policy choice.

Also in this domain, the perspective of relative authority can be fruitful in assessing the respective role of the different EU actors. What is more, very few researches investigated the interplay between global regulators and EU ones.[16] This chapter argues that the authority of EU financial regulators is not only 'relative' when taking into account other EU institutions or agencies. It is 'relative' also because of the impact that rules established by global regulators have on the EU's regulatory autonomy. This means, for instance, that a profound revision of the rules about capital requirements does not take place within the rule-making activity of the European agency for banking, the EBA, but within the transnational regulatory network, the BCBS (in which the EBA and the European Commission take part). Hence, a proper understanding of the limits of the powers and authority of the new EU financial bodies needs to take into account the global/EU interplay. Taking into account the global/EU interplay is relevant also in order to address both the legitimacy of the global regulators and of the new EU financial architecture.

The focus of the analysis will be twofold. First, the features of the new European financial architecture might provide useful insights for addressing the shortcoming of the global financial architecture.[17] This statement might sound counterintuitive, given the controversies on the legitimacy of the EU agencies themselves. However, the Court of Justice of the European Union (CJEU) judgment in *Esma/Short selling* suggested that different paradigms of legitimation for EU agencies can and do coexist.[18] Albeit raising some criticism,[19] the approach of the CJEU intends to link the legitimacy of the agencies with procedural requirements, subject to judicial review. Compared to other agencies, often lacking a well-developed

[16] The EU Parliament commissioned a number of papers in order to fully understand the EU role in international economic for a: www.europarl.europa.eu/thinktank/en/document.html?reference=IPOL_STU(2015)542193; see also L Quaglia, *The European Union and Global Financial Regulation* (Oxford, Oxford University Press, 2014) and D Mugge (ed), *Europe and the Governance of Global Finance* (Oxford, Oxford University Press, 2014).

[17] For this type of perspective, but looking at the global economic governance executive and in particular at the European Council, see J Wouters and T Ramopoulos, 'The G20 And Global Economic Governance: Lessons From Multi-Level European Governance?' (2012) 15 *Journal of International Economic Law* 751.

[18] Case C-270/12 *United Kingdom of Great Britain and Northern Ireland v European Parliament and Council of the European Union (ESMA-shortselling case)* [2014] EU:C:2014:18.

[19] M Scholten and M van Rijsbergen, 'The Limits of Agencification in the European Union' (2014) 15 *German Law Journal* 1223.

procedural legal framework,[20] the financial ones seem better placed, having put in place a well-shaped procedural framework. From this point of view, the European financial architecture, in spite of its shortcomings, might even contain lessons for confronting the global architecture.

Second, the analysis complements current debates on the legitimacy of the EU agencies themselves. The legitimacy of EU agencies in general is a highly debated topic.[21] Given the relevant regulatory and supervisory powers that financial agencies enjoy, doubts and criticism about the legitimacy of these new bodies is particularly widespread.[22] The object of *Esma/Short selling* were precisely the boundaries within which the delegation of powers to the financial agencies is legitimate. Shedding light on the impact of global regulators within the EU shifts the terms of the debate on the legitimacy of the EU bodies. If the activity of the latter is effectively shaped by the global regulators, then efforts intended to ensure that EU agencies' activity is legitimate should be extended accordingly.

In order to conduct an analysis focused on the allocation of authority between the different actors engaging in financial regulation, a clarification of the type of rules adopted by the global regulators is needed. The first part of the chapter will thus be devoted to analysing the features of global financial standards, clarifying in which sense they have a 'hard' impact (section II). Second, the chapter will examine the current fragmentation of powers in global regulation, showing how powers shifted over time and giving account of the increasing centralisation of powers in the FSB, raising several problems regarding its interaction with the G20 (section III). Third, it will be shown how public authority is divided in the financial domain at the EU level, and how the authority of EU institutions is limited because of the impact of global rules (section IV). Lastly, the legitimacy of both the global and EU regulators will be discussed (sections V and VI, respectively). Section VII concludes.

II. A Preliminary Caveat: Global Financial Standards between Soft and Hard Law

In order to fully understand the scope of the powers of global financial regulators, as well as their influence within the EU, it is necessary to clarify the

[20] E Chiti, 'European Agencies' Rulemaking: Powers, Procedures and Assessment' (2013) 19 *European Law Journal* 93.

[21] M Everson, C Monda and E Vos (eds), *EU Agencies In Between Institutions And Member States* (Alphen a/d Rijn, Wolters Kluwer, 2014); M Egeberg and J Trondal, 'EU-level Agencies: New Executive Centre Formation or Vehicles for National Control?' (2011) 18 *Journal of European Public Policy* 868; M Scholten, *The Political Accountability of EU Agencies: Learning from the US Experience* (Maastricht, Universitaire Pers Maastricht, 2014).

[22] C Harlow, 'Editorial: Transparency, accountability and the Privileges of Power' (2016) 22 *European Law Journal* 273, 276.

features of global financial standards. There is no agreement on the definition of standards between standard-setters, especially on whether instruments may be qualified as standards if they are, even from a purely formal point of view, mandatory.[23] The scientific debate looks divided as well. Some scholars tend to contrast standardisation and regulation on the basis of the binding force of the latter,[24] others tend to refuse such a restrictive definition of standards.[25]

Generally, global financial standards are at first drafted as voluntary, purely soft law. For instance, when the BCBS or the IOSCO publish a standard, national regulatory authorities participating in these networks are expected to implement these standards through rule-making acts. Drivers of compliance are identified in the standard-setting bodies' expertise[26] and capacity of persuasion.[27] In principle, the same drivers work also for implementation by national authorities that do not participate in the network. Next to other workings of power this could explain why, for example, the Basel capital accords were applied worldwide.[28]

International organisations leverage several mechanisms to improve the implementation of global financial standards; mechanisms that, according to some commentators, make the adoption of the standards 'essentially mandatory'.[29] A first mechanism leading to this result is conditionality, often used by IMF.[30]

[23] For example, while the WTO TBT Agreement, Annex 2, para 1, contrasts standards, which are deemed to be voluntary, with technical regulations, that are, on the contrary, mandatory, the ISO and the IEC consider as standards also mandatory rules. For a comment, see OECD, 'Regulatory Reform and International Standardization', www.oecd.org/tad/benefitlib/1955309.pdf.

[24] D Kerwer, 'Rules That May Use: Standards and Global Regulation' (2015) 18 *Governance* 611.

[25] KW Abbott and D Snidal, 'Hard and Soft in International Governance' (2000) 54 *International Organization* 421, 421 and 434; see also, about the advantages of soft law contrasted to hard law, D Shelton, 'Introduction: Law, Non-Law and the Problem of "Soft Law"' in D Shelton (ed), *Commitment and Compliance. The Role of Non-Binding Norms in the International Legal System* (Oxford, Oxford University Press, 1999); S Charnovitz, 'International Standards and the WTO, The George Washington Law School Public Law and Legal Theory' (2005) GWU Law School Legal Studies Research Paper 133, 6 http://ssrn.com/abstract=694346; HV Morais, 'The Quest for International Standards: Global Governance vs Sovereignty, The Quest for International Standards: Global Governance vs Sovereignty' (2002) 50 *University of Kansas Law Review* 779 and D Zaring, 'International Law by Other Means: The Twilight Existence of International Financial Regulatory Organizations' (1998) 33 *Texas International Law Journal* 281.

[26] D Kerwer, 'Standardising as Governance: the Case of Credit Rating Agencies' in A Heritier (ed), *Common Goods: Reinventing European and International Governance* (Lanham, Rowman & Littlefield Publishers, 2002).

[27] A-M Slaughter, *A New World Order* (Princeton, Princeton University Press, 2009) 213.

[28] According to some studies, more than 100 States complied with the 1988 Capital Accord: PP Jackson, 'Capital Requirements and Bank Behaviour: the Impact of the Basel Accord' (1998) Basel Committee on Banking Supervision Working Papers 1/1999, 1, www.bis.org/publ/bcbs_wp01.pdf. Even though the financial crisis which started in 2008 slowed down the implementation process, Basel II, published in 2004, was implemented in more than 80 jurisdictions: BIS, 'Implementation of the new capital adequacy framework in non-Basel Committee member countries: Summary of responses to the 2006 follow-up Questionnaire on Basel II implementation', www.bis.org/fsi/fsipapers06.htm. According to the Financial Stability Institute, Basel III is being implemented in 98 non-BCBS countries: FSI, 'Survey. Basel II, 2.5 and III Implementation' (2015), www.bis.org/fsi/fsiop2015.pdf.

[29] RP Delonis, 'International Financial Standards and Codes: Mandatory Regulation Without Representation' (2004) 36 *International Law and Politics* 563.

[30] ibid.

Second, monitor compliance has for long been an influential mechanism. This is the case of the Reports on the Observance of Standards and Codes ('ROSCs'), part of the Financial Sector Assessment Program ('FSAP').[31] The most recent mechanism intended to foster the implementation of the standards are the FSB peer reviews, put in place in the aftermath of the crisis.[32]

Albeit formally soft law, global financial standards have a 'hard impact'.[33] This hard impact can be a matter of perception, as in the case of peer reviews putting in place soft pressure to comply, or it can result from formal incorporation in binding acts. This is often the case of the EU, where Basel capital accords were incorporated in the Capital Requirements Directive. Also the Credit rating agencies ('CRAs') Regulation draws widely upon IOSCO standards.[34] Increasingly so, the incorporation of global standards through legislative binding acts in the EU appears to be the preferential method of implementation when standards are perceived as crucial for financial stability. This means that there is a huge difference in the implementation process in the EU and, for example, in the US. While US regulatory authorities participating in a network implement a global standard through an act of rule-making, in the EU the implementation of global standards goes through the approval of a directive or a regulation, and the (newly established) European agencies exercise their (circumscribed, as it will be seen[35]) rule-making prerogatives further specifying these EU legislative acts. The degree of specificity of global financial standards can notably vary between broad principles and some highly specific standards.

III. The Fragmentation of Powers in the Global Financial Regulatory Architecture

A. The Evolution of Global Financial Regulators and the Separation of Powers before the Crisis

Transnational cooperation between banking authorities dates back to 1974, when the Basel Committee on Banking Supervision ('BCBS') was established by the G10 central banks. The BCBS started drafting the first standards on banking at the end of the decade, and eventually evolved into the most powerful and

[31] See IMF-World Bank, 'International Standards: Strengthening Surveillance, Domestic Institutions, and International Markets' (2003) 3, www.worldbank.org/ifa/intlstandards.pdf.

[32] See s III.B.

[33] Slaughter, above n 29, 224; See also Brummer, above n 4, 268–70.

[34] For an analysis of EU financial regulations implementing global standards, see De Bellis, above n 3.

[35] See s IV.A.

well-known transgovernmental regulatory network.[36] Also the origins of the BCBS counterpart for securities, the IOSCO, date back to 1974, when the Inter-american Association of Securities Commissions was established.[37] In 1983, after the Banco Ambrosiano crisis, this association was transformed in a universal network.[38] The International Association of Insurance Supervisors ('IAIS') was established in 1994 and sets standards for insurance.[39] Similar to the IOSCO and contrary to the BCBS, the IAIS is a universal network.

In the mid-1990s, the G7 and the IFIs started to be involved in global financial governance. In the Halifax Summit in 1995, the G7 recognised, for the first time, the significance of the cooperation taking place within the BCBS and the IOSCO. At the 1996 Lyon Summit, the G7 identified the broad objectives the standard-setting activities should have.[40] During the late 1990s, the G7 was increasingly involved in the shaping of the financial reform agenda,[41] considering financial standards-setting and dissemination crucial components.[42] Moreover, the G7 explicitly called on the IMF and the World Bank to 'monitor, in close co-operation with the standard-setting bodies, the implementation of these codes and standards' and 'to work closely together to provide advice and, where necessary, assistance to countries to help them meet these internationally agreed codes and standards'.[43] In such a context, the IMF and the World Bank developed specific programmes aimed at fostering compliance with global financial standards (the FSAP mentioned above[44]).

In the aftermath of the Asian financial crisis, two new bodies were established. First, the G20, bringing together G10 countries and emerging ones, was a step forward in the direction of more inclusiveness and representation.[45] Yet, until 2008 it

[36] About BCBS's history, structure and activity, see DR Wood, *Governing Global Banking. The Basel Committee and the Politics of Financial Globalization* (Aldershot, Ashgate Publishing, 2005).

[37] About IOSCO, see AA Sommer Jr, 'Iosco: its Mission and Achievement' (1996–97) 17 *Northwestern Journal of International Law & Business* 15; and C Bummer, 'Post-American Securities Regulation' (2010) 98 *California Law Review* 327.

[38] J Braithwaite and P Drahos, *Global Business Regulation* (Cambridge, Cambridge University Press, 2000) 88 and 143.

[39] Kapstein, above n 2.

[40] G7, 'Economic Communiqué: Making a Success of Globalization for the Benefit of All' (Lyon Summit Economic Communique, 1996), http://europa.eu/rapid/press-release_DOC-96-5_en.htm.

[41] See W Murden, 'Banking Supervision and Government Policy: the Role of Regulators in International Financial Reform' (1999) 4 *Fordham Finance, Securities and Tax Law Forum* 35, 36–37.

[42] IMF, 'Declaration of G7 Finance Ministers and Central Bank Governors' (30 October 1998) www.imf.org/external/np/g7/103098dc.htm.

[43] ibid.

[44] ibid, para 1.

[45] Such as Argentina, Brazil, China, India, Indonesia, Korea, Mexico, Russia, Saudi Arabia, South Africa and Turkey. RD Germain, 'Global Financial Governance and the Problem of Inclusion' (2011) 7 *Global Governance* 411.

met only as a group of financial ministers. Second, the Financial Stability Forum (FSF) was set up, a network aimed at bringing together, on the one hand, international financial institutions and TRNs, and, on the other hand, representatives of advanced economies' national authorities. The FSF was a very informal body, which did not have any statute or bylaws. Its main task was the one of promotion, coordination and information exchange among authorities responsible for financial stability.[46] It lacked autonomous standard-setting powers.

Before the crisis, there was thus a tripartite separation of powers: the TRNs were recognised as the standard-setting bodies; the G7 took over the agenda-setting task and asked the standard-setters to report on their activity; the IFIs were called to establish themselves as standard enforcers. The role of the G20 was limited and the FSF had a merely coordination task.

B. Concentrating Powers: The FSB as the Centre of Global Financial Governance

After the global financial crisis of 2007/2008, a debate about the most appropriate reforms of financial governance took place. It was argued that flexibility and voluntary standard setting had proven unsatisfactory and that a radically new and stronger mechanism was needed.[47] Some authors advocated the establishment of a World Financial Authority with binding powers.[48] However, the approach of broadening and strengthening existing institutions prevailed. The BCBS membership, originally limited to G10 authorities, was broadened to include representatives from the G20 countries.[49] Most notably, the two bodies that had been established in the late 1990s, the G20 and the FSF, were reinforced. The choice of tightening a dispersed system of financial regulation, instead of setting up a new authority, is at the core of the current financial architecture.

As mentioned above, until 2008, the G20 met only as a group of financial ministers. It is only in November 2008 that the first G20 political summit took place in Washington. The originally named Financial Stability *Forum* was

[46] See G7, 'Statement by the G7 Finance Ministers and Central Bank Governors' (Washington DC, 3 October 1998) para 3, www.g8.utoronto.ca/finance/fm100398.htm.

[47] See B Eichengreen, 'Not a New Bretton Woods but a New Bretton Woods Process' in B Eichengreen and R Baldwin (eds), *What G20 Leaders Must Do to Stabilise our Economy and Fix the Financial System* (London, Centre for Economic Policy Research, 2008) 25–26.

[48] See H Davies, 'Global Financial Regulation After The Credit Crisis' (2010) 1 *Global Policy* 185, 186–87.

[49] Central bank governors and heads of supervision from Argentina, Indonesia, Saudi Arabia, South Africa and Turkey, together with Hong Kong and Singapore are now members of the Committee: see BCBS, 'Basel Committee Broadens its Membership' (Press Release, 10 June 2009) www.bis.org/press/p090610.htm.

reorganised as Financial Stability Board ('FSB') after the G20 London Summit in April 2009.[50] In order to assess how these reforms resulted in powers shifting in global financial regulators, the new role of the FSB—the new 'head' of global regulation, according to some observers[51]—must be examined in its interactions with the G20.

The reorganisation of 2009 modified both the structure and the functions of the Board. As for the membership, the Board brings together the IFIs and the transnational networks, on the one hand, and national authorities, on the other hand. The latter are not only from G10 countries plus Australia, Hong Kong, Netherlands, Singapore and Switzerland (which were already members of the Forum), but also from Argentina, Brazil, China, India, Indonesia, Korea, Messico, Russia, Saudi Arabia, South Africa, Spain and Turkey.[52] In this way, FSB membership corresponds to the one of the G20. Also the EU Commission and the ECB have been admitted. As for the type of national authorities admitted, they are diverse, including treasury departments, central banks and supervisory authorities. However, not all member jurisdictions have three representatives. According to article 11 of the FSB Charter, '[t]he number of seats in the Plenary [the decision-making body of the FSB] assigned to Member jurisdictions reflects the size of the national economy, financial market activity and national financial stability arrangements of the corresponding member jurisdiction'. As a result of the application of these general criteria, G7 and BRICS countries have three representatives, while other countries have one or two. In this second scenario, only the central bank or the financial ministry are represented. Currently, the Plenary comprises 70 members.[53]

The structure and the mandate of the Board are clearly set forth in its founding Charter:[54] a big change from the complete informality of the FSF, which did not have a Charter, nor bylaws or a statute. The Plenary, which takes decisions by consensus, is the decision-making body of the FSB, adopting the reports and standards.[55] The Plenary also establishes Standing Committees and working groups: it is within these committees that the drafting of the reports and the

[50] See FSB, 'Financial Stability Forum re-established as the Financial Stability Board' (Press Release, 2 April 2009) www.financialstabilityboard.org/press/pr_090402b.pdf.

[51] Black, above n 10.

[52] See FSF, 'The Financial Stability Forum decides to broaden its membership' (Press Release, 12 March 2009) www.financialstabilityboard.org/press/pr_090312b.pdf.

[53] Members of the Financial Stability Board, www.fsb.org/about/organisation-and-governance/members-of-the-financial-stability-board.

[54] The Charter was adopted in 2009 and amended in 2012: see FSB, *Financial Stability Board Charter* (June 2012) www.financialstabilityboard.org/publications/r_120809.pdf.

[55] FSB Charter, art. 9.

standards take place, while the Plenary endorses their activity.[56] However, not only a mere formalisation took place. On the contrary, the mandate of the Board was significantly broadened.[57] As a result, the FSB seems to play a threefold role in global financial governance: a) it identifies priorities and actions to be taken (which it has been doing by not only preparing periodic reports, but also by publishing recommendations and guidelines); b) it coordinates the activity of the standard setting bodies; c) it monitors the implementation of the standards through peer reviews. In contrast to the division of powers before the global financial crisis, two tasks are now particularly relevant: the FSB directly sets some standards, and it is involved in standards implementation through peer review programmes.

The FSB standard-setting activity of the last years focused on issues that are commonly identified as crucial in triggering the crisis and in its exploitation. That is the case of the sets of recommendations about over the counter ('OTC') derivatives, which are intended to overcome the lack of transparency of the derivatives market. The recommendations on systemically significant financial institutions ('SIFI') and on effective resolution regimes for financial institutions, aim at overcoming the 'too big to fail' problem. Two main observations can be made: first, the FSB standard activity does not substitute the TRNs in their areas of competence, but focuses on specific problems; second, the FSB standard setting activity was more frequent in the immediate aftermath of the crisis than in most recent years (most standards were drafted in the years 2010–2011).[58]

On the contrary, the FSB activity as a standard enforcer increased over the years. In 2010, the FSB launched the 'Strengthening Adherence to International Standards' project, aimed at fostering the implementation of standards.[59] It is based on two types of peer reviews: thematic, ie focused on specific sets of standards (for example, peer reviews on compliance with FSB Principles on compensation have been conducted), and country specific.[60]

56 FSB Charter, art. 14–16.

57 Its most relevant tasks are: assessing the vulnerabilities affecting the global financial system and identifying related citations needed to address them and their outcomes; promoting coordination and information exchange among authorities responsible for financial stability; monitoring market developments; monitoring best practice in meeting regulatory standards; undertaking joint strategic reviews of the policy development work of the international standard setting bodies to ensure their work is timely, coordinated, focused on priorities and addressing gaps; collaborating with the International Monetary Fund ('IMF') to conduct Early Warning Exercises; promoting member jurisdictions' implementation of agreed commitments, standards and policy recommendations through monitoring of implementation, peer review and disclosure. FSB Charter, art 2, para 1.

58 See www.financialstabilityboard.org/publications/policy-documents/?mt_page=1.

59 See FSB, 'Framework for Strengthening Adherence to International Standards' (9 January 2010) http://www.fsb.org/wp-content/uploads/r_100109a.pdf?page_moved=1.

60 FSB, 'Handbook for FSB Peer Reviews' (12 March 2015) 3 www.fsb.org/2015/03/handbook-for-fsb-peer-reviews.

As mentioned above, the FSB sets its own standards, but they are intended to fill the gaps of the rules established by other standard-setters. Similarly, the FSB clearly states that its peer reviews do not substitute existing assessment mechanisms, but build on them. The FSB takes part in standard-setting and standard enforcement, but does not substitute the other actors exercising these types of powers. In this way, the tripartite separation of powers that could be sketched before the crisis looks much more blurred in the current framework. A crucial point which needs to be further disentangled in order to fully assess the role of the FSB is its relationship with the G20. In particular: how far do the G20 powers go in directing and controlling the FSB?

C. The Limits of Concentration: Assessing the G20 Role Vis-à-vis the FSB

After 2008, the G20 started playing a leading role and the link between the G20 and the re-established FSB has been strengthened. It is now set forth clearly in the FSB Charter. According to Article 4 of the Charter, the FSB has to periodically report progress in its work to the Finance Ministers and Central Bank Governors of the Group of Twenty, and to Heads of State and Governments of the Group of Twenty. This provision can be better understood in the context of provisions governing the relationship of the FSB with the standard-setting bodies. On the one hand, the mandate of the FSB includes 'undertaking joint strategic reviews of the policy development work of the international standard setting bodies to ensure their work is timely, coordinated, focused on priorities and addressing gaps'.[61] On the other hand, the standard-setting bodies have an obligation to report to the FSB.[62]

Hence, the FSB Charter tentatively sketches a division of powers as follows: the FSB identifies the priorities, coordinates the standard-setting activity, so that it corresponds to such priorities and, subsequently, gives account through periodic reports to the G20 (both at the ministerial and political level). The TRNs (but also other standard-setters as the International Accounting Standard Board (IASB)) carry on the standard-setting activity. The G20 endorses the priorities identified by the FSB and is the recipient of the reports. However, a deeper understanding of the interactions taking place between the Board and the G20 requires a closer look at their activity in the last years. Even though usually the Board plays a crucial preliminary function, so that the G20's role is often limited to a simple endorsement

[61] FSB Charter, art 2, para 1.

[62] FSB Charter, art 6, para 3: 'the standard setting bodies will report to the FSB on their work without prejudice to their existing reporting arrangements or their independence. This process should not undermine the independence of the standard setting process but strengthen support for strong standard setting by providing a broader accountability framework'.

of the Board's activity, it shows that the G20 has stepped in when crucial issues were being discussed.

The specific impact of the G20 can be understood in light of the process that led to the drafting of FSB standards about SIFIs, which aimed at addressing the 'too big to fail' problem, probably the key issue of current reforms.[63] Bail-outs heavily affected public finances. On the one hand, banks must be made resolvable: that is the aim of resolution regimes.[64] On the other hand, some have argued that such an approach would be ineffective: given the complexity and interconnectedness of SIFIs, they should be restricted in the activities that present too high risk-taking and hence conflicts of interest.[65] Hence, structural reforms are advocated.[66] The difference between the two approaches is self-evident: resolution regimes aim at making markets work, while the approval of structural reforms entails a radical change from the model of supervision which has been enacted in the last 30 years—a 'revised' version of the separation of investment and commercial banking. The second approach is at the basis of the Volcker rule in the US and the Vilckers Report in the UK. The new EU rules[67] about the resolution of banks adopt the first type of approach,[68] while a proposal for a regulation on banking structural reform was adopted by the Commission in January 2014, but no agreement was reached on the point.[69]

The FSB 'Recommendations reducing the moral hazard posed by systemically important financial institutions' do not advocate for structural reforms.[70]

[63] J Carmassi, E Luchetti and S Micossi, 'Overcoming Too-Big-To-Fail: A Regulatory Framework to Limit Moral Hazard and Free Riding in the Financial Sector' (CEPS Task force Reports, March 2010) 5 http://ssrn.com/abstract=1610214.

[64] DW Arner and JJ Norton, 'Building a Frame Work to Address Failure of Complex Global Financial Institutions' (2009) 39 *Hong Kong Law Journal* 95.

[65] See Group of Thirty, 'Financial Reform: A Framework for Financial Stability' (January 2009) www.group30.org/images/PDF/Financial_Reform-A_Framework_for_Financial_Stability.pdf. See also N Roubini and S Mihm, *Crisis Economics. A Crash Course in the Future of Finance* (New York, The Penguin Press, 2010) 266.

[66] See High-level Expert Group on reforming the structure of the EU banking sector: Final report, Brussels, Oct. 2012 (so called Liikanen Report), available at http://ec.europa.eu/internal_market/bank/docs/high-level_expert_group/report_en.pdf, 88.

[67] Dir 2014/59/EU of the European Parliament and of the Council of 15 May 2014 establishing a framework for the recovery and resolution of credit institutions and investment firms and amending Council Dir 82/891/EEC, and Dirs 2001/24/EC, 2002/47/EC, 2004/25/EC, 2005/56/EC, 2007/36/EC, 2011/35/EU, 2012/30/EU and 2013/36/EU, and Regs (EU) No 1093/2010 and (EU) No 648/2012, of the European Parliament and of the Council.

[68] They are intended to make banks resolvable, ie to make market work, and avoid incentives to excessive risk taking. Communication from the Commission, 'An EU Framework for Crisis Management in the Financial Sector' (20 October 2010) 2, http://ec.europa.eu/internal_market/bank/docs/crisis-management/framework/com2010_579_en.pdf; J Carmassi, E Luchetti, and S Micossi, 'Overcoming Too-Big-To-Fail' (Centre for European Policy Studies Paper, 2010) 10, http://aei.pitt.edu/14484/1/TFR_Bank_Crisis_Resolution.pdf.

[69] Proposal for a Regulation Of The European Parliament And Of The Council on structural measures improving the resilience of EU credit institutions, COM/2014/043 final.

[70] See FSB, 'Reducing the moral hazard posed by systemically important financial institutions' (20 October 2010) www.fsb.org/wp-content/uploads/r_101111a.pdf?page_moved=1.

However, in its preliminary documents on the issue, the FSB clearly considered that structural measures could be necessary in order to make a systemically significant institution resolvable.[71] Later on, though, the FSB documents focused exclusively on resolution regimes, and considered monitoring structural reforms adopted at the national level with the sole purpose of avoiding the risk that they lead to a fragmentation of financial markets.[72] It is not easy to assess whether this change was autonomously adopted by the Board, or whether it resulted from pressures coming from the G20. However, it must be recalled that in the same year the IMF had suggested the adoption of financial levies for SIFIs,[73] a proposal endorsed by the FSB[74] but rejected by the G20, because of a lack of consent between its members[75] (eventually leading France, Germany and the UK to adopt a separate statement).[76] This suggests that, even though preliminary and highly technical work is conducted by the FSB (or, as for fiscal matters connected with financial regulation, by the IMF), the political decisions remain in the realm of the G20. The boundaries of the respective roles of the G20 (purely political body) and the FSB (hybrid body, partly political and partly technical) in agenda-setting remains uncertain and the dynamics governing this power are not transparent. No clear separation of powers is in place in global financial regulation.

IV. The Distribution of Powers in the EU Financial Regulatory Architecture

In global financial regulation, horizontal powers can be distinguished between agenda-setting, standard-setting and standard-enforcement—between the identification of the priorities for the elaboration of guidelines, policies and recommendations; the drafting and elaboration of guidelines and recommendations; as well as the use of instruments intended to verify the degree of implementation of these guidelines and recommendations within national jurisdictions. These

[71] FSB, 'Progress on the global regulatory reform agenda. Letter to G20 Ministers and Governors' (19 April 2010) 2, www.fsb.org/wp-content/uploads/l_100423.pdf. See FSB, 'Interim Report on reducing the moral hazard posed by systemically important financial institutions' (27 June 2010) 5, www.financialstabilityboard.org/publications/r_100627b.pdf.

[72] See FSB, 'Structural Banking Reforms. Cross-border consistencies and global financial stability implications' (Report to G20 Leaders for the November 2014 Summit, 27 October 2014).

[73] See IMF, 'A Fair And Substantial Contribution By The Financial Sector. Final Report For The G-20' (June 2010), www.imf.org/external/np/g20/pdf/062710b.pdf.

[74] FSB, above n 74, 2.

[75] Si v J Kirton, 'The G20's Approach to Financial Risk and Risk Management' (June 2010) 17–18, www.g20.utoronto.ca/biblio/kirton-cccpc-2010.pdf.

[76] W Lewis, 'Joint statement by the French, UK and German Governments on bank levies' (*Propertyreporter.co.uk*, 22 June 2010) www.propertyreporter.co.uk/finance/joint-statement-by-french-uk-and-german-govs-on-bank-levies.html?DT=0.

powers are allocated *horizontally* within different global regulators (TRNs, FSB, G20). The basic *vertical* division of powers at the core of the transnational regulatory networks, as opposed to traditional treaty-based arrangements, is that national regulatory authorities taking part in the network (say, the FED participating in the BCBS) participate in the standard-setting activity and later in implementing the standard, bypassing parliamentary ratification.[77] While this model prevails in US practice, the implementation of global standards in the EU follows a different path due to the lack, until recently, of financial regulatory agencies and the differences of the powers given to the newly established agencies when compared to their US counterparts.

A. The ESFS, the EBU, and the Division of Regulation, Supervision, and Resolution

In the EU context, the tentative dividing line is not the one between agenda-setting, standard-setting and standard-enforcement but between regulation—ie rule-making—and supervision—ie ensuring that 'rules applicable to the financial sector are adequately implemented'.[78] According to Niamh Moloney, '[t]he relationship between "rules on the books" (law-making) and "rules in action" (supervision and enforcement) is, of course, symbiotic'; however, even though the line between rules and supervisory practices is blurring, this distinction is necessary to explain EU financial reforms.[79]

As mentioned above, the current architecture is the result of two different reforms: the ESFS, put in place in 2010, and comprising the three ESAs (EBA, ESMA, and EIOPA), the Joint Committee of the ESAs and the national authorities,[80] and the EBU, started in 2013, and based on the SSM and the SRM.[81] The system

[77] P-H Verdier, 'US Implementation of Basel II: Lessons for Informal International Lawmaking' in J Pauwelyn et al (eds), *Informal International Lawmaking* (Oxford, Oxford University Press, 2012) 437.

[78] N Moloney, 'The European Securities and Markets Authority and Institutional Design for the EU Financial Market—a Tale of Two Competences: Part (2) Rules in Action' (2011) 12 *European Business Organization Law Review* 177, 179.

[79] N Moloney, 'The European Securities and Markets Authority and Institutional Design for the EU Financial Market: a Tale of Two Competences: Part (1) Rule-making' (2011) 12 *European Business Organization Law Review* 41, 42.

[80] Also the European Systemic Risk Board ('ESRB'), falling outside the scope of this paper, is part of the ESFS. About the features of the ESFS, see E Ferran, 'Understanding the New Institutional Architecture of EU Financial Market Supervision' in E Wymeersch, KJ Hopt and G Ferrarini (eds), *Rethinking Financial Regulation and Supervision in Times of Crisis* (Oxford, Oxford University Press, 2012) 111–58; E Wymeersch, 'The European Financial Supervisory Authorities or ESAs' in Wymeersch, Hopt and Ferrarini (eds), ibid 232–317; M Everson, 'A Technology of Expertise: EU Financial Services Agencies' (2012) LEQS Paper No 49.

[81] About the EBU, see B Wolfers and T Voland, 'Level the Playing Field: The New Supervision of Credit Institutions by the European Central Bank' (2014) 51 *Common Market Law Review* 1463; E Ferran and V Babis, 'The European Single Supervisory Mechanism' (2013) 13 *Journal of Corporate*

resulting from the setting up of the ESFS—applying to all Member States—and the EBU—applying to banking institutions of the euro-area[82]—has been described as a two-track or a dual one:[83] within the ESFs, the three financial agencies have been given broad regulatory powers, while financial supervision is—as a general rule—in the domain of national competent authorities ('NCAs'). Within the EBU, on the contrary, the ECB—not a newly established European agency, but an established EU institution—has been given supervisory powers on 'significant' banking institutions across the Euro Area (non-significant institutions falling under the supervisory competences of the NCAs).[84] As a first, simplified assessment of the division of competences in the EU after the crisis is the following: as for banking in the euro-area, the EBA has the regulatory role and the ECB is entrusted with direct banking supervisory functions under the SSM (NCAs being competent for supervision on non-significant banking institutions); in the areas of securities and insurance, ESMA and EIOPA have regulatory competences, while NCAs retain supervisory tasks.

Before moving on to showing how the dividing lines of competences are much more blurred than this first sketch suggests, one last clarification needs to be drawn. Within the Banking Union the EU decided to separate day to day supervision from public intervention when a credit institution in crisis needs to be resolved. The separation between supervision and resolution is at the basis of the distinction between the SSM and the SRM. In the SSM, the EU body entrusted with new powers is the ECB, while in the SRM the European body responsible to manage the orderly resolution of significant credit institutions is a new European agency, the SRB. However, as the analysis will now clarify, also the authority of the SRB is 'relative', in that its powers are limited by the powers given to the Commission, the Council and to the ECB when deciding whether and how to resolve a bank.

Law Studies 255; E Wymeersch, 'The Single Supervisory Mechanism or "SSM", Part One of the Banking Union' (2014) Financial Law Institute Universiteit Gent Working Paper No 1/2014, papers.ssrn.com/sol3/papers.cfm?abstract_id=2397800; GA Ferrarini and L Chiarella, 'Common Banking Supervision in the Eurozone: Strengths and Weaknesses' (2013) ECGI-Law Working Paper No 223/2013, http://ssrn.com/abstract=2309897 or http://dx.doi.org/10.2139/ssrn.2309897; E Barucci and M Messori (eds), *The European Banking Union* (Florence, Passigli, 2014).

[82] And of the non-Euro States freely adhering to it.

[83] See GL Tosato, 'The Governance Of The Banking Sector In The Eu—A Dual System, in The European Banking Union' in Barucci and Messori (eds), above n 86, 4. I explored this issue more in depth elsewhere: see M De Bellis, 'European Financial Supervision after the Crisis: Multi-Speed Models within a Two-Track Framework' in E Chiti and G Vesperini (eds), *The Administrative Architecture of Financial Integration. Institutional Design, Legal Issues, Perspectives* (Bologna, il Mulino, 2015) 61–92.

[84] In order to avoid conflicts of interests, a specific Supervisory Board ('SB') responsible for supervisory matters has been set up within the ECB, providing for organisational separation of the staff competent for supervisory tasks from the staff responsible for carrying out monetary policy functions: Reg (EU) No 1024/2013, recital 65 and art 25.

B. The Blurring Division of Competences

As far as regulation is concerned, the rule-making powers of the ESAs comprise the adoption of technical regulations and the drafting of guidelines and recommendations. The latter are soft law tools.[85] Technical regulations can be of two types: technical standards or implementing standards. In order to have a binding effect the technical standards must be endorsed by the Commission, which can reject or amend the regulation. Technical standards are endorsed by the Commission as delegated acts under Article 290 TFEU, while implementing standards are endorsed as implementing acts under Article 291 TFEU.[86] The rule-making activity of the ESAs is thus not completely autonomous, and the Commission retains significant powers.

As for supervision, even though the ESAs are mainly regulatory bodies, they are also entrusted with some supervisory powers. First, the ESA regulations do entrust the three financial agencies with direct supervisory powers in three exceptional cases: in order to ensure consistent application of EU law by NCAs; in emergency situations' and in case of disagreement between competent authorities in cross border situations.[87] Second, sector regulations gave the ESMA direct supervisory powers in the areas of credit rating agencies, short selling of credit default swaps and trade repositories.[88] As a result, the distinction drawn above does not reflect accurately the current framework. As mentioned above, for banking supervision in the EBU, the ECB is the supervisory authority only as far as 'significant' credit institutions are concerned (assessed on the basis of the criteria of size, importance for the economy and significance of cross-border activities, and roughly corresponding to 130 institutions).[89] NCAs are competent for supervision over non-significant institutions.

As for banking resolution, the same criterion—the significance of the institution—applies for the division of competences between national authorities and the SRB.[90] Yet, this pattern is further complicated because, in addition, the Commission and the Council have strong powers in deciding on the resolution of banks[91] while the ECB plays a key role in assessing whether the resolution procedure has to be started.[92] As Bassan put it, the three EU institutions—the ECB, the Commission and the Council—'revolve around a new agency (SRM), that

[85] Reg 1093/2010, art 10-15.

[86] For a comment, see Ferran, above n 85, 46.

[87] ESA Regs, arts 17–19.

[88] Regs (EU) No 513/2011 of the European Parliament and of the Council of 11 May 2011 amending Reg (EC) No 1060/2009 on credit rating agencies, art 30, and No 648/2012 of the European Parliament and of the Council of 4 July 2012 on OTC derivatives, central counterparties and trade repositories. On the role of ESMA, see Moloney, above nn 83 and 84.

[89] See Council Reg (EU) No 1024/2013, art 6, para 4.

[90] Reg (EU) No 806/2014, art 7.

[91] See further, Board Reg (EU) No 806/2014, art 18, para 7.

[92] Reg (EU) No 806/2014, art 18, para 2.

has neither the power to initiate (this is up to the ECB) nor the power to decide (entrusted to the Commission and—in a way—to the Council)'.[93]

As a result, within the two main architectures—the ESFS and the EBU—there is not one single model according to which functions are divided between European and national authorities, and between different EU agencies and institutions.

Regulation is in the domain of the European financial authorities in the three sectors—banking, securities and insurance—in both the Euro area and outside it. But the Commission can reject or amend the technical standards drafted by the ESAs. The separation of regulation from supervision in the building of the new financial architecture is in any event rather problematic. In particular in the area of banking it leads to considerable overlaps and potential conflicts between the EBA—which is in principle entrusted with rule-making—and the ECB—to which some specific regulatory powers are nevertheless given under the SSM.[94]

The distribution of supervisory competences varies not only according to the specific sector (banking versus other areas of financial markets). As for banking in the euro-area, the ECB and the NCAs share competences, depending on the type of institution (significant or non-significant) concerned.[95] In other sectors—securities and insurance—the division of competences is even more blurred, since direct supervisory powers have been given for some specific operations or institutions (the powers of the ESMA in the areas of CRAs and of derivatives are a case in point). However, for all the three sectors of financial markets, and both in the euro area and outside it, the EU financial agencies have direct supervisory powers under exceptional circumstances.

As for the resolution of credit institutions, the vertical division of competences between the new EU agency SRB and the national authorities is further complicated horizontally, because the SRB has to coordinate with other EU institutions.

C. How 'Relative' is EU Authority in Financial Matters? The Impact of Global Standards on EU Regulation

The authority of EU financial regulators is not only 'relative' when taking into account other EU institutions or agencies, it is 'relative' also because of the impact

[93] See F Bassan, 'The Resolution Procedure: Misunderstanding the Institutional Balance' in Barucci and Messori (eds), above n 86, 40.

[94] About the rule-making powers of the ECB within the ESFS, see EL Camilli, 'The Governance of EU Regulatory Powers in the Banking Sector' in E Chiti and G Vesperini (eds), *The Administrative Architecture of Financial Integration. Institutional Design, Legal Issues, Perspectives* (Bologna, Il Mulino, 2015) 52.

[95] Yet, in both contexts the ECB plays a strong oversight role (for non-significant institutions, giving instructions to the NCAs and being able to attract the competence upon itself in order to ensure consistent supervision), so that the SSM puts in place an unprecedented and strong model of integration.

that rules established by global regulators have on their regulatory autonomy. The tendency of EU institutions to comply with global standards can be traced back to the 1990s and is particularly striking in the area of banking regulation. Directive 93/6/EEC, implementing the first capital accord approved by the Basel Committee in the 1980s, clearly stated that such directive 'forms part of the wider international effort to bring about approximation of the rules in force regarding the supervision of investment firms and credit institutions'.[96] When the Basel Committee revised its standard for capital requirements of banks, this tendency went even further. According to Enrico Camilli, the approval of the Capital Requirement Directive ('CRD') was 'a mere copycat exercise of decisions agreed in the secretive Swiss club by National authorities'.[97] The dramatic impact of global standards on the drafting of the EU Directive was recognised by the EU Parliament. In a Resolution of 2003, it criticised that 'the Basel Accord and other international agreements laying down a framework for legislation at EU level came into existence without any form of democratic mandate or control by the European Parliament'.[98] And it emphasised that, in future, 'questions with such far-reaching political implications should not be determined in advance by expert committees alone'.[99]

The impact of global standards continued over time and can be considered as a constant feature that is not limited to this sector.[100] This is the case of the Banking Recovery and Resolution Directive ('BRRD') no 2014/59/EU, implementing the FSB Key Attributes of Effective Resolution Regimes for Financial Institutions ('Key Attributes').[101] Moreover, the European Markets Infrastructure Regulation ('EMIR') implements the FSB recommendations for OTC Derivatives Market

[96] Council Dir 93/6/EEC of 15 March 1993 on the capital adequacy of investments firms and credit Institutions.

[97] EL Camilli, 'Basel-Brussels One Way? The EU in the Legalization Process of Basel Soft Law' in E Chiti and BG Mattarella (eds), *Global Administrative Law and EU Administrative Law: Relationships. Legal Issues and Comparison* (Berlin, Springer, 2011) 324.

[98] European Parliament resolution on the adequacy of banks' own funds (Basel II) (2001/2257(INI)) 2 September 2003, 2001/2257(INI) para 4, www.europarl.europa.eu/sides/getDoc.do?pubRef=-//EP//TEXT+TA+P5-TA-2003-0358+0+DOC+XML+V0//EN.

[99] ibid.

[100] See for example EBA Europe, 'Esas Publish Final Draft Technical Standards On Margin Requirements For Non-Centrally Cleared Derivatives' (8 March 2016) www.eba.europa.eu/-/esas-publish-final-draft-technical-standards-on-margin-requirements-for-non-centrally-cleared-otc-derivatives.

[101] Dir 2014/59/EU of the European Parliament and of the Council of 15 May 2014 establishing a framework for the recovery and resolution of credit institutions and investment firms and amending Council Directive 82/891/EEC, and Dirs 2001/24/EC, 2002/47/EC, 2004/25/EC, 2005/56/EC, 2007/36/EC, 2011/35/EU, 2012/30/EU and 2013/36/EU, and Regs (EU) No 1093/2010 and (EU) No 648/2012, of the European Parliament and of the Council. Also see L Stanghellini, 'La disciplina delle crisi bancarie: la prospettiva europea' in Banca d'Italia, 'Dal Testo unico bancario all'Unione bancaria: tecniche normative e allocazione di poteri. Atti del convegno tenutosi a Roma il 16 settembre 2013' (2014) 75 *Quaderno di ricerca giuridica* 157.

Reforms,[102] and the Credit rating agencies ('CRAs') Regulation complies with the IOSCO Code of conduct for credit rating agencies.[103]

Concerns about the impact of global harmonisation of financial rules notably led the European Parliament ('EP') to adopt a new resolution in 2016, about the EU's role in the framework of international financial, monetary and regulatory institutions and bodies. The goal of the EP is precisely the one of ensuring that 'national parliaments and the European Parliament should not be reduced to a role of mere rubberstamping'.[104] Hence, it is the EU institutions themselves that recognise their authority as 'relative' because of the limitations stemming from the activity of global bodies.

This point is crucial also from a research perspective that is attuned to legitimacy issues. Global standards, despite their form of soft law, are perceived as binding and the drafting of directives and regulations implementing global standards is often a formal process that does not lead to a real public debate that could result in departing from global guidelines. The strengthening of the EU's role in the decision-making process of global standard-setting bodies and institutions then becomes crucial. Hence, current debates on the legitimacy of EU financial agencies should be complemented by an in-depth analysis of the global/EU linkage. The chapter will now turn to addressing the legitimacy issue of global and EU regulators and how they interact.

V. Global Financial Governance and Legitimacy Concerns

The perspective of relative authority, used in this contribution, helps in understanding how the powers are assigned among the different regulators and shows the main weaknesses in the current framework. Instead of being clearly divided among the different actors, powers are assigned along blurring lines of competences. Given the different structures and procedures followed by the various bodies, some guiding criteria can be advanced on how powers should

[102] Reg (EU) No 648/2012 of the European Parliament and of the Council of 4 July 2012 on OTC derivatives, central counterparties and trade repositories. See FSB, 'OTC Derivatives Market Reforms Seventh Progress Report on Implementation' (8 April 2014) for an analysis of the correspondence between EMIR provisions and FSB standards, www.fsb.org/wp-content/uploads/r_140408.pdf?page_moved=1.

[103] Reg 1060/2009; See FSB, 'IMN Survey of National Progress in the Implementation of G20/FSB Recommendations, Jurisdiction: EU Commission' (2013) 42, indicating the regulation as the act of primary legislation implementing the IOSCO Code.

[104] European Parliament, 'Resolution on the EU role in the framework of international financial, monetary and regulatory institutions and bodies (2015/2060(INI))' (12 April 2016) www.europarl.europa.eu/sides/getDoc.do?pubRef=-//EP//NONSGML+TA+P8-TA-2016-0108+0+DOC+PDF+V0//EN.

be articulated. However, this desire for clarification encounters both practical limitations, and difficulties stemming from the nature of the powers involved (subsection A below). The legitimacy of the regulators must hence be strengthened also with instruments different from the articulation of powers, especially instruments intended to increase the inclusiveness of the regulators, their respect of due process, and eventually the establishment of instruments of judicial control (subsection B). The analysis will show that also the EU financial regulatory architecture can contribute to this legitimacy enhancing agenda and might even constitute an inspiring template.

A. The Limits to a Clear Articulation of Competences

As mentioned, the current allocation of authority goes roughly as follows: the FSB and the G20 are responsible for agenda-setting; transnational regulatory networks such as the Basel Committee set the standards; the IMF, the World Bank and the FSB monitor the implementation of the standards. The lines of division of powers between the different actors, however, are extremely blurred. First of all, the interaction of the FSB and the G20 in agenda-setting is not clear. As discussed above, while the Board usually identifies the priorities to be met and the G20 endorses them, the G20 can also play a more active role. Second, the criteria adopted by the FSB when deciding whether to proceed in setting a standard autonomously (instead of delegating it to a TRN) are not specified, even though it seemed more active in this regard right after the crisis, than in more recent times.

Given the highly differentiated structures and composition of the various bodies, some of them appear to be better suited to exercise one type of power—standard-setting or agenda-setting—than other bodies. These uncertain lines of competences look problematic and a case for a clearer-cut articulation of powers in financial governance could be made.[105] The G20, comprising the heads of State or Government, is a purely political body. The FSB has a mixed nature, since financial ministries are part of it together with the central bank governors and supervisory authorities. Ideally, the identification of priorities and the guiding principles should be in the domain of political bodies, and the specification and implementation should be done by technical ones. This would not necessarily mean a centralisation of the agenda-setting in the G20, but a clearer correspondence between the type of tasks that the FSB is executing and its composition could be envisaged.

As has also been mentioned, the drafting of the reports and standards takes place in the Standing Committees and working groups, while the Plenary endorses their work. As far as the composition of the committees and groups is concerned,

[105] J Waldron, 'Separation of Powers in Thought and Practice' (2013) 54 *Boston College Law Review* 433, 434.

the FSB Procedural Guidelines take into account criteria of balanced geographical representation, but do not distinguish between ministries' representatives and regulatory authorities' representatives, so that currently the composition of the groups involves both. In order to enhance a correspondence between the ground of legitimation of this body and the type of tasks it executes, the composition of the groups entrusted with the standard-setting and standard implementation tasks could be restricted to national regulatory authorities, leaving to the General Assembly, where political representatives sit, the approval of the documents and the identification of the priorities. The TRNs, made up of specialised domestic authorities directly interacting with each other,[106] appear to be the appropriate forum for standard setting, because of their technical expertise.[107]

However, a clearer articulation of competences, inspired to a correspondence between the type of functions and the composition and grounds of legitimacy of the regulator, is not easy to pursue in practice. In the immediate aftermath of the global financial crisis in 2008, the building of a world financial organisation was suggested, but it was rejected.[108] Notwithstanding the undeniable momentum—in terms of the awareness of the unprecedented scope and consequences of the crisis—political willingness to bind to a on international agreement and cede sovereignty was lacking. This type of resistance might apply less to the type of reform suggested above, not aimed at building a treaty-based organisation. A reform pointing at a more specific division of competences among existing institutions could hence have higher possibilities of success. However, a second reason for the failure of that more ambitious project can be traced: as Eyal Benvenisti and George W Downs point out, the fragmentation of powers in different networks can favour stronger countries that can choose the venue that is more favourable to pursue their interests in a given circumstance.[109] If this latter interpretation is correct, also a less ambitious reform such as the one suggested above might encounter fierce

[106] See K Raustiala, 'The Architecture of International Cooperation: Transgovernmental Networks and the Future of International Law' (2002) 43 *Virginia Journal of International Law* 1, 4–5.

[107] See D Zaring, 'International Law by Other Means: The Twilight Existence of International Financial Regulatory Organizations' (1998) 33 *Texas International Law Journal* 281; ibid, 'Informal Procedure, Hard and Soft in International Administration' (2005) 5 *The University of Chicago International Law Journal* 547; P-H Verdier, 'Transnational Regulatory Networks and Their Limits' (2009) 34 *Yale Journal of International Law* 113; and MJ Warning, *Transnational Public Governance. Networks, Law and Legitimacy* (New York, Palgrave, 2009).

[108] Eichengreen, *Out of the Box Thoughts About the International Financial Architecture*, 18-20 (IMF Working Papers, 2009 1–26), available at SSRN: http://ssrn.com/abstract=1415173; see also, calling for a financial administrative law agency, EJ Pan, 'Challenge of International Cooperation and Institutional Design in Financial Supervision: Beyond Transgovernmental Networks' (2010) 11 *Chicago Journal of International Law* 243 263–73. Other authors, on the contrary, suggest incremental reforms of the current setting are preferable, because of efficiency concerns: Brummer, above n 4, 311–24 and Wouters and Ramopoulos, above n 17,774.

[109] See E Benvenisti and G W Downs, 'The Empire's New Clothes: Political Economy and the Fragmentation of International Law' (2007) 60 *Stanford Law Review* 595–631, at 597–98 (warning on the opportunity to investigate the role of intentionality in the existence of fragmented system of regulation).

opposition, since, clarifying the respective domain of each actor and respective responsibility, it could diminish the capacity of the States of switching regimes.

Moreover, an obstacle to a clearer allocation of competences in global financial governance stems also from a basic uncertainly of the whole system: it is the difficulty of distinguishing between global rules equivalent to legislative acts from those that could be assimilated to administrative rule-making. This unclear distinction is rather problematic also in the domestic legal orders[110] and it is very well-known within the institutional framework of the EU.[111] International rule-making often implies fundamental policy choices: this was the case, already before the crisis, of the first two Basel capital accords. The broadening of the agenda of global financial reforms after 2008 increased the scope and impact of global rules. For example, the 'too big to fail' problem is closely connected to questions of how to spend public money. The revision of the Basel Committee rules on capital requirements for banks can affect the costs of bank lending and hence the recovery of the economy. If the legislative power cannot be clearly separated from the administrative one, then also determining in a clear cut way what a political body should do vis-à-vis technical ones is more complicated. Both technical expertise and political support are needed in the shaping of global financial rules, even if it still seems reasonable that political bodies—such as the G20 and the ministerial components of the FSB—should be key in identifying the priorities, while technical experts should specify the policies in detail.

B. The Legitimacy of Global Financial Regulation: Perspectives and Research Agenda

A clear articulation of competences between political and technical bodies is difficult to achieve, because of the practicability of reforms. Moreover, as discussed above, the exercise of financial rule-making involves not only technical expertise, but also fundamental policy choices. Because of this interconnection, the criteria for enhancing the legitimacy of regulators should ideally both enhance their inclusiveness, and ensure due process. In this regard, the perspective of relative authority does not exclude other research perspectives that have been advanced in recent years in order to address the legitimacy problems of the exercise of public authority.[112] A legitimacy framework for global financial

[110] B Ackerman, 'Good-bye Montesquieu' in S Rose-Ackerman and PL Lindseth (eds), *Comparative Administrative Law* (Cheltenham, Edward Elgar Publishing, 2010) 128–33.

[111] See J Mendes and I Venzke, 'Introduction' (this volume).

[112] On the research perspective on public authority, see A von Bogdandy and I Venzke, *In Whose Name? A Public Law Theory of International Adjudication* (Oxford, Oxford University Press, 2014). On the Global administrative Law (GAL) normative project, see the opening framework essay B Kingsbury et al, 'The Emergence of Global Administrative Law' (2005) 68 *Law & Contemporary Problems* 15; for the most recent developments of the scholarship, see 'Symposium: Through the lens of time: Global Administrative Law after 10 years' (2015) 13 *International Journal of Constitutional Law* 463.

regulators requires extensive future research; here, only the key elements to build on can be sketched.

The first element is the one of representation. While the TRNs for securities and insurance—IOSCO and the IAIS—have universal membership, the membership of both the FSB and the Basel Committee is limited to national authorities coming from G20 countries. It has been argued that the FSB, given its ambition to establish itself as the centre of global financial regulation, should broaden its representativeness beyond the G20 countries.[113] Because of the strong linkages between the FSB and the G20, discussed above, such an enlargement, to be effective, should involve both institutions. However, while the FSB experimented with various systems to involve authorities of countries outside its membership (for example, through a system of regional conferences), the G20 is much more reluctant to open its activity to countries not represented in it. From this point of view, the strengthening of the representativeness of FSB might require making the Board more autonomous from the G20. If this separation were the case, then the political input and endorsement should be centred in the FSB general body, the Assembly, reformed in its composition in order to represent only the political components (instead of its current mixed composition, while the regulatory authorities would constitute the working groups and committees).

Second, at the national level the grounds of legitimation of administrations lie not only in their technical expertise, but also in the formalised procedures they follow.[114] In the past years, the TRNs enhanced their transparency and started following notice and comment procedures.[115] Also the FSB, according to its Charter, should provide for consultation (even if this is stated in rather vague terms).[116] However, in order to effectively increase the legitimacy of a global regulator, procedural requirements should be clearly defined, comprising transparency, participation and duty to give reason, and should not be granted on a case by case basis, but officially recognised.[117]

Moreover, after the crisis the effectiveness of the TRNs was questioned and it was argued that such failure was the result of a regulatory capture.[118] Well-known

[113] Black, above n 10, 20 and 27.

[114] See S Rose-Ackerman (this volume).

[115] MS Barr and GP Miller, 'Global Administrative Law: the View from Basel' (2006) 17 *European Journal of International Law* 15 (arguing that enhanced due process of the networks had successfully addressed accountability concerns). For a critical point of view on the networks, see M Shapiro, '"Deliberative", "Independent" Technocracy v Democratic Politics: Will the Globe Echo the EU?' (2005) 68 *Law & Contemporary Problems* 342, S Picciotto, 'Networks in International Economic Integration: Fragmented States and the Dilemmas of Neo-Liberalism' (1997) 17 *Northwestern Journal of International Law & Business* 1014, and BS Chimni, 'International Institutions Today: An Imperial Global State in the Making' (2004) 15 *European Journal of International Law* 1–37.

[116] FSB Charter, art 6.

[117] M De Bellis, 'Global Financial Standards and Regulatory Failure: Lessons for Reforms' in G della Cananea and A Sandulli (eds), *Global Standards for Public Authorities* (Napoli, Editoriale Scientifica, 2012) 73–107.

[118] D Wood, above n 39, 150.

and extensively investigated in domestic legal systems,[119] the risk of a regulatory capture seems even stronger in the global arena.[120] An effective tool in order to counterbalance the pressures coming from the financial industry is the one of setting up a stakeholders' group, in which also academics and consumer associations must have a seat. As will be discussed in the following section, this instrument has been adopted at the EU level, and it is one of the features for which the EU architecture could constitute a model for the global one, for purposes of enhancing its legitimacy.

Third, contrary to other areas of global regulation, where a proliferation of global courts can be traced,[121] in the area of global financial regulation there is no dispute settlement body, probably because the main addresses of the standards are the national regulatory authorities, and not directly private parties. However, if procedural due process is to be conducive to an increased legitimacy of the global regulators, a judicial control is crucial. For both the shaping of procedural rules for global financial regulation, and for building a system of judicial control, the EU financial architecture can work as an inspiring model.

VI. The EU Financial Regulatory Architecture and the Global Financial Architecture: Source of Inspiration or Part of the Solution?

A. Lessons from the EU Architecture for the Global One?

The argument that the new EU financial architecture might work as a source of inspiration might sound odd, given the widespread criticism involving EU agencies in general,[122] and the recent controversial exercise of powers by the

[119] For a general overview of the risks of the interest representation model, see RB Stewart, 'The Reformation of American Administrative Law' (1975) 88 *Harvard Law Review* 1667. For regulatory capture in financial regulation, LG Baxter, '"Capture" in Financial Regulation: Can We Channel It Toward the Common Good?' (2011) 21 *Cornell Journal Law and Public Policy* 175.

[120] M De Bellis, 'Global Financial Regulation. The Challenges Ahead and GAL, in Global Administrative Law: An Italian perspective' (2012) European University Institute (EUI) Robert Schuman Centre for Advanced Studies (RSCAS) Policy Papers 2012/04, 41–49, http://cadmus.eui.eu/bitstream/handle/1814/22374/RSCAS_PP_2012_04.pdf?sequence=1.

[121] A von Bogdandy and I Venzke, 'In Whose Name? An Investigation of International Courts' Public Authority and its Democratic Justification' (2012) 23 *European Journal of International Law* 7; S Cassese, *I Tribunali di Babele. I giudici alla ricerca di un nuovo ordine globale* (Roma, Saggine, 2009).

[122] About the long standing debate on the accountability of EU agencies, see M Everson, C Monda, E Vos (eds), above n 21; M Busuioc, *European Agencies. Law and Practices of Accountability* (Oxford, Oxford University Press, 2013).

ESMA[123] in particular. However, as mentioned at the outset, the CJEU judgment in *Esma/Short selling* shows that different paradigms of legitimation for EU agencies are not mutually exclusive. In particular, the approach of the CJEU links the legitimacy of the delegation of powers to ESMA with compliance with procedural requirements, subject to judicial review. The use of a procedural paradigm to legitimate the activity of regulatory agencies is common in national jurisdictions as well. From this point of view, the ESAs appear to be particularly well-equipped, compared to other EU agencies.

While EU agencies often lack a well-developed procedural legal framework,[124] the financial ones do follow a comprehensive procedural framework.[125] A full assessment of the potentiality of these procedural instruments, of how they connect and are part of a 'complex accountability'[126] framework of the EU financial agencies and of how this complex accountability framework could constitute a useful benchmark in assessing the one of global financial regulators fall beyond the scope of this chapter. However, some hints can be given within the continuous search for surrogate devices for democracy that is at the core of the debates on legitimacy beyond the State.[127] The research perspective of relative authority is here understood as a useful instrument to disentangle and better focus the legitimacy issues connected with the different actors, but does not exclude—and can actually be combined—with the use of other research perspectives, such as those focused on the potentiality of procedural instruments—for example, transparency, participation and giving reasons—in order to address the legitimacy concerns raising from the activity of global and EU regulators.[128]

First of all, the accountability of the ESAs is based on an obligation to report upon request of the Parliament (thus, not on an annual basis),[129] and on financial accountability.[130] The accountability standards of the SSM go far beyond the model used by the ESAs, including: an obligation to report on an annual basis to

[123] Case C-270/12 *United Kingdom of Great Britain and Northern Ireland (Esma-shortselling case)* [2014] EU:C:2014:18. For a comment, see E Vos, and M Everson, 'European Agencies: What About the Institutional Balance?' (2014) Maastricht Faculty of Law Working Paper No 4 SSRN: https://ssrn.com/abstract=2467469 orhttp://dx.doi.org/10.2139/ssrn.2467469.

[124] E Chiti, 'European Agencies' Rulemaking: Powers, Procedures and Assessment' (2013) 19 *European Law Journal* 93, 94.

[125] See M De Bellis, 'Procedural Rule-Making Of European Supervisory Agencies (Esas): An Effective Tool For Legitimacy?' (2016) Working paper to be presented at the Academic Research Network on Agencification of EU Executive Governance (TARN) conference on Constitutionality, powers and legitimacy of EU agencies or agency-like bodies.

[126] JL Mashaw, 'Structuring a "Dense Complexity": Accountability and the Project of Administrative Law' (2005) in *Issues in Legal Scholarship: The Reformation of American Administrative Law* (Berkeley, Berkeley Electronic Press, 2005).

[127] JHH Weiler, 'The Geology of International Law—Governance, Democracy and Legitimacy' (2004) 64 *ZaöRV* 547, 561.

[128] See s IV of this chapter.

[129] Reg (EU) 1093/2010, 1094/2010, 1095/2010, art 50.

[130] Since the budget of the EBA comes partially from contributions of national authorities and partially from the EU: see Reg (EU) 1093/2010, 1094/2010, 1095/2010, art 62.

the Parliament, the Council and the Euro Group; an obligation to participate in a hearing upon request of the Parliament; an obligation to hold confidential oral discussions behind closed doors with the chair and the vice-chair of the competent committee of the Parliament; the obligation to cooperate sincerely with any Parliamentary investigation.[131] Moreover, the ECB and the Parliament shall conclude appropriate arrangements on the processes of democratic accountability, including access to information.[132] There are obviously limits in how far this framework can work as an inspiration, given the lack of a global financial legislature with direct representation. However, should the FSB be reformed, reporting obligations could be clarified in a similar sense. Moreover, the ESAs rule-making follows a very detailed procedure, combining oral and written participation, transparency and duty to give reasons, that could constitute a blueprint in shaping the due process of the global standard setters. Lastly, each of the ESAs is required to establish, under its founding regulations, a Stakeholders Group, which, providing for a more balanced representation of all the interests at stake, can counterbalance risks of regulatory capture.[133]

B. EU Participation in Global Regulation: Addressing the Legitimacy Deficit of EU Agencies' Relative Authority

Debates on the legitimacy of EU agencies are widespread and focus on the impact of 'agencification' on the institutional balance within the EU. With this chapter, I tried to shed light on a neglected facet of the legitimacy concerns connected with financial agencies, ie showing how the exercise of regulatory authority on financial issues by EU bodies is limited by the exercise of authority in this domain at the global level. This suggests that a key—albeit neglected—element in legitimacy debates is the one of EU bodies' representation in global fora, and of their participation in the drafting of global rules, a phase that proves to be crucial, given the limitations to the scope of the autonomy of EU bodies in the implementation of the standards.

How do EU agencies and institutions participate in global regulators? Currently, there is a mismatch in institutional participation of EU bodies in global ones, for two reasons. First, some EU Member States participate in these regulators, so that some national interests are autonomously represented. As a result, there is no single voice channelling EU interests. Second, when the EU is represented, the participating body is often the Commission. The ECB or European agencies were not admitted until very recently, because of these bodies' development over time.

[131] Reg (EU) No 1024/2013, art 20, paras 2, 5, 8 and 9.
[132] Reg (EU) No 1024/2013, art 20, para 9.
[133] See M De Bellis, above n 131, 10–11.

Two examples show this mismatch. Since the BCBS, originally comprising the G10 Central Bank governors, enlarged its membership in 2009 to include representatives from all the G20 countries,[134] the banking supervisory authorities of nine EU Member States are members of the Committee.[135] As for EU institutions, the Commission has long lasting observer status. Recently, however, the ECB and the SSM have been given full membership in the Committee, while the EBA has been recognised observer status.[136] A similar pattern emerges within the FSB. As for the Member States, six are represented in the Plenary and in all the Standing Committees (in which the actual standard-setting work takes place).[137] The EU Commission is member of the Plenary and of two Standing Committees, while the ECB is represented in the Assembly and one Standing Committee.[138]

The high number of representatives that could 'voice' EU interests is one potential strength of EU participation in global regulators. However, it has been pointed out that the actual impact of the EU has been weaker than what it could have been, because there were divisions between national representatives.[139]

As for EU representatives, the Commission's participation in both the BCBS and the FSB is a heritage of the lack, until recently, of EU financial agencies. The recent admission of the ECB, the SSM and the EBA, in the BCBS, and of the ECB in the FSB matches the growing centralisation of banking regulatory and supervisory competences in the EU. However, this type of representation does not mirror the current division of powers in the EU: for example, the agency competent for banking regulation, the EBA, has been recognised only observer status,[140] while the ECB, competent for banking supervision, enjoys full member status. However, this mismatch can be understood in light of the blurring of competences between the EBA and the ECB, discussed above, and the stronger independence of the ECB, recognised in the Treaty. Moreover, the limits of the rule-making powers of the EBA (subject to the Commission's endorsement) would impair its activity

[134] Argentina, Indonesia, Saudi Arabia, South Africa and Turkey, together with Hong Kong and Singapore.

[135] Belgium, France, Germany, Italy, Luxembourg, The Netherlands, Spain, Sweden, and the United Kingdom.

[136] Basel Committee membership, www.bis.org/bcbs/membership.htm.

[137] Of which three have full membership, involving three seats corresponding to the central bank governor, the ministry of finance and the supervisory authority (France, Germany, Italy and United Kingdom), while two have two seats (Spain and the Netherlands; their supervisory authority is not represented): www.fsb.org/about/fsb-members.

[138] France, Germany, are represented in all the standing committee, and the United Kingdom in three, Italy, Spain and the Netherlands in two: see EU Parliament, Directorate general for Internal Policies, 'The European Union's Role in International Economic Fora Paper 2: the FSB' (June 2015) 15, www.europarl.europa.eu/thinktank/en/document.html?reference=IPOL_STU(2015)542191.

[139] For the BCBS, EU Parliament, Directorate general for Internal Policies, 'The European Union's Role in Economic Fora Paper 5: the BCBS' (May 2015) (In-depth policy analysis prepared by L Quaglia for the ECN Committee) 17–18, www.europarl.europa.eu/RegData/etudes/IDAN/2015/542194/IPOL_IDA(2015)542194_EN.pdf. For the FSB, see EU Parliament, Directorate general for Internal Policies, *The European Union's Role in International Economic Fora Paper 2: the FSB*, 2015., 15.

[140] Basel Committee Membership, www.bis.org/bcbs/membership.htm.

in the network.[141] Lastly, the very fact that the implementation of standards goes through the legislative process makes the Commission's role in the Committee necessary for the time being—no matter how baroque the architecture looks.

In its 2016 Resolution, the European Parliament considers this misalignment in representation as worrisome, in particular as national representatives of EU Member States often assume positions in international fora that are contrary to decisions adopted in the EU by majority vote.[142] However, if the diagnosis is clear—fragmentation leads to a weak representation of EU interests—the recipe is not easy to identify. The EP considers the Commission to be the actor representing the interests of the EU as a whole.[143] As for representation in the transnational network for banking, however, it calls for Member States to accept a single representation via the SSM.[144] It does not clarify whether this single representation would mean that the Commission should also give up its seat.

If the instrument better suited to address the legitimacy gap of EU agencies or institutions resulting from the impact of global regulators on their authority is correctly identified in the EP Resolution—ie, fostering EU participation in global fora—the shaping of the most appropriate institutional representation model is not easy, because of the very unclear current horizontal division of competences across different bodies in the EU financial architecture. However, it is necessary to put in place clear and transparent reporting obligations of the EU body (agency or Commission) representing the EU in the global network to the EU Parliament so that an instrument, which is intended to guarantee that EU interests are effectively taken into account within global networks, evolves into an instrument that could render the decisions taken within global networks more legitimate for EU constituencies.[145]

VII. Concluding Remarks

Global financial regulation appears fragmented in a number of different networks and clubs. Lines dividing the competences of the different bodies are blurring, even though they can roughly be described as entrusting transnational regulatory networks with standard setting, and the G20 and the FSB with the tasks of setting the agenda and identifying priorities and guiding principles. Efforts geared

[141] For an overview of EU agencies' external actions, see A Ott, E Vos and F Coman-Kund, 'European Agencies on the Global Scene: EU and International Law Perspectives' in Everson, Monda, Vos (eds), above n 21.

[142] European Parliament, above n 109, para 10.

[143] ibid, para 11.

[144] ibid, para 19.

[145] For a fuller discussion of this point, see M De Bellis, 'Reinforcing EU financial bodies' participation in global networks: addressing legitimacy gaps?', paper presented at the TARN Workshop, *External dimension of EU agencies and bodies*, University of Luxembourg, Luxembourg, 27–28 June 2017.

towards a clearer articulation of powers encounter many limits. Given the variety of powers that each of these bodies exercises, often implying fundamental policy choices, the legitimacy of these bodies should be grounded on both even representation and on procedural standards.

Within the complex financial regulatory architecture established in the EU in the aftermath of the crisis, the public authority of EU bodies is relative not only horizontally (because of the number of EU actors intervening in financial regulation), but also vertically, as limited by global regulators. The focus on the interplay between global and EU regulation helps to address the legitimacy gaps emerging both at the global and at the EU level.

First, the new EU financial architecture—as for some of its specific institutional features—can possibly provide lessons for the global financial architecture, hence contributing to fostering its legitimacy. This is the case of reporting obligations, due process, and the setting up of a stakeholders group, providing a channel for participation of neglected interests and attempting to counterbalance the risk of regulatory capture.

Second, shedding light on the impact of global regulators within the EU shifts the terms of the debate on the legitimacy of the EU bodies themselves. If the activity of the latter is effectively shaped by global regulation, then efforts intended to ensure that EU agencies' activity is legitimate need to extend accordingly. From this perspective, the analysis attempts to complement the debate on the legitimacy of EU regulators.

12

Relative Authority and Institutional Decision-making in World Trade Law and International Investment Law

DIANE A DESIERTO

All social laws are, in the last resort, laws for the protection of individuals; all laws for the protection of individuals are, in a true sense, social laws.[1]

Once negotiations are engaged, the interests of actors shape the scope and content of rules. There will be the offensive and defensive sector interests, the interests of various (often) competing central government departments, the interests of sub-central governments, independent regulatory bodies, consumers ...[2]

I. Public Authority in Trade and Investment Rule-making

Postmodern[3] trade and investment rule-making are, inimitably, examples of the exercise of international public authority.[4] The 1994 Marrakesh Declaration that

[1] *Application of the Convention of 1902 governing the Guardianship of Infants (Netherlands v Sweden)* (Merits) [1958] ICJ Rep 55, Separate Opinion of Sir Judge Hersch Lauterpacht, para 15.

[2] S Woolcock, 'Introduction: The Interaction between Levels of Rule-making in International Trade and Investment' in S Woolcock (ed), *Trade and Investment Rule-Making: The Role of Regional and Bilateral Agreements* (Tokyo, United Nations University Press, 2006) 16.

[3] Trade and investment norms between States have a particularly long genealogy. See P Garnsey, K Hopkins and CR Whittaker (eds), *Trade in the Ancient Economy* (Berkeley, University of California Press, 1983) ix–xxv (Introduction); 'Investment and Commercial Banks' in J Mokyr (ed), *The Oxford Encyclopedia of Economic History* vol III (Oxford, Oxford University Press, 2003); K Miles, *The Origins of International Investment Law: Empire, Environment and the Safeguarding of Capital* (Cambridge, Cambridge University Press, 2013) 17–70 (on foreign investment rules during the early nineteenth and twentieth centuries). For purposes of this chapter, however, I limit the analysis of separation of powers to the trade and investment rule-making systems to those trade and investment treaties and/or institutions that arose or were established after World War II.

[4] See A von Bogdandy, P Dann and M Goldmann, 'Developing the Publicness of Public International Law: Towards a Legal Framework for Global Governance Activities' (2008) 9 *German Law Journal* 1383

heralded the establishment of the World Trade Organization (WTO) identified various public interest concerns of the Member States in doing so, from the 'widespread desire to operate in a fairer and more open multilateral trading system for the benefit and welfare of their peoples',[5] the need for a 'more balanced and integrated global trade partnership',[6] to the importance of 'provisions conferring differential and more favourable treatment for developing economies, including special attention to the particular situation of least-developed countries'.[7] Similarly, Contracting States to the 1965 Convention on the Settlement of Investment Disputes between States and Nationals of Other States (otherwise known as the ICSID Convention) expressed public interest concerns such as 'the need for international cooperation for economic development, and the role of private international investment therein,[8] as well as 'attaching particular importance to the availability of facilities for international conciliation or arbitration to which Contracting States and nationals of other Contracting States may submit such disputes if they so desire'.[9] Scholars have already made the argument that various institutions, organs, and standards-setting boards of the WTO system,[10] as well as international tribunals in the international investment system,[11] concretely wield some form of international public authority.

This chapter focuses on scrutinising relative authority in trade and investment rule-making processes, by the authoritative decision-makers[12] within each regime.[13] Despite their structural, normative and institutional differences, trade

('We consider as international public authority any authority exercised on the basis of a competence instituted by a common international act of public authorities, mostly states, to further a goal which they define, and are authorized to define, as a public interest. The "publicness" of an exercise of authority, as well as its international character, therefore depends on its *legal basis*.').

[5] Marrakesh Declaration of 15 April 1994, para 2, www.wto.org/english/docs_e/legal_e/marrakesh_decl_e.pdf.

[6] ibid, para 4.

[7] ibid, para 5.

[8] Convention on the Settlement of Investment Disputes between States and Nationals of Other States (ICSID Convention), 575 UNTS 159 (1965), Preamble, first para.

[9] ibid, Preamble,4th para.

[10] See J Windsor, 'The WTO Committee on Trade in Financial Services: The Exercise of Public Authority within an Informational Forum'; I Feichtner, 'The Administration of the Vocabulary of International Trade: The Adaptation of WTO Schedules to Changes in the Harmonized System'; RA Pereira, 'Why Would International Administrative Activity Be Any Less Legitimate? A Study of the Codex Alimentarius Commission'; all in A von Bogdandy, R Wolfrum, J von Bernstorff, P Dann, and M Goldmann (eds), *The Exercise of Public Authority by International Institutions: Advancing International Institutional Law* (Heidelberg, Springer, 2010).

[11] A Kulick, *Global Public Interest in International Investment Law* (Cambridge, Cambridge University Press, 2012) 97.

[12] HD Lasswell and MS McDougal, *Jurisprudence for a Free Society: Studies in Law, Science, and Policy* (The Hague, Martinus Nijhoff, 1992) 323.

[13] I have discussed in detail the differences between bases of obligation, authoritative decision-makers, and constitutive decision-making processes in world trade law as opposed to international investment law, in DA Desierto, 'Public Policy Design in International Investment and Trade Law: Community Expectations and Functional Decision-Making' (2014) 26 *Florida Journal of International Law* 52–149.

rule-making and investment rule-making both occur through the exercise of international public authority, because these rule-making processes affect not just States' regulatory freedoms, but more crucially, individuals' actual felt entitlement to civil, political, economic, social and cultural rights and freedoms. While trade rules might appear primarily concerned with ensuring foreign market access and reaching for equal terms of competition between similarly situated market participants,[14] the formulation, application, and interpretation of world trade rules cannot be examined in sharp isolation from the effects they generate upon the entire spectrum of qualitative factors that affect individuals' real freedoms today—whether it be environmental conditions, food safety standards, consumer choice and welfare, labour and employment conditions in producing goods—in short, the whole realm of State regulation of economic activity, the factors of production, and the determinants of market access and terms of competition, which comprise the constituent elements of meaningful human development.[15] Likewise, beyond the establishment of rules for States' treatment of foreign investment and the protection of investors, international investment rules[16] can also affect the exercise of States' regulatory discretion and fiscal abilities to respond to public policy crises.[17] Because States purposely delegate and vest authority upon various inter-State and non-State actors to define, apply, interpret and refine world trade and international investment rules to serve broad public objectives, international public authority is arguably inherent and intrinsic to trade and investment rule-making. While both world trade law and international investment law are related disciplines within international economic law,[18] their rule-making processes and institutions are not identical.[19]

[14] See JH Jackson, *Sovereignty, the WTO, and the Changing Fundamentals of International Law* (Cambridge, Cambridge University Press, 2006) 84–90 (on the numerous social goals and objectives of the WTO system beside mainly achieving reciprocal market access).

[15] See A Sen, *Development as Freedom* (Oxford, Oxford University Press, 1999) 3 (on the concept of development as 'a process of expanding the real freedoms that people enjoy'); P van den Bossche and W Zdouc, *The Law and Policy of the World Trade Organization* (Cambridge, Cambridge University Press, 2013) 35.

[16] For the counter-argument that the content of international investment rules ultimately converge towards a multilateralist architecture, see SW Schill, *The Multilateralization of International Investment Law* (Cambridge, Cambridge University Press, 2009).

[17] DA Desierto, *Public Policy in International Economic Law: The ICESCR in Trade, Finance, and Investment* (Oxford, Oxford University Press, 2015) 308–34.

[18] Scholars have written about the trade-investment relationship variably, with some indicating unanimity between these fields, others indicating a trend towards potential convergence. See ME Footer, 'On the Laws of Attraction: Examining the Relationship between Foreign Investment and International Trade'; T Broude, 'Investment and Trade: the "Lottie and Lisa" of International Economic Law?'; DP Steger, 'International Trade and Investment: Towards a Common Regime?'; and C Tietje, 'Perspectives on the Interaction between International Trade and Investment Regulation' all in R Echandi and P Sauve (eds), *Prospects in International Investment Law and Policy: World Trade Forum* (Cambridge, Cambridge University Press, 2013).

[19] I have written elsewhere about the separate functional trajectories of international investment and world trade law. Desierto, above n 14.

This chapter uses the lens of separation of powers analysis[20] to examine the nature of rule-making processes within the WTO system and the international investment system,[21] and to show how relative authority operates differently for each, largely due to varying degrees of importance attached by authoritative decision-makers to the legitimacy assets of inclusiveness, functional specialisation and rights protection.

II. Trade and Investment Rules, Decisions, and Authoritative Decision-makers

The single undertaking approach to the multilateral agreements administered by the WTO,[22] taken alongside the different functional hats worn by the General Council (eg acting both as a political quasi-legislative organ for the WTO Members, as well as discharging judicial functions as the Dispute Settlement Body), enable a more centralised environment for the creation and interpretation of world trade rules.[23] Other agents for rule-making in the WTO, such as technical bodies and standards-generating boards, act under a clear mandate from trade law treaties to which States expressly confer consent.[24] In contrast, international investment rules are drawn from a more variable constellation of authoritative

[20] This is certainly not the first attempt to use separation of powers analysis for these treaty regimes. See L Bartels, 'The Separation of Powers in the WTO: How to Avoid Judicial Activism' (2004) 53 *International and Comparative Law Quarterly* 861; JL Dunoff, 'Constitutional Conceits: The WTO's 'Constitution' and the Discipline of International Law' (2016) 17 *European Journal of International Law* 3 (2006) 647–75; C Moellers, *The Three Branches: A Comparative Model of Separation of Powers* (Oxford, Oxford University Press, 2013) 204–09. In contrast, classic separation of powers theory has not been as readily transposable into international investment law. See G van Harten, 'Investment Treaty Arbitration, Procedural Fairness, and the Rule of Law' in SW Schill (ed), *International Investment Law and Comparative Public Law* (New York, Oxford University Press, 2010) 63.

[21] On the process of international investment rule-making, see J Zhan, J Weber and J Karl, 'International Investment Rulemaking at the Beginning of the Twenty-First Century: Stocktaking and Options for the Way Forward' in JE Alvarez and KP Sauvant (eds), *The Evolving International Investment Regime: Expectations, Realities, Options* (Oxford, Oxford University Press, 2011). On the process of world trade rule-making, see C-D Ehlermann and L Ehring, 'Decision-Making in the World Trade Organization: Is the Consensus Practice of the World Trade Organization Adequate for Making, Revising, and Implementing Rules on International Trade?' (2005) 8 *Journal of International Economic Law* 51; T Cottier, 'A Two-Tier Approach to WTO Decision-Making' in DP Steger (ed), *Redesigning the World Trade Organization for the Twenty-First Century* (Ottawa, Wilfrid Laurer University Press, 2009) www.10.iadb.org/intal/intalcdi/PE/2010/05075.pdf.

[22] See SE Rolland, *Development at the WTO* (Oxford, Oxford University Press, 2012) 223.

[23] On the argument that WTO adjudication is 'institutionally sensitive' to the work of other international organisations as well as other organs within the WTO, see M Foltea, *International Organizations in WTO Dispute Settlement: How Much Institutional Sensitivity?* (Cambridge, Cambridge University Press, 2012) 23–51.

[24] ibid, fn 25, 172–82; S Bernstein and E Hannah, 'Non-State Global Standard Setting and the WTO: Legitimacy and the Need for Regulatory Space' (2008) 11 *Journal of International Economic Law* 575.

rule-makers. While the web of over 3,000 bilateral investment treaties and regional investment agreements to date are concluded on an inter-State basis, there are also other dispersed rule-makers in the investment system that militate against centralised norm-creation and norm-interpretation,[25] such as individual arbitral tribunals (whether constituted within or outside the auspices of the Convention on the Settlement of Investment Disputes between States and Nationals of Other States, otherwise known as the ICSID Convention);[26] the domestic and regional regulatory agencies that draw up foreign investment legislation and model foreign investment contract clauses; as well as international organisations (such as the UN Conference on Trade and Development's Investment and Enterprise Division)[27] and non-governmental organisations (NGOs) (such as the International Institute for Sustainable Development) that put forward and propose model investment treaty language for States to adopt, including particular interpretations of investment treaty protection standards.[28]

Rule-making in world trade law and international investment law occurs beyond the production of 'hard law' treaty standards. The global regulation of complex economic activities such as trade and investment involves constituencies beyond States,[29] such as treaty regime participants and beneficiaries that may be non-State entities (including institutional or individual investors, exporters, commodity exchanges, public interest NGOs), as well as related international institutions (for example, development banks and financial institutions, regional economic cooperation organisations).[30] What stands distinct from both these treaty regimes is that their supple governance architectures appear to accommodate other sources of rules or operational norms.[31] For example, treaty norms may themselves

[25] The argument has been made that international investment law-making or rule-making is ultimately either directly exercised by States, or exercised on behalf of States through various forms of agency. See JW Yackee, 'Controlling the International Investment Law Agency' (2012) 53 *Harvard International Law Journal* 392.

[26] SW Schill, *The Multilateralization of International Investment Law* (Cambridge, Cambridge University Press, 2009) 277.

[27] P Muchlinski, 'Policy Issues' in P Muchlinski, F Ortino, and C Schreuer (eds), *The Oxford Handbook of International Investment Law* (Oxford, Oxford University Press, 2008) 8–9.

[28] On the role of NGOs in the development of soft law instruments such as model treaties in international investment law, see A Bjorklund, 'Assessing the Effectiveness of Soft Law Instruments in International Investment Law' in AK Bjorklund and A Reinisch (eds), *International Investment Law and Soft Law* (Cheltenham, Edward Elgar Publishing, 2012) 65.

[29] See EA Fogarty, *States, Nonstate Actors, and Global Governance: Projecting Polities* (London, Routledge, 2013) 81–156 (on the interlocking roles of States and non-State actors in the global investment and trade regimes).

[30] See MP Maduro, 'The Constitution of the Global Market' in FG Snyder (ed), *Regional and Global Regulation of International Trade* (Oxford, Hart Publishing, 2002) 49–70; S Young and T Brewer, 'Multilateral Investment Rules, Multinationals and the Global Economy' in NA Phelps and J Alden (eds), *Foreign Direct Investment and the Global Economy: Corporate and Institutional Dynamics of Global-Localisation* (London, Regional Studies Association, 1999).

[31] In this I recognise Hans Kelsen's differentiation between 'legal norms' and 'rules of law'. See H Kelsen, *Principles of International Law* (New York, Rinehart & Company Inc, 1952), 6 ('Legal norms are issued by legal authorities, rules of law are statements made by the legal science, which is not a legal authority and hence not competent to issue legal norms prescribing or permitting human behavior.').

allow and provide for subordinate sources of rule-making, such as, in trade law, Article 3 of the Sanitary and Phytosanitary Measures (SPS) Agreement, which purposely contemplates harmonisation and incorporation of diverse sources of rules (eg 'international standards, guidelines, and recommendations'),[32] or in international investment law, Article 42(1) of the ICSID Convention which allows for the possible application of rules of international law to an investor-State dispute.[33]

Decisions of political organs or bodies within these treaty regimes also wield some influence over the interpretive content of treaty standards. Although the WTO Appellate Body has specifically refused to establish a 'principle of institutional balance'[34] as part of the applicable law in disputes between Members, it remains conscious of the effect of the political organs' pronouncements on the interpretation of WTO law.[35] While other special bodies within the WTO system may be called upon to conduct some form of assessment or functional review of a Member State's measures, in practice the WTO panels and the Appellate Body strive for uniform interpretation and still conduct a full de novo review of those same matters already scrutinised by other WTO bodies.[36] Similarly, while investor-State tribunals have accepted submissions and considered documents pertaining to other regional political organs (such as the European Commission) in regard to the interpretation of international investment agreement (IIA) treaty standards,[37] they have not held themselves automatically bound by them as to foreclose any degree of review as warranted under their arbitral mandates.[38]

[32] See Agreement on the Application of Sanitary and Phytosanitary Measures ('SPS Agreement') arts 3(1) to 3(3).

[33] ICSID Convention art 42(1) ('The Tribunal shall decide a dispute in accordance with such rules of law as may be agreed by the parties. In the absence of such agreement, the Tribunal shall apply the law of the Contracting State party to the dispute (including its rules on the conflict of laws) and such rules of international law as may be applicable.').

[34] *India-Quantitative Restrictions on Imports of Agricultural, Textile and Industrial Products,* Panel Report adopted 23 August 1999 WT/DS90/AB/R, paras 10–28 and 98–105, where the Appellate Body nonetheless recognised in para 103 that it was 'cognizant of the competence of the BOP Committee and the General Council with respect to balance of payments restrictions under Article XVIII:12 of the GATT 1994 and the BOP Understanding. However, we see no conflict between that competence and the competence of panels.'

[35] I van Damme, *Treaty Interpretation by the WTO Appellate Body* (New York, Oxford University Press, 2009) 121–24.

[36] M Oesch, *Standards of Review in WTO Dispute Resolution* (New York, Oxford University Press, 2003) 175–77.

[37] See for example *Eastern Sugar BV v Czech Republic,* Partial Award and partial dissenting opinion of 27 March 2007 SCC Case No 088/2004, paras 117–28 and 172–73. Note that the argument has been made that 'the significant degree of differentiation of EU law from general international law combined with the exclusive jurisdiction of the ECJ, which is a public court, point towards the need for the exercise of self-restraint and deference of arbitral tribunals regarding the compatibility of EU or Member State IIAs with EU law'. See A Dimopoulos, *EU Foreign Investment Law* (New York, Oxford University Press, 2011) 334.

[38] *See Eureko BV v Slovakia,* Award on Jurisdiction of 26 October 2010, Arbitrability and Suspension, PCA Case No 2008-13, paras 286–92, noting at para 289 that 'in principle the EU legal doctrines, including those of supremacy, precedence, direct effect, direct applicability, are part of the body of EU law that might fall to be applied by the Tribunal in this case under Article 8(6) of the BIT', but in

Finally, it is also notable that within these treaty regimes, States themselves have reserved their power and authority to use political organs to directly determine the interpretive content of treaty standards. Article IX:2 of the WTO Agreement recognises that the Ministerial Conference and General Council

> shall have the exclusive authority to adopt interpretations of this Agreement and of the Multilateral Trade Agreements. In the case of an interpretation of a Multilateral Trade Agreement in Annex 1, they shall exercise their authority on the basis of a recommendation by the Council overseeing the functioning of that Agreement. The decision to adopt an interpretation shall be taken by a three-fourths majority of the Members ...[39]

Similar provisions exist for authoritative interpretations to be issued for international investment agreements,[40] most famously in the case of Chapter 11 (Investment) of the North American Free Trade Commission's issuance of a Note of Interpretation in regard to the 'fair and equitable treatment' standard under NAFTA Article 1105(1).[41] Among its numerous recommendations for States to assert control over investment treaty interpretation, the UN Conference on Trade and Development (UNCTAD) has recommended the establishment of 'IIA institutions' which would

> consist of representatives from the State parties and are charged with the task of monitoring the implementation of the treaty and issuing interpretive statements on treaty provisions. The existence of such standing bodies facilitates the exchange of views and formulation of common interpretations.[42]

para 292 it did not deem it appropriate to suspend arbitration proceedings 'until the EU Commission and/or the ECJ have come to a decision on the EU law aspects of the infringement case. While the Tribunal wishes to organise its proceedings with full regard for considerations of mutual respect and comity as regards other courts and institutions, it does not consider that the questions in issue in the infringement case are so far coextensive with the claims in the present case that it is appropriate to suspend its proceedings now. Should it become evident at a later stage that the relationship between the two sets of proceedings is so close as to be a cause of procedural unfairness or serious inefficiency, the Tribunal will reconsider the question of suspension'.

[39] WTO Agreement art IX:2. Note, however, that this power has not yet been exercised. See PJ Kuijper, 'The Court and the Appellate Body: between Constitutionalism and Dispute Settlement' ('There can be no doubt that this power can be used by the political organs to "correct" an interpretation of a particular provision of the WTO agreements given by the AB that they regard as too adventurous. Given that such an authoritative interpretation would need three-fourths of the votes of all Members in order to be validly adopted, it is obvious that Members will have recourse to it only in extreme situations, in which there is widespread and very strongly held support for such an interpretation. A real "corrective interpretation" of a panel or AB report thus has not occurred so far.') in SE Gaines, BE Olsen, and KE Sorensen, *Liberalising Trade in the EU and the WTO: A Legal Comparison* (Cambridge, Cambridge University Press, 2012) 107.

[40] See D Desierto, 'Joint Decisions by State Parties: Fair Control of Tribunal Interpretations?' (*Kluwer Arbitration Blog*, 8 June 2012) http://kluwerarbitrationblog.com/blog/2012/06/08/joint-decisions-by-state-parties-fair-control-of-tribunal-interpretations.

[41] See R Klager, *'Fair and Equitable Treatment' in International Investment Law* (Cambridge, Cambridge University Press, 2011) 70–81.

[42] UNCTAD, *Interpretation of IIAs: What States Can Do* (IIA Issues Note No 3, December 2011) 11http://unctad.org/en/docs/webdiaeia2011d10_en.pdf.

Notwithstanding the foregoing rule-making commonalities, however, there remains no identity between rule-making and rule-makers in the WTO system as opposed to the international investment system. The robust proliferation of trade law rules under the WTO system and its institutions at least lends itself to centralisation and harmonisation among trade law rule-makers. The same cannot be said of international investment rules, which arise from an uncoordinated and disjoint cohort of rule-makers, resulting in a diffusion of variable treaty standards and domestic and regional rules governing foreign investment.

International investment law arose from States' piecemeal conclusion of bilateral or regional investment treaties, tailored according to States' own foreign policy agendas, economic priorities and political programmes,[43] with the few capital-exporting States often having more leverage over the contents of treaty drafts than capital-recipient States.[44] Long before the controversial collapse of multilateral negotiations in 1997 in regard to the proposed Multilateral Agreement on Investment (MAI),[45] States had already been concluding IIAs on a bilateral basis, beginning with the first bilateral investment treaty (BIT) concluded by Germany and Pakistan in 1959 and entering into force in 1962.[46] Piecemeal and individualised treaty negotiation for over half a century resulted in many 'generations'[47] of investment treaties—often characterised by high standards of investor protection with scarcely any counterpart investor obligations;[48] few host State mechanisms to feasibly calibrate their protection obligations in light of good faith governmental regulation;[49] and a marked dearth of institutions for the

[43] KJ Vandevelde, 'A Brief History of International Investment Agreements' (2005) 12 *UC Davis Journal of International Law & Policy* 157.

[44] See K Miles, 'International Investment Law: Origins, Imperialism and Conceptualizing the Environment' (2010) 21 *Colorado Journal of International Environmental Law & Policy* 1; Vandevelde, ibid, 19–74; AA Ghouri, 'The Evolution of Bilateral Investment Treaties, Investment Treaty Arbitration, and International Investment Law' (2011) 14 *International Arbitration Law Review* 189.

[45] See E Neumayer, 'Multilateral Agreement on Investment: Lessons for the WTO from the failed OECD Negotiatons' (1999) 46 *Wirtschaftspolitische Blätter* 618; KC Shadlen, 'Resources, Rules and International Political Economy: the Politics of Development in the WTO' 124–28 (viewing developing countries' ability to block the MAI as somewhat of a favourable outcome) in S Joseph, D Kinley, and J Waincymer (eds), *The World Trade Organization and Human Rights: Interdisciplinary Perspectives* (Cheltenham, Edward Elgar Publishing, 2009) (hereafter, 'Joseph, Kinley, and Waincymer 2009'). Trebilcock and Howse have also described the political dynamics that took over the MAI negotiations and ultimately led to their breakdown. See M Trebilcock, R Howse and A Eliason, *The Regulation of International Trade* 4th edn (London, Routledge, 1995) 458–60.

[46] UNCTAD, *The Entry Into Force of Bilateral Investment Treaties (BITs)* (IIA Monitor No 3, 2006) 3 www.unctad.org/en/Docs/webiteiia20069_en.pdf.

[47] See J Pauwelyn, 'Rational Design or Accidental Evolution? The Emergence of International Investment Law', ch 1 in Z Douglas, J Pauwelyn, and JE Viñuales (eds), *The Foundations of International Investment Law: Bringing Theory into Practice* (Cambridge, Cambridge University Press, 2014).

[48] See A Roberts, 'Triangular Treaties: The Extent and Limits of Investment Treaty Rights' (2015) 56 *Harvard Journal of International Law* 353, 372; T Allee and C Peinhardt, 'Revisiting 'Rational Design': Preferences, Power, and the Design of Bilateral Investment Treaties' (2010) unpublished paper, www.princeton.edu/~pcglobal/conferences/ptas/Allee_pta_paper.pdf.

[49] See M Wagner, 'Regulatory Space in International Trade Law and Investment Law' (2014) 36 *University of Pennsylvania Journal* 71–84.

interpretation, oversight and monitoring of investment contract performance that could mitigate or avoid investor-State disputes.[50]

Moreover, the political decisions and compromises made in the negotiation of investment treaties are not publicly disclosed or formally centralised, unlike the relative publicity of the WTO's negotiation agenda.[51] Neither are there any prescribed mechanisms for investment treaty compliance monitoring where all affected State and non-State actors can provide inputs, unlike the trade policy consultations processes at the WTO. The interpretation of IIA standards is not, by any means, institutionally or formally centralised across individual investor-State arbitral tribunals (which do not uniformly abide by a system of precedent or *jurisprudence constante*),[52] unlike the WTO's Dispute Settlement Understanding (DSU) system that provides for the creation of dispute panels whose reports could be reviewed by a single Appellate Body.[53] Because States have, until recently, historically concluded their own investment treaty programmes away from the shadow of any multilateral economic agreement negotiations,[54] IIA standards have tended to reflect considerable textual diversity, albeit generally containing common features (such as legal standards of protection and dispute settlement provisions that enable investors to directly sue host States for IIA breaches).[55] Because each IIA must be taken according to its own terms, it is difficult to generalise that IIAs all possess identical institutional or structural features for monitoring IIA compliance, for establishing recourse to dispute settlement procedures, or for standardising IIA interpretations of States' spaces of regulatory freedom[56] between arbitral tribunals in investor-State arbitration and the actual States Parties to the IIAs.

[50] See recommendations in UNCTAD, *Investor-State Disputes: Prevention and Alternatives to Arbitration* (United Nations, 2010) 65–98.

[51] B Hoekman and M Kostecki, *The Political Economy of the World Trading System: WTO and Beyond* (Oxford, Oxford University Press, 2001) 100–44.

[52] See AK Bjorklund, 'Can International Investment Law Be Restated? Or Is Jurisprudence Constante the El Dorado of Investment Lawyers?' in AK Bjorklund (ed), *Yearbook on International Investment Law & Policy 2014–2015* (Oxford University Press, 2016) 101–10.

[53] See CL Davis, *Why Adjudicate? Enforcing Trade Rules at the WTO* (Princeton, Princeton University Press, 2012) 244–57.

[54] There are only a few regional investment treaties negotiated as part of trade groupings. See among others Investment Agreement for the COMESA (Common Market for Eastern and Southern Africa) http://vi.unctad.org/files/wksp/ilawksp08/docs/wednesday/Exercise%20Materials/invagreecomesa.pdf; North American Free Trade Agreement (NAFTA) ch 11 (Investment); Central America Free Trade Agreement (CAFTA) ch 10 (Investment); Association of Southeast Asian (ASEAN) Comprehensive Investment Agreement. See A Falsafi, 'Regional trade and Investment Agreements: Liberalizing Investment in a Preferential Climate' (2008) 36 *Syracuse Journal of International Law and Commerce* 43.

[55] Stephan Schill has long demonstrated the emergence of a 'multilateralised' system from the universe of bilateral treaties. See SW Schill, The Multilateralization of International Investment Law: Emergence of a Multilateral System of Investment Protection on Bilateral Grounds (2010) 2 *Trade Law & Development* 1.

[56] On vast literature involving the question of investment arbitral tribunals' degree of deference to domestic judicial review findings, see C Henckels, 'Indirect Expropriation and the Right to Regulate: Revisiting Proportionality Analysis and the Standard of Review in Investor State Arbitration' (2012) 15 *Journal of International Economic Law* 223; SW Schill, 'Enhancing International Investment Law's Legitimacy: Conceptual and Methodological Foundations of New Public Law Approach' (2011)

Unlike the coordinative processes between political and legal organs of the WTO, there are no formal institutions in international investment law that could centralise and coordinate foreign investment policy-making undertaken by all States, with the IIA interpretations emerging from a constantly growing corpus of investor-State arbitral jurisprudence. While investment arbitral tribunals usually observe a sense of precedent,[57] this is not formally required of them within the terms of their arbitral function or mandate. The consent of the disputing parties—a foreign investor and the host State—determines and shapes the jurisdiction of the investment arbitral tribunal.[58] In the particular case of arbitration administered through the 1965 Convention on the Settlement of Investments Disputes Between States and Nationals of Other States (otherwise known as the ICSID Convention),[59] the jurisdiction of the arbitral tribunal depends upon the fulfillment of the requirements in Article 25 of the ICSID Convention—written consent, either through direct agreement of the parties, national legislation of the host State that enables investor recourse to ICSID arbitration, or an IIA between the host State and the investor's State of nationality that provides for consent to ICSID jurisdiction.[60]

Unlike the extended litigation procedures in the WTO, there is no counterpart standing body (like the Dispute Settlement Body) that ensures the enforcement of ICSID arbitral awards. While the ICSID Convention makes it obligatory for all States Parties to the ICSID Convention recognise and enforce ICSID awards,[61] there is no international body or organ that oversees the practical procedures for enforcement of ICSID awards—rather, as with the 1958 New York Convention on Recognition and Enforcement of Arbitral Awards, it is the party seeking enforcement that must submit the ICSID award to the local court or authority charged with enforcement of ICSID awards in the State concerned.[62] Excluding

52 *Virginia Journal of International Law* 57; W Burke-White and A von Staden, 'Private Litigation in a Public Law Sphere: The Standard of Review in Investor-State Arbitrations' (2010) 35 *Yale Journal of International Law* 283; R Moloo and J Jacinto, 'Standards of Review and Reviewing Standards: Public Interest Regulation in International Investment Law' in KP Sauvant (ed), *Yearbook of International Investment Law and Policy* 2011–2012 (New York, Oxford University Press, 2013) draft version http://papers.ssrn.com/sol3/papers.cfm?abstract_id=2036243.

[57] Desierto, above n 18. See also A Reinisch, 'The Role of Precedent in ICSID Arbitration' (2008) *Austrian Arbitration Yearbook* 495; WMC Weidemaier, 'Toward A Theory of Precedent in Arbitration' (2010) 51 *William and Mary Law Review* 1895.

[58] On the primary principle of consent in international arbitration, see WM Reisman, 'The Breakdown of the Control Mechanism in ICSID Arbitration' (1989) 1989 *Duke Law Journal* 739.

[59] See C Schreuer, L Malintoppi, A Reinisch, and A Sinclair, *The ICSID Convention: A Commentary* (Cambridge, Cambridge University Press, 2011) [hereafter, 'ICSID Commentary'].

[60] ICSID Convention, art 25. See also, C Schreuer, *ICSID: Consent to Arbitration* (2003) http://unctad.org/en/docs/edmmisc232add2_en.pdf.

[61] ICSID Convention, art 54.

[62] Note that initiating the investment arbitration through ICSID (as opposed to ad hoc arbitration under UNCITRAL arbitration rules), has been observed by some as *not* necessarily a predictive indicator of future enforcement success. See F Baetens, 'Enforcement of Arbitral Awards: 'To ICSID or not to ICSID' is NOT the Question' in T Weiler and I Laird (eds), *The Future of ICSID, Juris Arbitration Series* (The Hague, Martinus Nijhoff Publishers, 2013).

Argentina's particular circumstances and its current policy of non-payment in around 40 pending or concluded arbitrations,[63] enforcement of ICSID awards has been reported to be fairly successful.[64] States have only recently started introducing structural innovations to retain control over IIA interpretation and the rulemaking process, such as 1) ad hoc joint decision mechanisms; 2) treaty-based institutional commissions; 3) inter-State consultative mechanisms; 4) incorporation of other subject matter-specific treaties (eg environmental, labour, human rights); and 5) inter-State bilateral appellate mechanisms to review arbitral awards under the IIA's investor-State dispute settlement mechanism, or the outright omission of investor-State dispute settlement mechanisms under the IIA.[65]

In sum, relative authority in world trade law has vastly different contours and possibilities from that of international investment law. The regular interactions of the WTO's political organs that negotiate trade agreements and review individual trade policies of Member States, with the fairly centralised jurisprudence of the WTO Appellate Body and panels, can collectively infuse a clearer vision of relative authority, where authoritative decision-makers within this system can enhance their legitimacy by: 1) demonstrating the virtues of the functional specialisations developed across and within this system of administration, implementation and interpretation of the WTO covered agreements;[66] 2) identifying the paths to institutional reform that seek to expand the WTO's inclusiveness to *all* non-State stakeholders such as non-governmental organizations, and not just to the WTO Members;[67] and 3) reviewing institutional possibilities for enhanced protection and vindication of individual or group rights even within this Member-driven organisation.[68] On the other hand, the disjoint architecture of international investment law makes judgments about relative authority—particularly *which* authoritative decision-maker prevails—quite unpredictable. Because international investment law rule-making is primarily driven by States in bilateral or regional treaty configurations while international investment law adjudication takes place through individualised investor-State arbitral tribunals, there are very disparate opportunities for enhancing legitimacy assets of functional specialisation, inclusiveness and rights protection.

[63] See VJT Perez, 'Diplomatic Protection Revival for Failure to Comply with Investment Arbitration Awards' (2012) 3 *Journal of International Dispute Settlement* 445.

[64] AR Parra, 'The Enforcement of ICSID Arbitral Awards' in RD Bishop (ed), *Enforcement of Arbitral Awards Against Sovereigns* (New York, Juris Publishing, 2009).

[65] For a recent general survey on approaches for States to control the interpretation of their IIAs, see UNCTAD, *Interpretation of IIAs: What States Can Do* (IIA Issues Note No 3, December 2011) http://unctad.org/en/Docs/webdiaeia2011d10_en.pdf.

[66] See HR Fabri, 'About the Sense and Direction of Multilateralism in International Trade Law' in HP Hestermeyer, D Konig, N Matz-Luck, V Roben, A Seibert-Fohr, P Tobias-Stoll and S Voneky (eds), *Coexistence, Cooperation, and Solidarity: Liber Amicorum Rudiger Wolfrum* (The Hague, Martinus Nijhoff, 2012) 285.

[67] See S Charnovitz, 'Participation of Non-Governmental Organizations in the World Trade Organization' (1996) 17 *University of Pennsylvania Journal of International Economic Law* 331.

[68] R Howse and M Mutua, 'Protecting Human Rights in a Global Economy: Challenges for the World Trade Organization' in H Stokke et al (eds), *Human Rights in Development Yearbook 1999/2000: The Millennium Edition* (The Hague, Martinus Nijhoff, 2001).

III. Legitimacy Assets, Accountability, and Reform in Trade and Investment

Considering the abject dissimilarity between the rule-making processes and authoritative rule-makers in the WTO system and the international investment system, how then does separation of powers analysis contribute to examining the legitimacy of global trade and investment rule-making, and the exercise of international public authority by these treaty regimes' respective rule-makers? Recognising that neither rule-making system encapsulates a perfect closed version of legislation under classic separation of powers theory,[69] one can focus on delegation doctrine contextualised in the modern regulatory state[70] to scrutinise how the institutional, formal and informal rule-makers within the trade and investment systems deploy their authority arising from the consent of States to these treaty regimes. Hans Kelsen's description of the concept of separation of powers being of 'a relative character'[71] is also appropriate to this analysis, since law-creation and law-application in the global trade and investment regimes are not hermetically distinct processes. As already discussed, institutions within these regimes primarily vested with the executive function (such as the Ministerial Conference and General Council in the WTO system, in contrast with the host States tasked with implementing IIA standards of protection in the international investment system), and those institutions entrusted with the judicial function (such as the WTO panels and Appellate Body in the DSB, in contrast with the investor-State arbitral tribunals and the administering arbitral institutions such as the Centre for Settlement of Investment Disputes or ICSID), could also end up discharging rule-making or legislative functions. Kelsen's conception of the doctrine of separation of powers accepts these kinds of blended functions across political and judicial institutions.[72]

While States author the treaty standards and norms governing global trade and investment, in practice, the implementation of these standards also trigger considerable rule-making by other political institutions, such as, for trade law, the WTO General Council and Ministerial Conference, the sectoral Councils, the universe of standard-setting agencies and technical bodies involved in the SPS, TBT, TRIPS, GATT, GATS, Agriculture, and other WTO covered agreements; and for

[69] To recall, under separation of powers 'the legislative power includes the power, through the enactment of laws, to specify the ends and means of public policy, but it does not include the executive power to administer and enforce those laws or the judicial power to resolve cases arising under them.' RE Levy, *The Power to Legislate* (Westport, Greenwood Publishing, 2006) 138.

[70] See S Rose-Ackerman, 'The Regulatory State' in M Rosenfeld and A Sajo (eds), *The Oxford Handbook of Comparative Constitutional Law* (Oxford, Oxford University Press, 2012).

[71] H Kelsen, *General Theory of Law and State* (Cambridge, Harvard University Press, 1945) 269.

[72] ibid, fn 146, 270–72.

investment law, numerous host State and home State ministries, agencies, and domestic legislatures that pass foreign investment legislation, design rules governing foreign investment contracting and due diligence processes, as well as determine the contours of their preferred investor-State dispute settlement mechanisms.[73] The same functional reasons for delegation—the need for agency expertise; the lack of time and resources for States to directly undertake, monitor, and coordinate rule-making; as well as the value of removing implementation decisions from more political forums[74]—may also be applied to explain the proliferation of rule-makers and rule-making beyond States' formulation of treaty standards in the global trade and investment regimes. To the extent that non-delegation doctrine also makes itself amenable to critiques of public participation in the regulatory process,[75] and is also subject to some form of judicial review,[76] one could test the legitimacy of trade and investment rule-making as exercises of international public authority.

Current proposals to reform both treaty-based regimes can be evaluated through scrutiny of the role of legitimacy assets of inclusiveness, functional specialisation, and protection of rights in trade and investment law. First, I examine *internal checking functions* within the respective architectures of trade and investment rule-making to ascertain how constituencies within each treaty regime can elicit accountability from rule-makers, specifically to detect if capacities exist for institutional override or amendment of delegated actions,[77] as well as to examine whether public participation in the rulemaking process addresses the inevitable democratic deficit between individuals directly impacted by trade and investment rules and the States that enact and implement such rules.[78] Second, I move on to potential *external constraints* on rule-making, specifically from the standpoint of dispute-driven interpretations of trade and investment rules by each regime's respective institutions discharging the adjudicative function. I show that judicial deference operates differently in the dispute settlement forums in the WTO

[73] One scholar refers to a generalised model of 'multilevel regulatory governance', where 'the capacity of each level to carry out the regulatory function must be verified. It must be based on the comparative advantage of each level. There needs to be coordination between different levels of government before the transfer of power. This would lead to an ongoing process of a dynamic separation of powers. The key element in the new situation is coherence. In the absence of coherence there is a risk of contradictory rules, excessive regulation or regulatory gaps …'. B Gavin, 'Reconciling Regionalism and Multilateralism: Towards Multilevel Trade Governance' in P de Lombaerde (ed), *Multilateralism, Regionalism, and Bilateralism in Trade and Investment* (Dordrecht, Springer, 2007) 64–65.

[74] ibid, fn 145, 673.

[75] ibid, 680.

[76] ibid, 682.

[77] See CA Bradley, *International Law in the US Legal System* 2nd edn (Oxford, Oxford University Press, 2015) ch 4.

[78] See A Boyle and K McCall Smith, 'Transparency in International Law-Making' in A Bianchi and A Peters (eds), *Transparency in International Law* (Cambridge, Cambridge University Press, November 2013).

system as it does in the international investment arbitration system largely due to differences in institutional mandate and structural design of tribunals (eg the DSU mandate to the panels and the Appellate Body, in contrast with the arbitral mandate under the ICSID Convention), which conceivably paints an inconsistent portrait of expectations of legitimacy of global trade and investment rule-making. Understanding these differences of expectations should help to foreground how one conceptualises relative authority in each treaty regime.

A. Internal Checking Functions and External Constraints on Trade Rule-making

Consensus decision-making at the WTO, while facially equal with a vote for each Member, does not, in reality operate under terms of equality for all.[79] The consensus rule under Article IX:1 of the WTO Agreement is often criticised for policy gridlocks that end up being prohibitive against making any prompt rule changes for the world trading system:[80] 'consensus reinforces conservative tendencies in the system. Proposals for change can be adopted only if unopposed.'[81] Mustering the required majority vote (2/3 or 3/4, depending on the decision) if consensus cannot be reached for certain decisions is certainly not an easy matter for any single Member or cluster of Members.[82] Any Member can submit proposals for amendments to the WTO Agreement and its accompanying Multilateral Trade Agreements, for example, but the amendment proposal will be decided by consensus.[83] While the WTO Ministerial Conference and the General Council 'have the exclusive authority to adopt interpretations'[84] of the WTO Agreement and its accompanying Multilateral Trade Agreements, the consensus (or in some cases, the alternative of 2/3 or 3/4 majority voting rules) ensure that few interpretations could easily be 'legislated' into the system without very significant support from the WTO's 164 Members. The WTO's 'Green Room' politics—small gatherings of representatives of up to 30 Members—have been hailed as a necessity for

[79] C-D Ehlermann and L Ehring, 'Decision-Making in the World Trade Organization: Is the Consensus Practice of the World Trade Organization Adequate for Making, Revising, and Implementing Rules of International Trade?' (2005) 8 *Journal of International Economic Law* 51; W Guan, 'Consensus Yet Not Consented: A Critique of the WTO Decision-Making by Consensus' (2014) 17 *Journal of International Economic Law* 77.

[80] See T Cottier, 'A Two-Tier Approach to WTO Decision-Making' in DP Steger (ed), *Redesigning the World Trade Organization for the Twenty-First Century* (Waterloo, Wilfrid Laurier University Press, 2010).

[81] See BM Hoekman and PC Mavroidis, *World Trade Organization (WTO): Law, Economics, and Politics* (New York, Routledge, 2015) 29.

[82] JH Jackson, *Sovereignty, the WTO, and Changing Fundamentals of International Law* (Cambridge, Cambridge University Press, 2006) 114–15.

[83] See WTO Agreement, art X.

[84] ibid, art IX:2.

consensus building, but they have also been seen as favouring representation from large and high-income Member countries, at the expense of representation for low-income and middle-income developing countries.[85]

Admittedly, the WTO has gone far to build in public participation at various levels of rule-making throughout its bureaucracy. As Gabrielle Marceau and Mikella Hurley rightly observe, there is now widespread public access to WTO documentation,[86] the possibility of NGOs and other civil society actors submitting amicus briefs in pending disputes at the WTO Dispute Settlement Mechanism, as well as public participation and consultations in WTO adjudicating bodies, committees, and councils.[87] These innovations, however, nonetheless remain limited since they are not formally constitutionalised through the WTO's founding instruments—given institutional constraints and lack of resources to cope with the demands of greater openness, and the

> low level of institutional differentiation of the WTO political branch … political organs in the WTO are spread on two tracks—the regular bodies and the negotiating groups—that often have overlapping competences … result[ing] in a negotiating process that is largely informal and obscures the progress and modalities of negotiations.[88]

The WTO remains every bit as much a Member-driven and Member-governed organisation, even if the States that comprise its membership sometimes permit limited avenues for public participation.

Even the notion of 'deference'[89] to national sovereignty or local decision-making (alternatively, the 'principle of subsidiarity'[90])—as a form of external constraint on WTO rule-making through the WTO dispute settlement tribunals' standards of review[91]—has to be understood within a context of institutional and political competences at the WTO. To the extent that WTO dispute settlement tribunals can issue recommendations on how to bring a challenged measure to consistency with WTO rules, the scope and contours of their recommendation can realistically create practical limits or operational boundaries to the extent of deference that the tribunal will observe over how the Member exercises its legislative discretion

[85] See K Jones, 'Green Room Politics and the WTO's Crisis of Representation' (2009) 9 *Progress in Development Studies* 349; K Jones, *The Doha Blues: Institutional Crisis and Reform in the WTO* (New York, Oxford University Press, 2009) ch 4.

[86] See also R Wolfe, 'Letting the sunshine in at the WTO: How transparency brings the trading system to life' (2013) World Trade Organization Economics and Statistics Division Staff Working Paper ERSD—2013-03, www.wto.org/english/res_e/reser_e/ersd201303_e.pdf.

[87] G Marceau and M Hurley, 'Transparency and Public Participation in the WTO: A Report Card on WTO Transparency Mechanisms' (2012) 4 *Trade Law & Development* 19.

[88] Y Bonzon, *Public Participation and Legitimacy in the WTO* (Cambridge, Cambridge University Press, 2014) 269.

[89] See SP Croley and JH Jackson, 'WTO Dispute Procedures, Standard of Review, and Deference to National Governments' (1996) 90 *American Journal of International Law* 193.

[90] T Cottier, *The Challenge of WTO Law: Collected Essays* (London, Cameron May, 2007) 464.

[91] M Oesch, *Standards of Review in WTO Dispute Resolution* (Oxford, Oxford University Press, 2003) 29.

to change the offending or challenged measure.[92] Tomer Broude argues that the standards or mechanisms for deference in the WTO

> are selective and strategic, not systemic, and that they more often than not serve to counteract the anxieties of the multilateral decision-making machinery, providing it with sources of enhanced legitimacy in its give-and-take with other actors (the Membership in particular) over influence and governance. Simultaneously, this selective subsidiarity does not clearly work to either empower or disempower national (or regional) systems, and it is in this respect that the deference becomes dialectical.[93]

The evolution of internal checks and external constraints on WTO rule-making—whether from direct negotiations of trade policy at the political organs or from the influence of trade dispute adjudication by the WTO judicial organs—demonstrate discrete inroads in attempting greater spaces of inclusiveness and public participation for non-governmental civil society actors, notwithstanding the WTO's institutional mandate as a Member-driven and Member-governed organisation;[94] continued reliance on functional specialisations as the axiom of multilateral rule-making emerging from the proposals of technical committees, councils, groups, and other expert bodies within the WTO system, for review and adoption by the Members;[95] and some growing recognition of the need to develop balanced protection of individual rights while ensuring Members' continued compliance and consistency with world trade rules.[96] The more centralised and identifiable structure of relative authority at the WTO, at the very least, enables discourses on WTO reforms that seek to bolster and strengthen these legitimacy assets of inclusiveness, functional specialisations, and protection of rights in the world trade system. As the next section will show, this is not at all the same environment in the diffuse and dispersed world of international investment law rule-making.

B. Internal Checking Functions and External Constraints on Investment Rule-making

States draw up international investment treaties and the terms of their foreign investment contracts, always according to their own internal treaty negotiation

[92] D Lovric, *Deference to the Legislature in WTO Challenges to Legislation* (Alphen aan den Rijn, Kluwer Law International, 2010) 50.

[93] T Broude, 'Selective Subsidiarity and Dialectic Deference in the World Trade Organization' (2016) 79 *Law and Contemporary Problems* 53, 58.

[94] See K Suominen, *Enhancing Coherence and Inclusiveness in the Global Trading System in the Era of Regionalism* (2016) ICTSD Policy Options Paper www3.weforum.org/docs/E15/WEF_Regional%20trade%20Agreements_2015_1401.pdf.

[95] See M Elsig, BM Hoekman and J Pauwelyn, 'Thinking about the performance of the World Trade Organization: A discussion across disciplines' (2016) EUI/RSCAS 2016/13 Global Governance Programme-212, http://cadmus.eui.eu/bitstream/handle/1814/39012/RSCAS_2016_13.pdf?sequence=1.

[96] See SA Aaronson and JP Chauffour, *The Wedding of Trade and Human Rights: Marriage of Convenience or Permanent Match?* www.wto.org/english/res_e/publications_e/wtr11_forum_e/wtr11_15feb11_e.htm.

processes, and following their own levels of transparency mandated under their respective domestic laws to their respective constituencies.[97] Disputes between States and investors also impact the nature of future rules written for the international investment system.[98] Non-governmental organisations, civic society groups, or other members of the public are thus compelled to rely on domestic laws to try and gain access to information on investment treaty negotiations, much more to even try and provide inputs to the contents of investment treaties being concluded on their behalf by their respective States.[99] While there is now an UNCITRAL Convention on Transparency in Treaty-Based Investor-State Arbitration,[100] there is no international law norm that compels States to disclose the records or contents of investment treaty negotiations to third party groups within their respective territories. The European Commission's comprehensive online consultation process on the investment chapter of the proposed Transatlantic Trade and Investment Partnership (TTIP) was voluntarily done, and not legally compelled.[101]

Some international investment treaties contain different formulations of transparency obligations imposed on host States and/or home States, often pertaining to the transparency of information that affects the legal and regulatory framework affecting investments.[102] However, this is not the kind of transparency that non-State groups need to feasibly check the lawfulness or legitimacy of the bargain that host States and home States reach to facilitate and protect foreign investment under investment treaties. Constitutional checks on the government's abuse of the treaty-making power, for example, remain very much a matter of strategically using 'structural, political, and diplomatic checks on the exercise of the power itself'.[103] There is little by way of the State's constitutional treaty-making power that non-State groups, communities and organisations can realistically constrain other than through domestic constitutional remedies as well, if these exist. It is, after all, not an easy task to try and compel States to disclose the contents of their trade and

[97] See UNCTAD, *International Investment Rule-Making: Stocktaking, Challenges, and the Way Forward* (United Nations, 2008); L Cotula, 'Investment treaties and citizens' power: lessons from experience' (*IIED*, 2015) www.iied.org/investment-treaties-citizens-power-lessons-experience.

[98] UNCTAD, *Investor-State Dispute Settlement and Impact on Investment Rulemaking* (United Nations, 2007) http://unctad.org/en/docs/iteiia20073_en.pdf.

[99] See JE Alvarez and KP Sauvant, *The Evolving International Investment Regime: Expectations, Realities, Options* (New York, Oxford University Press, 2011) 34 (noting that civil society groups remain 'nothing more than a critical voice asking for change' in the international investment system).

[100] United Nations Convention on Transparency in Treaty-Based Investor-State Arbitration (New York, 2014) [the Mauritius Convention], www.uncitral.org/uncitral/uncitral_texts/arbitration/2014Transparency_Convention.html.

[101] See European Commission, 'Online Public Consultation on Investment Protection and Investor-State Dispute Settlement (ISDS) in the Transatlantic Trade and Investment Partnership' (*Trade.ec.europa.eu*, 2014) http://trade.ec.europa.eu/consultations/index.cfm?consul_id=179.

[102] See UNCTAD, *Transparency, UNCTAD Series on International Investment Agreements II* (United Nations, 2012) 19–24, http://unctad.org/en/PublicationsLibrary/unctaddiaeia2011d6_en.pdf.

[103] See O Hathaway, S Amdur, C Choy, S Deger-Sen, J Paredes, S Pei and HN Proctor, 'The Treaty Power: Its History, Scope, and Limits' (2013) 98 *Cornell Law Review* 239.

economic negotiations. For example, in *Stichting Corporate Europe Observatory v European Commission*, the 10th Chamber of the Court of Justice of the European Union rejected the appeal filed by petitioners seeking access to documents relating to trade negotiations between the EU and the Republic of India.[104] Thus, whether it be matters of treaty renegotiation, renewal, consolidation, amendment, denunciation, it is States that will continue to decide these matters according to their respective constitutional powers. Internal checks against these forms of State rule-making (whether through treaties or sovereign contracts) depend on the domestic legal and constitutional system in place, and how far third parties or non-State groups can act to constrain and limit the discretionary exercise of the treaty power. The terms of the actual investment treaties themselves—of which there are as of this writing over 3000—also vary considerably in matters of amendment, treaty expiration and renewal, and mechanisms (if any) for oversight and monitoring of treaty implementation.[105] Because there is ultimately no centralised, institutional or mandatory legal framework through which non-State civil society actors and other interested groups can mediate public participation, obtain access to information about, and provide input into the investment treaty-making process, there are few real opportunities to deepen, enhance, or vindicate the legitimacy assets of inclusiveness, functional specialisation, or the protection of individual or group rights throughout the international investment system.

Even public participation (or amicus submissions) in investor-State disputes remains, to date, very much a rudimentary matter decided on a case-by-case basis by arbitral tribunals, and often, they appear quite ineffectual in actual dispute settlement outcomes. The International Centre for Settlement of Investment Disputes (ICSID) crafted rules for the limited participation of non-disputing parties,[106] but while there is 'no record of any abuse of this system … there is also no evidence that non-disputing parties have actually assisted the decision-making of tribunals.'[107] Investor-state arbitral tribunals also operate fairly autonomously of any other tribunals, with arbitral consent generally restricted to individual investor-State disputes brought before the particular tribunal. Caroline Henckels has powerfully argued in favour of an 'institutionally sensitive approach to

[104] Case C-399/13P *Stichting Corporate Europe Observatory v European Commission*, Appeals—EC Regulation No 1049/2001 [2015] EU:C:2015:360.

[105] See UNCTAD, *International Investment Policymaking in Transition: Challenges and Opportunities of Treaty Renewal* (IIA Issues Note No 4, June 2013).

[106] See T Ishikawa, 'Third Party Participation in Investment Treaty Arbitration' (2010) 59 *International and Comparative Law Quarterly* 373; E Levine, 'Amicus Curiae in International Investment Arbitration: The Implications of an Increase in Third-Party Participation' (2011) 29 *Berkeley Journal of International Law* 200; K Fach Gomez, 'Rethinking the Role of Amicus Curiae in International Investment Arbitration: How to Draw the Line Favorably for the Public Interest' (2012) 35 *Fordham International Law Journal* 513.

[107] E Obadia, 'Extension of Proceedings Beyond the Original Parties: Non-Disputing Party Participation in Investment Arbitration' (2007) 22 *ICSID Review* 349.

proportionality analysis in investor-State arbitration' (or a mode of deference that tribunals should observe in evaluating the exercise of regulatory autonomy by host States),[108] but what is tacitly admitted in this position is that it is up to the individual discretion exercised by each arbitral tribunal, in any particular investor-State dispute, the extent to which it will defer to the host State's design of its regulatory measure in order to evaluate host State liability for causing injury to foreign investors. Unlike the WTO dispute settlement system that, at least, has the harmonising or stabilising influence of an Appellate Body and the direct adoption of panel or Appellate Body reports by the Dispute Settlement Body (which is also composed of the same WTO Members that draw up world trade policies through their membership in the same General Council and the Trade Policy Review Body), investor-State arbitral tribunals retain considerable latitude to differ on the width and spaces of developing a *jurisprudence constante* in investor-State arbitral jurisprudence.[109] Where WTO tribunals have a direct impact on world trade rules by bringing offending Member measures to conform with the requirements of foreign market access, investor-State arbitral tribunals have no such far-reaching and decisive policy consequence on host States, other than the attenuated policy and regulatory impacts of the tribunal's power to determine the alleged compensability of investor losses incurred through host State acts and exercises of regulatory power.[110]

To this end, it is not too far off the mark to observe that there is a significant democratic deficit when it comes to the ability of non-State actors (specifically individuals, groups, local communities) to directly affect or influence the contents of States' investment treaty-making or investment rule-making, much less investment treaty adjudication through investor-State arbitration. The international investment system (at least to the extent that it *is* somewhat of a system of similar or blended norms[111]) does not entrench or prioritise significant legitimacy assets of inclusiveness, functional specialisations, or the protection of rights of individuals (other than foreign investors). To the extent that non-State actors can politically mobilise and use any domestic legal remedies to influence States' rule-making and treaty-making behaviour, they could, in theory, create concrete impact on the rules and rule-making processes of international investment law. Beyond what States actually provide within the terms of their investment treaties

[108] C Henckels, *Proportionality and Deference in Investor-State Arbitration: Balancing Investment Protection and Regulatory Autonomy* (Cambridge, Cambridge University Press, 2015) 126–71.

[109] G Bucheler, *Proportionality in Investor-State Arbitration* (New York, Oxford University Press, 2015) 96 ('there is no stare decisis rule in international investment arbitration … arbitral tribunals are not bound to adopt the solutions other tribunals have developed—even if the underlying circumstances are similar or identical.').

[110] DA Desierto, 'Public Policy in International Investment and Trade Law: Community Expectations and Functional Decision-Making' (2014) 26 *Florida Journal of International Law* 51.

[111] SW Schill, *The Multilateralization of International Investment Law* (Cambridge, Cambridge University Press, 2009) 362–78.

and investment contracts, however, there is a dearth of avenues or feasible channels for non-State actors such as individuals (other than investors who are purposeful beneficiaries of the investment treaty system), civil society groups, and local communities to affect the relative authority wielded by States in the international investment rule-making and dispute settlement system.

IV. Conclusion

Relative authority in the treaty-based systems of world trade law and international investment law cannot be fully visualised without a distinct consciousness of the differences between the political and institutional terrains in each of these systems. Using separation of powers theory, one can locate and identify institutions in the WTO system that discharge the executive, legislative and judicial functions. In contrast, in a purely State-driven system as the international investment treaty-making process, there are no clear institutions that uniquely, distinctly or consistently discharge executive, legislative, and judicial functions. States write investment treaties as a part of foreign policy—often without reference, access to information, or mandatory input from all affected non-State internal stakeholders and communities—and the implementation of these treaty commitments is left up to host States and home States assuming commitments under these treaties. Adjudication of investor-State disputes through individually constituted investor-State arbitral tribunals that decide particular disputes can also inhibit the direct transmission of investor-State jurisprudence to the content of international investment treaty policies of States. The WTO system—regardless of the rigidity of its processes or the perceived inflexibility of its institutions—at least contains identifiable focal points for strengthening the legitimacy assets of inclusiveness, functional specialisation, and the protection of rights of individuals and groups. The diffuse, disorganised, and dispersed international investment system, on the other hand, makes the strength of these legitimacy assets completely dependent on the will of the governing elites in States and authoritative decision-makers in individual investor-State arbitral disputes—who ultimately have the greatest influence and impact on how the rules, policies and treaties of international investment are to be written.

INDEX

www.ingramcontent.com/pod-product-compliance
Ingram Content Group UK Ltd.
Pitfield, Milton Keynes, MK11 3LW, UK
UKHW020905190926
475560UK00010B/277

9 781509 911936